AWAKENING UNIVERSE,

EMERGING PERSONHOOD

THE POWER OF CONTEMPLATION

IN AN EVOLVING UNIVERSE

AWAKENING UNIVERSE,

EMERGING PERSONHOOD

THE POWER OF CONTEMPLATION

IN AN EVOLVING UNIVERSE

❖

MARY CONROW COELHO

Wyndham Hall Press
Lima, Ohio 45806

AWAKENING UNIVERSE, EMERGING PERSONHOOD
The Power of Contemplation in an Evolving Universe

By Mary Conrow Coelho

First Edition

ISBN 1-55605-354-1
Library of Congress 2002

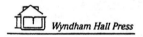 *Wyndham Hall Press*

Printed in The United States of America

For my late husband,
Jaime B. Coelho

and the brother I did not know,
David Conrow

CONTENTS

PREFACE

ALTHOUGH THIS book is written in "scholarly" fashion, with careful citations of the sources of quotations and some ideas, it is at the same time my personal story. It develops a 'way of seeing' that brings together what were initially three largely separate, though critically important, aspects of my world. It is about their integration within the context of the new origin story, the story of the evolutionary universe. The 'way of seeing' that is developed is not only of very great personal importance, it also addresses a critical need in a fragmented culture.

The first world of great interest for me was the natural world and the study of biology. In college and through my twenties, I identified myself as a biologist. After a major in the subject in college, I worked in a renal physiology research laboratory, taught high school biology, and completed a Master's degree in teaching biology at Teachers College, Columbia University. It was in those years that I developed a profound sense of the integrity and the exquisite delicacy of detail and balance of the organic world. One summer during college, I took a course in Invertebrate Zoology at The Marine Biological Laboratory in Woods Hole, Massachusetts, and became fascinated by a cluster of tiny, transparent hydra clinging to a submerged piling. Their minuscule tentacles waved gently in the current, waiting for passing food particles. I realized their life was completely integral to the sea and dependent on it.

But I also fell into the negative side of science, the side that tends to recognize as valid knowledge only that which has been quantified, measured, and proved by experimental methods. I thought there was only one way of knowing and I lived for a period with the reduced and narrowed worldview that results from failure to recognize the limits of the valid knowledge which science does obtain. For me, the world thus became stripped of its interiority. In the words of Thomas Berry, "the earth [was] no longer a communion of subjects. It had becomes a collection of objects to be adjusted to in an external manner." (Swimme and Berry, p. 199) When nature has been made an object though science and technology, it is hard to conceive how the human being, so closely related to other animals and so much a part of the natural world, can find a fully satisfying, meaningful place in life.

The second aspect of my life of central importance to me was the personal search for the sacred, for the numinous, powerful reality I was privileged to have known. It held great promise for the transformation of my life, for great beauty, meaning, and dignity. My first encounter with it, a mystical experience described in these pages, was so attractive that I felt compelled to leave the biological world (impossible, of course, in the larger context), and enroll at Union Theological Seminary in New York City—despite the fact that this meant leaving behind a career I loved and the many years I had spent preparing for it. But I did abandon biology, so I thought, including even some important questions. One concerned how my spiritual hopes and hungers could be valued in an evolutionary world, which I had been taught was governed by random, chance phenomena; another concerned the behavior of matter, in particular, how there could be physical healings if matter is adequately described only in the mechanistic terms I had been taught. Even in college, I had had questions about the relation between the Biblical worldview I studied in required bible classes and the worldview of science. Knowing nothing about mythic meaning, I badgered a Catholic friend with questions. I would ask, for example, how, if every human being has sixty-four chromosomes, could Jesus have been born of a virgin and still have the full complement. In a broad sense, this type of question is like those that motivated the writing of this book, because it sought to honor the integrity of the natural order and yet it reflected an abiding interest in questions of meaning and spirit.

At Union, I immersed myself in a new world, taking courses in theology, the history of Christianity, the bible, preaching, and in the depth psychologies. After obtaining my Master of Divinity degree, I helped develop the programs in spiritual direction at General Theological Seminary in New York City, and worked on the staff of those programs for four years. Not satisfied with what I had studied at Union, I went on to Fordham University, where, pursuant to obtaining a Ph.D. degree in historical theology, I was able to take courses in medieval mysticism, Franciscan spirituality, and the Spanish mystics that provided the opportunity to study people like Meister Eckhart, Richard of St. Victor, Saint Francis, Saint Bonaventure, Saint Teresa of Avila, and Saint John of the Cross. I was often moved and excited to learn of the possibilities of the contemplative journey and the implications of what the contemplative tradition teaches about human identity, especially when studies in mysticism were coupled with the depth psychology of Carl Jung.

I largely forgot about biology, although ecological concern about the natural world often came to the fore. For example, one day a few years ago a tree surgeon came to my home to trim a diseased dogwood, and to cut down two small, severely diseased Canadian hemlocks. I commented that it was worrisome to have the hemlocks dying, and he said that it is not just the hemlocks that are threatened, but also the ash, the dogwood, the elm, and the sumac. The ash, he added, is the most common tree in the eastern United States, and its absence will be very great loss. In past years he had seen one species of tree at a time threatened, but never so many at once. "Without trees, it will be a desert," he said. I wondered what would happen if our beloved oaks and maples were also to fall ill because, as the tree surgeon said, and contrary to many people's assumptions, trees can not take an unlimited amount of stress.

My alarm about the environment has deep, personal roots. The farm on which I grew up in New Jersey was one of many in an extensive agricultural area in the central and southern portions of the Garden State. Now the entire county, once filled with peach and apple orchards and fields of tomatoes and corn, has gone over to housing developments and shopping malls. I once hoped that this change was an isolated situation, because of the proximity of the area to Philadelphia, but I have heard too many times of people whose childhood homes in once rural areas have suffered the same fate. Although the population grows and there is indeed need for more housing, there remains the genuine loss of the scattered forests that remained, the frogs, the sunfish, and the great blue heron who enjoyed our pond, the songbirds in the fields and woods, the barn owl that frequented our barn and the great horned owl that sometimes came to our hemlocks.

It was while watching one of the videos of Brian Swimme's *Canticle to the Cosmos*, which describes the insights and ideas from the new story of the evolutionary universe and the new cosmology, that my two worlds suddenly began to come together. I was seated in a darkened room in a church in New York City with perhaps fifteen other people, watching and listening, when I heard Brian Swimme say: "The same dynamics that formed the mountains and formed the continents are the dynamics that eventuated into humans. We don't live on the planet but in and as this bio-spiritual planet." I saw that the belonging I sought in the spiritual world also pertained fully to the natural world, indeed to the Earth and the whole cosmos. I immediately imagined known and unknown active and dynamic forces within my body that were sustaining and forming my identity, far below my conscious awareness. I felt a surge of energy as those words brought a knowing that connected deeply to my being. It was a kind of illumination, an intellectual (in the classic meaning of that word, in which the intellect can be a pathway to the sacred) illumination of knowledge of the depth of my belonging to the universe and the Earth. To my very great excitement and near disbelief, I glimpsed a unified vision.

In the words quoted above and in other insights from the video series, I had come upon an integration of body and spirit from the story of the 13-billion-year history of the universe that I had hardly realized was missing in my life. The desacralization of the world of science and the nearly exclusive focus of religion on human affairs had made an integrated view of things inaccessible for me. Now I saw the healing of this most dangerous fragmentation as essential to the future of the Earth—and that the new story of the evolutionary universe is a remarkable origin story, offering a healing worldview and vision. It offers great wisdom because it is at once the story of the wisdom and creativity of the natural order and of the intrinsic wisdom of our hearts and bodies. I was ecstatic for weeks after seeing the video. I thought to myself many times during that period, "Everyone has to know this story." I understood why origin stories are so important: They confer an identity otherwise hidden in our daily comings and going. A cosmology is not just a theoretical enterprise, but a way also to gain our bearings in the inner world. I painted a large tree of life, filled with many creatures, against a background depicting the enfolded Mystery, since that was an image that seemed to express what I had come to know. An important reason we have not been able to free ourselves from the deep split between spirit and matter that plagues Western culture is that we have not had a cosmological origin story to orient our culture to a proper human/Earth/spirit relationship. Without a powerful, agreed upon story we have not been able to dream together as a culture. As Brian Swimme and Thomas Berry point out in the *The Universe Story*, the fate of the Earth now depends on whether humankind all together can find again its true place and role in nature and in nurturing the Gaian biosphere.

It isn't enough, however, just to know the story and to grasp some of the remarkable insights that the epic of evolution and the new cosmology offer. There remains the further step of realizing our own individual participation in the unfolding story, especially in its creative and sacred dimensions. There is a great loss if the evolutionary epic is experienced as an impersonal account about which we have some knowledge; instead we are invited to understand that it is an ongoing, living story in which we, in all dimensions of our being, are an integral part. It can offer us genuine salvation by awakening and engaging our divine depths and bringing us into participation in the Earth as a single sacred community.

But why are so many people so deeply alienated from the Earth, both in its physical and spiritual dimensions? This brings us to the third major aspect of the book and of my life, which is the world of psychological wounding. My parents lost a four-year-old boy, my brother David, to spinal meningitis when I was an infant. As a consequence, I was not welcomed in a loving, joyful way into the human family. I experienced this loss of embrace and love as a betrayal, the very fundamental betrayal of not being received and granted the appropriate and much needed love and attention that is every child's birthright. It was this wound that compelled me in my adult years to try to understand my inner psychological situation and to search for a satisfying physical, interpersonal, and spiritual belonging. Faithful friends, a loyal husband, and a Jungian analyst able to relate to my neediness, have all been essential in my learning how personal, psychological healing is integral to the search for a profound "at homeness" in the world.

So the final sections of the book are about getting our internal house in order. It seems clear that our own inner dividedness can keep us from entering and participating fully in the larger sacred totality of which we are an intrinsic part. As, in the context of the universe story, we seek through various pathways of healing to reawaken to the infinite sacred spaciousness within us, we also awaken to the sacredness of the world. In so doing, we will discover anew our human capacity for entering into the larger community of life.

Now, at the beginning of the twenty-first century, when the ecological threat is so serious, the inner journey becomes an ethical imperative. If we can follow the journey that awakens us to the sacred dimension of our being, it can bring with it the spiritual transformation necessary to evoke a profound change in our manner of relating to the threatened Earth and the needs of humanity. It is of key importance to know that the heart of the religious life and the search for personal healing can be understood as integral to the person who came into being out of the unfolding Earth and universe. For, as is widely observed, the roots of the ecological crisis lie within; thus an adequate response to it will not come without a fundamental change in spirituality. Through the universe story and our integration into it by means of the traditions of the contemplative pathway and of depth psychology, we will touch the deepest energetic resources of our being and have the vision to insist that our spiritual and physical home no longer be destroyed by human ignorance and rapaciousness. We will no longer have the illusion that our spirit will not be destroyed along with the natural world. If we can awaken to a deep love and awe for ourselves, and for the Earth, we will not let it be destroyed.

This is a critical evolutionary moment. We wonder if it will be possible to stop the ecological holocaust that is upon us, the greatest holocaust since the dinosaur extinction. I believe that the beauty and power of the new story, the knowledge of our belonging within it, and the hope and vision the story can awaken, will bring forth the caring and love that bear the psychic energy needed to co-create with the Earth a viable future. This must be a future in which human activities on the Earth are in alignment with the forces functioning thoughout. It is towards the articulation of this vision that this book is directed.

Mary Conrow Coelho
New York City
August, 2002

ACKNOWLEDGEMENTS

IT WOULD TAKE too many pages to acknowledge the many teachers, guides, retreat leaders, conference lecturers, authors, family members, and friends who have contributed in innumerable ways over the years to the personal and intellectual foundations of this book. In regard to more immediate sources, several seminal opportunities to ask questions and to clarify ideas with Thomas Berry, Brian Swimme, and Ewert Cousins were invaluable. I am a member of an "epic of evolution" group that meets monthly around our common excitement and interest. The gatherings with Ralph Copleman, Jennifer Morgan, Andy Smith, Susan Curry, Jack Heckleman (before he moved), Bob Wallis, and Maria Myers have been nourishing and enriching. I am indebted to my womens' spirituality group—Mary Virginia Stieb-Hales, Edith Tavon, and Jean Sutton—which carefully and warm-heartedly read and discussed an early version of this book. I thank the participants in workshops at Friends General Conference and other places for their responses to some of the material presented here. I am especially indebted to Joyce Richardson and Bob McGahey, who have shared in the leadership of some workshops. Several people read early versions of the manuscript, offering comments and corrections and helping in many other important ways. The readers were Jaime Coelho, DeDee Rigg, Louis Gropp, Ewert Cousins, Pat Reber, Kenneth and Margaret Conrow, Maria Myers, and Nancy Wright. Finally, I especially thank Corona Machemer, who not only edited the manuscript with great insight and skill, but designed and "made" the pages of the book for publication. Of course, any errors that remain are my own.

I

THE EPIC
OF EVOLUTION

1

IT'S A NEW STORY

Life in Europe, India and America has taught and shown me that there are no more urgent questions than the ultimate important issues, that there is no more felt need and no more torturing thirst than the desire to tackle human problems not only in a universal, global manner, but also in their ultimate meaning and at the level of their deepest roots.

— Raimundo Panikkar

WE ARE MOST fortunate to live in a time when the story of the evolutionary universe is available to us. Teilhard de Chardin, who was a paleontologist as well as a philosopher of religion, was convinced that the discovery that we live in an evolutionary universe, with the concomitant change in our conception of time (things do not just repeat themselves) is the most significant event in 2 million years of hominid intelligence. (Swimme 1985, tape 10) Understood only in the twentieth century, the story traces the unfolding of the universe from the great flaring forth an estimated 13 billion years ago to its the present magnificent, diversified state. It reveals that the universe is a developing reality going through a series of irreversible changes. No other culture knew this, but now we actually have some of the details. Awed and almost unbelieving, many people are seeking to comprehend and celebrate the mystery and beauty. *The new universe story is becoming one of the formative components of a shift in consciousness, as it radically reorders our fundamental perception of things.*[*] It offers insights and images of a world only occasionally glimpsed in earlier times by humanity's most gifted visionaries and philosophers, whose perceptions may now be seen in the context of the evolutionary universe. It is an origin story of great majesty and power. It describes the coming into being over many

[*] Throughout this book, passages in italics mark certain aspects of the universe story that have significance for the 'way of seeing' being developed. Terms of special significance are enclosed by single quotes.

hundreds of millions of years of a universe that is staggering in its immensity, including as it does perhaps 100 billion galaxies. The grandeur and creativity the story reveals were never dreamed of in our most imaginative origin stories. We learn from it that we are differentiated out of the primordial substance of the great flaring forth at the beginning and thus partake of that same creativity and grandeur. Awakening to the depth of our belonging to the creative heart of things and to its great diversity and beauty gives us a noble self-understanding, offering the potential for a transformation of ourselves and our relationships to each other and to all the natural world.

Many of us are familiar with parts of the story: When, for example, we observe the layers of sedimentary rock exposed as the road we are on cuts through a hillside, or note the similarities among the skeletons of different animals in a natural history museum, we are "reading" a paragraph or two. But because the story was discovered by Western science, we are likely to hear it as an impersonal story, no more than a further elaboration of scientific knowledge. Consequently, we may fail to identify with it, to hear it as the life-giving, empowering origin story that it is. We wonder how individuality can possibly be supremely valued in the context of this unfathomably large universe. And there may remain a nagging fear that our most profound, life-changing religious experiences and spiritual longings will be negated if this new story, coming out of "hard" science, is embraced as a common origin story. Hasn't modern science already deprived us of our primordial sense of belonging to a spiritual world? We fear embrace of this story will be another step in an ongoing, severe narrowing of human spiritual and aesthetic identity already reduced by technology, statistics, consumerism, behaviorism, and a denuded environment. Won't the essential amorality in much of science and its objectifying of the natural world further pervade culture? If the story is to be widely embraced it is urgent that these fears and questions be addressed.

The story must be told and comprehended in such a way that there is a central place for humanity's spiritual striving and mystical experiences, because religious insights and experiences have been, throughout history, at the defining core of individual life and culture. We are unlikely to emerge sound of body and mind from our ecological and human crises unless the sacred is brought again into our lives and into our relations with the Earth.

The Contemplative Tradition

It is essential to see that this new origin story does have a supremely personal place for the individual, including a place for a person's most cherished religious experiences and hopes. As preparation for recognizing this place, it will be important to appreciate and grasp the remarkable discoveries of people who have explored the inner life of the person. This study will draw largely on a Western contemplative tradition that has described a pathway to what is called the unitive life, in which the indwelling sacred depths of the individual are integrated with the personality, so that those depths find expression in the life of the person. Francis of Assisi, Richard of St. Victor, Bonaventure, Meister Eckhart, Teresa of Avila, John of the Cross, and uncounted others have discovered that the contemplative journey follows a natural progression from awakening experiences, through transformation of the personality, illuminative insights, and the lower levels of contemplative prayer to the attainment, perhaps, of the unitive life, the fulfillment of the contemplative journey. Jesus of Nazareth entered into the unitive life. His life and teachings, along with reflections on his life by Christians are among the foundations of the contemplative tradition.

There are radical claims in this contemplative tradition that raise compelling and intriguing questions about the nature of God and the person. What, for example, did Eckhart mean when he wrote: "Therefore I am the cause of myself in the order of being which is eternal?" Can the Son be born in the soul as Eckhart suggests? Catherine of Genoa wrote: "My Me is God, nor do I recognize any other me except my God himself." It was said of Jesus that he was fully human and fully divine. Insights like these invite a thoughtful and careful questioning of our basic assumptions. We actually will find support for many of the radical insights of the contemplative/mystical tradition in the context of the new origin story. If the awakened contemplative way of being can be seen as integral to this story, a powerful, life-giving vision emerges to our delighted hearts.

To truly embrace the remarkable identity of the person that modern science, through the new origin story, and the contemplative heritage of the West both reveal by their distinct ways of knowing, it will be necessary to understand that the inner structure of the personality can be receptive to the comprehensive, creative ordering powers of the Earth and the universe, a dimension of what we call God. To this end the self-organizing powers of the universe and the relation of these to traditional ideas of soul and Carl Jung's insights into the Self will be considered; then the pathway to the healing of the personality will be described, so that we may be empowered by awakening to our full creativity, and to our love as a form of the dynamic Earth and Universe. With such healing and integration, the individual can make a genuine creative contribution to the unfolding of the earth and all its inhabitants.

Although, in this work, the individuals used as examples of people who have entered fully into the contemplative life are drawn largely from the Hebrew/Christian tradition, the very nature of the integration into the new story of the evolutionary universe developed here shows that the sacred depths of the person cannot be unique to people who identify with Christianity. Other individuals in other traditions might have been chosen as examples; it is only lack of time and opportunity to carefully study the writings of people in other traditions that precludes extensive use of their experience.

A *Theoria*: A 'Way of Seeing'

In this book, insights derived from both the new universe story and the Western contemplative tradition are knit together in what might be called a *theoria* or a worldview. A *theoria* is primarily an insight or way of looking at the world, and not a form of definitive knowledge of how the world is. (Bohm 1983, p. 4) The word *theory*, which has the same root as *theater*, derives from the Greek *theoria*, meaning "to view, to behold, to make a spectacle." In Neoplatonism, the philosophy based on the thought of Plotinus (chapter 5), the term originally meant the intellectual vision of truth, which the Greek philosophers regarded as the supreme objective of the person of wisdom. (Keating, p. 19) Ultimately we do not know reality as it is, so can offer no proof about the nature of things, but rather a 'way of seeing' that has internal congruence and is congruent with the implications of the new universe story, the insights of the Western contemplative tradition, and, it is hoped, with our own experience. However, there is a type of proof, which is the one of lived experimentation, explored in the final chapters of this book. The capacity for experiencing the validity of the 'way of seeing' develops from a difficult journey that is itself an essential dimension of human self-understanding in the context of the new story and the contemplative tradition. We may gradually understand, 'see' and become different over the course of the years.

The *theoria* developed in this book will, for some people, challenge long-held religious assumptions. But such challenges, and the revolutions in belief they demand, are inevitable. Following the thought of Alfred North Whitehead in addressing the complexities of the relationship between religion and science, theologian Laurence Wilmot writes in his book *Whitehead and God* that "religion will not regain its old power until it can face change in the same spirit as science does; its principles may indeed be eternal, but its thought- forms and modes of expression must change with the advance of knowledge." (p.12) Tradition itself insists that our insights must be framed in our best knowledge of the universe. Brian Swimme, mathematical cosmologist and director of the Center for the Story of the Universe at the California Institute of Integral Studies in San Francisco, puts the question: How convincing are teachings and theologies that are framed by worldviews no longer regarded as real? (1990, p. 87)

Although from time to time theological topics will be discussed, the 'way of seeing' offered here is not a strictly traditional theology. Focus on theology as a separate discipline tends to abstract the divine dimension from the whole, leaving the "mere physical world" devoid of a rooted and integral relationship with the "numinous," a highly valued, healing and renewing realm. Besides, such a theology contradicts, in the case of Christianity, its incarnational insight. Nor is the integration being sought a scientific cosmology involving only adherence to a narrowly scientific interpretation of the implications of the new universe story. Although not contradicting science, incorporating the remarkable personal experiential, spiritual discoveries of the Western contemplative tradition in the story will amplify it and reveal its deeply personal, spiritual dimensions. Fortunately, and not coincidentally, as we shall see, the new cosmology does have in its assumptions the space and place for development of this profoundly personal dimension. If the awakened contemplative state is understood as a condition or state of being that is integral to the new universe story, we have a powerful synthesis. This is what this 'way of seeing' is about!

Though changes in our beliefs about matter and about God may be inevitable, they do not come easily. The continuing controversy over the validity of Darwin's insights demonstrates just how difficult it is for people to abandon long-held assumptions. As discussed in more detail later in this book (chapters 2 and 10), since evolution has been taught in an exclusively mechanistic manner, some of the resistance to Darwin's ideas is well-founded; there is a great need for a nuanced teaching of evolution. Nonetheless there is a price for failure to change our ideas: In *Process Theology* (1976), theologians John B. Cobb and David Ray Griffin point out that the tendency to conform to or reenact one's past can deepen habits that are inappropriate to the new situation. To be free from the past, however, is to be able to respond to the new possibility given in the new moment. Following Whitehead, Cobb and Griffin write:

> The new possibility is the opportunity to incorporate the past in a new way. There is no moment that is not constituted by a synthesis of elements from the past. If to be free from the past were to exclude the past, the present would be entirely vacuous. The power of the new is that it makes possible a greater inclusion of elements from the past that otherwise would prove incompatible and exclude each other from their potential contribution. (p. 83)

In other words, our religions could remain true to their essence if their traditions were to be reconceived within the larger context of the evolutionary universe. Brian Swimme writes: "It would not mean shrinking away from the central religious truths. On the contrary, expressed within the context of the dynamics of the developing universe, the essential truths of religion would find a far vaster and more profound form." The recasting would not be a compromise but a surprising and creative fulfillment, "one whose significance goes beyond today's most optimistic evaluation of the value of religion." (1996, p. 12)

Another compelling motivation for the search to embrace a new 'way of seeing' is the universal human need to form a coherent picture of the world and to find our place within it. The integration proposed in this book may seem quite ambitious, but as Quaker writer and spiritual guide John Yungblut wrote, it is a religious intuition to be implicitly trusted to seek one harmonious vision that integrates the integrity of the natural order and religious insight.[1] (1974, p. iv) Our desire is to see the whole picture without removing ourselves from it. (Kushner, p. 51) But such a coherent picture has not been available in recent centuries in the West. Indeed, we are convinced that the human is without significant relationship to the universe. (Swimme 1985, tape 8) Consequently, we are alienated from the integrated system of the cosmos, and the result is an estrangement that is costly to our psychological and spiritual well-being. Psychoanalyst Otto Rank believed we have become neurotic as a result. (Fox 1985, p. 36) Erich Neumann, a Jungian analyst, has asked if consciousness has lost its link with the whole and is thus deteriorating. (1954,

p. 384) A person isolated from the cosmos does not recognize that she is an integral part of a powerful, creative universe, so she is weakened and her full birth as part of the unfolding universe is aborted. We urgently need a relinking, a *religio*, of the person to the Earth and the All-Nourishing Abyss. It is a profoundly healing vision that is sought.

Ecological Consequences

Tragically, the consequences of the deeply dualistic Western worldview that places spirit in a realm separate from what we call matter have extended far beyond individual confusions. When we do not see the natural world as part of a dynamic cosmos that creates beings of varying complexity with subjective depth, we treat it as an object; we do not love it, care for it, and nurture it. The price has been immense. Jungian analyst Anthony Stevens expresses it well:

> Not only has it meant the sacrifice of our place at the centre of the universe, and the rupture—for the first time in the history of our species—of the mythological bonds linking us to The Great Architect Of All Creation, but it has, more terrifyingly, opened the Pandora's box of technological madness, the prospect of gross overpopulation, world-wide famine, mineral exhaustion, global pollution, and nuclear catastrophe, which may well cause the demise of Christendom to coincide with the destruction of life on this planet, as the Book of Revelation so confidently predicts.[2] (1983, pp. 30–31)

There is no need to elaborate further on the contents of Pandora's box except to mention the probable extinction, largely at our hands, of ten thousand or more species per year, the untested manipulation of the genetic code in our foods, and the destruction of forests. We are not only extinguishing present forms of life, we are eliminating the very conditions for the renewal of life in some of its more elaborate forms. (Swimme and Berry, p. 246)

We must risk fresh vision, while carrying forward many great ancient insights, because we realize the degradation of our mental and physical environs is largely the product of how each of us perceives, and thus acts in, the world around us. Human beings collectively have taken a determinative role in shaping the future direction of the Earth, a role formerly played by the much slower evolutionary processes. Embracing new images and new insights is a personal and community process that takes its own time, but there is great urgency to the work of revisioning demanded by the new universe story, because the insights it offers about the Earth and the person, some new and some old, can be central ingredients in creating a viable human/Earth future. Einstein wisely warned us that we cannot solve problems within the same consciousness in which they were created. The world we create is a direct outgrowth of our beliefs. We must expect and even rejoice in the offering of fresh insights, for we are still learning to be human; after all, in evolutionary terms, it has taken no more that the blinking of an eye for human beings to arrive at our current position of overwhelming influence.

A Vision of the Whole

Spiritual hunger, and the need to satisfy it, has been such a powerful force throughout history that it must find full expression in our telling of the new universe story. We seek to be faithful to both the revelations of the epic of evolution and to people's innermost, personal spiritual life, including the contemplative experiences not only of well-known people like Meister Eckhart and Saint Teresa of Avila, but of many who are little known, like Claire Owens, a housewife. In the end theology, personal spirituality, and cosmology must be considered simultaneously, and they must mutually inform each other. We seek a picture of "how things are" that is compatible with contemporary knowledge but yet does not diminish or devalue the power of the search for God (the meaning of this word will be explored) and the transformed human heart.

We seek, then, a union of theology, personal spirituality, and the new cosmology in what, in Christian terms, is a radically incarnational worldview. It is a vision of the whole that values differentiation without destroying unity; it values matter without becoming materialistic; it values unity without demanding uniformity; it values spirit without degrading matter; it values the present without disregarding the past; it values the future without failing to look honestly at the present out of which the future will unfold. We seek a unitive vision of the richness and depth and intrinsic worth of the whole and of the parts within the whole.

---

[1] Jungian analyst Erich Neumann observed that it is a characteristic of every individual, under all circumstances, to create for himself a consciously constellated and synthetically constructed view of the world, however great or small in scope. (1954, pp. 557–58)

[2] The world's human population has climbed to more than 6 billion. In 1987 it passed 5 billion, having doubled since 1950. Even now we are not caring for all our children: Every year about 11 million children under the age of five die from hunger or hunger-related disease. (Steger and Bowermaster 1990, p. 25)

2

THE EVOLVING UNIVERSE

This story, as told in its galactic expansion, its Earth Formation, its life emergence, and its self-reflective consciousness, fulfill in our times the role of the mythic accounts of the universe that existed in earlier times, when human awareness was dominated by a spatial mode of consciousness.

— Thomas Berry

IN A DISCOVERY that sent shock waves through the scientific community, Edwin P. Hubble observed in 1929 that galaxies are hurtling away from our galaxy and from each other at the rate of tens of thousands of kilometers per second. Einstein's field equations, written in 1914, had predicted that the universe is not static; it is either expanding or contracting. However, he resisted this implication, so profoundly in conflict with the assumption of centuries, and forced an adjustment into the equations. Now we know that the whole universe, everything that is, is in a state of dynamic inflation and evolutionary change. (Barrow and Tipler, p. 368)

With acceptance of the fact that the universe is expanding came the realization that the expansion must have had a beginning. Calculating the rate of expansion, including the evidence that distant galaxies are moving away at a faster rate than those nearer to us, and reversing time, astronomers were astounded to discover that all the celestial conglomerates of stars (galaxies) would simultaneously converge into a single point after some 13 billion years. Slowly, with important contributions from astronomy, physics, chemistry, biology, and paleontology, a coherent story of the birth and development of the universe began to emerge.

The retrospective tracing of all matter to a single original center is the basis for the model of the beginning referred to as the "Big Bang." According to this theory, a hot, dense, "restless sea" of elementary particles (quarks, electrons, etc.) and radiant energy (photons) made up the original substance of the universe. It was this "quark soup," this "fireball" the size of a grapefruit, that would eventually transform itself, over billions of years, into galaxies, stars, our solar system, and the Earth with its living beings. "Restless sea." "Quark soup." "Fireball." We fumble for metaphors to describe these mysteries, for which there is now scientific evidence. The deeper mystery of what came before is not yet (and may never be) fully explored by science, although in chapter 8, below, there are some reflections on the topic.

There was no existing space into which this primeval material unfolded; rather space/time itself unfurled as the material expanded and differentiated. Each place of the universe was part of the initial fireball. This understanding alone changes our way of seeing things quite profoundly. Instead of thinking of the universe as a background in which we exist, we realize we are an organized form, one among many, of the continually emerging totality. What was once the original fireball, now highly differentiated, surrounds us and comprises our very being.

The Big Bang theory received strong support with the discovery in 1964 of the actual radiation that issued from the expanding fireball when freely moving particles of light—photons—escaped.[1] Other predictions emanating from this model, such as the abundance of the lightest elements, hydrogen and helium, and their proportions in the Universe, have been confirmed by actual findings.

It is thought that about one second after the beginning, the energy level (temperature) and density of the expanding fireball had fallen to the point where certain elementary subatomic particles of matter (quarks) could be held together by the strong nuclear force to form the neutrons and protons that would eventually, after the "capture" of electrons, comprise the nuclei of atoms.[2] One proton comprises the nucleus of hydrogen. *This is the only time in the history of the universe that hydrogen nuclei were created.* It is called primordial hydrogen. Somewhat later (10 to 500 seconds) nuclei of helium, consisting of two protons and two neutrons, came into existence through nuclear fusion.[3] Thus the primordial energy yielded up by the fireball as it expands and cools is "captured" and converted into matter—"contained" in the nuclei of all the atoms that will ever be.

In this synthesis of hydrogen and helium nuclei, radiant energy is becoming matter. "Hydrogen atoms" Brian Swimme writes, "rage with energy from the fireball, symphonic storms of energy held together in communities extremely reluctant to give this energy up." (1984, p. 169) Everything we see around us was created out of energy as the cosmos expanded and cooled and became matter.

Following the formation of hydrogen and helium nuclei, in the first three minutes after the Big Bang, there was a long period—several hundred thousand years—before the actual atoms of hydrogen and helium could form. For this to happen electrons had to become associated with the nuclei. But the universe was still so compact (dense) and so hot, with photons of radiation (energy) greatly outnumbering the elementary particles of matter, that no sooner would electrons and nuclei assemble than the fierce radiation would scatter them.

As the universe aged from 300,000 to a million years, expanding and cooling all the while, the radiation era gradually ended. Photons no longer interacted constantly with particles (especially electrons) and could move about freely, generally passing unhindered through space.[4] It is these freely moving photons that are the very low level radiation that was detected in 1964. At the same time, electrons, free from interacting with photons, could be captured by the nuclei, and the actual atoms of hydrogen and helium formed; eventually matter composed of atoms came to dominate radiation as the principal constituent of the universe. Note that an atom is a very complex reality that is a million times larger than the elementary particles that constitute it.

An atom is a group of particles that organize themselves into a whole and coherent system. This is an early example of the creation of complex forms, a process that will be found throughout the story.

Over the ensuing billion years, large conglomerates of hydrogen and helium became prominent, drawn together by small variations in the gravitational field that just exceeded the expansion force.[5] These became the galaxies, which are the basic systems of the universe. In a process little understood, galaxies were created by the billions—as many as 200 billion. Galaxies are not forming now nor have they been for the past 10 billion years.

Within the developing galaxies, dense cores formed, where the tremendous temperature and pressure again caused hydrogen protons to be fused into the larger nuclei of helium. Once a nucleus of helium is formed, less energy is needed to hold it together; the excess is released in the form of radiant energy or light (new photons), and the conglomerates began to shine. What were dark, amorphous clumps of matter became stars. Most galaxies would eventually hold within their organizing power some 100 billion stars, more stars than people who have ever lived on Earth. Here we see the reverse of the process occurring in the first seconds of the universe. Whereas earlier, radiant energy was captured in atomic nuclei, now, with fusion occurring inside stars, matter becomes energy.

Stars convert hydrogen to helium at a relatively slow rate. Since the time when stars first formed, only two or three percent of the hydrogen in the universe has been "consumed" by their nuclear "fires." Still, the hydrogen in any particular star will be exhausted after a period of time lasting from millions to billions of years, depending on the size of the star. New young stars are continually forming, however, and this life cycle of stars, including their death, that turns out to be very fortunate for our own existence, as we shall see.

Cosmologists marvel at the enormous array of features that must be precisely in tune for the universe to complexify and reach a life-supporting stage, and then create a vast array of intelligent beings, including the human variety with its self-

reflexive consciousness. Among these fine-tuned features, sometimes called "meaningful coincidences," are the velocity of expansion of the universe and the degree of gravitational attraction opposing that expansion. Too slow an expansion—and too slow is only one trillionth percent more slowly—and the universe would have collapsed before much differentiation could emerge; too rapid, and all matter would have remained in a diffuse state, without coalescing into stars and planets. (Swimme and Berry, p. 18) The "coincidences" also include the so-called constants of nature, among which are the mass of the electron, the electric charge of the proton, and the strength of the nuclear forces. If the strengths of the nuclear forces had been minutely different, life as we know it could not have developed, because life requires an abundance of hydrogen and carbon atoms, and, it turns out, a very precise balance of nuclear forces is required to preserve these atoms. If the strong nuclear force, which glues the protons in the atomic nucleus together, had been only slightly greater, the conversion of primordial hydrogen to helium would have been almost complete, leaving insufficient hydrogen for star formation. There would have been no sun.

This all shows that for adequate differentiation the universe needs to be quite special: sufficiently long lived, with sufficient gravity to permit star formation in the face of continuing expansion, and with physico-chemical forces of a certain configuration. There is an elegant order, as Brian Swimme notes, such that protons were given the opportunity to become stars. It is so delicate that the universe would not unfold if altered. Given all this precise fine-tuning, some scientists believe that a complex universe including intelligent beings could have emerged only if the laws of physics were very close to what they are. The anthropic principle, as defined by cosmologists, proposes that the emergence of some form of intelligent reflec-

tion of the universe on itself was implicit in the universe from the beginning.[6]

Nucleosynthesis in Stars

The next major step in the story occurs inside very large stars, eight to twenty times the size of our sun, where we see a further step in the differentiation and complexification of the primordial material of the Big Bang. (In smaller stars important cycles also occur, but we will not discuss them in this telling of the story.) For billions of years stars maintain a dynamic equilibrium, balancing the contracting force of gravity and the expansive energy of the fusion reactions. When the supply of hydrogen is exhausted in a star, gravity gains the upper hand, and a phase of collapse begins. With the increased pressure and temperature of the collapse, helium atoms, which had been stable while hydrogen was burning, begin themselves to fuse. Again, energy is released, preventing further collapse, while, depending on the size of the star, atoms of carbon, oxygen and calcium are synthesized. In the largest stars, over millions of years, there is fusion of still heavier elements, ending with the formation of iron. Without this synthesis of elements within stars, no elements other than hydrogen and helium could have existed except in trace amounts.

In the synthesis of carbon there is another example of the remarkable fine-tuning of the universe. Carbon is made in stars by the simultaneous collision and successful fusion of three helium nuclei, an event too rare to explain the abundance of carbon, were it not for a special "resonance" that greatly facilitates this fusion.[7] *This coincidence, however, is not sufficient, because carbon could then be lost by further processing to oxygen, which only requires collision and fusion of two nuclei, one carbon and one helium; remarkably no resonance exists for this particular step, thus allowing many carbon nuclei to survive. (Barrow and Tipler, pp. 251–53)*

Once an iron core is formed, the end of the large star is near. Nuclear fusion involving iron does not produce energy, so that iron plays the role of a fire extinguisher in stellar evolution, damping the inferno in the star's core. The equilibrium sustaining the star is gone, pressure and temperature increase unchecked, and the star collapses. In a series of cataclysmic reactions, within a few seconds elements heavier than iron (initially only the nuclei of atoms) are formed and the star explodes in a titanic release of energy and matter: a supernova shining dramatically in the sky. It is by means of this explosive cosmic event that the nuclei of uranium and other heavier elements synthesized in the star and thrown, together with the lighter elements, into space. As the cloud formed in the explosion cools, the nuclei acquire electrons, and become atoms. The explosion of the supernova is a creative event producing the material for the future evolution of the universe. Although the star dies, its death is the basis for future creative events.

The cloud of elements from a supernova drifts through space, mixing with other clouds of matter and with primordial hydrogen, to form a nebula (cloud) that now contains a large mixture of elements, not just hydrogen and helium as in the first conglomerations of matter. When our sun, a second or third generation medium-sized star, was formed from a nebula in the Milky Way galaxy, some small percentage of the nebula fell into orbit around the star, condensed, and formed planets, including the Earth. Planetary formation may be a natural process in the early life of a star. It is known that the sun could not have been created after the Earth; rather, the Earth was formed in some way out of the same nebular material. It has been determined that our sun is close to 5 billion years old. The age of all the solid bodies in the solar system that have been measured—the Earth, the moon and meteorites—is about 4.6 billion years.

The sun converts 4 million tons of matter into radiant energy (photons) each second, and has enough hydrogen to burn for another 5 billion years. The Earth receives only a billionth of the sun's total energy output, yet this provides the energy for almost all the biosphere, the part of our world in which life exists. All the unfolding of life on Earth depends on the Earth's sensitivity to this abundant energy. Note that this stupendous, daily supply of energy, which results from the thermonuclear fusion of primordial hydrogen atoms, is the very energy of the original fireball.

We are involved in a universe of unfathomable size and one in which there are incomprehensibly powerful energy exchanges. While we go about our daily activities we are usually not aware of the numinous energetic realities in which we are embedded. This is one reason why this story is so important: it keeps present for us the fact that as living beings we are participants in a powerful energetic totality. If we knew this, perhaps we would not allow our lives to be trivialized. Sometimes people feel intimidated by the immensity of the universe and the enormity of the forces. But we must recognize that it takes these very large, complex structures, the powerful interaction of energies and such a long history, to create and sustain the life and the consciousness we have and that we find around us. Since the universe has been expanding continuously, its size must be commensurate with its age; thus, the mere fact that the universe supports human life means that it has to be huge. We could not live in a small universe, the size, for example, of the Milky Way galaxy alone.

The Earth

The story continues as we turn to the unfolding of the cloud of elements that condensed around the sun to form our planet.[8] It is the story of the most remarkable transformation of that condensing "dust" to become today's Earth: the crustal rocks and core, the atmosphere, the seas, the rivers, the teeming variety of life. Figure 1 is an overview of the history of the Earth from its birth to the present that helps us comprehend the vast time involved. It depicts something of the Earth as it would look from space every 100 million years, showing its gradual transformation. There are 46 Earths in the diagram, making the total of 4.6 billion years, the time since the Earth solidified.

Fig. 1. THE EARTH'S LONG TRANSFORMATION

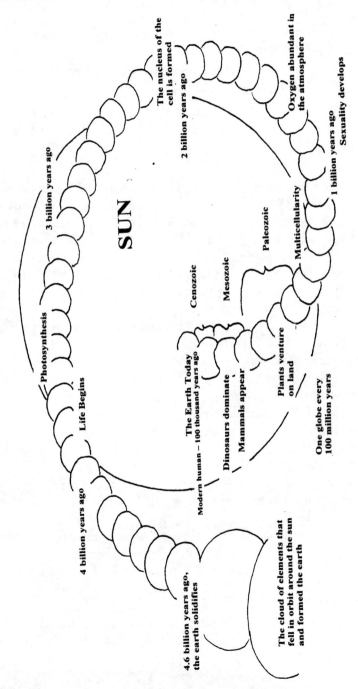

The broad perspective of the diagram encourages us to ponder the remarkable transformation that the Earth has undergone. We must ask how the Earth got from a cooling, condensing nebula of elements formed in the stars to oceans, birds and human beings. It is an important change in human consciousness to begin to seek understanding of this transformation which has been an enterprise involving very great creativity.

For the first half a billion years, while the Earth was condensing from the cloud of elements around the sun, it suffered the shock of collisions with meteors and planetoids that kept it boiling day and night. Colliding comets brought quantities of water in the form of ice. During this period the Earth was cooling and, as it did, the heavier elements such as iron and nickel began to settle to form a super-thick metallic core. The lighter elements floated to the surface, forming a granite crust that has been compared to the skin that forms on a steaming pudding. The early, turbulent atmosphere of methane, hydrogen, ammonia and carbon dioxide (CO_2) formed largely from the release of these gases from the Earth's interior through fissures and volcanoes.

By about 3.9 billion years ago, the temperature of the Earth had fallen below the boiling point of water so it was cool enough for transient shallow oceans to form on the unstable crust. And very soon after that—3.8 to 4.0 billion years ago—life began. The microscopic bacteria-like microorganisms, the form of life on Earth for millions of years, were the ancient ancestors of all the life on Earth.

The discovery that life appeared so very early in the history of the Earth is major new knowledge. Until quite recently it was thought to have begun only about 600 million years ago, because that was the extent of the record of visible fossils in ancient rocks. We now know that it took more than 3 billion years for life forms to complexify to the point where their fossils could be readily observed, and still longer to attain their present beauty and bounty.

One of the consequences of the broad perspective offered by our new knowledge of the epic of evolution is that we witness the emergence of life out of the early conditions of the Earth. We realize that there must be a continuum between life and the "non-living," when we remember that all things, whether living or not, are descendants of the nebular material that formed our sun and the planets. The Earth itself emerged into life, the story tells us. This is remarkable indeed. David Bohm, a quantum physicist and speculative thinker whose work we will consider in the next chapter, wrestled with the mysterious relationship between the living and the "non-living." He thought that everything in the universe is alive and that the emergence of life is not a foreign or radical change but is implicit in what we call inanimate matter. (Briggs and Peat, p. 126) Or perhaps, in order to preserve our common assumption that we can tell what is alive, it is better to say that life must be approached "as a variation of the matter question, for life is simply one more thing matter does, given the right circumstances." (Rue, p. 65) Chemist James Lovelock, who proposed the Gaia hypothesis (see chapter 10), suggests that the distinction between living and non-living matter "is merely a hierarchy of intensity going from the "material" environment of the rocks and atmosphere to the living cells." (Quoted, with commentary, in Barlow 1991, p. 18.)

Many ingenious ideas are offered to explain how life began and how cells and their complex components developed. Perhaps the complex molecules that would come to be parts of larger biomolecules, and eventually cells, were formed on deep-sea hydrothermal vents, or perhaps on talcum powder-sized specks of interstellar dust that had been pulsed by radiation from stars and come to Earth with comets and meteors. (Goodenough, p. 20) The Earth was in a position with respect to the Sun that granted it a temperature range where complex molecules could be formed. We don't know how these complex molecules (sugars, amino acids, and nucleotides), together with water, carbon dioxide, and other small molecules (like formaldehyde, methane, and hydrogen sulfide), formed the larger biomolecules. One of these, ribonucleic acid (RNA), is essential to the formation of cells because it has the ability to copy itself and also the ability to carry instructions for making more RNA and for making a surrounding membrane. It is thought the earliest cells had self-replicating RNA molecules with a membrane. Later, DNA (another information-carrying molecule), protein synthesis, and biochemical pathways facilitated by enzymes (proteins) complexified the developing cell. In general we can say that life as we know it emerged from "non-living" matter when chemical systems integrated the functions of energy transformation, information processing, and self-replication. (Rue, p. 67)

The early individual bacteria-like cells would not have been visible to the naked eye, although cabbage-shaped colonies of them, sometimes several meters high, would have been. Fossil mounds of these colonies, called stromatolites, have been found around the world, including in Australia, Kansas and South Africa. They are made of thin mats of the bodies of the early single-celled organisms and fine layers of mud. When very thin slices of the layered stromatolites are cut and studied under a microscope, the body walls of the ancient microorganisms are clearly visible.

These earliest cells are now classified as prokaryotes. The word *prokaryote* means "before the true nucleus." All bacteria are prokaryotes and the prokaryotes (Monera kingdom) are one of the five kingdoms of the biological world. The others—the mostly unicellular protists, and the multicellular fungi, plants, and animals—are all eukaryotes, which means the cells all have a true nucleus, the development of which comes a bit later in the story.

It is not reductionist to say life emerged from the Earth, as it would have seemed to be in the context of an outdated, mecha-

nistic view of matter. Instead, this emergence of life from the Earth expands our sense of the mystery of matter, the mystery of the stuff of the universe. Life is intrinsic to the universe and emerges under the right conditions. Teilhard de Chardin spoke of life being asleep in matter, a promise from within, or, as Brian Swimme and his co-author, geologian Thomas Berry, put it in The Universe Story, *"the universe, when given a chance, will organize itself into complex and persistent patterns of activity." (p. 84) The universe apparently needed something like 8 or 9 billion years to be able to express itself in these early forms of life on Earth.*

The differentiation of life from these early prokaryotic cells to today's highly developed ecological systems, with complex interrelationships among plants and animals and the Earth and atmosphere, is a very long and complex story, occurring over more than 3 billion years. Many of the details are not known, for the record has been lost in the metamorphosing of organic sediments of the past. However, some of the major steps are known, and this allows us to reconstruct the outline, at least, of the great creativity of the Earth.

Relationship with the Sun

With the advent of life on Earth, new capacities have emerged in the universe. For example, the prokaryotic cells, as we have seen, can "remember" information in their molecules, including those patterns necessary to assemble other living cells. Perhaps even more significant was the development of the capacity to capture the energy from the sun, in the process we call photosynthesis.

This is a supreme achievement of creativity because a photon is an extremely fast-moving particle of light. If you do not capture the photon just right, it will "dissolve" into heat. It is a stupendous and permanent achievement to harness the sun's light, one that is central to the subsequent unfolding of life. (Swimme 1984, p. 103).

Whether the very earliest cells carried on photosynthesis, or derived energy from inorganic reactions, or lived off the energy-rich organic molecules in the primeval seas is unknown. Nonetheless, the early microorganisms had very soon fashioned molecules, called chlorophyll, to capture photons from the sun, and convert the energy in them into energy in organic molecules capable of supporting life. Thus does the energy coming from the thermonuclear reactions of the primordial hydrogen in the sun sustain life on Earth.

It is important to pause here to ponder what is happening when the molecules that can capture the photons of the sun are created. We need to remember that both the prokaryote and the sun itself are composed of the elementary particles of the primary fireball, which were subsequently differentiated into hydrogen and helium atoms, and then into other elements, during the life cycle of early, large stars. These elements become part of the chlorophyll molecule and the biochemical pathways that capture the photons coming from the nuclear fusion of primordial hydrogen in the sun. There has thus developed a remarkable sensitivity and interrelationship between one differentiated part of the universe and another part of the universe: a new intensity of communion. This communion is a fundamental characteristic of the universe.

The advent of life on Earth with photosynthetic powers has profound influence on the entire Earth system. As prokaryotes became able to take CO_2 out of the air in the process of photosynthesis, the CO_2 level of the atmosphere declined. An atmosphere with a high level of CO_2 prevents thermal radiation from the Earth's surface, so as the cells pulled CO_2 out of the air, the temperature of the entire Earth declined. By 2.3 billion years ago, Earth had entered an era of glaciation that spread an immense cover of ice across the continents. The photosynthetic process, developed in microorganisms, thus became an important factor in determining the climate of the Earth.

The prokaryotes also gradually altered planetary dynamics in another vital way: one product of photosynthesis is oxygen. Initially the oxygen released during photosynthesis did not affect the oxygen level in the atmosphere because it was absorbed into the rocks as iron was oxidized and because it reacted with various elements in the primitive atmosphere. But eventually as these "oxygen sinks" were filled, and about 2.7 billion years ago, oxygen began to accumulate in the atmosphere; it became relatively abundant about 1.2 billion years ago. One very important consequence was that free oxygen in the upper reaches of the atmosphere was reconfigured by solar energy into ozone. This protected the Earth from ultraviolet radiation, which is highly damaging to the complex molecules of life, and so made possible life's eventual expansion beyond the protective seas.

Cells with More Energy

A further consequence of the presence of oxygen in the atmosphere came from the fact that oxygen is highly reactive, because it is in perpetual "need" of electrons that it seeks from other compounds, potentially harming them. This reactivity made it destructive to the life forms of the time, which had developed in an oxygen-poor atmosphere. Its presence created a crisis so severe that it threatened the very existence of life itself. Instead, faced with the crisis, life transformed. A type of bacteria (cyano-bacteria, formerly called blue-green algae) capable of using the oxygen in respiration developed. Respiration releases energy (measured as the amount of the energy-carrying molecule called ATP that is produced)[9] for the cell from fuel molecules like simple sugars and from the oxygen itself; the process releases carbon dioxide into the atmosphere. As a consequence of the development of respiration, a new source of energy, which provides fifteen times the energy of the previous type of metabolism, was at hand, laying the foundation for the appearance of more complex life. It was a change that marked the end of an old regime, as the foundation was laid for more than 2 billion years of further creativity. It is possible that the biosphere (the life on the planet) could have remained in a rudimentary state without the threat from oxygen.

One type of early bacteria that began to carry out respiration is with us today in the cells of our bodies. It is now widely accepted that such bacteria began to live symbiotically with cells that were unable to use oxygen in this manner. There is a great deal of convincing evidence that these symbiotic bacteria became the mitochondria, organelles found today in all plant and animal cells.[10] Mitochondria are often called the powerhouse of the cell because the reactions of respiration and the production of ATP occur inside them. The fact that mitochondria have their own DNA and that they divide independently of the cell they inhabit, strongly supports the idea that they were once independent organisms. Now no longer free-living bacteria, millions of descendants of these ancient organisms in our body, some in every cell. A liver cell, which has modest energy requirements, has about 2,500 mitochondria, making up about 25 percent of its volume, whereas a heart muscle cell has several times as many very large mitochondria. (Curtis and Barnes, p. 119) Thus, the history of the Earth is living in our bodies in a most central and intimate way. Mitochondria are the ancient bacteria, but they are also part of us.

Developments in the Oxygenated Seas

The first radically new creation within the oxygenated system was the true nucleus. Cells with a true nucleus, called eukaryotic cells, appeared no later than 1.3 billion years ago (Eldredge, p. 56) and possibly as early as 1.8 to 2 billion years ago. (Knoll, p. 67) With the nucleus came mitosis, a sophisticated process that divides the genetic material in the cell to pass it on to the daughter cells. Eukaryotic cells are in many ways more efficient and capable of a greater range of function than simple prokaryotic cells. Within one-celled eukaryotic creatures there occur several thousand different *types* of chemical reactions. (Rue, p. 66) Since all the cells in our body are eukaryotic, we are descended from an early eukaryotic cell, a protist. Yet, in spite of this development, the prokaryotes, the bacteria or Monera, are still very much with us, in our bodies and all around us. The old is often not eliminated with the advent of the new.

Roughly a billion years ago, a eukaryotic cell consumed its living neighbor. The Earth began "eating itself alive." (Swimme and Berry, p. 104) As heterotrophy (Gr. *heteros*: different; Gr. *trophos*: nutrition) became established, a primordial mouth developed, with many elaborations of that form following. Predator/prey relationships evolved that became central parts of complex ecosystems.

Another major development of this eon was the beginning of sexual reproduction.[11] In the process, the genetic information in the nuclei of two individuals is mingled; the DNA "cards" are shuffled and dealt again in such a way that great variation becomes possible. Mutations from errors in copying the DNA, and from other sources discussed below, also contribute significantly to variation. A mutation may be lethal or it may result in beneficial traits that enable the organism to thrive and pass the mutation along in the genetic line. Eukaryotic sex is both ancient and ubiquitous; it is found in all the phyla that trace back to the Cambrian, the first period of the Paleozoic (see below). (Goodenough, p. 117)

About the same time sexuality appeared, so did multicellularity. With sexuality in multicellular organisims, the genetic information in the nucleus of cells of the parents (their genome) is entrusted to immature offspring, making the survival of these progeny of the highest importance. A plant, for example, nurtures the fertilized egg, the seed, by surrounding it with protective coats or with attractive fleshy fruits. Reptiles, birds and mammals use incredible energy and ingenuity to assure the survival of their offspring.

With the development of sex the death of individuals begins in the evolutionary story. For billions of years death was not a biological necessity; not the inevitable ending of life. There is no death programmed into the life cycle of bacteria or protists. Such organisms divide to form either clones or mutations of themselves with no residue. The earliest creatures might have been killed, crushed or starved to death, but they never died "naturally." They had a kind of immortality, which is found in their single-celled descendants on Earth today. But in sexual organisms, since the genetic information is carried forward to the next generation by special cells called gametes (egg and sperm or their equivalents), immortality is handed over to the germ line. (Goodenough, p. 148) The arrival of the next generation assures the continuity of the genetic information. The absence of death in the earliest creatures means it is possible that clones of the earliest bacteria (prokaryotes) are still with us. Their particular genetic pattern could be more than 3 billion years old.

Complex Multicellular Life

Complex multicellular life developed some 670 million years ago. (Eldredge, p.58) However, the great efflorescence of plants and animals that were large enough to be visible later to the naked eye as fossils began 570 million years ago. It isn't known exactly why this astounding development occurred at this time, although the radiation of large plants and animals may be linked to an increase in oxygen, embedded in an even larger framework of tectonic, climactic, and biogeochemical changes. (Knoll, p. 73) It seems that once the basic systems were in place, life took off in an almost wild explosion. Multicellularity made possible great success in motility and predation, as cells specialized to achieve these purposes. Sexual eukaryotes adopted the evolutionary pattern known as speciation, which segregates organisms into those that will and will not mate with one another. A higher order of self-organization was also achieved. (See chapter 10.) The self-organizing processes that are part of multicellularity enabled the appearance in the universe of individuals capable of training thousands of cells to function in accord with the organism's particular aims.

In his book The Garden of Ediacara, *paleontologist Mark McMenamin describes the strange Ediacaran animals that arose some 670 million years ago and flourished for about 100 million years. The name comes from a strata of fossils found in the Ediacaran Hills of Australia and a rock formation known as the Burgess Shale in the Canadian Rockies. These animals have not survived. Their evolution was cut short by the trilobites and brachypods of the later Cambrian explosion, which supplanted them. One reason they are of interest is that they indicate that multicellularity may well have arisen more than once, for in general the Ediacaran animals appear not to be closely related to later animals, although they have protist (single-celled) ancestors in common. The Ediacaran were often flat, segmented, and leaflike, and lacked internal tubular structures. Yet in these strange creatures McMenamin finds evidence of cerebralization, which he suggests supports the idea that there is a directionality in evolution.[12] He writes: "There must be something about the structure of the material world that causes matter to organize in this particular and very interesting way. In other words, it would appear that life evokes mind. There is indeed some kind of evolutionary directionality and vital potency." (p. 270)*

Directionality had been suggested earlier by Teilhard de Chardin, who observed the emergence of common characteristics in three separate branches of Chinese mole rats that had followed independent evolutionary trajectories after the branches of the family tree diverged.[13] He concluded that the appearance of similar traits in all three lineages indicated directionality in evolution. Many scientists disputed this interpretation, however, claiming that the supposed directionality could be explained by the common genetic inheritance of the three lines before the divergence and by similar selection pressures. But, as McMenamin writes, it could be that matter organizes in ways that are not determined only by the genetics and selection pressures. Ideas about a creative ordering will be discussed in chapters 10 and 13.

The Paleozoic Era (Gr. *palaios*: old, ancient)

The period of abundant fossil evidence has been divided into three major geologic eras: Paleozoic (570 to 230 million years ago), Mesozoic (230 to 66 million years ago) and Cenozoic (66 million years ago to the present): ancient, middle and modern life respectively. Each of these eras is further subdivided into periods of millions of years. The group of species found in the fossil record of a particular period and geographic area are sometimes called Cuvierian packages, after the French naturalist Baron Georges Cuvier (1769–1831). A division of geological time with a beginning and an end is determined by the presence of characteristic fauna and flora (the Cuvierian package) that typify the particular period. Commonly the marked change in the flora and fauna from one period to the next is caused by extinction episodes. The packages of life—biological systems—of one period diversify and flourish, only to vanish, leaving remnants to seed the next evolutionary and ecological diversification, the next populating of the bioregion or globe. New ecosystems and new species replace the old. This is an important recognition. It means that human beings today are part of Cuvierian packages in each particular ecosystem in which they dwell.

As we review some of the most important creative events in the last 570 million years, we need to hold in mind that it is part of human history. We are not directly descended from all the various animals, but we are related to the complex ecosystems that supported the forms to which we do have direct genetic link.

In the early Paleozoic, invertebrates (no backbone) dominated the seas. There were no land dwellers, and no vertebrates. During this era there was a veritable explosion in the numbers and varieties of marine invertebrates: among others, the crinoids (relatives of modern starfish); the brachiopods (bivalves but not mollusks; and the brachiopods' "cousins," the bryozoans all came on the scene. At the same time, bacterial crusts and lichens were pioneering the land.

Plants were the first larger life forms to venture onto dry land, some 400 million years ago. Up to this point—for 90% of Earth's history—life had remained in the oceans. It was the development of stiff-walled woody cells, which could resist the flattening power of gravity, that was essential for the invasion of land. In addition, structures specialized for transporting fluids made it possible to handle the water shortage that came with the transition from the seas to land. The first land plants quite early diverged into at least two separate lineages. One was a group (the bryophytes) which includes the mosses; the other was the vascular plants, which have a well-developed vascular system that transports water, minerals, sugars, and other nutrients throughout the plant body, allowing a much greater size.

The Paleozoic saw forests of ferns, giant horsetails, lycopods and one group of gymnosperms (meaning "naked seed," in contrast with later seeds, which would be encased) that thrived in the great swamps covering the warm land. There were no deciduous trees, as we know them, nor any true conifers. Coal deposits, formed by the compression of buried, decomposed vegetable matter, originated during this period.

The appearance of gymnosperms, later represented primarily by the conifers, marks a major development, since they could bring the male and female gametes together to create a seed without the moist surface that mosses and ferns require. This, together with the needle-like leaves that protect them from water loss, allowed them to overcome the threat of aridity on the vast land masses. They would soon spread rapidly across the continents.

The first animals to live on land developed an external skeleton that could keep water within and also offer protection. These were the arthropods (jointed legs), a grouping that includes the enormous multitude of insects and spiders, as well as crabs and lobsters. Amphibians also developed during the very long Paleozoic, and at the end of the period the reptiles appeared. Two adaptations characteristic of reptiles allowed them to forsake the vicinity of water and become the predominant terrestrial vertebrate: a watertight skin and the amniotic egg, with its encapsulated water supply and nourishment for the embryo. The appearance of warm-blooded animals further energized this migration across the land. At the boundary between the upper Paleozoic and the lower Mesozoic, fossils of warm-blooded mammal-like reptiles have been discovered—reptiles because they laid eggs and lacked the ha ir and other features of their mammalian descendants. (Eldredge, p.95)

At the end of the era of ancient life, 230 million years ago, there was a mass extinction, one of five major extinctions that decimated land and sea species. It was a global event, the most devastating of all the extinctions, during which more than 90% and maybe even 96% of all the species on Earth disappeared. Perhaps some huge extraterrestrial object collided with the Earth and drastically altered the atmosphere, although direct evidence for this has not been found.[14] There is evidence of a progressive, "stepped," cumulative extinction, partly triggered by sea level decline. (Eldredge, pp. 97–98). The descendants of the survivors moved into the next era, the Mesozoic (230 to 266 million years ago), popularly known as the age of reptiles.

Following extinctions, new species develop. It is thought that perhaps 99% of all species the Earth has produced are now extinct, yet there are 30 to 80 million species living today. (Eldredge, p.22) Such is the creativity of the Earth.

The Mesozoic Era (Gr. *mesos*: in the middle)

Dinosaurs dominated life on the surface of the Earth for 145 million years, yielding just enough space for mammals to cling to existence. Fossil evidence indicates it was the dinosaurs who developed parental care of the young. The dinosaurs have been described as the Earth's experiment with giantism. If a convenient unit of size is an elephant (roughly five tons), a Diplodocus is two or three elephants and a Barosaurus is eight elephants. The giants weighed as much as ten to twenty elephants. Their diet, except for the carnivorous dinosaurs, was the forests of ferns that were a dominant feature of the Mesozoic.

Primitive mammals appeared about 200 million years ago. Birds also evolved in the Mesozoic, diverging, it is now believed, from therapod dinosaurs about 150 million years ago. The first marsupial mammals appeared 124 million years ago.

Mammals differed from dinosaurs in having body fur instead of scales, giving live birth instead of laying reptilian eggs, and having mammary glands to supply nourishment to their highly dependent young. (Reptile young are nourished in the egg and when "born," are capable of independent living.)

In The Universe Story, *Brian Swimme and Thomas Berry point out that the "new mammalian mode of nourishing the young in the earliest period of their existence outside the womb was immensely significant for the future psychological formation of the mammalian species. This bodily intimacy during pregnancy and after birth can be associated with the distinctive emotional qualities that develop in this line of descent." (p. 122)*

About 100 million years ago, during the last period of the Mesozoic, another major development occurred: the emergence of flowering plants. In *The Immense Journey*, Loren Eiseley calls this a soundless, violent explosion (p. 51), for although there is evidence flowering plants may have developed at the end of the Paleozoic, according to the fossil record they appear suddenly now in great numbers and spread very fast, dominating other plant life. The reason was their reproductive system, which was an order of magnitude more fruitful than that of gymnosperms: a conifer takes eighteen months to produce its seeds whereas a flower can grow a seed capable of producing the next generation in a few weeks.

Flowering plants are called angiosperms, which means "encased seed," or seeds within fruits. There are now 235,000 species of angiosperms, including not only plants with conspicuous flowers but also the great hardwood trees, all the fruits and vegetables, nuts and herbs, grains and grasses that are staples of the human diet and the basis of agricultural economies all over the world.

It is the covered seed that was critical for the development of other, later life forms. The appearance of flowers and seeds parallels the rise of birds and mammals. With the concentrated food energy in the seeds of grasses came the great mammalian herbivores, like mammoths, horses and bison. A symbiotic relationship between flowers and insects also developed, with the insect, attracted by the flower's nectar, transporting pollen from one flower to the next. Often the body shape and size of an insect is highly specific to a particular plant.

At the time when the flowers were "exploding" over the continents, there existed a mouse-like mammal from which humanity would eventually develop. It climbed into the trees 69 million years ago and led to the primates. Both these little mammals and the birds could be said, in hindsight, to have been be "awaiting" the mass extinction that, 66 million years ago, marked the transition from the Mesozoic to the Cenozoic and the end of the dinosaurs.[15] The impoverished fauna at the end of the Mesozoic left a clear field for mammalian expansion.

It now seems evident that it took the eradication of dinosaurs to give mammals a chance to take over. We have to abandon the notion that mammals superceded the great reptiles by dint of inherent superiority. (Eldredge, p. 102)

We are following a gradual increase in the complexity of plant and animal species. In the context of this new story, the question of the manner in which such complexity develops becomes an important subject of study. (See chapter 10.) Some scientists assert that it developed through random interactions, while others believe that although a vast amount of time has passed since the Big Bang, it has not been enough for the complexity we observe to have been built that way. According to astronomer Fred Hoyle the probability of the formation of complex organic molecules, let alone a living thing, through random events is about one in 10^{200}—equivalent to zero. (Coxhead, p. 132) Brian Swimme gives a figure of one in 10^{229} for the probability of arriving at the complexity of the Earth by *means of random collisions.* In fact, if we consider any of the largest structures of the cosmos, like galaxies, it seems clear that they are difficult or impossible to account for in a random and unbiased universe.*

The Cenozoic Era (Gr. *kaino*: recent) and the Hominids

The Cenozoic, which began about 66 million years ago, and may now be ending, has been a time of stupendous creativity. Within 12 million years of the mass extinction at the end of the Mesozoic, most of the living orders of mammals had already come into existence. The differentiation of the mammals gave rise to a variety of marsupials and about two dozen lines of placental mammals, including carnivores like lions and tigers; ungulates, which include horses and cows; rodents; and such diverse groups as whales and dolphins, bats and primates—and the family of species, the hominids, that would include the modern human.

That the mammal from which humanity would develop went early on into the trees is significant. Forest life seems to have advanced the psychic capacity of these ancestral primates: Swinging easily among tree branches demanded quickness of mind, frontal focus of the eyes and countenance, binocular vision for depth perception and eye-hand coordination, and the ability to focus attention—all qualities that were preserved when their hominid descendants moved out of the forest to the more open savanna. The eventual upright posture freed the hand from the task of walking and allowed an increased capacity for grasping. Other significant developments are the enlargement of the brain and the prolonged period of childhood prior to maturity. (Swimme and Berry, pp. 145–46) The oldest known hominid fossil, discovered in 2001 in Chad, in central Africa, is nearly 7 million years old. It is generally thought that our direct ancestors split off from the great ape lineage some 4 or 5 million years ago, although the great apes are considered to be in the same family, the *hominidae*, as those genera from whom our species is descended. It has also been generally accepted that the hominids

---

* Lecture at the Unitarian Universalist retreat center on Star Island, June 1997.

called australopithecines were the earliest group of primates to be part of the specifically human lineage. However, one suspects that older hominids in our lineage may yet be found; indeed, the fossil from Chad may turn out to be one.

The first australopithecine discovery was the Tuang child (*Australopithecus africanus*), found in South Africa in 1924. It took many years of controversy and the discovery of more australo-pithecine fossils for the child's humanlike features to be widely recognized by the paleo-anthropological community. "Lucy," who lived in what is now southern Ethiopia about 3.2 million years ago, was of this same species, and the hominids who made the famous footprints found in volcanic ash in the Rift valley in what is now northern Tanzania were also australopithecines (*Australopithecus afarensis*). The footprints are clear proof that 3.6 million years ago there were hominids who walked upright with a bipedal gait. Australopithecines lived until at least 1.4 million years ago; it is has been generally accepted that *A. Afarensis* gave rise to the genus *Homo*.[16]

It is now commonly believed that modern humans (*Homo sapiens*) probably arose in Africa 100,000 to 120,000 years ago, and migrated from there only 90,000 years ago, replacing various populations of the genus *Homo* like *Homo erectus*, which had previously come out of Africa and spread around the Eurasian world. By 40,000 years ago, *Homo sapiens* had migrated beyond the African-Eurasian world into Australia and by 20,000 years ago had reached North and South America.[17]

Modern humans bring a radical new type of self-reflexive consciousness to the Earth. Thomas Berry writes: "The human is that being in whom the universe activates, reflects upon, and celebrates itself in conscious self-awarness." (1987, p. 108, emphasis added)

For 4 or 5 million years our ancestors lived in groups of perhaps 40 individuals as wild hunter-gatherers—an integral part of local ecosystems and directly affected by general ecological events that simultaneously affected other species as well. There is little question that the abandonment of the hunter-gatherer life and the advent of a sedentary mode of existence, supported by cultivation and animal husbandry, changed the course of human economic adaptation for all time. (Eldredge, p. 203) The increase in food supply, and later developments yielding further increase, permitted the human population to soar; people now became active agents of environmental change. Also with the advent of life in settlements, humans could devote more time to the development of culture, to seeking fulfillment in art, music, dance and poetry, in religious life and in contemplation of the stars. It is in this realm that further rapid evolution now occurs.

Our Body as History's Museum

The various parts of the human body denoted in figure 2, on the next page, are creations of the early universe, the early Earth, and early organisms that have been carried forward within us. Only a very few of all the thousands of such links are marked. Patterns and forms developed hundreds and thousands of millennia ago live in the present in us. And, of course, a similar diagram could be made for every plant and every other animal, living or now extinct.

One example of the organic bond of descent already discussed is that of the mitochondria: Once independent microorganisms, they are now found in every cell of the human body. People could not live without them. Most remarkably, we are multi-cellular organisms. The very cells in our body are directly descended from single-celled organisms of the early Earth.

Another striking example of the body as history's museum is the level of concentration of salt in the cells in our body. It is much lower than that found in today's oceans, but is believed to be the same as that of the seas when life first emerged on land. This level was subsequently maintained in most terrestrial beings, while the oceans became progressively more concentrated (and therefore saltier).

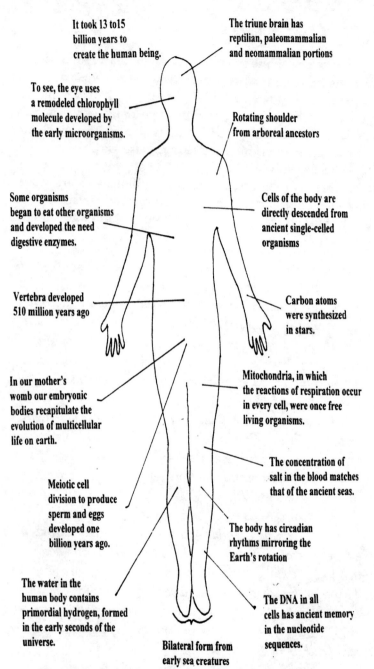

It took 13 to15 billion years to create the human being.

The triune brain has reptilian, paleomammalian and neomammalian portions

To see, the eye uses a remodeled chlorophyll molecule developed by the early microorganisms.

Rotating shoulder from arboreal ancestors

Some organisms began to eat other organisms and developed the need digestive enzymes.

Cells of the body are directly descended from ancient single-celled organisms

Vertebra developed 510 million years ago

Carbon atoms were synthesized in stars.

In our mother's womb our embryonic bodies recapitulate the evolution of multicellular life on earth.

Mitochondria, in which the reactions of respiration occur in every cell, were once free living organisms.

The concentration of salt in the blood matches that of the ancient seas.

Meiotic cell division to produce sperm and eggs developed one billion years ago.

The body has circadian rhythms mirroring the Earth's rotation

The water in the human body contains primordial hydrogen, formed in the early seconds of the universe.

The DNA in all cells has ancient memory in the nucleotide sequences.

Bilateral form from early sea creatures

Fig. 2. HUMAN BEINGS WERE MOTHERED OUT OF THE EARTH AND UNIVERSE.

An organic bond of descent of particular interest to the theme of this book, is the continuity from earlier vertebrate beings of the structures of the human brain. In his book The Triune Brain in Evolution, *neuroscientist Paul MacLean describes the human brain as a hierarchical organization of three brains that reflect developments identified respectively with reptiles (reptilian), early mammals (paleomammalian), and late mammals (neomammalian). As the human brain has developed to its great size, it has retained the chemical features and patterns of anatomical organization of the three basic formations. (p. 14) In their evolutionary development they were separated from each other by innumerable generations covering millions of years. The three brains are radically different in structure and in chemistry and are capable of operating somewhat independently. (p. 9) A schematic diagram of the three brains taken from MacLean's work is shown in figure 3.*

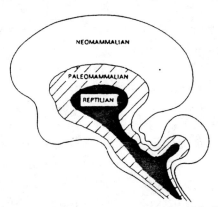

Fig. 3. The Triune Brain, courtesy Paul MacLean.

Each of the three formations in the triune brain has its own special intelligences, its own subjectivity, its own sense of time and space, its own memory, motor, and other functions.[18] *(p. 9) Yet they are interconnected—amalgamated and interfaced in* complex and splendid ways into a single brain. The designation "triune brain" indicates that the three formations are not completely autonomous and also that the relationship among the three together makes a functioning unit that is very much greater than the sum of its parts, because the exchange of information among the three brain types means that each derives a greater amount of information than if it were operating alone. (p. 9)

A long story could be told about each of points of continuity shown in figure 2, and about all the countless points that are not labeled in the diagram. Human beings were indeed born out of the Earth and universe. Each person is a part of the Earth that got up and walked. Rabbi Lawrence Kushner has termed us "creation's museum," because we contain within us the most ancient creations of the Earth and universe. We have an interior archeology. The history of the universe is "written" in our bodies, an ancient history that we are just now learning to read. So there is a lot more to these matters than simply knowing the history: We are made of it; it is made of us. (Kushner, pp. 85–87)

The person is a living form of something incomparably old and thus is, in this sense, also most ancient. The human being is both ancient and new. It is important not to let a misconception springing from the short span of our individual lives result any longer in a false devaluation of ancient matter, the ancient Earth, the ancient soil, the ancient water and the ancient body. The "finite" world of matter is actually not passing, although it continually changes form. (See chapter 10.) Individual lives are brief, but a person, one of the present forms of the ancient Earth, is not "finite" because the person is a form of this ancient Earth. It is no longer appropriate to think of matter and the body as a passing container for spirit. Matter and its forms are *ancient and part of the continuous unfolding in the ever changing, ongoing 'present now.'*

---

[1] It had been predicted in 1948, by cosmologist Ralph Alpher, with Robert C. Herman, that the hot fireball of the Big Bang should leave an "echo," a glimmer of its former self, in the present-day universe. Alpher and Herman calculated that the adiabatic (occurring without loss or gain of heat) expansion of the universe should have cooled the heat radiation from the hot initial state down to a level of approximately 5 K, or thereabouts, by the present, some fifteen billion years after the initial Bang. What was actually discovered was a radiation of 3 K, an extraordinarily close figure.

[2] Initially both particles and antiparticles emerged out of the vacuum. These collided with each other and vanished. There was a very small excess of particles over antiparticles, only one in a billion. This meant that as the fireball expanded and the collision rate dropped, there remained sufficient numbers of unscathed particles for the universe to persist.

[3] Actually, hydrogen nuclei do not fuse directly, because of the low probability that two separate protons and two separate neutrons will come together in a single collision; instead, deuterium is first formed by the fusion of one proton and one neutron, then two atoms of deuterium combine to form one of helium.

[4] The period during which nuclei and electrons combined to form atoms is often called the epoch of decoupling, for it was during this period that the radiation background parted company with normal matter. At early times, when matter was ionized, the universe was filled with large numbers of free electrons, which interacted frequently with electromagnetic radiation of all wavelengths. As a result, a photon could not travel far before encountering an electron and scattering off it. In effect, the universe was opaque to radiation (rather like the deep interior of a star like the Sun). Matter and radiation were strongly "tied," or coupled, to one another by these interactions. When the electrons combined with nuclei to form atoms of hydrogen and helium, however, only certain wavelengths of radiation—the ones corresponding to the spectral lines of those atoms—could interact with matter. Radiation of other wavelengths could travel virtually forever without being absorbed. The universe became nearly transparent. (Chaisson, p. 472)

[5] It is debated how such large structures as galaxies arose from the seemingly smooth and featureless beginning. Recently broad "wrinkles" in the form of temperature fluctuations in the microwave radiation have been detected. These variations in topography are large enough to create the gravity to attract more and more matter. (*New York Times*, April 24, 1992)

[6] The Anthropic Principle argues that the present structure of the universe, with its delicate adjustment of nature's constants, seems to favor life and consciousness. There is a weak and strong version. "The Weak Anthropic Principle notes this as *a fact*. Out of all the possible values the physical constants of the universe might have had, they seem, improbably, to have arrived at the narrow range of constants that favor the existence of carbon-based life forms.

Some critics accuse the Weak Anthropic Principle of being a tautology: because we are here, it *must* be possible that we can be here. The Strong Anthropic Principle goes further. It claims necessity for the presence of people like us: the universe must have those properties that allow life to develop at some stage in its history—and this requires explanation. (Marshall and Zohar, pp.43–44) Physicist Paul Davies states that the "strong anthropic principle can therefore be regarded as a sort of organizing meta-principle, because it arranges the laws themselves so as to permit complex organization to arise." (Davies 1988, p. 163)

[7] Actually, two atoms of helium combine to form one atom of beryllium, then a third helium atom combines with the beryllium to form carbon.

[8] Important sources for this section were *The Universe Story*, by Brian Swimme and Thomas Berry, and the fifth edition of *Biology*, by Helena Curtis and N. Sue Barnes.

[9] ATP is an abbreviation for adenosine triphosphate. It is the main energy-carrying molecule by which organisms make energy available for chemical synthesis, muscular contraction, transport across membranes and other kinds of work in the cell.

[10] Specifically, the mitochondria, the basal bodies of the flagella (hairlike extensions by which a single cell moves), and the photosynthetic organelles can all be considered to have derived from free-living cells. The eukaryotic cell is the result of the evolution of the ancient symbiont.

[11] It is postulated that sexual reproduction had its origins when a predator cell was able to digest the cell walls of its prey, as well as some of the prey's cytoplasm, but not the nucleus with its genetic treasures. From the combination of the two nuclei new possibilities emerged. (Swimme and Berry, p. 105)

[12] An orthogenesis (appearance of similar characteristics in groups related but already separated) of cerebralization is clearly present in many metazoan phyla; not only in vertebrates but also in arthropods, mollusks, annelids, and also in such lower metazoan as flatworms. Patterns of evolution in these phyla seem to confirm Teilhard's hypothesis. But it may also be contradicted: as a matter of fact, it is possible to find among metazoans some phyla that do not show any tendency to cerebralization. (Galleni, p. 160)

[13] First, all rats experienced an increase in size. Second, each lineage developed continuous molar growth. Third, all the rats evolved fusion of the cervical vertebrae.

[14] While no direct evidence that a meteor impact may have set off the catastrophic extinctions at the end of the Paleozoic has been found (no trace of a crater, for instance), scientists have found, in the extinction layer, soccer-ball-shaped carbon molecules that have within them a mix of helium and argon gas that is unlike anything that could form naturally on Earth. It is believed that the gases and carbon molecules were formed billion of years ago in an ancient star, blown into interstellar space and later carried to Earth aboard the killer meteor. The meteor's impact would then have set off the chain of events that so decimated the land and sea species. (*New York Times*, February 23, 2001)

[15] The high level of iridium found in deposits from the boundary period between the two eras—thirty times more than was expected—suggests bombardment by a large meteorite or a series of them, because meteorites contain iridium in high concentrations. This would have caused prolonged climate change. The event might have been volcanic, but it is more likely to have been extraterrestrial. The catastrophe was clearly not the only cause of the extinction, however: There had been a significant loss of dinosaur species and other species well before the actual boundary of the two eras.

[16] Another ancient australopithecine, more primitive than *A. afarensis*, has been discovered and dated to 4.4 million years ago. (*New York Times*, September 22, 1994) It is *A. ramidus*, thought to lie close to the point of divergence between the lineages leading to the African apes and the human line. It was quite small and chimpanzee like, and it is not known if it walked upright, but it still has characteristics that put it on the human side of the divergence.

The skull from Chad, which has been assigned to an entirely new genus and species (*Sahelanthropus tchadensis*) but is generally called Toumai ("hope of life" in the local language), has caused a stir among paleontologists because, though it is twice as old as Lucy (and its brain capacity is comparable to that of a chimpanzee), its face appears to be more humanlike than Lucy's. (*New York Times*, August 6, 2002)

[17] Based on unusual Australian fossils that have small bones and thin skulls and that have recently been shown by mitochondrial-DNA analysis to be 60,000 years old (instead of 30,000, as previously thought), anthropologist Alan Thorne challenges the out-of-Africa hypothesis. In his view, 120,000 years was not enough time for *Homo sapiens* to "leave Africa, dash up to China, evolve from rugged Africans into small-framed Asians, invent boats, sail to Australia, march to the interior, get sick and die." He believes that *Homo sapiens*, which he identifies with *Homo erectus*, came out of Africa almost 2 million years ago and

dispersed throughout Europe and Asia, and that all the later varieties of *Homo*, including the Neanderthals, were *Homo sapiens* too. According to this theory of "regional continuity," instead of successive migrations out of Africa by different species of hominids, beginning with *Homo erectus* and culminating with *Home sapiens*, which wiped out all the others, there was one migration followed by regional variation, with sexual intermingling occurring when migrants from different regions encountered each other, as happens today. (*Discover*, August 2002, pp. 52–57)

[18] A portion of the human brain, the R-complex ("R" for "Reptilian"; see fig. 3), is the oldest from an evolutionary point of view and is the most interior in the human brain, just as the oldest growth of a tree is hidden in the most interior rings. It is characterized by distinctive anatomical and biochemical features consistently present in reptiles, birds and mammals but absent in the lower fish brain. Study of the anatomy of the reptilian portion of the brain in vertebrates shows it has remained remarkably unchanged over evolution. The R-complex in the human has the same pattern of organization as that of a major part of the reptilian forebrain. It has the same cerebral tissues as the reptilian brain (deBeauport, p. 265) and it governs some types of behavior initially developed by and experimented with by reptiles. The structures of the reptilian forebrain are thought to be the basis for the integrated performance by reptiles of daily master routines and subroutines. A master routine in the reptile world would be, for example, emergence from the den, basking, defecating and then foraging and hunting, in that order. Each day one particular type of lizard, which Paul MacLean studied, engaged in a routine of seven sequences of behavior that were performed with almost clocklike regularity although there were times when courtship activity or the defense of territory interfered with this master routine. (MacLean, p. 220) We can see that the evolutionary development of the reptilian brain involved the development of capacities to enable the animal to survive and thrive on land. These behaviors have been carried forward, with some maintained and some modified by evolutionarily newer portions of the human brain.

The structures added to the brain as animals transitional between reptiles and mammals developed are called the paleomammalian formation, or limbic system. The limbic system has three main anatomical subdivisions and is the common denominator in the brain of all contemporary mammals. The behavioral developments arising with mammals and associated with the newer part of the limbic system were (1) nursing in conjunction with maternal care (2) audiovocal communication for maintaining maternal-offspring contact (also developed in birds) and (3) play.

The neocortex is the newest structure of the human brain from an evolutionary perspective. A well-developed neocortex is found only in the brains of higher mammals so it is referred to as the neomammalian formation. It is the expansion and differentiation of the cerebral cortex creating the neocortex that most clearly distinguishes the brain of mammals from that of reptiles and birds. (p. 251) The evolution of the neocortex involves the elaboration of the visual, auditory and somatic systems which provide refined information of happenings in the external environment fitting the needs of mammalian life. (p. 513) Together with certain other parts of the brain it has afforded a progressive capacity for problem solving, fine analysis, concentration, learning, planning and memory of details. It also provides the basis for complex social behavior along with evolutionarily older parts of the brain. It makes possible human language abilities, the use of metaphor and communication of subjective states. In addition, differentiation in function developed between the right and left hemisphere of the neocortex. It is the development of left hemisphere dominance that is responsible for rational empirical thinking and the use of language and speech.

3

AN UNBROKEN WHOLENESS

The true physics is that which will, one day, achieve the inclusion of man in his wholeness in a coherent picture of the world.

— Pierre Teilhard de Chardin

THE STORY OF the unfolding of the universe from the primal fireball to its present magnificent efflorescence is a narrative of epic proportions. It encompasses energies ranging from the brilliant supernova observed by the Chinese in 1054, which was visible in the daytime for twenty-three days and bright enough to read by at night, to the invisible world of atoms and microorganisms and to the human experiences of love and tenderness toward a spouse, a child, or the infirm. Our urgent task, begun in the last chapter, is to consider the story as it has emerged from science, and to give it a full, sympathetic hearing, carefully pondering and digesting some of its revelations so that they may become familiar to us and gradually penetrate our imagination and change our consciousness. These reflections will prepare us to understand how we may integrate it with the highly personal, experiential material of the contemplative/mystical tradition.

Figure 4 summarizes the continuous unfolding of the primal material of the universe into the present, complex differentiated state of the Earth within which we have awakened to consciousness.[1] It helps make clear the fact that *everything that exists is a differentiated form of the fireball*. From the beginning, after its brief period of almost formless radiation, the universe articulated itself in unique, identifiable, intelligible constellations or patterns of energy. (T. Berry 1988, p. 106) Brian Swimme has offered a short version of the new story: "You take hydrogen gas, and you leave it alone, and it turns into rosebushes, giraffes and humans." (2001, p. 40)

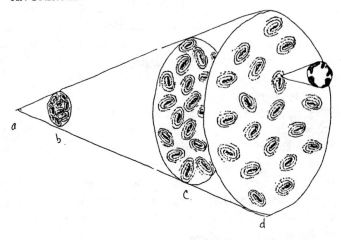

Fig. 4. The continuous unfolding of the universe from the primordial fireball (a), 13 billion years before the present differentiated situation at (d). About 1 billion years after the Big Bang (b), galaxies formed; 4.5 billion years ago (c) our solar system emerged in the Milky Way galaxy.

Systems theorist Eric Jantsch points out in his book *The Self-Organizing Universe* that at the beginning of the expansion of the universe, in the mold of unimaginable temperatures and extreme density, the *simplicity and unity of nature manifests itself directly.* (p. 78, emphasis added) Out of the hot, dense initial energetic event, everything will unfold as time and space unfold—stars, galaxies, the Earth, ourselves.

It seems impossible as we look at the world around us, at the seemingly infinite diversity of rocks, people, insects, trees and flowers, coupled with the confusion of man-made cars and houses and television sets sitting lifeless on the surface of the Earth, that it could all actually arise from a common origin. Murders and mayhem, disease and destructive storms, don't encourage the perception of ongoing unity. Furthermore, we have derived the attitude from Western scientific endeavor that we can study an isolated unit and know it fully, with the result that we find it extremely difficult to recognize the fact that things are not fully understood apart from their participation in the unfolding whole. When in this book, we turn to the manner of the generation of distinct forms like cells and trees (chapters 10, 11), we will see that their differentiation does not result in a separation of the form from the unity. This will prove important when we consider the contemplative life of the individual person in the context of the new story.

We do not see the unity only from the broad perspective of the story. According to David Bohm, both relativity theory and quantum theory destroy mechanistic, atomic assumptions concerning the nature of the universe and reveal it to be an unbroken wholeness or holomovement.[2] David Bohm (1917–1992) was a theoretical physicist who wrote a number of highly regarded books, including a textbook on quantum physics[3] and, more pertinent to our focus, the work titled *Wholeness and the Implicate Order*. A man who knew both Einstein and Krishnamurti well, he tried to paint a comprehensive picture of the world using his knowledge, as a quantum physicist, of its inner workings. Instead of the usual picture of objects related to each other in an external manner, he presents a wholistic perspective from the inside, so to speak. It is a compelling conception of things, coming out of scientific work, that describes an internally interconnected world. *The shift in perspective Bohm offers is heartening and helps us begin to conceive how complex beings can be internally integrated into the internal dynamics of the unfolding cosmos*, a topic central to the integration of the contemplative tradition with the new story.

What is the holomovement? The prefix, from the Greek *holos*, whole, is used as it is in the word *holography* (described later in this chapter) to indicate that the fundamental ordering of the holomovement is present throughout every part of it. By combining the prefix with the word *movement* in the term he coined, Bohm indicates the dynamic, flowing nature of the universe. The holomovement, then, is a universal flowing movement that carries the patterns and the order out of which all forms of the material universe emerge. Given that the world is a holomovement, "whatever part, element or aspect, we may abstract in thought, this still enfolds the whole and is therefore intrinsically related to the totality from which it has been abstracted." (Bohm 1983, p. 172)

The holomovement includes what Bohm calls the *plenum*, the immense "'sea" of energy, measurable and immeasurable, that is the ground of the existence of everything. Since the holomovement includes the measurable and the immeasurable, the universe is "open-ended" and infinite, not a measurable, fixed something.

Bohm's particular interest as a physicist was to describe the overall law, the order or patterns inherent throughout the cosmic web. It is a notion of order which is not to be understood solely in terms of the mechanical laws that describe the interaction of objects in time and space—the laws by which we fly to the moon. These are a subset of the larger order. The full law governing the holomovement is only vaguely discernible at present and, Bohm suggests, is probably unknowable in its totality.

The Implicate Order

The word *implicate* means "to fold inward," just as *multiplication* means to fold many times. The implicate order refers to the enfolded information in each region of time and space which underlies the various manifestations of the explicate, or unfolded order, including matter, energy, life, and consciousness. A glimpse of what Bohm means by the term can be gleaned by considering radio waves, which "carry" the visual image that can appear on the television screen. The information enfolded (implicated) in electromagnetic radio waves is unfolded (explicated) by the circuitry of the television set. "Points that are near each other in the visual image are not necessarily 'near' in the order of the signal. Thus, the radio wave carries the visual image in an implicate order. The function of the receiver is then to *explicate* this order, i.e. to 'unfold' it in the form of a visual image." (Bohm 1983, p.149) Comparably, Bohm says that the visible world is a manifestation or display of an implicate order. A very similar idea of an ordering realm will be found in Plotinus's conception of the *Nous*, often translated Mind. (See chapter 5.) The extent of the implicate order is not known because our knowledge simply fades out at a certain point. Bohm refers to an immense "sea," or *plenum* as the implicate ground which is beyond time. The ocean of energy is not primarily in space and time at all. (Bohm and Weber, 1978, p. 30)

The implicate order is autonomously active (Bohm 1983, p. 185): Out of this ground each moment is projected into the explicate order. It is an order which both folds and unfolds (Bohm and Weber 1981, p.23); thus it is fundamental to the flux and creativity of the holomovement. Bohm takes the view that neither matter nor mind is fundamental: rather there is something unknown, which he calls the deeper or implicate ground. (Bohm and Weber 1982, p. 37) His ideas of the implicate order include the assumption that "the ground of all being is somehow permeated with a supreme intelligence that is creative," the evidence for which he finds in "the tremendous order in the universe and in ourselves and the brain." (McInnis, p.7)

The Explicate Order Manifests the Implicate Order

Bohm calls our ordinary notions of time and space, and the distinct objects present to our senses, the explicate or unfolded order. It is the manifest world. One can imagine the relationship of the explicate order to the implicate order by considering the way clouds, which hold a stable, visible form for a period, are an explicate manifestation of the movement of the atmosphere and wind. Similarly, according to Bohm, matter can be regarded as flowing out of the law of the implicate order of the holomovement. Elementary particles are projections of this higher-dimensional reality, the implicate order (Bohm 1983, pp. 185–86). As matter forms, it manifests the implicate order to our senses and thought. As images form in the mind, they too manifest the implicate order. (Bohm and Weber 1978, pp. 28, 33) What is manifest is, as it were, abstracted from and floating in the holomovement.[4] From atoms and cells to people and their capacities, in fact all entities are forms of the holomovement. Yet it is important to keep in mind that only a small part of implicate order is expressed in an explicate fashion.[5] (Bohm and Weber 1978, p. 26)

Another valuable image of the relationship of the explicate to the implicate order is to conceive of the visible, manifest world (explicate order) as a sheet or two-dimensional plane within the implicate three-dimensional space, although such a conception offers no more than an intimations of the multidimensional reality that the implicate order is. Comparably, is a photograph of a person the actual person? Obviously not, but Bohm suggests that our daily conception of ourselves is similarly limited, by our failure to recognize the enfolded implicate order. Contemplatives urge us in similar way, to awaken from a limited consciousness.

Another valuable image from Bohm illustrates the dependence of a particular form on the larger holomovement. Consider a fountain in an Italian square. The explicate shape of the display, the overall shape we admire as tourists, is an expression of the constant folding and unfolding of the stream of water that flows through it. Thus are all objects in daily life dependent on the whole order. And through this image we also see that it is the implicate order that is autonomously active, that the explicate flows out of a law of the implicate order. (Bohm 1983, p. 185)

Form: An Intrinsic Part of the Whole

In our daily world, forms or bodies (Bohm calls them "relatively autonomous subtotalities") are exterior to each other and interact through local forces. The mechanistic order of classic cause-and-effect physics, which many of us studied in high school and college, describes the behavior of these relatively stable forms in the explicate order. In the prevailing, mechanistic philosophy of much of the Western world, these forms are not considered subtotalities, but are assumed to be separate and independent and are taken as constituting the basic reality. (Bohm 1983, p. 178) For Bohm, however, the laws that describe the movements of billiard balls and planets in classical physics, or those describing particles and fields in quantum physics, are always limited and made stable by a larger law of the whole. It is the implicate order that is the fundamental, autonomously active reality. Quite contrary to "common sense," what makes subtotals stable is not their separateness but the movement in the whole. (Briggs and Peat, p. 120) Everything, including human beings, is to be explained in terms of forms derived from the flux of this holo-movement. (Bohm 1983, pp. 11, 178, 192; Bohm and Weber 1978, p. 46) If we push causality to the limit, Bohm writes, we are led back to finding its explanation in the whole. He explains: "We ordinarily think of an effect as having one, or a few causes. *In fact, the cause for any one thing is everything else.*" (Briggs and Peat, p. 96, emphasis added) We think that when we swing the tennis racket and hit the ball, the swing is all that is involved in sending the ball over the net. But actually the moon, gravity, the air and the distant mountains all also affect the flight of a tennis ball. The universe as a whole is a moving, causal network.

In general, the manner in which something forms and maintains itself in the holomovement depends on its place and function in the whole. Just as the Gulf Stream depends for its stability on the ocean, the stability of a stone is not derived only from the forces within the atoms but from the movement of the whole. It is always the whole that is manifesting. (Bohm and Weber 1978, p.26) This is most intriguing and enlightening insight, for it means that our lives can manifest what is actually going on in the dynamics of the holomovement. The whole may act in each aspect. We get a sense of the completeness of our belonging to a dynamic and "alive" whole.

Characteristics of a Hologram

Since, according to Bohm and his interpretation of quantum physics, the fundamental ordering of the holomovement is present throughout every part of it, it has the characteristics of a hologram. A holographic plate, which is comparable to an exposed film, has imprinted everywhere on it the record of interference patterns from split laser beams that have been reflected off a mirror and off the subject being "photographed." If a holographic plate is projected using laser light, the original three-dimensional image is reproduced. Most remarkably, if the plate is broken up, and any *piece* of it is projected, the entire image is again reproduced, although with less detail and from fewer angles than when the plate was intact. The key feature of holography, then, is that each piece of the plate contains information about the whole object that was "photographed," or, in Bohm's language, light from every part of the object is enfolded within each region of the plate. To imagine how this is possible, the following illustration is helpful. Visualize the concentric circles of ripples made by a pebble thrown into the smooth surface of a pond. Throw two pebbles and the spreading concentric circles will cross each other and create interference patterns; throw in a handful of pebbles and, when the interference patterns are at their maximum, take a photograph of the surface of the pond. That photograph is like a hologram because the interference pattern in whatever portion of the surface of the pond is photographed carries information about the whole situation. This feature (that a piece of the plate contains information about the whole object) is like the universe, Bohm writes, in that "the totality of existence is enfolded with each region of space (and time)." (1983, p. 172) The encoding pattern of matter and energy spreads ceaselessly throughout the universe—with "each region in space, no matter how small . . . containing . . . the pattern of the whole, including all the past and with implications for all the future." (Briggs and Peat, p. 111) All the matter in our bodies, from the first, enfolds the universe in some way. Consciousness too, having a common ground with matter and being enfolded with matter, as we shall discuss momentarily, likewise enfolds the universe in some manner. Here in the holographic nature of things, we find one way of addressing one of the central concerns of this book, because the person, as a subtotality, has enfolded within her the implicate orders, including the implicate ground, the *plenum*. This opens the door to integrating contemplation with the new physics and the universe story.

We need to pause to ponder this astounding insight into the universe, this idea that the whole is enfolded in each region, although from a distinct perspective. The information in the part may not include every detail of the whole, but it is about the whole; it refers to the whole. (Bohm and Weber 1978, p. 46) At first, we may think this is impossible, or we may put the idea aside as only a philosophical abstraction, or we may assume it concerns only the quantum level of the physical world and so does not affect our lives as complex people among large, separate, solid objects. But in fact it is something we can experience everyday. One occasion would be to go outdoors and look at the night sky. David Bohm writes:

> Consider, for example, how on looking at the night sky, we are able to discern structures covering immense stretches of space and time, which are in some sense contained in the movements of light in the tiny space encompassed by the eye (and also how instruments, such as optical and radio telescopes, can discern more and more of this totality, contained in each region of space.) (Bohm 1983, pp. 148–49)

The stars and galaxies we see in the night sky are millions of light-years away. The Andromeda galaxy, visible to the naked eye, is nearly 3 million light-years away. These distant objects are visible to us even though we couldn't travel to them in many lifetimes. Astronomers do not have to get into spaceships and go out into interstellar space to collect their information. Instead they learn about the universe by studying the information that comes to them in *the small space in front of their telescope*. Incredibly, most incredibly indeed, *right in front of our eyes*, as well as in front of our neighbor's eyes, and those of the person in China, is *a wealth of information about the immense night sky*! The same information, or very similar information allowing for a different angle of vision, is in front of millions of people's eyes. The information is then unfolded by the eye and brain. Furthermore, in the space in front of the eye, there is information about the past, including, as has been learned only in the past century, information about the very early universe in the background microwave radiation, although it is not visible to the human eye.[6] (See chapter 2.) This illustrates most convincingly that there is information about the whole in the part. What was initially difficult to believe becomes most enlightening. It illustrates what David Bohm writes: "Various energies such as light, sound etc. are continually enfolding information in principle concerning the entire universe of matter into each region of space." (1983, p. 197) This is also true of aspects of consciousness. It is not just the information to be found in front of the eye—the information that interests the astronomer—that compels our attention. The *plenum*, the implicate ground of consciousness according to Bohm, is also found everywhere throughout time and space.

Consciousness within the Holomovement

Bohm's conception of the holomovement also includes clarifying insights about consciousness and the relation between consciousness and matter. The source of consciousness (which for Bohm includes thoughts, emotions, desires, will—the whole of mental and psychic life) lies in the nonmanifest. (Bohm and Weber 1978, p. 33) Consciousness in his thought does not just arise from the complexities of the physical brain (which would make it an epiphenomenon of matter), as some mechanistic thinkers hold. Bohm suggests there is a relationship between human thought and the patterns of the implicate order similar to that between the manifest, explicate order and the implicate order. Thus in the same way the cloud in the sky is an explicate form of the nonmanifest wind and atmosphere, certain aspects of consciousness are a manifestation of some intrinsic mind in the implicate order. Images, as noted, manifest the implicate order.

Too often, our consciousness is restricted to the explicate order. Most of us have been trained through practical requirements and acculturation to screen out and suppress vast dimensions of our own implicate nature. (Briggs and Peat, p. 129) This is in marked contrast to the experience of mystics, of some children, of members of indigenous cultures, and of some artists. Almost everyone, says Bohm, at some time or other experiences the implicate order. On occasions when a person has insight into the implicate order it may take explicate form as a poem, a theory, or a sigh. The wind moves and changes the cloud. The artist calls the flux of the implicate order "intuition" or "inspiration." Insight, involving an active intelligence, bypasses our routinized rational thoughts and can transform our habitual thought patterns. Insight is a leap to the explicate order from the holomovement. A significant insight, as when Einstein wrote down his field equations for relativity theory, is not insight belonging to a particular person, but is the movement of the whole expressing itself in explicate forms through that person (e.g. Einstein) and his prepared and inquiring mind. (Briggs and Peat, p. 131) This universal quality of such insights is also true of many mystical experiences, which involve intuitive knowings. Thus many contemplative insights have similar content and a universal appeal, since they arise from the movement of the whole expressing itself as the insight/experience of the particular person.

The Relationship between Matter and Consciousness

Bohm believes that both matter and consciousness are rooted in the implicate order, they are not ultimately to be seen as distinct, fundamentally separate substances. Rather, they are different aspects of one whole and unbroken movement. Though they are not the same, they are intimately related and inextricably linked as mutually enfolding aspects of one overall order. (Bohm 1983, pp. 11, 197, 208) Bohm writes: "In the implicate order we have to say that mind enfolds matter in general and therefore the body in particular. Similarly, the body enfolds not only the mind but also in some sense the entire material universe." (p. 209) This is not at all foreign to human experience, in which consciousness commonly affects one's physical state, and the physical state often affects the content of consciousness.

Bohm's thought dramatically confronts the widespread assumption that our consciousness markedly separates us from other living beings, and instead suggests that human consciousness, however developed it is in some ways, is part of the fundamental order in the holomovement. The sense of separation, so acute in Western culture, is in part a legacy of the thought of René Descartes, who separated matter and consciousness to the extent that there was no basis in his philosophy for any relationship between them except by means of God, who, being outside of and beyond matter and consciousness (both of which He had indeed created), is able to give to consciousness 'clear and distinct notions' that are currently applicable about matter. (Bohm 1983, p. 197) Animals are relegated to the domain of matter alone and humans are encouraged to treat their own bodies in a mechanical way. In today's world, the belief in a God external to the universe who would take care of this requirement of connecting body and consciousness has been abandoned in many circles, but because of the lingering influence of the Cartesian assumptions, insights like those of David Bohm are desperately needed. We are only beginning to grasp the complex interrelationship of consciousness and body and to leave behind the highly destructive legacy of Descartes and others.

With recent developments in biochemistry and physiology, we have discovered the intimate relationship of the emotional life and matter. Opiates like opium, heroin, codeine and Demerol and certain drugs like cocaine produce euphoria by affecting those areas of the brain involved with emotion. It was postulated that these drugs were mimicking endogenous (internal) natural substances, since otherwise the brain cells would not be so responsive to them. Then, in 1973, the brain receptors for opiates were discovered and shortly thereafter, peptides (a type of protein) exhibiting morphine-like activity were isolated from pig brain. This led scientists to realize that the body produces its own "morphines," which were named endorphins (for "endogenous morphines"). These and many other peptides later found in the nervous system were collectively named "neuropeptides." More than fifty have been identified to date. A great concentration of receptors for neuropeptides exists in those areas of the brain known to be concerned with emotion. Candace B. Pert, former chief of the Brain Biochemistry Section of the National Institute of Mental Health, and her associates have identified neuropeptides as the biochemical substrate of emotion. (Pert et al., 1985) So, to our surprise, a dimension of consciousness, emotion, is caused by a molecule, either by endogenous substances or by mimics. In this example consciousness is not directing inert matter, as we would have expected; instead the opposite is true: The manipulator is manipulated.

The story does not end here. Pert and her co-workers have found that not only brain cells, but all cells in the body, carry on their surface receptors for these neuropeptides. When a particular neuropeptide attaches to a receptor on a cell membrane it "wiggles and changes in such a way that things start to happen"; ions start pouring in, and other changes occur depending on where the receptor is located. (Pert in Moyers, p. 179) In the case of morphine there is constriction of the pupil, slower respiration, a reduction of intestinal motility and pain-suppression. When morphine attaches to the receptors in the brain, euphoria is experienced. As descendants of Descartes, we are shocked to discover that the same molecules involved with the conscious experience of emotion are also involved with regulation of bodily activities, even including immune responses.[7] But it is indisputable: A mental, emotional event cannot be separated from the biochemistry of the brain or from that of the other bodily activities. Consciousness and matter are intimately related.

Candace Pert herself observed that emotion seems to exist in at least two realms: the local events involving neuropeptides and the more wholistic reactions across the entire body. The latter, it will be proposed in later chapters, involves comprehensive, self-organizing dimensions arising in the implicate order. (See chapters 10, 11.) These organizing powers are of great importance in the integration we seek.

The Part and the Whole

Ultimately, David Bohm says, the entire universe has to be understood as a single undivided whole, in which categorization into separately and independently existent parts has no fundamental status. (Bohm 1983, p. 174) Bohm's great emphasis on unity would seem to deny the importance of individuality and difference. How, then, is Bohm's thought to be reconciled with Carl Jung's admonition in his essay "The Meaning of Psychology for Modern Man" (1934) that "the essential thing is the life of the individual . . . here alone do the great transformations first take place. . . . We make our own epoch"? (CW vol. 10, par. 315) Although Bohm emphasizes the wholeness, he does not suggest the universe is one giant undifferentiated blob. He warns against dividing what cannot be divided—and uniting what we cannot unite. He in fact accords great importance to the individual, because the person is empowered by participation in the implicate order, which is autonomously active and, hence, autonomously active in the individual. The individual is a form of the holomovement and can express its patterns and movement. This greatly enhances the significance of the individual, who is not an isolated part depending only on family and cultural definitions. An understanding of unity and diversity that addresses the relationship of the individual (the "semiautonomous subtotality") to the whole, is a central issue in this book.

It is a very great moment now, at the beginning of the twenty-first century, to be able to begin once again to embrace with confidence the wholeness and the presence of the implicate ground of our very being, much the way an earlier age embraced Plotinus's insight into the *Nous* (chapter 5) and Christians affirmed the presence of the *logos* in Jesus of Nazareth (chapter 13). To understand this means to redefine us, healing the entire order of Western fragmentation.

---

[1]Although the diagram illustrates the continuous, unbroken unfolding, it is inadequate both with regard to the shape of the universe, which is unknown, and because it falsely suggests that the universe is moving through time, the

horizontal axis. Instead, the universe is expanding and gradually becoming more complex. The universe does not develop into *preexistent time*, a very important insight from the new story that is key to our inquiry. (See chapter 4.) Nor does it move into preexistent space, as was discussed.

[2] For why Bohm believes this to be so, see Bohm 1983, pp. 172–76.

[3] *Quantum Theory* (Englewood Cliffs, N.J.: Prentice-Hall, 1951). Another textbook, *Causality and Chance in Modern Physics*, (Princeton, N.J.: Van Nostrand, 1957) has become a classic in the field of quantum mechanics.

[4] The general thrust of Bohm's thought is not unique. "In Einstein's vision, the universe is like an organism in which each part is the manifestation of the whole. What appears to be separate and independent is in fact the excitation of a nonlinear field, excitation that is sustained for a time and then are merged back into the ground that gave them birth." (Peat 1987, p. 76)

[5] This is in contrast to the Cartesian view that the whole of the order is at least potentially manifest, though we may not know how to make it manifest on our own, and might need microscopes and telescopes and various instruments. (Bohm and Weber 1978, p. 26)

[6] "If we think of the light in any particular part, it contains obviously the entire past of those waves which came from everywhere to reach that part." (Bohm and Weber 1978, p. 46)

[7] The immune system was considered an independent, autonomous system. However, it is now known that human monocytes, white blood cells that migrate to disturbed sites to attack infectious agents, can be guided in the laboratory by the concentration of certain neuropeptides involved in emotion. (Pert et al., p. 824S) Emotional states that lead to a reduction in neuropeptide levels may, therefore, have the potential to decrease the effectiveness of the immune system. Such a mechanism may explain the observation that people who feel isolated are more prone to disease, while those participating in group therapies that support emotional life may improve their immune responses.

4

"THE PRESENT
IS THE ONLY THING
THAT HAS NO END"

The central core of mystical experience seems to be the conviction, or insight, that the immediate now, whatever its nature, is the goal and fulfillment of all living.

— Alan Watt

THE STORY OF the evolutionary universe opens the door to a most important insight into time. It is central to understanding the possibilities of the contemplative life in a time-developmental universe because the realization of the 'fullness of the present now' is the core of the contemplative life. To identify with the new story and incorporate the person and the world around us within it, it is critical not to limit our understanding of time to numbers on a clock or the date on the calendar. Our dominant images and largely unconscious ideas about time profoundly influence our assumptions about the possibilities of the moment, including those of a contemplative nature.

Imagine being able to watch the Earth from a satellite and to observe in rapid succession the changes it has undergone over its 4.5 billion year history. You could watch the early Earth cool, watch rocks form, see the mounds of one-celled organisms at the edge of the shallow seas, the constant churning with mountains rising and eroding, tectonic plates floating across the mantle, glaciers advancing and retreating and inland seas growing over the land and then receding. Finally, during the last tenth of the total time, you could observe various multicellular plants and animals developing in the seas and then watch plants spread over the land, followed by a succession of more plants and animals as complex ecosystems develop. This churning succession of forms can be imaginatively stopped it at any moment, for example, when there were only one-celled organisms, and the total state of affairs of the Earth at that moment carefully examined. The unfolding can be stopped later to watch the dinosaurs roaming or to admire the new flowers, and, on each occasion, to explore the total state of affairs of the Earth. As you proceed with this undertaking you will be astonished to realize that on each occasion, this particular state of affairs is all there is. There cannot be a past that still exists, because *all* the "material" of the Earth is caught up in the 'present now,' the present total state of affairs.

Although past forms are carried forward to the present, it remains true, as Erwin Schrödinger wrote in *Science and Humanism*, that "for eternally and always there is only *now*, one and the same now; the present is the only thing that has no end." (p. 22) Things are just the way they are right now. The many complexities and changes in the visible forms do not alter the fundamental insight that *there is only the 'present now,' which is the current state of affairs, incorporating both new emergent forms and forms of the past that have been carried forward, making a whole that changes moment by moment.* Each successive present is different, or has the potential to be different, so the possibility of change is incorporated in Schrödinger's statement. There was an earlier state of affairs, which we call an earlier time, but it is crucial to realize that the unique situation when that particular configuration existed is no longer to be found in the next moment. When this insight is coupled with the inseparable presence of the implicate order and the autonomously active *plenum*, a realization of great importance about the fullness of the possibility of each 'present now' emerges.

Since many of the forms of the past are carried forward, their presence has important, frequently determinative implications for the future. (Briggs and Peat, p. 111) Often the state of affairs is little changed over many years, and we can be confident of considerable continuity but the state of affairs in what is yet to unfold is not completely contained in the present because the new may also appear, sometimes out of chaos. This potential for creativity and the appearance of novelty is a central feature of the evolutionary universe—one that we had not known before the discovery of the evolutionary epic.

The Nature of Time

This succession of one state of affairs followed by another gives us insight into the nature of time. Time is not independent of the state of affairs at each moment, contrary to the impression suggested by the movement of a clock ticking on a shelf. Rather, time denotes this continually changing state of affairs and the progressive, irreversible complexification, accompanied on occasion by extinctions. As David Bohm explains, one of the basic features of time is this sequence by which there comes a later movement that contains the earlier movements in its past but not the other way around. (Bohm and Weber 1978, p. 45)

Time is not external to our lives. We are not marching through time as measured by the calendar on which a child crosses out the dates as she anticipates a birthday. Our bodies and our psyches are immersed in time, and time and space are dimensions of the unfolding whole of the Big Bang, inseparable from the *plenum*. Time is a quality of the mystery. Space is a quality of the mystery. "Space and time erupt together with mass and energy in the primordial mystery of the universe's flaring forth." (Swimme 1996, p. 85)

The Jews recognized that in events in history there was a revelation of meaning. They gradually developed a sequential, progressive conception of time, in contrast to the cyclical views of earlier cultures. The historical process was regarded as essential to the realization of identity of that people and their important values. In the same manner that a Jew, even in the Diaspora, derives identity from belonging to the long and troubled history of Israel, every human being gains a remarkable identity from belonging to the Earth, with its most ancient, dramatic and creative history.

We commonly affix a date to each successive occasion of the ongoing changing state of affairs. This creates chronological time.

We all agree that December 30, 2000, is the date given to the state of affairs when there was a fifteen-inch snowstorm in New York City. Chronological time is a very important social construction, imposed to signify, in equal segments, the ongoing changing state of affairs (which does not change at a fixed rate). It is clearly of central importance in ordering our daily lives and our knowledge of past events (periods of mountain building, wars, our family and personal history) and in aiding our ability to anticipate the future. It is recognized that humanity has escaped from the eternal present of the animal world into knowledge of past and future. (Eisley, pp. 120–21) However, just as there are no dividing lines between countries marked on the Earth, so a particular state of affairs of the Earth has no intrinsic date. The condition of the Earth when flowers appeared is simply assigned the date of 130 million years ago.

We tend to think of the past configuration of things, with a certain number of years assigned to it, as somehow still existing, as if the actual past were still present with us. We see a two-thousand-year-old Roman aqueduct in southern France, and believe we see the past. The aqueduct we see *is* the aqueduct built in 19 B.C.E. in Nimes by the Romans, of course, but we only see it as it exists now, as part of the present, in its eroded, aged condition. It is one of the successful forms of the past that has been carried forward into the present, in this case because humans have valued its preservation. As a result, it is a form that is part of the present now. Not all the aqueducts have been carried forward. Indeed, most Roman structures have eroded and been broken up, so only a very few exist in the present.

Most rainforests are not being carried forward into the future in spite of their unparalleled diversity and beauty and their vital role in climate patterns. The 'present now' when our grandchildren are adults may be seriously degraded without them.

After living for an extended period among traditional peoples in Indonesia and Nepal, author David Abram was shocked by his experience into a new 'way of seeing' with regard to time. He began to question beliefs that he had accepted as obvious and unshakable while growing up in the United States. One was the belief in an autonomous "past" and "future." The oral culture within which he lived and studied had not objectified space and time, which is what makes them seem to be independent of particular things and events of the corporeal present. Upon his return home Abram asked himself: Where *are* the invisible realms (of "past" and "future") that have so much power over the lives of my family and friends? Everyone appeared to be strangely unaware of happenings unfolding in and around them *in the present.* He realized that the present for most of us seems nothing more than a point, an infinitesimal now separating "the past" from "the future"; it is an assumption that severely inhibits awareness of the sensuous presence of the world. (Abram, pp. 201–2) *Americans seemed to live as if they were listening to a symphony just to hear the finale, whereas the point of the music is discerned in every moment of playing and listening to it.*

The Chime of the Moment

Chronological time leads us to focus on the rapid succession of events in human-centered culture, and as a result we fail to be aware of our total immersion in the 'present now,' with its full, complex, infinitely rich dimensions and with its particular character and state of affairs. We are encouraged by our culture to value sequential thinking more than the wholistic awareness that would awaken us to the 'present now.' If we could learn to attend to the 'present now,' we would recognize that, using physicist F. David Peat's phrase, "the particular configuration of the interplay of forces at an historical moment sounds a single chime." (1987, p. 88) The chime of a moment refers to its unique quality, to the central promise and activity that is occurring and the unique creative opportunity by which it is characterized. For example, scientists can look at the organic remains in an ancient rock and by their composition know its chime, the quality of that particular type of life on Earth. The conditions for creating life here on Earth are thought to have occurred once and are now unrecoverable. The situation in which life could emerge was the chime of that condition of the Earth. Imagine the marked change in the quality of the Earth when the first flowers began to bloom. There had not been such glorious color before. Or imagine the "chime" when the first birds began to fly and to sing from the trees. The advent of human beings brought another unique quality to the Earth. There was a different chime to life in Europe after the Berlin wall fell.

The Integrated Wholeness of Each 'Present Now'

Awareness of the integrated wholeness of each 'present now' and its particular chime for our lives and for our culture has been largely lost to us because of our alienation from our own subjective depths and from our roots in the ecological system in which we live and on which we depend. If we became able, through the contemplative pathway, to enter into the true, full time of things, into the total, unique, never-to-be-repeated situation, we could develop a more satisfactory relationship to the whole internally and to the life around us.

We must learn to live fully in this 'present now.' It is essential to a viable ecological future, for it is only out of full immersion in the now, in its psychological, physical and spiritual aspects, that we will find the knowledge about ourselves and about the present condition of things we need to make authentic choices. It is out of honest, compassionate, open participation in the present situation, the situation out of which the next configuration will unfold, that we can best cooperate with and join in an appropriate unfolding, whether it be a continuation (more or less) of the status quo or something new.

Al Chung-liang Huang's understanding of his classes in T'ai Chi, as recounted by Gary Zukav in *The Dancing Wu Li Masters*, reminds us that some people actually do live knowing the true nature of time:

> "Every lesson is the first lesson," Al Chung-liang Huang told me. "Every time we dance, we do it for the first time."
> "But surely you cannot be starting new each lesson," I said. "Lesson number two must be built on what you taught in

lesson number one, and lesson three likewise must be built on lessons one and two, and so on."

"When I say that every lesson is the first lesson," he replied, "it does not mean that we forget what we already know. It means that what we are doing is always new, because we are always doing it for the first time."

This is another characteristic of a Master. Whatever he does, he does with the enthusiasm of doing it for the first time. This is the source of his unlimited energy. Every lesson that he teaches (or learns) is a first lesson. Every dance that he dances, he dances for the first time. It is always new, personal and alive. (p. 9)

It has always been astonishing and memorable that near the end of his life, Saint Francis, then a revered person with a great many followers, said to his brothers in the newly forming community, "Let us begin, brothers, to serve the Lord our God, for up to now we have hardly progressed." (Bonaventure, *Life of St. Francis* 14. 1)

Meister Eckhart's teaching of a pathway of "letting go," "letting be," and "releasement" (chapter 18) was intended to enable entrance into a "now" that is always new. Flight from attachment is a way of being in the present, and Eckhart exhorted people to dwell in 'this present now,' as opposed to living in duration, in "before" and "after"—the one single Now of Eternity in which all Divine operations take place simultaneously. In the sermon "Jesus Entered," Eckhart preached: "Indeed, the now in which God made the first man, and the now in which the last man is to perish, and the now in which I am speaking are all equal in God and are nothing but one sole and the same now." (As quoted in Schürmann, p.6)

The Contemplative Tradition in the 'Present Now'

The insight about the nature of time from the new universe story becomes greatly enriched when we learn that even though "the originating power gave birth to the universe thirteen to fifteen billion years ago, this realm of power is not simply located there at that point of time, but is rather a condition of every moment of the universe, past, present and to come." (Swimme and Berry, p. 17) Our lives and the entire current state of affairs incorporate what is going on in the 'full depth of things.'(See chapter 8.) There is an "all at onceness," to use William James's phrase. It has been observed that when hurried people of the West, with its competitive culture, say they have no time, they have lost soul. The very utterance of such a phrase demonstrates alienation from the 'creative now.'

The contemplative tradition described in the next chapters will aid in awakening us to the unrecognized richness of the 'present now.' Such awakening can help counteract our dis-enchantment of nature, which is threatening our world with ecological disaster. Greater awareness of the fullness of the ongoing present will enable us to know the supreme value of the Earth and its many beings. We can recover a sense of the ineffable value of each moment, an ancient religious experience. Anthropologist Mircea Eliade observed that every ritual of ancient people had the character of happening at the very moment it was performed. (Eliade, p. 392) The Roman Catholic Church insists on the real Presence in the bread and wine in the mass. Quakers seek the presence of the Inner Light in their silent worship. We are invited by the contemplative traditions to seek to know this 'all at onceness' in our daily lives.

———————

II

THE CONTEMPLATIVE
TRADITION OF THE WEST

5

CONTEMPLATION: ESSENTIAL TO THE FULL HUMAN LIFE

What lies behind us and what lies before us are tiny matters compared to what lies within.

— Ralph Waldo Emerson

THE EPIC OF evolution offers compelling evidence of our roots in the Earth and the depth of our belonging to the unfolding story. People are part of a magnificent ongoing event, and can celebrate the great powers and creativity of the universe within which our lives and all that surrounds us have come into being. To begin to address specifically the question of a place in the story for our spiritual strivings and experiences, we turn now to the contemplative tradition, because it has extensively explored mystical/religious experience and its careful nurture to full mature expression. An understanding of its discoveries will prepare us to seek to integrate them with the revelations about the person and about the Earth from the new story.

In this discussion of contemplation, the word *God* will be used without, at this point, considering its meaning. It will be used as the contemplatives themselves use it, with the caveat that no facile assumptions be made about what a particular individual means by the word *God*. We should not assume that theologians and writers hundreds of years ago had a naïve conception of God. They lived prior to the great divide in Western culture, when mechanistic ideas of matter forced in some minds the adoption of a deistic conception of God, which denied that God is involved in any significant, ongoing way with the course of events in the world. Nor should we too readily assume that the word *soul* refers to a rarefied dimension of the person that is not integral to the body. It is important to try to hear fully what great contemplatives in the Western tradition say about the realms of human experience, which they so passionately and beautifully articulate without being put off by their terminology.

What Is Contemplation?

The word *contemplation* is often used carelessly to mean a relaxed but focused attention on something, or "a long loving look at the real." These meanings are inadequate and weaken a powerful Western tradition. To grasp the meaning of contemplation we turn first to the work of Plotinus (205–270 C.E.), a philosopher educated in Alexandria. He is one of the world's greatest mystical writers, who describes in a particularly clear and convincing way the essential, radical nature of contemplation. Plotinus's work is also of great interest because of his awareness of the inner, comprehensive levels of being (the *Nous*) that are the ordering and form-generating dimensions of the universe. This awareness, we will see in later chapters, is closely related to contemporary study of self-organizing and form-generation, or morphogenesis.

Plotinus was the founder of the comprehensive systems of philosophy called Neoplatonism, a term used since the early nineteenth century to refer to his thought and its further development or modification by his successors. Plotinus's understanding of contemplation had a formative influence on Christian mystical philosophy, particularly through his influence on the Christian thinkers known as the Cappadocian fathers—Basil of Caesarea, Gregory of Nazianzus, and Gregory of Nyssa—in the 4th century, on Augustine (354–430) and on the fifth-century theologian known as Dionysius the Areopagite. It was through Dionysius the Areopagite that the thought of Plotinus reached Meister Eckhart, whose work is often discussed in this book. Other sources for the Western contemplative tradition include the writings of Paul and the Gospel of John, in which the life in Christ consists of a dynamic union with God.[1] (Dupré

1989b, p. 4) There has also been much influence from Judaism and Islam.

The insights of Plotinus into the unseen, inner structure of the world and the person are initially difficult to appreciate and comprehend. His philosophy was constructed on the basis of religious experience, so the dimensions of being he describes are little spoken of in daily life. The fact that he wrote in Greek in another age adds to the difficulty. But fundamentally he is seeking to understand the divinity of the soul and to discern the pathway, through realms of interior experience "more inward to" or "above" discursive reasoning and sense perceptions, leading to restoration of the soul's relationship with the divine All or One. His writings about contemplation offer a stark statement of a person's incompleteness apart from her return to what he calls the One, wherein lies the fullness of our potential creativity, love and power.

Plotinus conceived of the world as consisting of the One (the Good or the Absolute), which is the infinite source that makes the existence of all things possible, and two levels of being, formed successively by emanation from the One. Emanation is a model of creation in which the world proceeds spontaneously from the fecundity of the One, with an ongoing process of partial separation from and return to the One; it is a timeless process of overflowing and outpouring, and should not, according to this tradition, be thought of in a temporal or spatial way. The One, at the center and core of being, is beyond the reach of thought or language, and can only be described by exclusion; that is, it is possible to say what it is not but not what it is. It is a positive reality of infinite richness, but since it has no form discernible to us, we cannot describe it. The first emanation from the One is the *Nous*, variously translated as Mind, Spirit, Intellect, or Intuitive thought, and the second is the *Psyche*, translated as World Soul. Both are present equally everywhere.

The *Nous*, or Mind, is of particular importance in the contemplative life because, according to philosopher A. H. Armstrong's interpretation of Plotinus, it can be experienced as the level of intuitive thought and insight in a person. The *Nous* is a level of divinity, the world of form and ideas that engenders the various forms of the sensible world.[2] It connotes a comprehensive ordering principle throughout the universe. It is certainly similar to Bohm's implicate order. In a later chapter the phrase "objective intelligence," suggested by F. David Peat, will be used to describe a contemporary understanding of this ordering realm.

There will be several occasions throughout this book when we will be concerned with the type of knowing that involves Mind (or Intellect). It is of particular interest in the integration we are seeking because these knowings involving the *Nous* are part of contemplative experience, in which the person *participates* in an alternative type of knowing that grasps its object immediately rather than seeking knowledge outside herself by discursive reasoning. It involves a direct, intimate knowing that brings with it awareness of a person's deep belonging to the world. We will give several examples of this type of knowing, often called intellectual knowing or illumination, in the next chapter. It is found not only in mystical/contemplative experience as a form of prayer but also in poetic, artistic and scientific insight. Sometimes contemplative experience involving *Nous* is grasped through symbols, as the patterns are known in an icon or some other image.

The *Psyche* (World Soul) is the great intermediary between the world of *Nous* (Mind) and the sense world, the representative of the former in the latter. The specific function of the World Soul is to organize and govern the visible cosmos, to reflect the order and beauty of the intelligible world (*Nous*), in which it unceasingly participates. The world is grounded in a timeless movement by the Soul, which suffuses it with intelligence, to become a living, and blessed thing. The individual soul is part of *Psyche,* neither higher nor lower than it; in fact, they are sisters, because they have a common origin that is prior to either of them. (Hellerman-Elgersma, p. 57) This means that the individual soul is constantly united with the divine *Nous* through its "summit," which makes a person capable of becoming united with the divine Mind (*Nous*) and then with the Good in mystical "ascent."

A Return to the Fullness of the Human Being

The One remains present in the two levels of being emanating from it (the *Nous* and *Psyche*) as their immanent core and thus the immanent core of all being. Nor are the levels of being formed by emanation from the One spatially separate or cut off from each other. A principle of emanation is that it is not complete without a "turning back," or conversion to the One. Without responding to the allure of the One, without awakening to the eros of the One and returning to it, a person is isolated from the totality and fullness of reality. That which is emanated needs to become integrated within its source. In the return, in unmediated rapport, the levels of being are informed and filled with content and become the totality of real existence. (Armstrong 1966, p. xx) For Plotinus, *this return to the fullness of being is contemplation*: The individual soul, participating in the Mind, experiences the Good through what Plotinus calls a "non-thinking," which is drunkenness and loving joy. (Hadot, p. 244)

The return in contemplation of both the Mind and the World Soul is not initiated by them; rather it is the One, first and foremost, that gives a power of return. (Armstrong 1979, p. 128) The One induces the Soul to return to that core within itself. Plotinus wrote: "The Soul loves the Good (the One) because it has been moved by Him to love from the beginning." (*Enneads* VI. 8. 31). With this "turning back" within the Soul and Mind in response to desire and love of the Good, and with the rediscovery of the totality of one's true self, there is contemplation. *Contemplation is the moment of embrace by the totality of real existence that includes the immanent core, the One. It is a returning to the heart of oneself. This is a great principle of the philosophy of Plotinus: "that all derived beings depend for their existence, their activity and their power to produce in their turn on their contemplation of the source." (Armstrong 1996, p. xx, emphasis added to quotation)*

In contemplation, a vital relationship with reality's core is being discovered. The realization does not occur outside the person (although it need not be contained within the person), as some have thought and on the basis of that misunderstanding, criticized Plotinus. The person is not climbing a hierarchical ladder outside himself. Rather, in Plotinus's thought each being contains within itself the whole intelligible world i.e. the world to which there is access through the intellect as distinguished from the material world perceived through the senses. Recall that David Bohm wrote, as a physicist, that there is information about the whole in the part (chapter 3). Likewise, Plotinus's higher life of unity must not be seen to describe something temporally or spatially apart from what he called the lower life of multiplicity, although by identifying the higher life of unity he is pointing to consciousness of a distinct dimension of being. Bohm points out that if we make distinctions (in Plotinus's case, between the One, the Mind and the World Soul) as guides to perception, this does not imply that they denote separately existing substances or entities. (1983, p. 7) Sometimes the ecstatic forms of this state of consciousness may temporarily obscure daily consciousness of the world of multiplicity and hence seem to indicate an existence apart from it. And sometimes there is a demeaning of the world of daily consciousness in his school of thought, because the contemplative experience is so highly valued. Plotinus's writings do betray some regret over "returning to the body" after experiences of contemplation, although for him the sense world is not an evil influence, as it is in some Gnostic understanding.[3] Such regret, however, does not necessarily accompany this philosophy. Meister Eckhart's insights into contemplation, described below, are similar to those of Plotinus. For him, there is no re-gret over returning to consciousness of the body after a repose in the divine, and no opposition between a higher world and a lower one to which consciousness returns. (Schürmann 1978a, p. 15)

Plotinus's writings are not concerned with a negative attitude toward the body, but with freeing people from distortion of consciousness.* Plotinus thought our values are distorted, that we receive superficial reflections of the Good and that we live in illusion. We fail to be awake to and to know what is most important. James Hollis, a Jungian analyist, writes that without access to depth, we remain superficial and without vitality. (Hollis p. 96) In addition, it is important to realize, as theologian Ewert Cousins indicates, that the great influence of "pagan Neoplatonism" is not a grafting of foreign ideas into the Judeo-Christian tradition because Jews, Christians, Muslims, and Platonists had all discovered the same spiritual universe. He argues from an integral perspective that finds a compatability between Greek metaphysics and the sacred texts of both Judaism and Christianity. (Cousins 1992, p. 27) They work within a common spiritual landscape.

Participation in Emanation

There is an important further step in Plotinus's thought: not only is there a return to the fullness of who we are in contemplation, but the person then participates in emanation. This is the basis of the active life of the contemplative. The One is productive goodness, so when there is a return to embrace the fullness of our identity we participate in this productivity. "Emanation is the overspill of contemplation, for goodness is always diffusive of itself and communicates to others what it has seen." (Knowles 1966, p. 84) With the return in contemplation we participate in the dynamic reality of life, a dynamism grounded in the One. We enter the fullness of living and productive power, not a state of moral perfection (Armstrong 1966, p. xx) Erich Neumann describes the experience of unity in contemplation as the occasion in which the self is made manifest as the "creative center" out of which both man and the world are generated. (Neumann 1968, pp. 411–12) We become productive and creative in a way impossible apart from contemplation. Here the person is concerned with the daily world that needs her care. Furthermore, there is a joy, which is the joy of life. In the ongoing

* Ewert Cousins: Lecture, Fordham University, 1982.

healing of our old habits and complexes, in the reaching out to other people, and in the creation of ideas and activities that bring forth new and reformed personal and cultural patterns, the emanation is realized in a particular person in daily life.

Now we can see the inadequacy of such definitions of contemplation as "a long, loving look at the real." Contemplation is not the mystique of the vision, in which one "looks at" the divine realm. "Looking" suggests we remain separate from the One or Source, and would seem to involve a conception of God as an entity external to the person or at least external to the central identity of the person. Plotinus's thought, in contrast, involves a wholistic conception: he spoke of the body *in* the soul, soul *in* the Mind (*Nous*) and Mind *in* the One. (Helleman-Elgersma, p. 33) In contemplation we enter into the totality of existence as we return to our Source, in which we find our essential being. In his writings on contemplation, Plotinus sought to teach the divinity of the soul and to restore its relationship to the divine One. He wrote about possibilities of actual human experience, and for us, in the twenty-first century, he offers a vastly expanded vision of the human being. Plotinus's insight into the nature of contemplation addresses the heart of the contemporary malaise of Western culture, in which people often consider themselves fully described as distinct physical beings governed by their DNA. Tragically, this involves the loss of our deepest self, as we are reduced to limited dimensions of our being.

Contemplation's Transformative Power in the Life of Saint Bonaventure

The radical transformative power of contemplative experience may be glimpsed in an event from the life of Saint Bonaventure (1217–1274). In 1259, this great contemplative, poet, and theologian, who was Minister General of the newly formed Franciscan order during a period of intense struggle between disputing factions, withdrew "under divine impulse" to Mount LaVerna in Tuscany, "seeking a place of quiet and desiring to find there peace of spirit." (*Soul's Journey*, Prologue 2) Years earlier, in 1224, at that same place, Saint Francis had had a vision of "a Seraph with six fiery and shining wings," with the figure of a crucified man between the wings. (*Life of St. Francis* 13. 3) Ewert Cousins describes this six-winged seraph as a cosmological, mystical symbol that functioned as an integrating mandala for Saint Francis at a time of crisis in his life, just two years before his death.* Thirty-five years later, when Bonaventure was reflecting on Francis's vision, he "saw at once that this vision represented our father's [Francis's] rapture in contemplation and the road by which this rapture is reached." (*Soul's Journey*, Prologue 2) Franciscan scholar Ignatius Brady suggests that "in the quiet and solitude, Bonaventure seems to have undergone a deeply spiritual experience where he obtained an insight into the mystery of the stigmatization of Saint Francis and came to a deeper understanding of the way the mind of man can ascend in . . . stages from the contemplation of creatures to the very mystery of God." (Brady, p. 60) This contemplative experience of the peace of ecstasy became, for him, the sole end to which Christian wisdom leads.

Bonaventure had gained an insight into the comprehensive order of the world that became the basis of his classic work, *The Soul's Journey into God*: The cosmological, mandalic vision in which Christ is the exemplar that makes it possible for the untrained eye, immersed in sensible things, to recognize God's power, wisdom and goodness, in nature and in the soul. His great synthetic vision incorporated the Christian revelation with the peculiarly Franciscan intuition of the presence of God in nature. At the end of *The Soul's Journey Into God*, the goal of the journey, mystical ecstasy and union with God, is realized. The illuminative power of contemplation is well illustrated.

Meister Eckhart

In the preaching and writing of the Rhineland mystic, the Dominican Meister Eckhart (1260–1327), we find a sophisticated theologian, a speculative philosopher, a writer, and a popular, bold preacher. A man of many talents, he was a scholar who held

* Lecture, Fordham University, 1982.

the prestigious title of Master of Theology at the University of Paris and later at the Studium Generale in Cologne, where he had once studied. He also held several important administrative positions in the Dominican Order. His sermons in German to the nuns of the Rhine Valley, who preserved them for us, are thought to be the most significant reflection of his ideas and the creative genius of his language, although his academic works in Latin constitute the doctrinal basis for understanding his thought. (Schürmann 1978a, p. xii) We do not have personal accounts from him of actual contemplative experiences, but his preaching is filled with remarkable insights about the deepest reaches of human experience. For example, he preached about a spiritual power in which God is fully verdant and flowering, in which "there reigns such a clear joy, so incomprehensibly great a joy, that no one can ever fully speak of it." (As quoted in Schürmann 1978a, p.5.) This is certainly speaking from experience.

Eckhart preached about an interior dimension of the person, having an unsurpassable intimacy to the person, which he called the "ground of the soul." It can neither be known mentally nor described in rational terms: It has no names and no form. The 'ground of the soul' is "below" or "beyond," yet encompasses the rational, intellectual, and emotional dimensions of the person, described in Eckhart's time as comprising the lower faculties of the sensible order and the higher faculties of the intellectual order. In the sermon "Jesus Went Up," Eckhart preached:

> I have sometimes said that there is a power in the spirit that alone is free. Sometimes I have said that it [the 'ground of the soul'] . . . is higher above this and that than heaven is above the Earth. And therefore I now give it finer names than I have ever given it before, and yet whatever fine names, whatever words we use, they are telling lies, and it is far above them. It is free of all names, it is bare of all forms, wholly empty and free, as God in himself is empty and free. It is so utterly one and simple, as God is one and simple, that man cannot in any way look into it. (1981, p. 180)[4]

In addition to "ground of the soul," Eckhart designated this dimension "abyss" or "essence of the mind" or "image of God," all terms referring to the same aspect of the person, eternally at rest, where the mind is closer to God than to the faculties, closer to God than to itself or to the world. (Schürmann 1978a, p. 150)

This understanding of the nature of the 'ground of the soul' is a key conception in Eckhart's thought, because the Godhead is also nameless, free of form or pattern or any distinctions that would separate it into parts.[5] It is the ultimate Reality, to which no one can give a name and which cannot be described with any image, although Eckhart refers to it as the Silent Desert, The Abyss of Mystery, the Source, the Root and "the God beyond God." Thus he describes the Godhead in the same terms as the 'ground of the soul.' It falsifies Eckhart's thought to say the 'ground of the soul' and the Godhead are "two" which must be "united." In fact, he taught that they are one with each other and already united; they are a nameless, naked unity—"God's ground and the soul's ground is one ground." (McGinn 1981a, p. 9) Here we find the basis for Eckhart's understanding of contemplation as a union that can be realized in the 'ground of the soul' in an alternative form of consciousness and in an active life pouring forth from the discovery of the 'ground of the soul.' Louis Dupré, Professor of Philosophy of Religion at Yale University, writes that unitive experience is "where knower and known are substantially united, that union no longer allows any distance for subject-object opposition." (1989b, pp. 10–11) This is in accord with what Eckhart taught and with the understanding of contemplation we have already found in Plotinus. The soul is truly divine in its innermost ground. This union, according to Eckhart, is not "in the soul," but in God. (Caputo, p. 214) "God's isness," Eckhart says, "is my isness, neither less nor more." In the sermon "Distinctions Are Lost in God," he preached:

> As I have often said, there is something in the soul so closely akin to God that it is already one with him and need never be united to him. . . . If one were wholly this, he would be both uncreated and unlike any creature. (1941, p. 205)

Eckhart also spoke of the nobility of the soul to signify a capacity for the ground of the mind to unite itself to the ground of God. (Schürmann 1978b, p. 299) However this nobility is not automatically realized. There must be an organic preparation. Evelyn Underhill (1875–1941), an Anglican whose classic book *Mysticism*, published in 1910, and other works have proved invaluable to modern seekers, is very clear on this, as are the writings of Teresa of Avila and so many others.

In *Mysticism, East and West*, German theologian Rudolf Otto tells us that Eckhart's search for a knowledge of Being, and knowledge of the relationship between the soul and God, is fundamentally impelled by a longing for "salvation." Meister Eckhart is intent on laying bare the nature of Being as a vehicle for declaring what is truly valuable. Otto writes: "That the soul is eternally one with the Eternal is not a scientifically interesting statement, but is that fact upon which the salvation of the soul depends."[6] (p. 34)

Eckhart and the Inquisitors

Near the end of his life, Meister Eckhart's teachings came under the scrutiny of the inquisitors of the Roman Catholic archbishop of Cologne, because he was thought to have preached, among other things, that there is an uncreated dimension of the human soul, an unorthodox statement in the Christian faith. There was a trial in which issues were raised that we are starkly encountering again in the context of the new cosmology. They involve the delineation of the parameters or limits of the human personality.[7] This question goes to the very heart of a theme of central concern in this search to understand who the human person is by seeking an integration of the contemplative life with the new universe story. How deeply do the roots of the human being sink into the universe, and to what degree do people take part in the creation of the fundamental direction of things on this Earth? The answer to this is the answer to the question whether the ongoing creative origination of the manifest world is taking place in part in human consciousness. Is the intrinsic creativity of the person and intrinsic capacity for love in the domain of God, in the domain of the human, or in both simultaneously? Is the 'ground of the soul,' in Eckhart's use of that phrase, universal human nature or does it transcend the human form? The answer to this depends on the stance from which we look at things, a stance now significantly changed by the new universe story. This is a central theme of the chapters that follow.

It is feared by some that if one does not maintain a careful distinction between the Creator and the created, one is necessarily implying that there is an automatic equivalence between the human will and mind and the "will and mind" of the Godhead. But this is not true. The assertion of a unity of the 'ground of the soul' and the Godhead does not means that a person will automatically be blessed or holy. All men and women, however, whether their actions be good or evil, possess the substantial unity within themselves. The manner in which the human will and mind are transformed so the person is prepared to actualize the divine reality in daily life is difficult to understand fully and to clarify, but is key to this integration. (See chapters 17–20.)

Contemplation Is an Inborn Human Capacity

It is critical to realize that the search for the contemplative life springs from the desire at the core of all religion to live within the experienced presence of God, in whatever degree. And, in fact, there is a great deal of evidence that the desire to so live can be satisfied to a remarkable extent, though we often do not have confidence that this type of life is available to us. However, when Evelyn Underhill defines mysticism as an organic process, she give us reason to suspect these doubts. She defines the contemplative/mystical journey as follows:

It is the name of that *organic process* which . . . is the art of establishing . . . conscious relation with the Absolute. The movement of the mystic consciousness towards this consummation is not merely the sudden admission to an overwhelming vision of Truth: though such dazzling glimpses may from time to time be vouchsafed to the soul. It is rather *an ordered movement* towards ever higher levels of reality, ever closer identification with the Infinite. (1955, pp. 81–82, emphasis added)

The fact that Underhill describes the mystical/contemplative pathway as an organic process and as an ordered movement means that it is a native human capacity, and therefore that the mystical/contemplative life is not an extraordinary talent of a select few. Gregory of Nyssa wrote that "the participation in the blessed life we hope for, is not, properly speaking, a retribution for virtue but the 'natural' and 'proper' life of the soul." (Quoted in Balas, p. 94.) The organic process is not dependent on intelligence and education, but is intrinsic to the capacities of all persons. It is often baffling and confusing to the rational mind and leaves the ego passive before the organic process. However, even though contemplation follows from a dynamic process that is part of the very fabric of the individual, it must be carefully nurtured. (See chapter 18.) This involves cooperation with the transformative process by means of conscious effort and commitment and the pursuit of a moral life; yet the contemplative life is not "earned," for it is based on the organic transformation of the personality.

Others besides Evelyn Underhill and Gregory of Nyssa have recognized that the contemplative journey toward the unitive life is not an exceptional process, but a natural one; it is the inclination of the body and psyche if given the opportunity and nurture. Carl Jung's life-long study of the unconscious of hundreds of subjects—normal, neurotic, psychotic—proved to him that mysticism is the natural tendency of the deeper unconscious. (Owens, p. 140) Louis Dupré writes of mystical experience: "The exceptional character of the mystical experience tempts us to isolate it from all others. But if its vision is unique, its foundation is not. For the mystical experience merely brings to full awareness the common religious principle that the soul itself rests on a divine basis." (1976, p. 93) As just mentioned, the mystical drive to live in the experienced presence of God (in whatever degree) belongs to the core of all religions. "Without this living flame to warm its life," Dupré asserts, "religion rapidly degenerates into moralism, ritualism, legalism, or pure speculations." (1989b, p. 7)

Often this organic process is blocked and stymied. It can recommence in a number of ways, which include a severe personal crisis that causes the breakdown of the daily ways of coping, physical illness, an "awakening" experience, or simply a persistent longing that impels a spiritual search. After an awakening of some kind there commonly ensue many years of gradual psychological, intellectual, and bodily healing, aided by a variety of modes of prayer and meditation, personal relationships, therapeutic work, study, body work, worship, and discipline, all accompanied by the many personal insights and illuminations that make up the organic process that is the contemplative/mystical pathway. The great explorers of this transformative process have identified stages of the journey that have classically been named "awakening," "purgation," "illumination," "dark night," and "union."[8] The purgative process is a period of healing of the personal unconscious, often lasting many years. It is followed by the lower levels of contemplation, which means the desire for the experienced presence of God is beginning to be fulfilled. The start of the lower levels of the contemplative life, according to Teresa of Avila, is by temporary recollection, which means the attention is drawn inwardly by God, pulling the senses and faculties from their dispersion. Even after initial experiences of contemplation, there will commonly be further need for healing, for the movement from purgation to illumination is never linear; the need to return to further healing processes will depend on the individual's personal history. Initial experience of recollection can gradually develop and mature into the prayers of quiet (chapter 7) and union, until the person enters the full contemplative life.

Perhaps the experience of Meister Eckhart, Teresa of Avila, and the many other contemplatives will be thought to be an exception, but Thomas Keating, who is a Cistercian monk, points out that the Christian tradition maintained uninterruptedly for the first fifteen centuries that contemplation is the normal development of the genuine spiritual life in response to listening to the word of God, and hence is open to all Christians. (Keating, pp. 19–20) This means that for many centuries there was in devout people a persistence of belief in the Christian experience of God's presence. Even the theologians of the Reformation, who resisted any pretense on man's part of appropriating God's nature, did not question the occurrence of some unification at the heart of the redemptive process. But too many have not understood or embraced the radical nature of this inner way of being, even though it is at the heart of the personal side of religious life. At our peril we ignore the implications of people's experience of the contemplative life. In fact, the implications of the new universe story urge us to take them seriously. The integration between the scientific and contemplative traditions being sought in this book is intended to make it more evident that various levels of contemplation can become part of the consciousness that is emerging in relation to the revelations of the new universe story.

---

[1] The French Catholic theologian and spiritual writer Louis Bouyer writes as follows about the concern that contemplation is an infiltration from Greek sources into the Judeo-Christian tradition, pointing out it must be determined what the Church Fathers and the great scholastics understood by this "knowledge," of which contemplation is the full flower. "Certainly, it is not the purely intellectual knowledge of Aristotle, nor the semi-esthetic knowledge of Plato (and to some extent the Neo-Platonists) but rather biblical knowledge, that is, the knowledge of God as inseparable from his love, and of that love penetrating us entirely and reflecting on all creation and on all our fellow men. To oppose Christian contemplation with the charity exalted by St. Paul (I Cor. 12) is to quarrel over words, since this contemplation is itself the flowering of charity and consists precisely of that which St. Paul gives in the same text as the characteristic of everlasting life. 'To know (God) as I have been known.' (v. 12) Christian contemplation in the highest sense must be considered as a superior awareness of the activity of grace in us, and therefore not only is it infused, but it is connected with the higher gifts of the Spirit." (1965, pp. 101–2)

[2] In Plotinus's thought the *Nous* is subordinate to the One, while in Christian Trinitarian thought it is equivalent to the Word or Son and is a dimension of the One God. Interestingly, Plotinus speaks of the *Nous* as the Father generating and perfecting souls.

[3] Plotinus always holds that the sense-world is good. However matter is often regarded as an evil, anarchic force. (Armstrong 1940, p. 83)

[4] While the works of most of the important classical and Medieval writers have been "standardized," with numbered paragraphs or verses, this is not the case for much of Eckhart. Hence, citations for his sermons and other works specify the edition being used.

[5] Godhead refers to the undifferentiated divine unity. By referring to the undifferentiated divine unity of the Godhead it is thought Eckhart moves beyond Trinitarian thought into emphasis on Godhead, God beyond God. In Sermon 52 "Blessed Are the Poor in Spirit," Eckhart tells us that the essence of mystical union is found in the nameless unity of the 'ground of the soul' with the ground of God beyond all Trinitarian relationships. However, other sermons say mystical union is with the Son, occurring with the birth of the Son in the soul. (Caputo, p. 217) Like most Christian theologians who drew upon the ancient theology of Greek fathers, Eckhart emphasized the unity of God, if not as higher than the Trinity, at least as logically prior to it. (C. Smith, p.46) Benedictine scholar Cyprian Smith offers a resolution by indicating that the Godhead is silent and unuttered, it has no name; when it utters itself, it becomes 'Father'; the utterance itself is Son; yet the two are totally one, both in each other and in the silent Abyss of Godhead from which they emerge and to which they return; this total oneness and unity is itself a Person , and is called Holy Spirit. Through the same Son, the Universe is uttered and becomes Creation. (C. Smith, p. 61)

[6] Otto goes on: "All affirmations and arguments in proof of the absolute unity, the complete simplicity and the perfect identity of the soul with God, all evidence and declamation against multiplicity, separateness, division and manifoldness—however much they sound like rational ontology—are . . . only ultimately significant because they are 'saving.'" (p. 34)

[7] The first of the last two articles of the bull of condemnation cites a statement of Eckhart's that is condemned: "There is something in the soul that is uncreated and not capable of creation; if the whole soul were such, it would be uncreated and not capable of creation and that is the intellect." (Eckhart 1981, p. 80) The issue of the identity of the intellect or the other faculties of the soul and their relationship to God arises in contemplative experience, when in illuminative experience the intellect penetrates into the Godhead, and discovers, according to Eckhart, the unity of the ground of the soul with God.

Eckhart did seek to avoid a violation of the distinction between the Creator and the created and still acknowledge illuminative experiences; he did this by inventing the new designations the "ground of the mind," the "citadel of the soul," "the spark of the soul" or the "castle in the mind" for the locus of oneness. He said in regard to the "spark of the soul" that it is "the highest peak of the soul which stands above time and knows nothing of time or of body." (Woods 1986, p. 59) This was also challenged by the inquisitors because it suggests a part of the soul is uncreated.

Eckhart denied his theology was unorthodox and explained in his Defense: "In the nakedness of his essence which is above every name, [God] penetrates and falls into the naked essence of the mind which is itself also without a proper name and which is elevated above the intellect and the will, as the essence is above the faculties. This is the castle into which Jesus enters, in his being rather than in his acting, giving graciously to the mind the divine and deiform being." (Schürmann 1978a, p. 46).

Reiner Schürmann writes that the charge of heresy against Eckhart was not accurate, since he did not teach that there was an identity between a dimension of the human soul and God but, rather, an imperative for such an identity to be accomplished. To speak of "something of the mind which is uncreated and uncreatable" is not at all the same as affirming that the operation of the detached mind, "in the mind" and not "of the mind," is identical with the divine operation. (1978a, p. 29) Throughout the ordeal of the trial Eckhart maintained he was not guilty of the charges against him, because heresy is a matter of the will, and it was his intention to remain and to die a faithful son of the Church.

[8] Evelyn Underhill has an extensive treatment of these stages in her classic book *Mysticism* (1955; orig. pub. 1910). See also, Maria Jaoudi's *Christian and Islamic Spirituality* (1993) for examples of these stages in those traditions.

6

THE BREAKTHROUGH EXPERIENCE

World and history are the place in which the numinous manifests itself, that numinous which transforms its elect by revelations and mystical encounters and through them renews the world.

— Erich Neumann

THE LANDSCAPE OF the individual broadens immensely when she actually touches into the 'ground of the soul.' Meister Eckhart referred to this as breakthrough; his insights into the subject will clarify its nature and a number of examples of breakthrough experiences will illustrate how profoundly a person is affected and why the new story must incorporate this type of experience and the life that may develop from it. Some fortunate few people do not need to experience breakthrough because they have been able to maintain from childhood a ready contact with the ground and sources of their personality. Others, for unknown reasons, seem never to have such an experience. But whatever our personal history, we can learn about the mystery of our lives from their occurrence.

Breakthrough into Silence and Emptiness

Breakthrough is a penetration of soul into the divine ground. It is uniting with the Silent Desert, a union understood, according to Eckhart, only in darkness and in silence, a kind of unknowing knowing, obscure and indescribable indeed, yet actual, of the enfolding presence of Reality. In its most fundamental form, breakthrough does not involve concepts or ideas but raw, naked unity. Although breakthrough may occur spontaneously, it more commonly happens after long preparation, which Eckhart described as a process of "letting be" and "releasement." He taught: "Your opening and His entering are but one moment."

Only in the "flowing back" of breakthrough is authentic personhood realized, because it means that the person begins to find the fullness of being based on the unity of the 'ground of the soul' and the Godhead. In breakthrough the person comes into possession of her full nature. Breakthrough is a brief "return" from alienation from full human identity. This is contemplation, the return necessary, as described by Plotinus, for the person to find the fullness of her potential creativity, love, and power.

The direct, unmediated experience of the 'ground of the soul' in breakthrough is felt to be superior and more veridical than daily consciousness. The very purpose of the mystical journey, Louis Dupré writes, is "to surpass consciousness and to rest in the dark source of the conscious self." (1980, p. 451) When this happens, it is highly valued and sometimes attributed to something beyond the bounds of personality, but that depends on how one defines the limits of personhood, a topic important to the considerations of this book. There is a great deal of evidence that the experience is a discovery of the fullness of personhood and a center of identity in 'this present now.'

Although initially breakthrough may involve particular types of experience in prayer and meditation, if there is an unfolding of the contemplative/mystical journey, the relationship with divinity is not something that occurs only when we are engaged in solitary meditation and prayer. God does not lie merely at the heart of our devotional and religious life but instead lies at the heart of our whole life and especially our day-to-day activities.

Breakthrough is a source of peace and acceptance of life, because of its fulfilling nature: a door has opened to knowing the fullness of 'this present now.' Key to this knowing, this acceptance of the fullness of the now, is the realization following Eckhart, that there is no opposition between a "higher" world known in breakthrough and the "lower" world of the senses to which the soul will redescend. (Schürmann 1978a, p.15) The use of the word "redescend" should not suggest that God lies outside the confines of the human person (though not limited to the confines of the person), so that after a breakthrough we must "lower" ourselves back into daily life. Rather, the "descent" involves the return to daily consciousness from the highly valued contemplative consciousness. In the mature contemplative life, there is no descent even in consciousness, because there has been an integration of the depth dimensions of the personality.

Eckhart and his predecessors in the Christian tradition largely adopted Trinitarian thought to describe the contemplative return. In the Christian tradition, breakthrough into unity with the divine life is not beyond the Trinity. (Dupré 1984, p. 32) However Eckhart sometimes spoke of breakthrough into the Godhead beyond God, seeming to stretch the bounds of Christian orthodoxy. We will see in chapter 13 the importance of Trinitarian thought, a pattern of insight not limited to Christianity, and why ideas of Godhead beyond God may not be adequate.

The Great Personal Value of Breakthrough

The examples of breakthrough given in the pages that follow are of many types: those involving naked unity with God and those accompanied by visions and auditions (hearing words) and various knowings or illuminations that the individual is certain are revelatory of the very order of existence. The body is often affected. The realizations are sometimes felt according to the symbols of personality: the person experiences meeting with Someone. Or sometimes the experience is of an impersonal life-giving Force, Light, Energy, or Heat. (Underhill 1942, p. 159) Breakthroughs often involve bliss, joy, healing and a sense of liberation, although some people experience fear. The examples that follow are far from an exhaustive survey of the great variety of experiences, but they will serve to show the importance of their content and to illustrate why the contemplative tradition in all its multifaceted expressions needs to be integrated into the new universe story.

Experiences of Bliss and Beatitude

A nearly universally attested characteristic of mystical experience is ecstasy, a sense of spiritual exaltation, bliss and beatitude, joy. Feelings of wonder, awe, reverence, humility, surrender and worship are often reported.

While on a visit to England in 1872, Richard M. Bucke, a Canadian doctor and psychologist, who was thirty-six at the time, had a breakthrough so profound that it became the center of his outlook on life. This is part of his record of the experience:

> I had spent the evening in a great city, with two friends, reading and discussing poetry and philosophy. We parted at midnight. I had a long drive in a hansom to my lodging. My mind, deeply under the influence of the ideas, images and emotions called up by reading and talk, was calm and peaceful. I was in a state of quiet, almost passive enjoyment, not actually thinking, but letting ideas, images, and emotions flow of themselves, as it were, through my mind. All at once, without warning of any kind, I found myself wrapped in a flame-colored cloud. For an instant I thought of fire, an immense conflagration somewhere close by in that great city; the next, I knew that the fire was within myself. Directly afterward there came upon me a *sense of exultation, of immense joyousness* accompanied or immediately followed by an intellectual illumination impossible to believe. . . . (In Coxhead, pp. 7–8, emphasis added)

In her classic work *The Interior Castle*, Teresa of Avila describes the beginning of contemplative prayer as an experience of ineffable blessing:

> It seems that since that heavenly water begins to rise from this spring I'm mentioning that is deep within us, it swells and expands our whole interior being, *producing ineffable blessings*; nor does the soul even understand what is given to it there. It perceives a fragrance, let us say for now, as though there were in that interior depth a brazier giving off sweet-smelling perfumes. No light is seen, nor is the place seen where the brazier is; but the warmth and the fragrant fumes spread through the entire soul and even often enough, as I have said, the body shares in them. See now that you understand me; no

the scent of any perfume, for the
...e than an experience of these things;
...nly so as to explain it to you. (IV. 2.

the great joy the detached person
...y that no one would be able to tear it
...ted in Schürmann 1978a, p. xv) In a
...n "Blessed Are the Poor in Spirit," he

essedness] does not consist in either
...ut that there is that in the soul from
which knowing ... loving flow; that something does not
know or love as do the powers of the soul. Whoever knows
this knows of what blessedness consists. (1981, p. 201)

Great Value and Worth of the Experience

Closely related to the exaltation and bliss is the great value
and worth of the experience for the individual. This type of
experience is related to worship, a word derived from the Anglo
Saxon word *weorth*, worth. A particularly lovely account of an
experience emphasizing its extraordinary value was written by
Johannes Anker-Larsen, a twentieth-century Dane:

I had been sitting in the garden working and had just finished.
That afternoon I was to go to Copenhagen, but it was still an
hour and a half before the departure of the train. The weather
was beautiful, the air clear and pure. I lighted a cigar and sat
down...I just sat there. Then it began to come, that infinite
tenderness, which is purer and deeper than that of lovers, or
of a father toward his child. It was in me, but it also came to
me, as the air came to my lungs. As usual the breathing
became sober and reverent, became as it were incorporeal;
I inhaled the tenderness, needless to say the cigar went out. I
did not cast it away like a sin. I simply had no use for it!

This deep tenderness which I felt, first within myself and
then even stronger around and above me...drew me into the

Eternal Now. That was my first actual meeting with Reality; because such is the real life; a Now that is and a Now which happens. . . . I sat in my garden but there was no place in the world where I was not.

A few pages later, he declares:

If I had all the food in the world in one dish, all the wine in the world in one glass, all its tobacco in one cigar . . . and all the honors of all the kings conferred upon me in one decoration, and the promise in addition that I should have all these things continuously, if only I were to renounce the possibility of experiencing again those meetings with the Eternal Now, and the illumination of life that they would bring—I would laugh heartily and throw the whole collection of trinkets on the dunghill. If I have forgotten anything else one might covet, I throw it after the rest. . . . (In Steere, p.27)

Anker-Larsen is hardly able to express how greatly he valued the experience. This is not uncommon, although not often articulated so strongly. His account calls to mind one of the teachings of Jesus of Nazareth which uses compelling images to express the value of what has been discovered:

The kingdom of heaven is like treasure hidden in a field; which a man found and covered up; then in his joy he goes and sells all that he has, and buys that field.

Again, the kingdom of heaven is like a merchant in search of fine pearls, who, on finding one pearl of great value, went and sold all that he had, and bought it. (Matt. 13: 43–45)

Johannes Anker-Larsen knows that the realm he encountered is utterly real, profoundly important and attractive, and that contact with it can bring real life. Others feel that their deepest being has been touched, and consequently the awakening of a desire that it be touched again so that life may have the meaning and richness it does not have otherwise. It is this desire that provides the motivation for undertaking of the contemplative pathway.

In his *Memoirs* Tennyson wrote of an experience which he induced through monotonous, repetitive meditation:

> I have never had any revelations through anaesthetics, but a kind of waking trance—this for lack of a better word—I have frequently had, quite up from boyhood, when I have been all alone. This has come upon me, as it were out of the intensity of the consciousness of individuality, individuality itself seemed to dissolve and fade away into boundless being, and this not a confused state but the clearest, the surest of the surest, utterly beyond words—where death was an almost laughable impossibility—the loss of personality (if so it were) seeming not extinction, but *the only true life*. I am ashamed of my feeble description. Have I not said the state is utterly beyond words? (As quoted in Idel and McGinn, p. 128, emphasis added)

The person discovers that life has a much greater significance than he or she had previously realized. As in Anker-Larsen's experience, we find confidence in the supreme intrinsic value and great worth of what has been made known to the person. In a study of "peak experiences" Abraham Maslow, one of the founders of humanistic psychology, discovered that the subject perceives the intrinsic value of being, described as wholeness, simplicity, honesty, goodness, effortlessness, playfulness, justice and self-sufficiency; characteristically, the subject's life henceforth is known to be worthwhile and self-validating. (Maslow, p. 78) This apprehension of something that is so greatly valued, intrinsic to our world, can completely transform one's sense of the worth of human life, and the worth of the Earth.

Gratuitousness

Scholars, William James among them, who have listed the characteristics of mystical experience are unanimous in asserting that they seem gratuitous, undeserved. The experience of discovering the presence of God has a quality of being a free gift from the perspective of the needy, perhaps isolated, ego. Gordon

Cosby, founder of the Church of the Savior in Washington, D.C., has preached: "We do know this whole order of being is a gracious reality. It is ready to flow into me if I can open to it as a gracious reality. . . . If one is to pray, it is necessary to take this terrible risk, this risk of assuming that this infinite life and energy, and power, ready to break into us, is gracious and is working and will work for our good." Often, because of popular emphasis on the exclusive transcendence of God, grace has seemed to come from outside the person. However, Louis Dupré writes: "Grace is not in the first place a created 'gift' added to nature but the gracious presence of God's self communicating Word through the Spirit." (1984, p.11) Thus grace brings us into the divine life. Because these experiences are unearned, they are a great gift to the ego, which no longer need feel estranged.

Healing

Breakthrough experiences are often healing to body and mind. Bernard of Clairvaux (1090–1153), the man who did most to establish the Cistercian Order, tells in one of his sermons on the "Song of Songs" how he knew the Word was present:

> He is the life and power (Heb 4:12), and as soon as he enters in he stirs my sleeping soul. He moves and soothes and pierces my heart (Sg 4:9) which was as hard as stone and riddled with disease (Sir 3:27; Ez 11:19; 36:26). And he begins to root up and destroy, to build and to plant, to water the dry places and light the dark corners (cf. Jer 1:10), to open what was closed, set what was cold on fire, to make the crooked straight and the rough places smooth (Is 40:4), so that my soul may bless the Lord and all that is within me praise his holy name (Ps 102.1). (*Sermons on the Song of Songs* 74. 6)

Teresa of Avila found healing in her experiences. On one occasion, when she felt lonely and abandoned by her friends, she heard the words: "Do not be afraid, for it is I." She then wrote:

> These words had so much power that from then on she could not doubt the vision, and she was left *very much strengthened*

and happy over such good company.* (*Interior Castle* VI. 8. 3, emphasis added)

Describing the effects of a type of ecstasy, she wrote:

> *Frequently the body is made healthy and stronger*—for it was really sick and full of great sufferings—because something wonderful is given to it in that prayer. The Lord sometimes desires, as I say, that the body enjoy it since the body is now obedient to what the soul desires. (*Book of Her Life*, 20. 21, emphasis added)

Naturalist John Muir wrote:

> No amount of word-making will ever make a single soul to know these mountains. As well seek to warm the naked and frost bitten by lectures on caloric and pictures of flame. One day's exposure to mountains is better than carloads of books. See how willingly Nature poses herself upon photographer's plates. No earthly chemicals are so sensitive as those of the human soul. All that is required is exposure, and purity of material. The pure in heart shall see God! . . . Come to the woods, for here is rest. . . . The galling harness of civilization drops off, and *we are healed ere we are aware.* (1983, pp. 27, 30, emphasis added)

Two criteria for authenticity of mystic experience, according to Rufus Jones, a Quaker philosopher and spiritual teacher, are "increase in the coherence of the personality which is noted as the life of the person takes on new depth, and the second is increase in psychic energy." (Quoted in Jones, p.17) The experience produces release from fixed unconscious patterns that have prevented the actualization of the person's highest potentialities. Writing from the perspective of psychotherapy, Harry Guntrip observes that religious experience and faith result in the most comprehensive and invulnerable security and the largest scope of self-actualization possible to men and women. (p. 198)

---

* When using themselves as examples, Teresa and some other Medieval mystics often referred to themselves in the third person.

Illuminations and Contemplative Knowings

Contemplative experience sometimes involves a type of intuitive knowing, which Louis Dupré describes as being with reality, not reflecting upon it. (Dupré 1989b, p.11) It is a direct, unmediated contact with, or participation in, ultimate reality. The knowing is an inherent part of the experience and is not derived from interpretation made afterwards. Plotinus incorporated this type of knowing at the level of *Nous* (or Mind or Intellect), which is a level humans can experience directly.

Such experiences of knowing have traditionally been called intellectual visions (they are not a visual perception), with "intellectual" used in the Neoplatonic sense, as in chapter 5. Thus they do not refer to daily, rational thought. They can be in a verbal or non-verbal form. In the verbal form, the insights sometimes seem to the person to be thoughts of God that have now become her own. Mention was just made of one verbal form, in which Teresa heard the words "Do not be afraid, for it is I," and felt that they were from God. Dupré observes that the impact of "intellectual visions is one of insight and even of all-surpassing insight." (1980, p. 458) John of the Cross called the knowledge given in contemplative experience a "knowledge of naked truth," that is, "an intellectual understanding or vision of truths about God, or to a vision of present, past, or future events, which bears great resemblance to the spirit of prophecy. . . ." ("Ascent of Mount Carmel" II. 26. 2; see also II. 25. 1)

A famous, classic example of this type of knowing is Ignatius of Loyola's description of what he experienced at the River Cardoner:

> As he sat there, the eyes of his understanding began to open. Without having any vision he understood—knew— many matters both spiritual and pertaining to the Faith and the realm of letters and that with such clearness that they seemed utterly new to him. There is no possibility of setting out in detail everything he then understood. The most that he can say is that he was given so great an enlightening of his mind

that if one were to put together all the helps he has received from God and all the things he has ever learned, they would not be the equal of what he received in that single illumination. He was left with his understanding so enlightened that he seemed to be another man with another mind than the one that was his before. (As quoted in Dupré 1980, p. 458)

Claire Myers Owens, a Connecticut housewife, had an experience when sitting at her desk, at a time of considerable inner distress at the state of the world and from several months of illness, which had left her body weak:

Extraordinary intuitive insights flashed across my mind. I seemed *to comprehend the nature of things*. I understood that the scheme of the universe was good, it was only man that was out of harmony with it. I was inherently good, not evil as our Western society taught me as a child; all people were intrinsically good. Neither time nor space existed on this plane. I saw into the past and observed man's endless struggle toward the light. Love and suffering and compassion for the whole human race so suffused me that I knew I never again could condemn any person no matter what he or she did. I also saw into the distant future and beheld man awakening gradually to the good in himself, in others, moving with the harmonious rhythm of the universe, creating a new golden age—in some sweet tomorrow. (As quoted in Coxhead, p. 35, emphasis added)

The following example involves an illumination concerning the nature of love and the infinite value of other people. It is somewhat unusual in that the experience was shared by three others besides the narrator, who is not identified:

One fine summer night in June, 1933 I was sitting on a lawn after dinner with three colleagues, two women and one man. We liked each other well enough but we were certainly not intimate friends, nor had any one of us a sexual interest in another. Incidentally, we had not drunk any alcohol. We were talking casually about everyday matters when, quite suddenly and unexpectedly, something happened. I felt myself invaded by a power which, though I consented to it, was irresistible and certainly not mine. *For the first time in my life I knew exactly—because thanks to the power, I was doing it—what it means to love one's neighbor as oneself.* I was also certain, though the conversation continued to be perfectly ordinary, that my three colleagues were having the same experience. (In the case of one of them, I was able later to confirm this.) My personal feelings towards them were unchanged—they were still colleagues, not intimate friends—but I felt their existence as themselves to be of infinite value and rejoiced in it. (In Freemantle, p. 30, emphasis added)

The same breakthrough in which R. M. Bucke experienced such great joyousness also included an intellectual illumination about matter, eternal life, and love:

I saw that the universe is not composed of dead matter, but on the contrary, a living Presence; I became conscious in myself of eternal life. It was not a conviction that I would have eternal life, but a consciousness that I possessed eternal life then; I saw that all men are immortal; that the cosmic order is such that without any peradventure all things work together for the good of each and all; that the foundation principle of the world, of all the worlds, is what we call love, and that the happiness of each and all is in the long run absolutely certain. (In Coxhead, p. 7)

Some scientists, including most notably the physicists Brian Josephson and David Bohm, believe that regular mystical insights achieved by meditative practices can be useful in the formulation of scientific theories. (Davies 1992, p. 227) Wolfgang Pauli attributed his discoveries to archetypal dream experience. (Berry and Clarke, p. 26) In the late 1960s, Fred Hoyle and a colleague were working on a cosmological theory of electromagnetism that involved difficult mathematics. Hoyle took a vacation and went hiking in the Scottish Highlands. He later wrote that somehow, while hiking,

> My awareness of the mathematics clarified, not a little, not even a lot, but as if a huge brilliant light had suddenly been switched on. How long did it take to become totally convinced that the problem was solved? Less than five seconds. It only remained to make sure that before the clarity faded I had enough of the essential steps stored safely in my recallable memory. (Quoted in Davies 1982, p. 229)

Hoyle described this as a truly religious event. It certainly shows the remarkable capacity for insight and creativity available to the person, and it seems likely that in their origin, such experiences are not too different from mystical experiences that involve the healing and reordering of the personality. These too are based on an emergence of the inner ordering of things.

Illuminations such as these are clearly not the rational, objective knowledge valued in the West; instead the mind has literally *perceived*, as directly as the senses ordinarily do. (Dupré 1980, p. 451) The new story of the evolutionary universe provides a context in which knowledge of this type can be valued and better understood. After all, as indicated in the initial discussion of the implications of the new universe story, the person and her consciousness are *integral to* the unfolding whole, so it should not be surprising that there could be various types of participatory knowledge directly perceived from our *integration in* the unfolding whole. This topic will be explored more extensively in the chapter titled "Knowings That Change Consciousness: Entrance into the Unitive Life" (chapter 19), since it is particularly important to the 'way of seeing' being explored. Such knowings, also called direct perceptions or illuminations, are often part of the contemplative pathway because of their transformative, personal significance: the knowledge of belonging and the confidence in the order of things that accompany them. Also, the topic is especially important because this type of knowing is traditionally considered to belong to a faculty of the soul, the intellect (the *Nous* in Plotinus's thought)[1]—a faculty foreign to contemporary psychology, which by and large has not been in touch with the mainstream spiritual wisdom.[*]

Experiences of the "Aliveness" of Nature and Inanimate Objects

Recall that, in the passage quoted above concerning the "intellectual illumination impossible to believe," which was the culmination of his breakthrough experience, Richard M. Bucke saw with great clarity that "*the universe is not composed of dead matter, but is on the contrary, a living Presence.*" (In Coxhead, p. 7, emphasis added)

Often when John Muir was climbing in the mountains he felt "ebullient life bursting forth from the rock and ice." This exhilarating vision affected every aspect of his climbing and elevated his mountaineering from the realm of simple sport to spiritual quest. (1986, p. 50)

A mystical insight came to a friend of mine while visiting Niagara Falls in 1987. The Horseshoe Falls on the Canadian side seemed to be calm, with the water falling quietly over the rim, while the American falls were filled with a great volume of racing water that leapt forward like a galloping horse. He said to himself, "That is God," as a deeply felt insight arose within him. He said later that he felt that the leaping falls evoked this insight in the same way that fountains have often evoked similar insights: Historically "fountain fullness" has been an image used for God.

A man of the last century, identified by philosopher William Stace as N.M., had an experience after taking mescaline, which he insisted did not "produce" the experience but only "inhibited the inhibitions which had previously prevented him from seeing things as they really are." (Stace, p. 71) Part of his experience is included here because it is illustrative of the "aliveness" of things; animate or inanimate, they are, he says, "*urgent* with life" (the emphatic *urgent* is N.M.'s):

[*] Ewert Cousins: personal communication, 1996.

The room in which I was standing looked out onto the back yards of a Negro tenement. The buildings were decrepit and ugly, the ground covered with boards, rags, and debris. Suddenly every object in my field of vision took on a curious and intense kind of existence of its own; that is, everything appeared to have an "inside"—to exist as I existed, having inwardness, a kind of individual life, and every object, seen under this aspect, appeared exceedingly beautiful. There was a cat out there, with its head lifted, effortlessly watching a wasp that moved without moving just above its head. Everything was *urgent* with life . . . which was the same in the cat, the wasp, the broken bottles, and merely manifested itself differently in these individuals (which did not therefore cease to be individuals, however). All things seemed to glow with a light that came from within them. (In Stace, pp. 71–72)

Luminosity and Fire from Within

In the third chapter of Exodus it is recorded that while Moses was keeping the flock of his father-in-law Jethro in the wilderness, "the angel of the Lord appeared to him in a flame of fire out of the midst of a bush; and he looked, and lo, the bush was burning, yet it was not consumed." (Ex. 3:2) Here is what Teilhard de Chardin wrote in *The Divine Milieu* (1960):

> *Throughout* my life, *by means of my life*, the world has little by little caught fire in my sight until, aflame all around me, it had become almost completely luminous from within. . . . Such has been my experience in contact with the earth—the diaphany of the Divine at the heart of the universe on fire . . . Christ; his heart; a fire: Capable of penetrating everything and, gradually, spreading everywhere. (p. 46n.)

John Yungblut comments that he wishes Teilhard had called this luminous diaphany of the Divine "God" rather than "Christ," in deference to the other living religions, but we see what he meant, since Christ was his God. (1995, p. 7)

Perhaps experiences of an inward light are closely related to these of an inner fire. We will give some examples in the next chapter in the discussion of the unitive life.

Experiences of Indigenous Peoples

The experiences of indigenous people as described by Mircea Eliade in *Patterns of Comparative Religion* seem to be akin to these experiences of "aliveness" and of an inward fire. Hierophanies (from the Greek *hieros*: powerful, supernatural, holy, sacred, and *phaneia*: to reveal, show, make known) occurred in relation to the sky, the sun, the moon, water, certain stones, the earth, vegetation; in fact, Eliade suggests, in the study of ancient peoples we have to learn to recognize hierophanies everywhere. Anything, at any given moment, can become a hierophany, although not everything in a particular culture. (p. 12)

Water was often the occasion for hierophanies: By their very nature springs and rivers display power, life, perpetual renewal; they *are* and they are *alive*. "Water flows and it is living." (p. 200) In myths, water was sometimes the source of all things, the whole of potentiality. (p.188) "Living water, the fountain of youth, the Water of Life, and the rest, are all mythological formulae for the same metaphysical and religious reality: life, strength and eternity are contained in water." (p. 193)

The indigenous peoples encountered an inexhaustible hierophany in the inaccessibility, infinity, and creative power of the sky, due largely to the rain that falls from it. These qualities were sometimes personified in certain supreme sky divinities and their hierophanies dramatized in various ways by myth. Hierophanies of the moon gave insight into the lunar characteristics of fertility and regeneration, of immortality through metamorphosis. There was an almost unlimited abundance of plant hierophanies among indigenous peoples. Various uses of vegetation in rituals, symbols, drama and myth all express the same conviction that "the plant world embodies (or signifies, or shares in) the reality of which life is made, which creates untiringly, which is ever reborn in an innumerable variety of forms, and is never worn out." (p. 324) All of these hierophanies and others were the basis of an intuitive insight into cosmic harmony and wholeness.

If the people Eliade describes had had an experience like that of the friend at Niagara Falls who had the insight "That is God," the falls would be sacred. We do not allow ourselves this great knowledge because our assumptions about the natural world and our relationship to it have been severely reduced. The falls are only matter in the narrow sense defined by the chemistry of water. The contemporary Western person has tragically lost this sensitivity to and appreciation of the sacred modalities of nature.

Unitive Visions

Sometimes in breakthrough experiences there is a perception of the world as transfigured and unified in one ultimate being. We find an example in a sermon of Meister Eckhart's: "The whole scattered world of lower things is gathered up to oneness when the soul climbs up to that life in which there are no opposites." (1941, p. 173) William Stace quotes a similar passage: "All that a man has here externally in multiplicity is intrinsically One. Here all blades of grass, wood and stone, all things are One. This is the deepest depth." (Stace, p. 63) In another place Eckhart wrote: "Say Lord, when is a man in mere understanding? I say to you 'when a man sees one thing separated from another.' And when is he above mere understanding? That I can tell you: 'When he sees all in all, then a man stands above mere understanding." (As quoted in Stace, p. 64) Before considering these assertions further, let us turn to some statements of a perception of unity similar to Eckhart's, but that name God.

Experiences That Name God

Angela of Foligno (c. 1249–1309), a Franciscan born in Italy only thirty years after the death of Saint Francis, gave the following report of an experience that names God:

After this I went into the church, and there did the Lord speak most sweetly and graciously unto me, whereat all my mind did greatly rejoice and take comfort. He said, "My beloved daughter," and many other things better still, and added, "No creature can console thee, only I alone, who desire to reveal My power unto thee."

And immediately the eyes of my soul were opened and I beheld the plenitude of God, whereby I did comprehend the whole world, both here and beyond the sea, and the abyss and all things else; and therein did I behold naught save the divine power in a manner assuredly indescribable, so that through excess of marveling the soul cried with a loud voice, saying, *"This whole world is full of God!"* Wherefore did I now comprehend that the world is but a small thing; I saw, moreover, that the power of God was above all things, and that *the whole world was filled with it.* (Quoted in Idel and McGinn, p. 136, emphasis added)

Teresa of Avila described knowing how everything is seen and contained in God:

Once while in prayer I was shown quickly, without my seeing any form—but it was totally clear representation— *how all things are seen in God and how He holds them all in Himself.* How to put this in writing, I don't know. But it was deeply impressed upon my soul, and it is one of the great favors the Lord has granted to me and one of those that have most embarrassed me and made me ashamed when I recalled the sins I committed. (*Book of Her Life* 40. 9, emphasis added)

This was an extremely important experience for Teresa, one that fundamentally influenced her understanding. (See chapter 7.)

About the year 1600 a young German shoemaker named Jakob Boehme (1575–1624), a Lutheran from Görlitz, had a shattering mystical experience, which became the vital center of his life and thought. He said it was "like the resurrection of the dead." (Stoudt, p. 58) The experience was initiated by a trance-like state of consciousness, the result of gazing at a burnished pewter plate in which the sun was reflected. The experience brought with it a peculiar and lucid vision of the inner reality of the world in which, as he said, he looked into the principles and deepest foundations of things as he gazed at the plate. "He believed that it was only a fancy, and in order to banish it from his mind he went out upon the green. But here he remarked that he gazed into the very heart of things, the very herbs and grass, and that actual Nature harmonized with what he had inwardly seen." (Quoted in Underhill 1955, p. 256). Boehme called the "very heart of things" God. "In the light my spirit saw through all things and into all creatures and *I recognized God in grass and plants*." (Quoted in Stace, p. 69, emphasis added)

The person identified as N.M. by William Stace wrote: "I had no doubt that I had seen God, that is, had seen all there is to see; yet it turned out to be the world that I looked at every day." (In Stace, p. 73)

There are also experiences that people have about their own person that bring, it seems, the same insight about God's immanence as those just cited, which occurred in relation to nature. From July 27, 1989, through March 3, 1990, a total of 220 days, a group of six international explorers crossed Antarctica with dog sleds. On the next to the last day of the crossing, sixteen miles from their destination, Keizo Funatsu, a Japanese member of the team, went out at 4:30 p.m. to feed the dogs, and found himself unable to return because the white-out conditions of a snowstorm prevented him from finding either his nearby tent or a ski marker he had left. Knowing not to wander blindly in the snow, and trusting his companions to search for him, Keizo buried himself in a snow ditch. When his party discovered he was lost, they made several attempts to find him that evening, but called the search off at 10:00 p.m. At daylight, they began to search again, sweeping areas with a radius of 350 feet, with men placed every 20 feet along a rope calling for the missing man. At 6:30 he was found. Keizo heard someone's voice and clambered exultantly out of the shallow snow ditch, shouting, "I am God, I am God." The account of this episode was edited in the *National Geographic* report of the expedition, so that Keizo is reported to have said, "I am alive." The story is recounted both ways in the book *Crossing Antarctica*, but it has been confirmed that he said, "I am God." (Steger and Bowermaster 1992)

The altered consciousness from which Keizo Funatsu proclaimed "I am God" probably resulted in part from acute sensory deprivation, a consequence of being buried in the snow. A number of meditative techniques seek the same "naughting" of daily consciousness to induce comparable experiences.

Keizo's insight is not unique. Others have made similar statements. Catherine of Genoa said "My name is God, nor do I know my selfhood save in Him." To say one is changed completely into pure God, as Catherine did, certainly indicates a state of consciousness markedly different from more ordinary modes. And while saying "I am God" is not indicative of a full human self-understanding, it is an important "take," and one honored in the integration of the new universe story and the contemplative tradition undertaken in this book.

These experiences and insights about nature and about the person are important because they indicate a great intimacy between God and the world; their interpretation goes to the heart of Western assumptions about God, nature and the person, and is, I believe, essential to finding our way to a viable future, to joy and to meaning in life. It will be our task to try to understand this intimacy in the context of the new universe story, which in turn will involve understanding the concept of simultaneous unity and difference that is central to the integration, as well as exploring a number of other topics, including changes dating from the last century in our assumptions about the nature of matter and recent discoveries about form generation.

---

[1] Augustine preserves the primacy of illumination in the act of knowledge but his influence wanes in the twelfth and thirteenthth centuries, especially with. Thomas Aquinas, who denied the possibility of the illumination of the mind by the Intellect and considered all knowledge as having an origin in the senses. This reduces the function of the intellect to that of a handmaid of faith rather than the means of sanctification. Nasr comments: "Had Thomism continued to be interpreted by a Meister Eckhart, the intellectual destiny of the West could have been different." (Nasr, p. 37)

7

THE UNITIVE LIFE,
UNITIVE EPISODES AND GESTURES

Oh, then, Soul, most beautiful among all the creatures, so anxious to know the dwelling place of your Beloved that you may go in quest of Him and be united with Him, now we are telling you that you yourself are His Dwelling and His secret chamber and hiding place.

— John of the Cross

PEOPLE WHO HAVE entered into the unitive life come to very important and highly informative experiences that signify a profoundly changed relationship to the world. An understanding of the unitive life as described by the tradition will lead us deeply into the heart of the personal side of the spiritual life. The reader is encouraged to be open to seeing a broad congruence between Bohm's thought about the whole being enfolded in each region and characteristics of the experiences of those who have entered into the unitive life.

The Unitive Life

The persistent explorers of the deepest ranges of the mystical/contemplative pathway made a remarkable discovery. According to Teresa of Avila, John Ruusbroec, Richard of St. Victor, Catherine of Genoa, Francis, and many others, a type of contemplation, that of union, can become a permanent condition. It is no longer the brief breakthrough; rather, after a process of personal transformation, union with the highest (or deepest) reality becomes a state of being, and this state of being is understood to be a permanent union, though God's presence may not always be fully sensed. (Dupré 1989b, pp. 11–12) Teresa of Avila writes of the unitive life, which she called spiritual marriage, that "it seemed to her, despite the trials she underwent and business affairs she had to attend to, that the essential part of her soul never moved from that room (the room of mystical marriage)." (IC VII. 1. 10)[1]

Meister Eckhart is not the only one who struggled over how to interpret and to communicate contemplative experiences within the accepted framework of thought in his time (see chapter 5). Jesus of Nazareth's assertion that "I and the Father are One" was severely challenged. And though Jesus claim of unity with the Father was ultimately accepted by Christianity, too often this acceptance was as an exception rather that as an opening of a new mode of human self-understanding and a new consciousness for all humankind. Jesus of Nazareth has, of course, profoundly shaped the contemplative tradition.

Jan van Ruusbroec, a fourteenth-century Flemish mystic, refers to God's direct communication to the soul in contemplation—without intermediary—as the essential unity. He declared that by their very nature people have an essential unity with God. He called it the "Imageless Ground," and wrote: "This is the nobility which we naturally possess in the essential unity of our spirit, which is at this level naturally united with God."[2] (1985, p. 118)[3] Through the Imageless Ground, the soul partakes in the divine life. (Dupré 1984, p. 35) Ruusbroec wrote: "To comprehend and understand God as he is in himself, above and beyond all likeness, is to be God with God, without intermediary."(1985, p. 146)

Friedrich von Hügel (1852–1925), the great modernist Catholic philosopher and theologian, believed we should reject any absolute qualitative difference between the soul's deepest possibilities and ideas of God, thus indicating the possibility of the return in contemplation to the fullness of our identity. It is also indicated by Rabbi Lawrence Kushner, who, drawing on the Hebrew Bible and the rabbinical tradition, writes in *The River of Light*:

There is a "place" from which all places can be seen. And "time" from which all time might be beheld. This place is in us and was once shown to us even as it is still within us to this day. . . . This place precedes life in this world and yet exists simultaneously with it. Its knowledge remains sealed in us. (p. 84)

The sources used to understand contemplation in this book are from the Western tradition, although it is important to note that in the Vedantic tradition the deeper self, unknowable yet attainable, is at once the core of all that is. The duality between man and Brahman is abolished yet this "ground of selfhood is experienced by the mystics not only as hidden but also as transcendent. It is the very point in which the soul is more than an individual soul." (Dupré 1980, p. 461)

Some writers in both the Christian and Hebrew traditions have been at pains to maintain a distinction between the person and God in order to be faithful to the biblical distinction between Creator and created. But in Christianity at least, this distinction is severely challenged and in fact contradicted by the radical Christian assertion that Jesus of Nazareth was fully divine and fully human, or in more theological language, that Christ was consubstantial with the Father.[4] The way the new universe story sheds light on this question of the limits of personhood will be carefully explored in the chapters that follow.

Teresa of Avila's Images of the Unitive Life

Teresa of Avila (1515–1582) uses several compelling images that help us to understand the unitive life. She was a Carmelite nun who led a major reform of her order in Spain, the beginning of which was the founding of a small, enclosed, reformed, discalced convent in Avila called St. Joseph. There were only twelve women living in it, so its members were free of the distractions and social demands of the large unreformed convent where Teresa had lived until age forty-seven with more than a hundred other women. At the convent of St. Joseph, the women were able to dedicate themselves to recollection and contemplative prayer. Teresa eventually founded sixteen reformed convents and wrote several books that have become classics. These include *The Book of Her Life* (L), which is her autobiography, *The Way of Perfection* (W), and *The Interior Castle* (IC). In her writing, Teresa sometimes professes a humility that seems false, and even low self-esteem, but her life and her writings show she was a great contemplative woman who led a very effective active life, reforming her order against entrenched resistance. She was canonized in 1622, and in 1970 she was declared a doctor of the Roman Catholic Church, which means that her writings have teaching authority for the church.

In 1577, when Teresa was sixty-two and in the midst of her reform efforts, she wrote *The Interior Castle*, a book based on the image of a castle made of clear crystal so that light from the center may permeate all the dwelling places if there is no obstruction and no sin. The central dwelling place, in the middle of the castle, is the place "where the very secret exchanges between God and the soul take place." (IC I. 1. 3) To understand the significance of the castle image it is important to realize that it is an archetypal mandala image.[5] (In Carl Jung's understanding, the mandala may be an image of the Self, and thus it concerns the ordering and healing of the Self/soul. There will be a discussion of the ordering power of the Self in chapter 12.)

The various rooms in the castle represent different ways of being within one's self and within God. Movement from room to room toward the central or seventh dwelling place represents changes in the nature of the relationship of the person to God. Christ, the image of God, dwells in the innermost, seventh dwelling place.

People outside the castle live in darkness because they have not yet begun to search for the Light and for a contemplative life. Those in the outer three dwelling places live in partial darkness; these are people who are attracted to the center and are moving toward it but are still quite distant from it. Most good Christians live in the third dwelling place which, Teresa says, is no small favor. However, she insists, there is no reason why entrance into the more interior dwelling places—those closer to the center—should be denied these souls. (IC III. 1. 5) As the person's capacity for relationship with that central inner reality changes, she moves more toward the center.

In the fourth dwelling place, the person begins to enter into a passively given relationship with the central reality. This marks the beginning of contemplative prayer, which is an alternative form of knowing and loving. It is called the prayer of quiet, because the person is further quieted and centered. (IC IV. 2. 4) The recollection of the senses and thoughts is more profound. Teresa says the experience of the prayer of quiet is like a fountain constructed at the very source of the water, which fills without making noise and overflows. Indeed, in this state of being, the water overflows through all the dwelling places and faculties until reaching the body. (IC IV. 2. 4) Describing this prayer, she writes: "I don't think the experience is something, as I say, that arises from the heart, but from another part, still more interior, as from something deep. I think this must be the center of the soul." (IC IV. 2. 5) As an early form of contemplation, however, the prayer of quiet is not a greatly exalted form. (L 22. 3 and L 28. 10) The higher forms of contemplation, called the prayers of union, are found in the last three dwelling places, the fifth, sixth, and seventh. Those reaching the fifth and sixth dwelling places have entered into occasional, temporary union with the central divine reality; the union becomes permanent when the person enters the seventh dwelling place. In union, the divine reality in the center of the castle becomes the life-giving center of the particular person. In Plotinus's thought, this is the return to the One.

The Development of the Image of the Interior Castle

A particular illuminative experience that was of great importance to Teresa will help us to grasp the meaning of the unitive life for her. She records an imageless intuition in the fortieth chapter of her autobiography, *The Book of Her Life*, as follows: "Once while in prayer I was shown quickly, without my seeing any form—but it was a totally clear representation—how all things are seen in God and how He holds them all in Himself."[6] (L 40. 9)

To try to better explain this experience, Teresa suggests the image of the Divinity as "a very clear diamond, much greater than all the world. . . . And we could say *everything we do is visible in this diamond* since it is of such a kind that it contains all things within itself; there is nothing that escapes its magnitude." (L 40. 10, emphasis added) When we put the image of the large diamond, in which everything we do occurs, together with Teresa's understanding that God is intimately within the soul, we see the basis of her understanding of union.

Late in her life, Teresa was ordered by her superiors to write another book, because her autobiography was in the hands of the inquisition and they feared it would not be released. At the time, she had tremendous responsibilities in the reformed order and lacked the energy and inspiration to write again. Then, suddenly she was energized by the image of the interior castle made of a diamond or of very clear crystal; she wrote *The Interior Castle* in the equivalent of two months, although with was a break of several months.

Teresa had first used the castle image in an earlier book, *The Way of Perfection*; here she describes the castle as an extremely rich palace that is within us, *built entirely of gold and precious stones*. The King dwells in the castle on a throne, which is your heart. (W 28. 9) When she reintroduces the image in *The Interior Castle*, written after she had the imageless vision just quoted, the castle is very significantly changed. Instead of the original gold and precious stones, it is now made entirely "of a diamond or of very clear crystal." (IC I. 1.1)

These images show the change in the 'way of seeing' the contemplative life brings. The perspective of the person in the early stages of the journey is that of one looking toward the center, where the King dwells in an inner room. God is in a place separate from where the individual stands, although he or she does receive light from the Center. When a person knows she lives within the castle made of a very clear diamond larger than the world there is a radical difference. Teresa writes: "He brought me *into the wine cellar*." (IC V. 1. 12, emphasis added) She no longer finds herself apart from that which is sought and no longer has to move anywhere in the castle. She no longer needs to make an effort to reach the center, because she finds herself already there. She is within God and God is within her.

Thus Teresa has combined in a single image the understanding that God dwells in the soul and that we dwell in God.[7] She writes this explicitly in *The Interior Castle*: "God so places Himself in the interior of that soul that when it returns to itself it can in no way doubt that it was in God [the diamond image] and God was in it [seated in the center of the palace]." (IC V. 1. 9) This is a brilliant image of the unitive life.

Images of Unitive Prayer

Teresa's careful description in *The Interior Castle* of the earlier forms of unitive experience also includes valuable images. All the more interior dwelling places in the castle, the fifth, sixth, and seventh, are where unitive experiences occur; the differences among them lie in the permanency of the union, which only in the seventh dwelling place becomes indissoluble. Teresa uses vivid images to illuminate the steps along the way. For examples, she describes the first unitive contact of the soul with God, in the fifth dwelling place, as like two wax candles put together at their tips so that they make only one light, but afterwards the two candles can be separated and they remain distinct. (IC VII. 2. 4) In book VI there is betrothal for marriage, which means there is a promise of more to come, but the presence of God is still punctuated by periods of seeming absence. In book VII spiritual marriage is consummated: The soul is made one with God and remains all the time in that center with God.[8] (VII. 2. 3–4) "What God communicates here to the soul in an instant is a secret so great and a favor so sublime—and the delight of the soul so extreme—that I don't know what to compare it to. . . . One can say no more—insofar as can be understood—than that the soul, I mean the spirit, is made one with God." (IC VII. 2. 3) In other words, God is now the soul's own possession and the soul draws without limit upon the resources of God for strength to sustain itself. (Dicken, p. 426)

Several images of union suggest that a dimension of the person is in some manner inseparable from God and that we may know this in contemplation:

> In the spiritual marriage the union is like what we have when rain falls from the sky into a river or fount; all is water, for the rain that fell from heaven cannot be divided or separated from the water of the river. Or it is like what we have when a little stream enters the sea, there is no means of separating the two. Or, like the bright light entering a room through two different windows; although the streams of light are separate when entering the room, they become one. (IC VII. 2. 4)

These images indicate that in Teresa's experience of union, the essence of the person is of the very same nature as God (an ontological or substantial union), which suggest in turn that her experience was like Eckhart's. She refers to the union as occurring "in the deepest center of the soul which must be where God himself dwells." (IC VII. 2. 3) She once wrote of her experience of "mystical marriage": "In my opinion there is no need of any door for Him to enter." (IC VII. 2. 3) If there is no need of a door, God must already be in some manner integral to the person. Similarly, she says the person can never be outside God "in whom there is no otherness." (As quoted in Kelley, p.52)

This unitive consciousness is believed to become permanent, running concurrently with, and in some way fused and integrated with the normal or common consciousness. (Stace, p. 61) Mystical marriage involves an integration within the person such that the usually unrecognized depths of the personality play a role in daily consciousness and inform the activities of everyday life. Although God's presence may not always be fully sensed—in Teresa's experience the "presence is not felt so fully, I mean so clearly, as when revealed the first time, or at other times when God grants the soul this gift" (IC VII. 1. 9)—Teresa felt calm and centered as she went about her many duties. The center of the soul remained untouched by what preoccupied the mind's surface. (IC VII. 2. 10)

Eckhart taught that the 'ground of the soul' and Godhead are united; they are the same reality.[9] Teresa is describing her personal discovery of this, as the analogy of the rain and river indicates. With the building of the castle, the person is prepared and the union is realized in inner experience. Furthermore, her unitive experiences are true contemplation, as Plotinus describes it. She enters the fullness of her being by a "return" to the center of the castle she dwells within; her very active and influential life indicates the return to a realm of generative power and creativity.

Before moving on we must be cognizant of questions about the belief of Teresa and Eckhart that unitive experience involves actual union with God. Martin Buber once experienced an undivided unity, which he initially thought was union with the primal being or Godhead. But he came to believe this was an exaggeration. He wrote:

> I can elicit from these experiences only that in them I reached an undifferentiable unity of myself without form or content. I may call this an original prebiographical unity and suppose that it is hidden unchanged beneath all biographical change, all development of the soul . . . existing but once, single, unique, irreducible, this creaturely one: one of the human souls and not the "soul of the All"; a defined and particular being and not "Being"; the creaturely basic unity of a creature."(As quoted in Merkur, pp. 142–43)

This is a question central to the integration we seek. We will ask, what is the content of the prebiographical unity? Might it not involve union with God? Is the "undifferentiable unity of myself" actually separate from the Ground of the whole, as Buber came to believe, or is Eckhart more accurate in his understanding that there can be a breakthrough into the 'ground of the soul' and the Godhead, which are one. The next chapters are written to inquire whether the new physics and insights from the new universe story shed light on this question and then, subsequently, whether assumptions from depth psychology about the origins of consciousness are informative.

Types of Unitive Experience

The manner or mode of the unitive experience is not the same for everyone; the three traditional types are the modes of knowledge, of love, and of light.

Knowledge

With regard to knowledge, one is struck on reading the mystics by the fact that they clearly believe they know something of greatest importance and they seek diligently to communicate it. It is one of the central themes of this book to discern something of the nature of this knowing in the context of the new story of the evolutionary universe and to see its central importance as humans seek to find a way into the future. David Bohm suggests that it involves a kind of "experience-knowledge" in which the experience and the knowledge constitute one process, the hyphen indicating that these are two inseparable aspects of one whole movement. (1983, p. 6) Similarly Louis Dupré recognizes it as a remarkable participatory kind of knowledge, which he describes as being *with* reality, not reflecting upon it. (1989b, p.11)[10] Dupré indicates compellingly the difference between this knowledge and the detached objective observation and measurement that is valued in the West to the near exclusion of other ways of knowing: "To understand the real as an object that reason places before the mind—rather than as a totality of which the mind constitutes an integral dynamic part—conflicts with the very essence of mystical experience." (1989b, p. 21) We will come back to this statement often, for it articulates well the type of knowing in which there is a "coincidence of being and knowing in an experience that precedes all mental differentiation." (Dupré 1980, p. 459)

Love

The unitive life may also be found through love. The unknown author of *The Cloud of Unknowing* was a person who entered into unitive experience drawn and guided by love. Some people abandon conceptual and imaginative knowledge so that it is love that knows God by unknowing. (Strollo, p.740) Union through love involves an affective experience of intense communion, a love that is considered the secret of the real. (Dupré 1989b, p.21) Richard M. Bucke said that he understood in his breakthrough experience, part of which was quoted in chapter 6, "that the foundation principle of the world, of all the worlds, is what we call love. ..." (In Coxhead, p. 7) In the unitive experience of love, people realize this foundation principle. They are in union with it. Other love mystics are Bernard of Clairvaux, John of the Cross, and Hadewijch of Brabant.

These unitive experiences of love sometime go beyond a union with an inner dimension of the person to involve love of specific creatures for their own sake. Saint Francis's nature mysticism was not of a generalized, theoretical type, but was a felt, radically individual recognition of the nature of the lamb, the earthworm and the moon. Thomas of Celano, the earliest biographer of Saint Francis, tells us that Francis removed little worms from the road lest they be crushed under foot. (*Second Life* 124. 165) In his great *Canticle of Brother Sun*, Francis called the moon and the water his sisters. He preached to the birds, telling them to praise their creator. (Bonaventure, *Life of St. Francis* 12. 3) Here we see a love of the finite as such, not just love for the infinite in the finite; it is the creature, e.g. the bird, which is divinely lovable, not only in its core, where, as Eckhart would say, it touched God's own nature, but also in its finitude, even in its imperfections. (Dupré and Wiseman, p. 15) This kind of insight will be crucial in our integration.

Although love mystics are distinguished from those emphasizing an alternative kind of knowing, it would be false to suggest that the actual experience of union is distinctly one kind or the other. Gregory the Great, who was pope from 590 to 604, and the father of Western spirituality in the Middle Ages, stressed the unity of love and cognition when he wrote that "love itself is knowledge." (Quoted in Dupré 1989b, p. 22) Love and knowledge converge in contemplation. Clearly there must be a knowing of what is loved and an affection or attraction to what is known.[11] Mystics constantly break through existing theological theories in order to stress the unity of love and cognition. (Dupré 1989b, p. 22) Eckhart wrote:

> Blessedness does not consist in either knowing or loving but that there is that in the soul from which knowing and loving flow; that something does not know or love as do the powers of the soul. Whoever knows this knows of what blessedness consists. (1981, p.201)

Light

The third type of unitive experience is an experience of brightness or light. Plotinus speaks of the Good as a light in which there is no distinct object, a light that we see in itself and not by means of some distinct organ. (Hadot, p. 246) According to Jan van Ruusbroec, the soul surpasses its createdness and participates actively in God's uncreated life, known as Light. Ruusbroec wrote:

> All those men who are raised up above their created being into a contemplative *Life* are one with this divine brightness and are that brightness itself. And they see, feel and find, even by means of this Divine Light, that, as regards their uncreated nature, they are that same simple ground from which the brightness without limit shines forth in a godlike manner, and which according to the simplicity of the essence remains in everlasting, mode-less simplicity. (Quoted in Dupré 1980, p.462)

This is congruent with the realization of Arthur M. Young (1905–1995), the mystic and mathematician, philosopher and technologist who invented the Bell Helicopter, that the light is not seen, it is seeing. (Cited in Kushner 1981, p. 105)

The experience of Claire M. Owens, the Connecticut housewife, had a unitive element involving light. We looked at part of her description of her experience, with regard to its illuminative aspects, in chapter 5. Now we turn to the beginning of it:

> Then the most incredible thing happened—the most frightening, beautiful, important experience of my entire life. I understood absolutely nothing of its meaning at the time.
>
> One morning I was writing at my desk in the quiet writing room of our quiet house in Connecticut. Suddenly everything within my sight vanished right away. No longer did I see my body, the furniture in the room, the white rain slating across the windows. No longer was I aware of where I was, the day or hour. Time and space ceased to exist.
>
> Suddenly the entire room was *filled with a great golden light, the whole world was filled with nothing but light.* There was nothing anywhere except this effulgent light and my own small kernel of the self. The ordinary "I" ceased to exist. Nothing of me remained but a mere nugget of consciousness. It felt as if some vast transcendent force was invading me without my volition, as if all the immanent good lying latent within began to pour forth in a stream, to form a moving circle with the universal principle. Myself began to dissolve into the light that was like a great golden all-pervasive fog. It was a mystical moment of union with the mysterious infinite, with all things, all people. (As quoted in Coxhead, pp. 35–36, emphasis added)

Marcelle Martin, a contemporary mystic, writes:

> I have had more than one experience of feeling filled with light, of feeling my physical body melt into the Light, of becoming aware of the world as atoms in motion, of a world in which all atoms, including those of the body, merge into and out of the forms taken by plants and animals, humans, rocks and other elements of Creation." (p. 14)

Although it might be thought that light is being used as an image of consciousness or of the Unknown, it is not. It refers instead to the actual "content," an intrinsic aspect, of the experience. It is a light qualitatively different from ordinary light known to the eyes. This is made clear in the quotation from Augustine below, where he says his experience of light did not involve the ordinary light visible to all flesh. It is this internal light that mystics often call God. Claire M. Owen calls her experience of light a mystical moment of union with the mysterious infinite. Pierre Hadot, discussing Plotinus's experience of light, says it involves an internal light that is a vision of pure presence beyond all determinate forms and all distinct objects. (Hadot, p. 241)

Augustine describes an overwhelming mystical experience involving light in the *Confessions*. It occurred after he had read some books of the Platonists, whom he addresses, during a period of intense search:

> I was admonished by all this to return to my own self, and, with you to guide me, I entered into the innermost part of myself, and I was able to do this because you were my helper. I entered and I saw with my soul's eye (such as it was) an unchangeable light shining above this eye of my soul and above my mind. It was not the ordinary light which is visible to all flesh, nor something of the same sort, only bigger, as though it might be our ordinary light shining much more brightly and filling everything, entirely different from anything of the kind. (VII. 10)

This experience freed Augustine from the materialism and dualism of his previous Manichaean position and led to his formal conversion to Christianity.

There are also experiences of "darkness" that do not refer simply to the absence of regular light. The darkness itself has the quality of intensity, fecundity, and immediacy.*

In all of these experiences there is either a participatory kind of knowledge, an intense communion of love or there is seeing such that the person is the brightness. They all show the depth of our embeddedness in the spiritual dimensions of our being and all must find a place in the new universe story.

---

* Ewert Cousins: personal communication, 1999.

Unitive Episodes and Gestures

The discovery of the unitive life again and again over the centuries is most instructive. But it is also important to recognize that we aren't concerned, in this book, only with some not too common, developed state of being. We are most interested in the mysticism of daily life and recognize that it is often compelling, simple episodes that speak to us of the sacred dimension in daily life. F. David Peat, in his book on synchronicity, writes of "gestures" whose meaning, like those of a ballet dancer, is contained in the movement of the whole person. (1987, p. 54) Gestures emerge out of the universe as a whole. Thus the smallest expression of caring, a morning glory on a fence, or a pewter plate, can be the occasion for glimpsing the total nature of things. We recognize that certain actions bring the sacred realm into daily life. The unity, the 'all at onceness,' we are describing may be recognized in a simple gesture or episode in someone's life.

Saint Francis kissing the lepers and preaching to the birds are such episodes. A man recognized something remarkable about Francis and laid down his cloak over a mud puddle for him to step on. A pope recognized that he would help reform the church. After his death, his body was carried in a funeral procession past the Poor Clares so that Clare and other sisters who loved him could be close to him one more time. The series of paintings by Giotto in the basilica of St. Francis in Assisi depict with iconographic integrity the sacred nature of the person and various events in his life.

In the film *Hasten Slowly*, Laurens Van der Post describes a remarkable experience when he was a prisoner of war in a Japanese prison camp during World War II. Once, he was the third person in a line of several prisoners being beaten, one by one, by a Japanese officer. As he was walking away after being beaten, he asked himself: "What can I do to stop this?" The answer came to him immediately: Return to the officer and offer himself to be beaten again. He did this. The man doing the beating was so confused that he took a half-hearted swing at Van der Post and then walked away. (Van der Post 1996)

The exodus of the Israelites from slavery in Egypt has spoken to countless generations of the possibilities of a new life for communities and for individuals under oppression. The father *running* to greet his prodigal son is a compelling image of forgiveness and of the embrace of change. The healing and teaching events in the life of Jesus of Nazareth have spoken of the indwelling divine dimension to many people, as has his crucifixion.

Conclusion

The contemplative tradition certainly provokes many questions about the nature of matter, the identity of the person and the meaning of the word God. It once seemed impossible to understand and accept the contemplative's claims, given Western assumptions about matter and God. But now this has changed. Within the new story of the evolutionary universe, and the new cosmology and new physics by which it is informed, the contemplative tradition finds a central place. We explore the foundation for this integration in the next section of this book.

---

[1] In this chapter, where quotations from the works of Teresa of Avila are cited extensively, the customary abbreviations for citations of her works will be used: IC for *The Interior Castle*, L for *The Book of Her Life* and W for *The Way of Perfection*. Be reminded that, when using herself as an example, Teresa often writes about herself in the third person.

[2] Ruusbroec notes that this essential unity of our spirit "renders us neither holy nor blessed, for all person, both good and bad, possess this unity within themselves; it is, however, the first principle of all holiness and blessedness. This, then, is the meeting and union between God and our spirit in our bare nature." (1985, p. 118)

[3] A standard edition of Ruusbroec's work is not yet available in English.

[4] Louis Dupré writes that this substantial unity in Christian thought is confirmed by Athanasius (c. 295–373), the person responsible for articulating the Trinity as we know it today. "If by the participation of the Spirit we become participants in the divine nature, then it would be foolish to say that the Spirit is of a created nature and not of a divine nature." (Quoted in Dupré 1984, p. 12)

[5] A city or a castle or a temple is often a symbol of the place of individuation. Such images are chosen by the psyche as symbols not only because of their form but, as Esther Harding observed in reference to the city, because they not only must be built, but having been built, must be kept in repair. (Harding, p. 414)

The mandala (from the Sanskrit *mandala*: circle) is a peripheral circle or square, usually connected with a focal center by at least four radial lines set like the arms of a cross. Mandala forms have been used universally in religious art, ritual, and architecture since Paleolithic times. (Elkin 1985, p. 76) Interestingly, Teresa's image of the interior castle has been shown to have Islamic sources. (Lopez-Baralt, p. 655)

[6] In addition to this unitive intuition, Teresa also had a locution in which she heard the words: "Don't try to hold Me within yourself, but try to hold yourself within Me." ("Spiritual Testimonies." No. 14: June 30, 1571)

[7] This conflation of two images seems to have occurred spontaneously in Teresa's mind, giving her the energy to write *The Interior Castle*

Her actual use of the image throughout *The Interior Castle* indicates that she understands that God dwells in the soul and the soul dwells in God. She tells us in Book I that the castle is the soul (IC I. 1. 5) and in the middle there is a royal chamber where the King stays. (IC I. 2. 8) Similarly she tells us in book VI that "the soul, while it is made one with God, is placed in this room of the empyreal heaven that we must have interiorly." (IC VI. 4. 8) Yet later in the same work she uses the image differently. She also writes in book VI: "Let's suppose that God is like an immense and beautiful dwelling place," which a sinner cannot leave to do evil deeds. (IC VI. 10. 3) This use of the image of God as the comprehensive dwelling place certainly reflects the intellectual vision that revealed to her how all things are seen in God and how He has them all in Himself. (L 40. 9)

[8] Mystical marriage is by no means an original metaphor. Pre-Christian and gnostic religions used the image of sacred and spiritual marriage between God and the soul to symbolize mystical union (Marcoulesco, p. 242)

[9] This unity of soul and Godhead is referred to as the given ontological or substantial unity, but the word substance, a translation of the Greek word *ousia*, is misleading. *Ousia* refers to "what this or that is itself." We will consider this further in chapter 13.

[10] Unitive experience of a type of knowing may involve entering into the source and coherence of all reality. For example, the experiential knowing expressed as "all is one" is an attempt to communicate an experience of cognitive union. This type of union is precisely the realization that the rest of the world is not in the first place an object of reason, but there is an experiential awakening to the integration of the person, and the mind of the person, into the whole. This type of knowing is clearly of the utmost importance in regard to a knowledge of belonging, and certainly has congruence with insights from the new universe

story. The new universe story can itself be evocative of this type of knowing.

[11] Sometimes it is objected that unitive experiences of love as in mystical marriage cannot involve substantial union because love has an object and hence there is a distinction maintained between lover and loved. The presence of both cognitive and affective dimensions in union answers this objection. Bernard McGinn, teacher at the Divinity School of the University of Chicago, says that even though there is a union, there is still a sense of relationship. Louis Dupré draws a distinction between two different concepts of union: one refers to a *unitas spiritus* (moral and psychological in orientation), the other to a *unitas indistinctionis* (ontologically oriented). The former consists of an interpersonal relation of love; the latter of an ontological or substantial union. The distinction is undeniable and significant. Equally significant, however, is that those Christian and Muslim mystics who consider the union to be ontological or in some way substantial nevertheless express themselves in interpersonal terms, while some of the most articulate exponents of love mysticism (such as John of the Cross, Teresa, and Hadewijch of Brabant) do not shy away from a terminology proper to substantial union. (1989b, p. 17–18)

III

THE FOUNDATIONS
OF INTEGRATION

8

THE GENERATIVE COSMOS

Theoretical and experimental physicists are now studying nothing at all–the vacuum. But that nothingness contains all of being.

— Heinz R. Pagels

A MAJOR REASON it is difficult for Western people to integrate their very personal spiritual experiences into a wholistic understanding of the world is our unexamined assumptions about the physical world around us and within us. We tend to think we are embedded in something that is limited to fixed and predictable patterns, because we learned the laws of physics and chemistry, and these allowed us to send men to the moon and develop the many medicines that alleviate our symptoms and sometimes cure our diseases. However, radical, unexpected discoveries made in the last century, as well as ancient intuitions long treasured by humankind, invite us to new possibilities. Some of these are found in David Bohm's thought about the holomovement and the autonomously active implicate order and *plenum*. In the context of the evolving Earth and these unexpected discoveries, our minds and hearts can begin to have confidence in a meaningful and creative place for human beings in the unfolding Earth story. It will not be necessary to become experts in the physics of the very small (quanta) to recognize that its findings revolutionize our ideas about matter. In addition, in this chapter some contemporary discoveries are considered together with ancient intuitions about a generative, formative power that gives rise to the manifest world (manifest, from the Latin *manus*: hand; the world we can hold in the hand).

Discoveries about the Very Small: Quantum Studies

It is known from quantum physics, a subfield of physics developed in the 1920s, that subatomic, elementary wave/

particles continually emerge and fall back into the quantum potential or quantum vacuum. This so-called vacuum is an undifferentiated, seemingly empty realm recently encountered empirically by mathematical and experimental techniques. Brian Swimme describes just how remarkable this discovery is by explaining that when elementary particles leap into existence out of the quantum vacuum and then disappear, this is *not* the phenomenon in which mass and energy can be transformed into one another, as in nuclear reactions. "I am speaking of something much more mysterious. I am saying that particles boil into existence out of sheer emptiness. That is simply the way the universe works. . . . The way particles spontaneously leap into existence is a radical discovery of our own lifetimes." (1984, pp. 36–38) "I am asking you to contemplate a universe where, somehow, being itself arises out of a field of 'fecund emptiness.'" (1996, p. 93) Particles usually erupt in pairs that will quickly interact and annihilate each other. Electrons and positrons, protons and anti-protons, all of these are flaring forth, and as quickly vanishing again. "Such creative and destructive activity takes place everywhere and at all times throughout the universe."(p. 93) It is happening trillions of times within us at each moment, so this matrix of fecundity is integral to our being.

The realm where this creation/destruction takes place is described as a vacuum because it is empty in the sense that we cannot detect forms and differentiations in it. Swimme describes it as nonvisible, which means it can never be seen.[1] Although this realm cannot be delineated by scientific methods of measurement, this does not mean it is empty of generative power. Thus the term "vacuum," suggesting emptiness, is misleading: This so-called vacuum is actually "the basal generative power of the universe." (1996, p. 94) If all the individual things of the universe were to evaporate, one would be left with an infinity of pure generative power. (p. 100)

Although little is known about this basal generative power, a number of physicists are considering a realm that lies beyond the mathematical laws and descriptions that have been abstracted from nature. F. David Peat writes about a generative power that "cannot lie within the mental or material worlds alone, but rather has its place in some, as yet unexplored, ground that lies beyond the distinctions of either." (Peat 1987, p. 88)

Jungian analyst Edward Whitmont tells us that Werner Heisenberg, one of the creators of quantum theory, has argued that at the deepest level of reality, the ground of the vacuum, there is "emptiness," equivalent to what the Buddhists call *sunyata*, prior to anything that "is." (Whitmont, p. 43)

David Bohm discusses the immense background energy which, according to calculations from quantum theory, is believed to be present in empty space. Bohm asserts that "empty space" has so much energy that it is full rather than empty, although its fullness is largely ignored, since no instrument can respond directly to this background energy. He equates it with the *plenum*, the same immense "sea" of energy that is the ground of the existence of everything (discussed in chapter 3), and estimates that the amount of energy in one cubic centimeter of the "vacuum" is greater than the total of the energy "contained" in all the matter in the known universe. Although some physicists think this figure must involve some error in the mathematical foundations of quantum theory, Bohm takes it seriously and includes in his thought the relationship between visible matter and this vast energy because he understands it to be the ground of the whole of reality. (Briggs and Peat, p. 132) The visible world, which necessarily dominates our attention, is a comparatively small pattern of excitation within this background *plenum*, rather like a ripple on an ocean. The Big Bang too, Bohm suggests, was actually just a "little ripple."[2] (Bohm 1983, p.192) Without the *plenum*, particles would disappear; hence, this vast sea of energy is a generative matrix, the source of manifest forms.

The discovery of a powerful realm of "emptiness" is not, of course, inconsequential for human identity. Brian Swimme describes the situation:

What I would like you to understand is that this plenary emptiness permeates you. You are more fecund emptiness than you are created particles. We can see this by examining one of your atoms. If you take a simple atom and make it as large as Yankee stadium, it would consist almost entirely of empty space. The center of the atom, the nucleus would be smaller than a baseball sitting out in center field. The outer parts of the atom would be tiny gnats buzzing about at an altitude higher than any pop fly Babe Ruth ever hit. And between the baseballs and gnats? Nothingness. All empty. Indeed, if all the space were taken out of you, you would be a million times smaller than the smallest grain of sand. (1984, p.37)

These insights into a powerful, ongoing, generative *plenum* permeating all the physical world are like a wide open window allowing fresh spring air to pour into the formerly constricted, mechanistic world of science. Suddenly, at the very core of science, there is a profound mystery: an ultimate no-thing-ness that is simultaneously a realm of generative potentiality. (Swimme 1989, p. 80) It becomes possible to begin to imagine that our ongoing, stable, reliable physical structure and psychological order have a certain fundamental "openness" to a larger, more comprehensive creative order.

Are We "Hiring Science as a Consultant for the Higher Reaches of Life"?

If these insights from quantum physics are included in our reflections about the contemplative life, are we, as Huston Smith, a philosopher of comparative religion, warns, in danger of "hiring science as a consultant for the higher reaches of life"? Is it true, as Smith argues, that nothing science discovers about the interstices of nature tells us anything directly about what lies beyond them? (Griffin and Smith, pp. 73, 84)

While it is true that scientists do not know the background energy by direct measurement, Smith is wrong in the sense that discoveries in the last century about the behavior of matter have pushed the inquiry of physicists into speculation about "what lies beyond." The new ideas about a generative *plenum* are concerned with a nonvisible realm that cannot be studied by the usual measurements of science. Also, Smith seems to be assuming a disjunction between "what lies beyond" and the manifest world. But this dualism is now challenged because of the intimacy between the elementary particles and the "fecund emptiness," and it has long been challenged by the fundamental incarnational insight of Christianity, which recognized the great intimacy of the divine and the human; we have just explored this intimacy in our examination of the contemplative tradition. Furthermore, the story of the evolutionary universe also has implications for our understanding of "what lies beyond," as we shall see in later chapters. This does not involve an assumption of equivalence between the scientist's inquiry into the quantum vacuum and traditional ideas about the divine. They will be seen to be different "takes," different windows, on the same nonvisible realm. To respond to Huston Smith's warning: Each of us can only draw insight from the weight of accumulated evidence derived from many sources, including science (particularly quantum theory and relativity theory), the arguments of the great philosophers, the native wisdom of some cultures and traditions, insights from the great classic religions, and our own personal experience. The implications of the new physics and the new universe story lead some to believe that we are dealing with a fundamental change in "gestalt" such that there are indeed scientists who are attempting to speak about the "higher reaches of life," although these reaches are not measuraable by traditional scientific methods. More congruent with the emerging worldview is the thought of Lawrence Kushner, who rejects such a disjunction between the "higher reaches" and the daily world in *The River of Light* (1981):

> Remember: one who is able to reach a rung of consciousness utterly unaware of oneself and aware only of the "outside world" (science), and one who is able to reach a rung of consciousness utterly unaware of the outside world and aware only of one's innermost self (spirit) will have arrived at the

same place. . . . And so it is that the traditions are very close. (p. 97)

So we continue to seek insight from science, turning now to discoveries in this century by astronomers about the beginning and the subsequent unfolding.

Discoveries in Astronomy

One of the key discoveries leading to the story of the evolutionary universe, as recounted in chapter 2, was the observation that clusters of galaxies are moving away in every direction from the supercluster of which the Earth is a part. As we have seen, this provided evidence in support of the surprising implication of Einstein's field theories that the universe is expanding. By measuring the speed with which the more distant galaxies are moving away and comparing them to the slower speed of closer ones, it was determined that everything that is can be traced back to a center, the cosmic explosion at the beginning of time.[3] All the energy that would ever exist in the entire course of time erupted as a single quantum—a singular gift of existence. (Swimme and Berry, p. 17) This is a most remarkable discovery. Swimme points out that "all this is new. None of the great figures of human history were aware of this. Not Plato or Aristotle, or the Hebrew prophets or Confucius or Thomas Aquinas or Liebniz or Newton or any other world-maker. We are the first generation to live with an empirical view of the origin of the universe." (1984, p. 28)

Astronomers and cosmologists do not know the source of this great flaring forth of primeval energy; while the realm of originating power is recognized, it is beyond the techniques of scientific measurement. Swimme suggests the primeval fireball came out of an empty realm, a mysterious order of reality, a no-thing-ness that is simultaneously the ultimate source of all things. (Swimme 1984, p. 36) All that has existence, even space-time, erupted out of nothing. From this fecund "emptiness," particles erupted and bonded together through time to give rise to the entire universe.

There is something further about the discovery of a great flaring forth that informs our inquiry. The remarkable consequence arising from this location of the physical birth of the universe is that as the cosmos expanded and continues to expand, *there is no place in the universe separate from the originating center, instant by instant.* This seems impossible, but Edwin Hubble's discovery that clusters of galaxies are moving away from the Earth in every direction speaks to this. Paul Davies, a physicist who writes lucidly about these matters in terms comprehensible to non-scientists, explains that it was by a systematic study of the pattern of motion and the way it varies with distance that Hubble showed that other galaxies are also moving apart from each other. (1984, p.14) Observers with telescopes on another planet in another supercluster, would, like us, discover themselves to be at the center, with the other superclusters hurtling away from them. This is the expansion predicted by Einstein's theories. Space emerges or stretches between the superclusters of galaxies and the universe expands. The universe simply grows in scale. (p. 15) The amazing thing is that these clusters, including our Virgo cluster and the Earth, remain at the originating center of which everything was a part in the beginning, even though it is now in expanded, differentiated form. In other words, the expansion is of such a nature that we do not go away from the center.

It is essential to try to comprehend this insight that today, at this moment, we are at the center, where the universe came into being. A helpful image has been suggested. Imagine yourself inside a ball of unleavened dough filled with raisins and that you are standing on one raisin. As the dough begins to rise, the raisins move away from one another in such a way that no matter which raisin you may be standing on, you will see the other raisins moving away from you in every direction. In the same way that all the raisins with you on yours began the expansion clustered together at the center—in fact comprised the center—we can imagine that every thing in the universe today was initially the dense, original flaring forth of the initial primal cosmic substance.

As the expansion continues and time and space unfurl, every place remains the center of the evolving universe although now in expanded form. Each person is situated in that very place, and is rooted in that very power, that brought forth all the matter and energy of the universe.[4] (Swimme 1996, p.104).

People once thought the Earth was at the geometric center of the universe. Copernicus, Galileo, and others dismantled the classic Ptolemaic scheme that placed the Earth at the center when they recognized that the Earth is a planet orbiting the sun. This is cited as one reason why people have lost a sense of significance and of knowing their place in the order of things.[5] Thus, this new recognition that we are indeed at the center (though not at a geometric center of traditional three-dimensional space) is of great psychological and spiritual significance. It is a different center, a center found throughout the universe and hence widely shared, but nonetheless a center of great importance to the complex beings that have evolved there.

This insight, that we are at the center of an expanding universe, can be brought together with evidence from quantum studies, as Brian Swimme has done. From quantum studies we learn that matter and energy continually emerge from and fall back into the quantum potential. Thus, the cosmic birth is not taking place away from where we are standing. (Swimme 1996, p. 83) From astronomy we learn that even though "the originating power gave birth to the universe fifteen billion years ago, this realm of power is not simply located there at that point in time but is rather a condition of every moment of the universe, past, present and to come." (Swimme and Berry, p. 17) "Taken together these two discoveries bring human understanding to a vista never before enjoyed: *Each child is situated in that very place and is rooted in that very power that brought forth all the matter and energy of the universe.*" (Swimme 1996, p. 104, emphasis added) This is key to our integration with the contemplative tradition.

It should be pointed out, however, that while it is true that this realm of power is a condition of every moment, not every place in the universe is actively creative. Rather, the creativity of a particular place depends on it being part of the domain of a self-organizing system. We will consider the role of such systems in chapters 10 and 11.

Origin Out of A Generative "Nothingness" in the Religious Tradition of the West

The recent insights and theories about the ongoing generation of the universe are new to modern science, impelled by observations of characteristics of matter and consciousness that can't be explained except as derived from a more encompassing matrix and order. But although this perspective is new to modern scientific thinking, religious traditions have long spoken of an unknowable, fecund, creative "nothingness." It seems most remarkable that within Western culture there is a strong and pervasive religious tradition that has taught that there is an "empty" realm, a "nothingness" that is a fecund, timeless, eternal, undifferentiated unitary source, the ultimate source of the manifest world. This tradition is particularly important since the quantum vacuum postulated by physicists has only recently been conceived, in contrast to the great centuries-long interest in this realm (which is at least in part related to the vacuum) by the religious traditions. Something of its nature is thus already known by the intrapsychic pathway of contemplation and speculative reflections on the experience of the contemplative. We may become familiar with it through consideration of the thought of a few individuals in this apophatic (from Greek: not speaking because of the limitations of language) tradition.

Using the word *nothingness* to refer to the fecund generative realm described by the Western contemplative tradition is confusing, but by saying what it is not—it is non-objectifiable, has no discernible form, and cannot be conceived of in representation—there results an affirmation of an ungraspable mystery, which is not other than itself. So the "negation" of language and thought is not a negation of the "nothingness" in itself, but a negation of the senses and reason as a means of knowing this realm. Those exploring most deeply the inner recesses of God's presence to the soul, Louis Dupré assures us, are the ones who most firmly assert our inability to grasp that presence in human cognition. (Dupré 1984, p. 21) The negation does not deny the person's capacity to know the generative realm in an alternative form of consciousness; indeed the mystic's accounts affirm that they do know it.

Mystics and contemplatives speak of entering a realm of darkness and silence, hence the sense of "nothingness," but they find this darkness and silence is not the only quality of the experience. Although there are moments of unity without distinction, this is not the final resting place, since "God's life knows no rest." (Dupré 1984, p. 31) The person is urged to move out again, a movement believed to have its roots in the very fecundity and creativity of the Generative Realm. This is described as the "birth of the son in the soul" in Eckhart's thought, and we will explore it further in chapter 20.

The tradition of not speaking or apophatism has roots in the Bible. The theophanies (from the Greek *theo*: God, and *phaneia*: manifestation, appearance) of Moses and Elias are apophatic; apophatism is found in the Old Testament prohibition of idols. In the fourth century, Gregory of Nyssa wrote *The Life of Moses*, in which Moses climbs the mountain and, by transcending all thought, enters the dark clouds of the invisible and incomprehensible God. He teaches that it is in the darkness that we find the light. This tradition was given great impetus in Western mystical theology by the works of the fifth-century theologian Dionysius the Areopagite, a writer who pseudonymously used the name of the biblical figure who was converted to Christianity by Saint Paul in Athens (Acts 17: 22).[6] Partly because of this attribution, his treatises assumed almost canonical authority in Christian theology. Thomas Aquinas quotes him some 1,700 times. Although he was a Christian writer, he was strongly influenced by Neoplatonic thought, which he used to explain humanity's ascent by God's grace to his presence. He conceived of the Supreme Godhead as the unknowable "dazzling obscurity" and as the Divine Darkness, the negation of all that the surface consciousness perceives. The phrase "cloud of unknowing" is his. In itself, he taught, the divine nature is beyond being, yet becomes manifest in all being as its cause: "And It is called the Universal Cause since all things came into being through Its bounty, whence all being springs. . . ." (*Divine Names* 1. 4)

It is most important that words like *darkness* and *desert* are not perceived to suggest that the Godhead lacks energy and fruitfulness. The realm of "nothingness" is for Eckhart and others a fertile, fecund ground. It is a *plenum*. It is a realm of generative potentiality that gives birth to phenomena. Eckhart follows the Neoplatonic emanation tradition of God as self-diffusive goodness, such that the Godhead is the hidden source from which all things proceed.

Jan van Ruusbroec described God as wayless abyss of fathomless beatitude and "a dark silence." However, as Louis Dupré explains, since God is dynamic, this does not represent a full experience of the nature of God. For Ruusbroec, the realm of silence and darkness is the Father; that is, a unity that becomes fertile, "a silence that must speak, a darkness that yields light."[7] (Dupré 1985, p. xiii) Since soul is understood to be an image of God (chapter 12), it partakes of the movements within God when the person reaches this place of silence. The contemplative moves with the Father's generative act into the perfect image of the Son. (p. xii)

Lawrence Kushner points out that in the Kabbala, a text of the Jewish mystical tradition, the ultimate name of God is *Ayn Sof*, not-finite or without end, utter Nothingness. (Kushner, pp. 38, 122) It is a unity independent of the opposites. "The source of all creation," Kushner writes, "is nothing." (p. 132)

Coincidence of Knowledge from Science and Religion

It is certainly significant that the teachings of theologians like Eckhart and Dionysius the Areopagite refer to a tradition of No-thing-ness that is an ongoing creative source of everything and that some physicists in this century refer to a "vacuum" of unmeasurable generative power that is the condition of every moment of the universe, past, present and future. Although there are important caveats to be aware of as this connection is made, it is heartening that for both there is a no-thing-ness that is simultaneously a realm of generative potentiality, the ultimate source of all things. (Swimme 1984, pp. 36–37) Both avenues of inquiry recognize that everything of the universe has its roots in the realm of originating power. The great wonder is that the empirical, rational journey of science should have come to an insight long carried within the spiritual traditions. It is remarkable that science found both a beginning and an ongoing non--material origin. With regard to the beginning, Swimme observes, it might have been discovered that there was no beginning, but an eternally flowing river of galaxies. (Swimme 1996, p. 81) (See chapter 9.)

Danger of Collapsing Modes of Consciousness

There is a danger if we collapse different modes of consciousness from distinct disciplines and different eras of human history. As Swimme point out, the "quantum vacuum," in all its specific quantum mechanical descriptions, was discovered by no one else but the physicists of the last century. The religious witness we have drawn from has a very long, independent history, with no influence from modern physics. It is a distinct tradition spanning centuries and drawing from both Hebrew and Greek culture and from lived human experience within these traditions. It would clearly be an error to try to make the ancient insights equivalent to the recent speculation about the vacuum and deeper levels of the implicate order. A complete coincidence of the insights of the scientific and theological traditions is not sought, but it is important to consider them as complementary explorations of *the same mysterious realm* that mutually inform one another.

It is important to our integration that some scientists have begun to inquire into a dimension of things previously left to theological inquiry, although they may have inquired only into limited dimensions of that realm. However, we must always be aware of the danger of importing inadequate conceptions from theology, colored by assumptions from outdated worldviews, to this integration and, just as important, be aware of the danger of being too influenced by reductionist science and the limited nature of scientific inquiry, which does not study or value, for example, the subjective breakthrough experiences into the realm of "Nothingness" that are so important to individuals. Any assumption that one discipline has exclusive claim to knowledge of the "nothingness" must be avoided, when in fact both science and contemplative religious people are apparently investigating or seeking to know the same dimension. After all, they investigate the same universe, and the openness of some scientists to including a science of mystery indicates that a comprehensive, integrating vision may be approached once again. But both traditions will and must continue their distinct paths of inquiry.

For an individual seeking an integrated vision and the fullness of personhood and the possibility of a viable human/Earth future within the context of the new story, however, recognition of the complementary exploration of the same realm is critical. With discoveries in both disciplines that reinforce each other, it is possible to entertain new ways (many of which are also old) to imagine ourselves and all of the Earth. The transition of human culture to a vision that embraces the new universe story can be facilitated by showing that such profound mystical experiences as those cited in chapter 6 can be integrated into the story. A 'way of seeing' like the one being offered in this book, is essential to facilitate the very great change in consciousness that is required of all of us in these dangerous times. And, of course, many people, including Alfred North Whitehead, Teilhard de Chardin, David Bohm, F. David Peat, Ewert Cousins, Louis Dupré, Thomas Berry, and Brian Swimme, on whom this 'way of seeing' depends, have laid the foundation for this type of integration.

Resistance from the Religious Traditions

Religious people often resist the incursion of science into realms that were once the exclusive domain of faith and belief.

The investigation of physicists into the quantum vacuum seems cold, impersonal and unrelated to religious life. But in later chapters it will be shown that it is eminently personal in the context of the experience of the individual. Also, with regard to the objection that the work of physicists is impersonal, there is hope that their conception of the generative realm will expand as they become concerned not only with the origin of matter but also with consciousness and the place of consciousness in the order of things. This involvement of physicists with consciousness will bring scientific inquiries closer to the explorations of the contemplative tradition.

Support for the Insights of Mysticism from Science

The great changes in astronomy and physics can be an impetus for many people to be more receptive to radical mystical/contemplative intuitions. Physicists can now agree with the mystics who have told us that our everyday perception of reality from our sense impressions is only one, rather circumscribed way of comprehending the world. They can begin to acknowledge that it is indeed possible that Jacob Boehme really *was* gazing into the very heart of things while looking at the pewter plate. Our sense impressions and daily experience of solid objects tell us of only one aspect of our being—not wrong but only one aspect. The physicists' investigations into the nature of matter require us to further rethink our assumptions about what matter might be and how it is related to what has just been described about the ongoing Origin. This we begin to do in the next chapter.

Naming the Fecund Nothingness

It is a problem to name that which is not an object and which is unknowable to rational consciousness. Still, we need words or phrases to refer to this realm attested to in religious sources and now by some physicists. Shouldn't we use the word *God*? But *God* is often used to refer to a distinct being, separate and above the Earth, although occasionally coming "down" and visiting; some inadequate conceptions of transcendence are attached to the word. The generative realm just explored is characterized by a type of transcendence that will be called "true transcendence" (chapter 17), but it is not a separate, distinct being. It is now recognized that *we live in a world in which space and time are intrinsic to the expanding, differentiating universe* that is itself permeated by the "nothingness," so God cannot be outside space and time (although this realm may have eternal aspects, as will be discussed later). Although there can still be what we call "true transcendence," God does not exert influence from outside the dynamic whole. Thus by not using the word *God* we underline the fact that the traditional worldview that nourished and sustained many of its meanings is gone.[8] But this does not mean that the reality people experienced is gone. A new vision of the whole is sought.

Although naming is difficult, for the sake of trying to understand and discuss the way things are, a word or phrase is needed. This is especially important in Western, materialistic culture, which often neglects the presence of this realm, especially in our everyday assumptions about matter, the Earth, and daily life. Names are necessary to facilitate human understanding of the full nature of things and human participation in the mysterious, hidden realm.

To signify the generative realm phrases will be used that indicate at once the unknowable, silent, no-thing aspect and also, simultaneously, the fecund, creative, generative aspect. They include Generative Nothingness, Fecund Nothingness, Plenary Emptiness and simply the word *plenum*. The compound word *Abyss/God* will be used frequently. By using *Abyss/God* rather than the word *God* alone, we avoid some common associations with the word *God*, and instead indicate the rationally unknowable realm of generative "nothingness" just discussed. Other dimensions of Abyss/God, such as the power to generate forms and create order, will be explored in later chapters. The word *Abyss* conveys the infinite depths of the originating power. By including *God* in the compund word we indicate, of course, that many traditional insights into this mysterious dimension of our lives are carried forward.

Also, phrases and images that indicate intimacy of the generative Nothingness with the daily world are valuable. Marguerite Ponete, a thirteenth-century Beguine, used the phrase "divine far Nearness." There is also the phrase "near Unknowable." The phrase "Womb of the Universe" suggests hiddenness, creativity, and nearness. Brian Swimme suggests the phrase "All-Nourishing Abyss."(Swimme 1996, p. 100) "All-Nourishing" captures the immediacy of the relationship between the emergent thing and Abyss, the ground from which it emerged.

---

[1] Swimme uses the word *nonvisible* to refer to the quantum vacuum, rather than *invisible*, because "many things are 'invisible' to us and yet capable of being seen. Individual atoms are too small for the unassisted human eye to detect, but such atoms can be seen if they are magnified sufficiently. The *nonvisible*, on the other hand, is that which can never be seen, because it is neither a material thing nor an energy constellation. In addition, the nonvisible world's nature differs so radically from that of the material world that it cannot even be *pictured*. It is both invisible and nonvisualizable. Even so, it is profoundly real and profoundly powerful." (1996, p. 97)

[2] Bohm notes that this immense background energy is largely discounted by scientists, since the philosophy informing scientists is that only what can be measured by an instrument can be considered real. Instruments do not directly respond to this background. But he says his thoughts on the "infinite sea of energy" are directly implied by contemporary physics. According to Bohm, it is almost unavoidable to infer it. (Bohm and Weber 1978, p. 30)

The size of the "little ripple" is a calculation derived from the number of waves (down to an extremely short wavelength of 10^{-33} cm) in any region. Each wavelength contributes to the total energy. (Briggs and Peat, p. 132; see also Bohm 1983, pp. 190–91 and Bohm and Weber 1978, pp. 29–30)

[3] There is further evidence from the second law of thermodynamics for a specific beginning of the universe as opposed to an eternally existing universe. If the universe has a finite stock of order, with an increase in entropy (a measure of disorder), thermodynamic equilibrium (total disorder; see chapter 10) would have eventually been reached. The universe cannot have existed forever, otherwise it would have reached its equilibrium end state an infinite time ago. (Davies 1984, p.11) If our universe has only been disordering itself for 15 or 18 billion years, that is nowhere near long enough to complete the process. (p. 20)

[4] This image of the expanding dough is not fully adequate because there is no point at the outer edge of the expansion of the universe, which the image of a rising loaf suggests; rather, each point is at the very center of the expansion.

[5] "People had linked the theological aspects of the traditional cosmology so closely with its detailed astronomical structure, and with the associated system of 'correspondences' that the rejection of those details at once brought the associated natural theology in question also." (Toulmin 1982, p. 231)

[6] Recent scholarship, finding direct quotes in his work from authors postdating the Dionysius in Athens, has discovered that this Dionysius was probably a fifth-century Syrian anchorite.

[7] For Ruusbroec, unlike Eckhart, the unity of divine life is not beyond the Trinity. For this reason, some theologians consider Ruusbroec a more orthodox theologian of the contemplative life.

[8] Theologian Gordon Kaufman writes that "indeed, the symbol 'God'...itself points to the great mystery of life, the deepest and most profound issues about which we do not know what to say." He continues: "Since much about the world (as we presently understand it) was completely unknown to our religious traditions, and this significantly affects the way in which God has been conceived, theologians dare not simply take over traditional ideas; we must be prepared to criticize every use and interpretation of the symbol 'God' that has appeared to date." (G. Kaufman, p. 29)

9

WE HAVE FOUND NO PRIMAL DUST

Western culture has a million ways of reinforcing the illusion that the world consists of inert stuff out there and that we are the active agents of change whose role is to get that stuff into shape . . .This is the assumption on which most modern education has been based, an education aimed at giving us the tools to exercise dominion over the earth.

— Parker Palmer

WHAT IS MATTER? Loyal Rue, who is a professor of philosophy and religion, once put this question to a physicist friend. With a glare of astonishment, the friend answered, "You're kidding, right?" When another physicist was asked the same question he answered, "I do not have the slightest idea." (Rue, p. 53) After recovering from the shock of these answers, we are intrigued and heartened because they invite us to examine our assumptions about matter. Our discoveries about the age of the Earth and the transformations it has undergone similarly call us to such a reexamination. As Rue points out, matter is not to be underestimated, never to be taken for granted.

It helps a great deal to have some images and ideas about the inner nature of the manifest, visible world in order to be able to imagine how the inner experiences of contemplative life may be integrated with the new story of the evolutionary universe. Some grasp of the remarkable discoveries of the last century about matter is necessary. To begin, we will consider discoveries about the relationship of the very small wave/particles that comprise matter to the *plenum*, the immense "sea" of background energy. Then, as we study the emergence of complex forms in the next chapters, and determine how the indwelling, generative *plenum* remains integral to complex beings, we can begin to see how the contemplatives' claim that they have entered a unitive life—

substantial union[1]—with that generative Abyss and its formative order might be accepted in the contemporary context.

Physicists once expected that a very small particle, a little piece of indestructible matter, would be found, and that, with knowledge of the forces acting on this particle, it would become possible predict and explain everything. Even though the universe might be very complex, with persistence we would able to describe it in a mechanical manner and, by learning the innermost workings of nature, gain the potential for great control over it. But many of us have known that if this were true, it meant that most spiritual ideas and hopes would have to be discarded, because the mechanisms would determine everything. Many people feared what life would be like when such assumptions were applied to psychology, as the behaviorist B. F. Skinner did, and we began to believe that people are simply programmed automata. Such a world would be quite dull, lacking in true adventure, and there would be a danger of some people being able to control our lives by virtue of their knowledge. Even more frightening, we would have no genuine freedom enabling us to object. Certainly some people would seek financial gain from this knowledge, as in manipulative advertising. It seemed that if the mechanistic view were true, then all the thought, spanning centuries, about meaning, creativity, and free choice must have been an illusion of an earlier, benighted period in human history.

But this fear has evaporated. Through the work of quantum physics, scientists have been forced to recognize that, as the structure of matter is probed in finer and finer detail, there are no finite particles with predictable patterns of behavior to be found. The smaller "pieces" no longer possess the traits of objects that can be described adequately in mechanistic terms alone. Thus, for example, although an electron can sometimes behave as if it were a compact little particle, physicists have found that it literally possesses no dimension. (Peat 1990) In *Breakfast at the Victory*, James Carse, a professor of the history and literature of religion, wrote: "We thought they [scientists] would find a primal dust, a swarm of lifeless identical realities, the atoms of Epicurus only smaller, that are the building units of all larger, composite beings. But in fact they are describing things more dreamlike than real, more made of empty space than substance." (p. 97)

To the world of physics, this discovery was an earthquake, very high on the Richter scale: It is scientifically non-viable to think of particles as having a complete, independent existence. Particles are radically dependent upon the ground from which they take form. There "occurs an incessant foaming, a flashing flame, a shining-forth-from and dissolving-back-into." (Swimme 1996, p. 101) Although every object in the universe is composed of various atoms, this does not mean reality is identical with these atoms, if they are conceived to be the indestructible atoms posited by the Greeks and Isaac Newton and latter-day physicists until the twentieth century. Since we have found no primal dust we can once again inquire into the levels of comprehensive order and energy out of which wave/particles emerge. Hence Plotinus's insights about an originating fecundity, the One (or a differentiated One, in the Trinitarian conception of Christianity), are no longer incompatible with the contemporary worldview of physicists.

Recall, from chapter 3, David Bohm's description of the relationship of wave/particles to the immense background energy as a comparatively small pattern of excitation "on top" of a background "emptiness," rather like a ripple on a vast sea. (1983, p. 191) He says that "elementary particles" are not ultimate substances; that is, they are not little bits of unchanging matter (no primal dust), for they "can be created, annihilated and transformed." Instead they are relatively autonomous forms, abstracted from some deeper level of movement. (p. 49) It is these very wave/particles, abstracted from a deeper level, that over the billions of years of evolution of the universe have become part of the complex, manifest world we know from day to day. The relatively autonomous excitation pattern over great periods of time gives rise to the approximately recurrent, stable, separate forms of the manifest order, which is more or less equivalent to what we commonly experience. (p. 192)

Bohm describes the "patterns of excitation" as being as inseparable from the deeper level as the vortex (whirlpool) is inseparable from the stream in which it forms. The whirlpool is not a separate thing at all, but a pattern or form of the whole stream. (1983, p. 10) F. David Peat offers the lovely suggestion that elementary particles may therefore be closer to the gestures of a dance or the movements of a piece of music than to "elementary building blocks of matter." (1987, p. 96) If the relationship between the "patterns of excitation" (the wave/particles) and the vast energy sea is indeed like the relationship of the whirlpool to the stream, then matter as we know it with our senses and by our measurements is most intimately related to some deeper level of movement.

However, someone may quickly object that a person or a tree is clearly more distinct and autonomous than the whirlpool in the flowing river. And, indeed, the image of a whirlpool forming in a stream is not entirely adequate to describe large complex beings that achieve a high degree of subjectivity and partial autonomy. Later chapters explore some recent ideas about how the great complexity of the visible, daily world has formed and how that process has not rent the fundamental inseparability and intimacy of the ongoing origin and the wave/particles that emerge from it. In *Science and Humanism* Erwin Schrödinger wrote that modern physics recognized that material substance is "nothing but pure shape, . . . not an individual speck of material." (pp. 20– 21)

Solitons

A helpful way of imagining the relation of particle/waves to the deeper level is to consider the phenomenon of solitons. A soliton is a solitary wave that provides an example of a distinct, localized form arising out of a background on which it subsists. The relationship of solitons to the background from which they emerge demonstrates how a part can emerge as an expression of the whole. One of the first observations of a soliton was made in 1834, when a man named J. Scott Russell, on horseback, followed a single wave for a mile or two as it rolled rapidly along a narrow channel of water. Such a wave is a local phenomenon that is born, persists as a pattern in space and time, and then dies back into the ground that has sustained it. Solitons have been discovered in a wide variety of situations, such as the operations of electrical circuits, the propagation of nerve impulses, and the vibration of atoms. The image is valuable because solitons are distinct and localized and appear to be independent units. However they are constantly sustained by the ground that gave them birth. (Peat 1987, p.75) It is thought that elementary wave/particles are like solitons that arise out of an underlying ground. Thus it is suggested that "elementary particles are not, in fact, the fundamental building blocks of matter but are the solitons of an underlying nonlinear quantum field." (Peat 1987, p. 74)

The Phenomenon of Presence

There is further evidence indicating that discrete atoms are not the basic building blocks they were once assumed to be. It has been discovered that matter has behaviors that can only be explained if atoms are understood in the context of comprehensive orders. One of the most revealing discoveries about particle/waves is the phenomenon of presence. It is not an entirely new idea in the world of science: there were features in the theories of Isaac Newton suggesting that the presence of a particle was coextensive with the universe. (Swimme and Berry, p. 27) However, it has been largely assumed in recent centuries that the nature of a thing, e.g. a proton, could be determined simply by considering a small region surrounding it. Quantum theory has proven something quite different.

In quantum physics one particle is said to be present to another if they are energetically coupled (for example, if they were part of one atomic nucleus and then became separated). There are two types of presence (referred to the parlance of physics as "causality"): local and nonlocal. Local causality is a well-entrenched principle, which states that distant events cannot instantaneously influence local objects without any mediation. (Pagels, p. 139) In the autumn, when we see leaves flying in the sunlight we know that the wind is blowing locally; wind blowing miles away will not make the leaves outside my window move until the disturbance reaches my area. Nonlocal causality, however, is outside our common daily experience; it occurs when two spatially separated particles are present to each other even though there is no mediation between them, such as another particle moving in space and time or some known force. A change introduced to one particle causes an instantaneous adjustment in the other particle, even though it may be at the other end of the galaxy. Physicists were not aware that established quantum theory called for nonlocal causality until Einstein, who was always looking for weaknesses in the theory, proposed a thought experiment in 1935, the so-called EPR (Einstein, Podolsky, Rosen) paradox, to point out what he saw as a flaw in quantum theory. But his challenge failed. Experiments were conducted that avoided any kind of local influence up to the speed of light, and demonstrated many times the non-local presence for interacting particles.[2] Thus scientists have established in repeatable experiments that "it is not viable to think of a particle or an event as being completely determined by its particular locale. Events taking place elsewhere in the universe are directly and instantaneously related to the physical parameter of the situation." (Swimme and Berry, p. 28) Furthermore, since "most particles or aggregates of particles that are ordinarily regarded as separate objects have interacted at some time in the past with other objects, . . . in some sense all these objects constitute an indivisible whole." (d'Espagnat, p. 180)

In sum, this discovery of non-local causality suggests that particles are immediately present to each other in a more comprehensive domain and are themselves in some manner part of that domain. This in turn indicates that from some point of view particles are part of a larger whole and are not separate and independent. Recall that Bohm spoke of particles as abstractions from the sea of energy "nothingness." "Every atomic particle is immediately present to every other atomic particle in a manner that enables us to say that the volume of each atom is the volume of the universe." (T. Berry 1988a, pp. 120–21)

Unbroken Wholeness

Both quantum mechanics and relativity theory, despite their differences, imply that the actual state of the universe is unbroken wholeness. (Bohm 1983, pp. 134, 176) Niels Bohr stated that particles are not separate "things," but are part of an indivisible system. (Talbot 1991, p. 37) Bohm writes: "The essential new quality implied by the quantum theory is nonlocality, i.e. that a system cannot be analyzed into parts whose basic properties do not depend on the whole system. This leads to the radically new notion of unbroken wholeness of the entire universe." (As quoted in Wolf, p. 177) These discoveries invite us to entertain a new way of imagining the relation of the part (as the person) to the whole: Because of them, we recognize that the individual is never found in an absolute sense. The manifest daily world of things and living beings in their inner dimension are directly open to and are part of the nonvisible depth of things.[3] This is key to the 'way of seeing' being developed. Although this nonvisible depth discovered by quantum physics cannot be equated with all that has been signified by the word *God*, a word that originated in a different cosmological context, both apply, however inadequately, to the same hidden, nonvisible, active dimension of things. The contemporary conception of an indwelling *plenum* is highly valuable, since as it speaks to the immanence of that nonvisible realm and the intimacy of that realm with the manifest world. It seems appropriate to assume that the *plenum* is a dimension of what we are calling Abyss/ God. This is congruent with a statement made by theologian Raimundo Panikkar, who observed that the fundamental unity of reality should not be overshadowed by the diversity of the whole universe: "*The variety of beings, including the theological difference between the divine and the created or God and the world should not overshadow the fundamental unity of reality.*" (Panikkar

1973, p. xv, emphasis added) Similarly, Whitehead speaks of God and creation as co-constituting a communal Reality. And like other insights considered here, this one is by no means an insight limited to the twentieth century. Thus, in the twelfth century, the Spanish-born Jewish sage Maimonides instructed us to "know that this universe, in its entirety is nothing else but one individual being. . . . The variety of its substances . . . . is like the variety of substances of a human being." (Quoted in Kushner , p. 80)

How Separate Are the Wave/Particles from the Source?

If wave/particles are "quantized ripples" of the great sea of energy "nothingness" (*quantized* simply means the energy comes in small, discrete packets), how should we think about the distinction or lack of distinction between the originating matrix and the wave/particles? In traditional language, to what degree is the Creator separate from the created? There is certainly some distinction between the originating matrix and the wave/ particles, because as wave/particles appear, the energy field is said to be taking form. And over evolutionary time, wave/particles have become part of complex structures that take on various quite distinct forms. Mountains can be very big and solid. On the other hand, as we have just seen, the existence of presence (non-local causality), and the fact that particles constantly emerge and fall back into the vacuum, would seem to indicate that the wave/ particles remain, in some manner, integral to the generative matrix. David Bohm calls particles modifications of the vacuum, which would indicate an apparent lack of clear separation between the particles and the matrix from which it comes. The evidence from quantum physics suggests that we cannot choose one position or the other: that is, choose whether the appearance of wave/particles is the appearance of something of a different order, or simply a form or modification of the originating matrix. Sometimes atoms will behave like relatively independent entities and it is convenient to treat them as if they were such, but in general, scientists have to face the fact that atoms are projections from higher-dimensional realities; that is, expressions of implicate orders. (Briggs and Peat, p. 124) And amazingly, we will see that that this is not incongruent with Christian incarnational insight, with unitive contemplative experiences and with related insights into unity and diversity. (See chapter 13.)

This research into the very small means that we may not make a complete separation, as some have done, between the Abyss/God (Creator) and the wave/particles (the created). To insist on such a separation is a remnant of a time when matter could be conceived of as composed of discrete atoms. It comes from a time when we did not know that the elementary wave/particles that become the complex forms of the day-to-day world are inseparable from the generative matrix of which they are modifications. To be able to embrace the significance of this for the person, we need more understanding of the manner in which complex beings are formed in an evolutionary universe and how they remain integral to the unfolding whole. Such understanding will speak to the continuing presence of the indwelling *plenum* in complex beings, and we will seek it in the next three chapters.

Reflections on the Beginning of the Universe

Although the beginning of the universe is shrouded in mystery and unknowable by observation and measurement, it is important to reflect briefly on it to avoid conceptions that can result in inadequate ideas about the relationship between the Abyss/God and the manifest world.

In the context of the new physics, which "found no primal dust," we cannot think of creation as producing an object (dust) in space. Nor did creation explode into an already existing space.[4] (Swimme 1996, p. 85). We cannot think of the Generative No-thing-ness as spatially outside the universe because space unfolds as the universe expands. Nor can we think of a creative Source before time, since time did not exist to be before. Neither space nor time can be extended back beyond the initial singularity.[5] Just as the Big Bang represents the creation of space, so it represents the creation of time. (Davies 1983, p. 18) It is noteworthy that in *The City of God* Augustine ridiculed the idea of God waiting for an infinite time and then deciding at some moment to create a universe: "The world was made, not in time, but together with time." (XI. 6) In *The Universe Story*, Brian Swimme and Thomas Berry suggest that "the realm of power that brings forth the universe is not itself an event in time nor a position in space but rather the very matrix out of which the conditions arise that enable the temporal events to occur in space." (p. 17) We have seen that it is an empty realm, a mysterious order of reality, a no-thing-ness that is the ultimate source. We have noted David Bohm's suggestion that the Big Bang is a "little ripple" in the vast sea of the immense background energy, the *plenum*.

The Nature of Making or Creating

For many people raised in Western Judeo-Christian culture, ideas about the beginning are informed by the first words of the biblical creation story in Genesis: "In the beginning God created the heavens and the Earth." It rings harmoniously in our ears, easily leading us to assume from our experience of creating and making that, notwithstanding its awesome dimensions, the beginning of the universe was of the same nature. We tend to conceive of making as the production of an object, of something other and separate from the maker, like the ceramic vase on the table we made in a pottery class (disregarding that we did not make the clay). But the word for "create" in the Genesis passage is the Hebrew word *bara*. It is not the common verb *asa* or "made." The word *bara* is used only with God as the subject, and its use here surely indicates that "creating" by God is thought of as a unique relationship. (Montefiore, p.18) Although we do not know exactly what this special verb meant, it is thought to express the constant relation subsisting between God and the world, whereby he maintains the world in being. This conception is not foreign to the contemporary worldview. Louis Dupré writes: "In confessing that God has created me, I affirm that, at some point, his act and my being coincide." (1984, p.33)

In *The River of Light*, Lawrence Kushner interprets the Genesis story of creation in a way that would seem to be congruent with the new story and the new physics in terms of the relationship between the One of Being and that which is created:

> The One of Being says, "Let there be Light." And with the same simple mystery that thought becomes speech and that intention becomes action or that energy becomes matter, "there was Light." Not a second idea or the next step but all part of the flow of one sentence. (The divisions between phrases and words and letters are a human invention.) Here the "let there be" and the "and there was" are both one totality. As the flame is joined to the burning coal, so the intention is joined to the creation. . . . All being, from space to time, matter to energy, intention to creation, is on one spectrum. Or, more correctly, different facets of one underlying reality. (pp. 102, 104)

In parts of the Biblical tradition, there is a great intimacy between the God of the Bible and the world. Everything in creation lives moment by moment by the breath of God. We "live and move and have our being" in God. (Acts 17:28)

Some Reflections

The failure to find any "primal dust" and discoveries about the intimacy between the manifest (the wave/particles) and the generative *plenum* are most important with regard to the identity of each person and that of the natural order. Even if it is difficult for people not trained in quantum physics (myself included) to understand what has been discovered about the very small, we can certainly grasp that this discipline demolishes any assumptions we may have about the nature of matter being inert stuff and limited to predictable laws of cause and effect. Its discoveries profoundly inform this investigation into an integration of the new universe story with the experience of the contemplative tradition, given the inner relationship of the manifest (i.e. what can be held in the hand) with the *plenum*.

In chapter 8 we considered the work of physicists regarding the vacuum and the experiences of contemplatives who have explored a generative "nothingness" as *complementary explorations of the same mysterious realm*. We can now point to a further exciting complementarity in the two traditions: the discovery of *the ongoing intimacy, indeed inseparability, between the Source and the manifest* that is encountered in both avenues of exploration. The intimacy discovered in the unitive life was discussed in chapter 7. Again, we do not equate the two realms of inquiry, but note the remarkable congruence of insight.

We also note that none of this was something people wanted to discover. Physicists strongly resisted accepting their inability to find a piece of solid, particulate matter and some contemplatives wanted to hide the experience that no longer allowed them to separate themselves from the Creator. We have described Meister Eckhart's troubles in regard to defining the limits of the person. The fact that contemplatives have discovered a pathway to a permanent union with Abyss/God within their person indicates that the nonvisible realm is present and may, with adequate preparation, become known in an alternative type of consciousness. (The question of our general lack of consciousness of this presence is a topic to be considered in chapters 15 and 16.) Eckhart's teaching about the noble identity of the person seems highly congruent with the inseparability between the *plenum* and the found by quantum physicists. And in chapter 7, we noted that Friedrich von Hügel believed we should reject any absolute qualitative difference between the soul's deepest possibilities and ideas of God. When Catherine of Genoa said, "My me is God," she had discovered the remarkable intimacy between herself and God. The same indwelling *plenum* has been recognized in the natural world. The person William Stace identified as N.M. wrote: "I had no doubt that I had seen God, that is, had seen all there is to see; yet it turned out to be the world that I looked at every day." (In Stace, p.73) These reflections are central to the 'way of seeing' (*theoria*) we are exploring. Indeed the discoveries of contemporary physics and contemplative experience seem to suggest that the 'way of seeing' we aim for, which embraces both, is possible.

---

[1] As noted also in chapter 7, substance is not used here, as it often is in English, to describe a physical material of which something is made. Rather substance comes from the translation of the Greek word *ousia* to *substancia*, in Latin. As we will discuss in chapter 13, it refers to "what this or that is in itself."

[2] Essential to quantum theory is that quantum wave/particles, e.g., electrons or photons, exist in a sort of limbo with respect to such properties as position, motion, spin, and polarity (the orientation of their vibration as waves) until a measurement is made. It postulates an observer-created reality in place of the classical objective reality. The EPR thought experiment can be described as follows, in simplified form: a source emits a pair of energetically-coupled (i.e., when one has spin up the other has spin down) particles, A and B, although the actual spin is in limbo until measured. These particles fly at the speed of light to opposite ends of the galaxy where measuring devices are located. Until a measurement is actually performed, particles A and B must be regarded as a single totality, even if light years apart. If at one location, particle A is found to have spin up; instantaneously particle B, now light-years away, is known to have spin down without the need for measurement or mediation. In an objective world this would be taken for granted; if you go on a trip and when you get there you discover you only brought one glove, you instantly know which glove you left at home without having to call there to find out. However, in the quantum world things are not defined until an observation is made. It is as if your glove were both right and left until you took it out of the suitcase and looked at it. The same would be true of the glove left at home; therefore, looking at the local glove would have instantly transformed the home glove into a definite form. But, how was the information communicated? According to Einstein's principle of special relativity, nothing can travel faster than the speed of light. The EPR analysis showed that quantum theory either made nonlocal causality possible or the theory was incomplete. Einstein favored the latter option, believing that future discoveries would provide the missing elements, such that nonlocal causality could once again be excluded from physical reality.

The implications of the EPR thought experiment were so disturbing that experimental verification was eagerly sought, but it was not until thirty years later that an avenue for testing nonlocality was discovered. J.S. Bell demonstrated that in the absence of nonlocal influences the probability of coincidental results for paired particles at distant locations under the conditions of the EPR experiment was subject to precise rules (the so-called "Bell's Theorem" or "Bell's Inequality"). Most importantly, if there is only local causality, the upper limit of the possible correlation will be lower than that predicted by quantum theory. Here then was an avenue for testing reality, and it became a matter of finding ways to run the EPR test of the flying particles. Intergalactic distances were obviously out of the question, but it turned out that the essential feature was that not enough time be available for communication between the particles at speeds up to the speed of light, to assure that "local" influences were eliminated. Any unexpected correlation would then have to be attributed to a nonlocal effect. Several such experiments have been conducted (for details see the review articles of Shimony and d'Espagnat), and the results overwhelmingly demonstrate that reality, while retaining an element of objectivity, must incorporate the element of nonlocality for interacting particles.

[3] As noted also in chapter 8 (note 1), Brian Swimme uses the term *nonvisible* to refer to that which can never be seen.(1996, p. 97)

[4] Physicists consider that space itself begins in the Big Bang. The expanding universe does not move into preexisting space and time. They think of space as infinitely shrunk in the beginning. (Davies 1983, p. 18) Even now, spaces between galaxies are thought of as "stretching" or being "inflated." The universe expands without having to expand into some external void.

As John Cobb notes: "In modern thought space-time is not to be thought of as a fixed receptacle which preexists events. Rather, energy events themselves are the ultimate reality." (1969, p. 163)

[5] The initial event is referred to as a singularity. This first instant of the Big Bang where space was infinitely shrunken, represents a boundary or edge in time at which space ceases to exist. Physicists call such a boundary a singularity. (Davies 1983, p. 18) Some cosmologists believe that the universe emerged without cause from a type of naked singularity. (Davies 1983, p. 56)

10

COMPLEX, CENTERED BEINGS
WITHIN THE UNFOLDING WHOLE

We need to understand that the evolutionary process is neither random nor determined but creative.

— Thomas Berry

ACCORDING TO the late paleontologist and essayist Stephen J. Gould, human beings are "a glorious evolutionary accident." (Kayzer et al.) This is a most disheartening description. Gould cites as one reason for his assertion the improbable, random crash of a six-mile-wide meteor into the Earth 66 million years ago, which is thought to have been a major factor in the extinction of the dinosaurs and the opening of niches for mammals. Without this fortuitous meteor, it is quite conceivable that human beings might not have emerged on this Earth, at least not at this time. Furthermore, some of us were taught, as students of biology, that it is random variations in DNA and also errors in its replication that result in the changes in the organism which are then acted upon by natural selection. French chemist Jacques Monod wrote: "Chance alone is at the source of every innovation of all creation in the biosphere." (Quoted in Capra 1996, p. 225) Gould's worldview is also that random events control evolution and render the process unpredictable.[1] To be an accident, even a glorious one, or to be the result of error and chance alone, denies people the possibility of living in a manner faithful to any fundamental order or intrinsic direction of things. Any intrinsic value and purpose for the person except that invented by the individual and the common consent and practical considerations of members of a particular culture is denied. It is a "dismal worldview in which evolution has no direction and no purpose." (McMenamin, p. 263) If the processes of evolution are all accidental and random, our search for a fundamental integrity to our individual lives is tragically undermined.

Clues to the inadequacy of the "glorious accident" way of seeing come directly from the larger context offered by the new universe story. As mentioned, there is essentially zero probability of achieving the complexity of the Earth from only random collisions of atoms and molecules. So there must be some creative, ordering process. But what do we know about how the multitude of diverse and complex beings develop? It is not enough to know that we share atoms coming from the stars with the entire Earth and all its living beings. We need to know if and to what degree a person is a participant in the creative, organizing processes. This brings us to the study of self-organization. Form generation through self-organization involves the creation of centered, complex beings: therefore, questions of soul and subjective identity are central to the topic.

Up until the mid-twentieth century the study of the origin of complex, non-living and living beings (forms) was not an issue for science, because the world was generally accepted to have been given from the hands of the Creator in final form, although marked by the cycles of the seasons and those of birth, life, and death. The study of form was the exclusive domain of philosophy and theology. Even evolutionary biologists of the nineteenth and early twentieth centuries, who sought to discover the common ancestors of various species and to trace lines of descent, did not know that all species are formed from the complexification of the elements synthesized in stars (and compounds derived from those elements) that fell into orbit around the sun and coalesced to form the Earth. It was with the discovery of the evolutionary universe that the question of how the great diversity and complexity of the world could have arisen from simple origins arose. Since the 1940s there has been intense research on and study of the form-generating powers of the universe by scientists in the new interrelated disciplines that include the science of complexity, systems theory, the science of dynamic systems, cybernetics, the study of dissipative structures, the study of autopoietic systems and non-linear thermodynamics. These disciplines seek to discover the principles and processes that are involved in the appearance and maintenance of forms and collective order.

Examples of Actual Generation of Form

It was from research with a specific type of chemical reaction that the spontaneous appearance of a simple form was first observed in the laboratory. In 1958, two Russian biophysicists discovered a chemical reaction, now called the Belousov-Zhabotinsky reaction, in which certain chemical reactants, when mixed, formed concentric and spiral "cells" on the surface of the solution.[2] The "cells" pulsed and remained stable, and as the reaction proceeded, periodically more "cells" formed. The manner in which the "cells" spontaneously appeared looked like the growth of a life form. (Briggs and Peat, p. 164; see also Davies 1988, p. 85) This reaction proved to be a simple example of a self-organizing system, an important characteristic of which is that its order in structure and function is not imposed by the environment but is established by the system itself. (Capra 1982, p. 269) A similar example of form generation occurs when a thin layer of liquid is heated uniformly from below. At a certain point there appears on the surface a very striking ordered pattern of hexagonal cells, like a honeycomb, called Bénard cells after the French physicist Henri Claude Bénard (1874–1939) who discovered them. These cells occur spontaneously in nature in many circumstances, such as in the flow of warm air from the surface of the Earth, which leaves its imprints on sand dunes in the desert and on arctic snowfields. (Capra 1996, p. 88) Both the Belousov-Zhabotinsky reaction and the formation of Bénard cells offer glimpses of the generation of forms that are not built slowly by the random conjunction of molecules, but appear spontaneously.

Everything is form, including atoms, cells, or human beings. A galaxy is a self-organizing system, organizing its stars into a non-equilibrium process,[3] drawing forth new stars from its interstellar materials. A star is a dynamic organization, centered within itself; it organizes hydrogen and helium and produces atomic elements and light. (Swimme and Berry, p. 75) The flame of a candle, certain thunderstorms, and tornados are all self--organizing systems. Brian Swimme states that there is no thing that exists outside unseen shaping activity. (Swimme 1984, p. 132) There is no matter without form. At all scales, the universe is far from equilibrium— self-designing at the edge of chaos. Wherever we look gradients of matter and energy create crucibles for self-organizing systems.

We began consideration of the topic of the generation of form in the discussion in chapter 3 of David Bohm's conception of an implicate order out of which the many forms of daily life have unfolded. His idea implies that form is not only the consequence of the known mechanical laws of physics and chemistry, but that there is an inner ordering and creative capacity in the universe. We explore this subject further now, difficult and elusive though it is. One reason it is difficult is that the form-generating capacity of the universe is not visible to the senses, although it is never absent from the visible world of our daily lives. We have taken it for granted but we can no longer do so in the context of an evolutionary universe.

Characteristics of Self-Organizing Systems

The maintenance of a fixed organization is a key characteristic of self-organizing systems, which in the case of a living being means staying alive. This is possible because energy constantly flows through the system from its environment. Matter and energy literally flow through the structure, which may be a living or a non-living self-organizing system. There is a continuous exchange providing the energy for regulating the system's processes in such a way that the integrity of the structure is maintained. Ilya Prigogine, Nobel Prize-winning systems theorist, gave these structures the name "dissipative structures" because they dissipate energy as heat, yet the organization is continually maintained with the import of energy, thereby achieving a dynamic, far-from-equilibrium stability over an extended period of time. (Equilibrium in living beings is equivalent to death; see endnote 3.) The many living, self-organizing systems of the Earth depend on the enormous quantity of radiant energy pouring upon us from that non-living self-organizing system, the sun, which has made possible, over the millennia, a great increase in order and complexity on the Earth.

Here, in our knowledge of this capacity of dissipative structures to maintain themselves over an extended period, there is an important difference in our 'way of seeing' now as compared to an earlier period, when the second law of thermodynamics alone molded our assumptions. The second law of thermodynamics requires that, in an isolated system, disorder (measured as entropy) must gradually increase. "Isolated" means that no energetic sources are acting on the system from the outside. The second law indicates that because disorder inevitably increases, a system left to itself will always run down, fall apart, and decay.[4] Applied to the entire universe, it predicts an eventual total loss of organization, i.e. death. This law occasioned great pessimism in the nineteenth century, because it presented a picture of a universe on a continuous downhill course after a stupendous created beginning. Fortunately, our perspective has now changed with the discovery that we live in an evolutionary universe which, over time, has differentiated and complexified to an astounding degree and continues to do so. While this appears to contradict the second law, on closer inspection it does not, because the second law does not preclude an increase in order in *parts* of the system. The important thing is that Prigogine and others have shown that even though the second law remains valid for the universe as a whole, under certain circumstances there are local situations in which order, rather than entropy, increases. This is part of the creativity of the Earth.

During World War II, Norbert Wiener (1894–1964), the American mathematician known for his theory of cybernetics, and others worked on self-guided missiles that find their target by receiving information (feedback) from a system that is monitoring their performance. The feedback concept, developed in the military, was recognized as applying to natural systems. An organism relates to its environment by monitoring the effects of its behavior using information received by its receptors. When we touch a hot stove we quickly change our behavior based on the feedback. We lose our balance if there is inadequate feedback from our joints and muscles. A lion chasing its prey depends on constant sensory feedback in order to capture its meal.

Another characteristic of self-organizing systems is that in critical, unstable conditions, new forms may emerge. Prigogine referred to matter organized far from equilibrium as "active matter." The matter has a "will of its own" such that it may leap into a new state of enhanced organization.[5] Disequilibrium, Prigogine claims, is the source of order in the universe; it brings order out of chaos. For this reason, self-organizing systems are said to be self-transcending. It is an order that is intrinsically unpredictable, at least by the known phenomenological laws of evolution. (Davies 1988, p. 89)

This indeterminacy (not known in advance) in the behavior of these systems when they are at points of instability changes our worldview. In the pre-quantum age of Newtonian physics, the prevailing idea was that the universe was fully predictable by the then-known laws or, at least, by future refinements of these laws. This confident view was shattered by the revelation of quantum mechanics that events at the atomic and subatomic level—for example, the specific motion of an electron or the radioactive decay of unstable nuclei—could not be predicted individually for any particular electron or nucleus, but only on a statistical basis that encompassed a large number of events. It was further shattered by the discovery of indeterminacy in the behavior of dissipative structures when they are at points of instability. We have left the determinism that has plagued human consciousness for so many decades, opening a place for change and the creation of a viable future.

The potential for the emergence of new forms is, of course, of central importance in the unfolding of the cosmos, including the evolution of life on Earth. The inherent tendency of self-organizing systems in chaotic situations to become changed, new forms makes the universe a place in which there is a predisposition toward novelty and surprise. This is evident, for example, in the unimaginable variety of insects that have developed over the millennia. As the universe unfolds it is "temporarily" (this could mean millions of years) manifest in globally stable structures (Jantsch, p.6), but then, often at critical points, through systemic fluctuation and an intrinsic form-generating capacity, there is an emergence of new structure and order resulting in more complex beings. An interesting dimension of these ideas about the development of changed, new forms, is that it has led to speculations about how life emerged here on Earth from the organic molecules that were its precursors.[6] It is observed that new structures and systems develop with unusual efficiency. (Davies 1988, p. 200) Stuart Kauffman, a leading thinker on the science of complexity and self-organization as applied to biology, believes that "the origin of life was not an enormously improbable event, but law-like and governed by new principles of self-organization in complex webs of catalysts." (Kauffman 1993, p. xvi)

Living Systems: Autopoiesis

An important theme throughout this book is the recognition that a considerable degree of human autonomy and self-determination exists simultaneously with imbeddedness in the unfolding unity of the Earth and universe. Living organisms, like non-living self-organizing systems, have the same characteristic flow of energy and matter through the system. However living organisms have more autonomy than non-living systems, a characteristic derived from their ability to continuously renew themselves by producing their own components.[7] In 1973 Humberto Maturana, a Chilean neuroscientist, coined the word *autopoiesis* from the Greek words, *auto* (self) and *poiesis* (creation, production) to describe the central feature of the organization of the living, which is autonomy. (Maturana and Varela 1980, p. xiv) An example of autopoiesis in a cell is the production by the DNA, in the cell nucleus, of RNA molecules which contain instructions for producing a group of special enzymes that can recognize, remove, and replace damaged sections of DNA in the same cell nucleus. This is clearly autopoietic, since the cell is making enzymes that repair the DNA, which itself codes the RNA for more of that same enzyme. (Capra 1996, p. 167) Gail Fleischaker, biologist and philosopher, has summarized the properties of an autopoietic network in terms of three criteria: the system must be self-bounded, self-generating, and self-perpetuating. (Capra 1996, p. 208)

The autopoietic capacity of cells and of multicellular organisms results in far greater stability and longevity than is possible, for example, for a tornado, a non-living self-organizing system. The stability consists in maintaining the same overall organization and structure in spite of ongoing processes and ongoing replacement of the components of the structure. There is organizational closure, which means a living system is self-organizing in the sense that its order and behavior are not imposed by the environment, but are established by the system itself. (Capra 1996, p. 167) Organizational closure provides an autopoietic system with partial autonomy vis-à-vis the environment. Yet the system is also fragile. A one-celled organism can maintain its functioning with some changes in the environment, keeping itself repaired and healthy, but with extreme heat or dryness or the loss of energy input from food over an extended period, it cannot survive. This also, of course, applies to human beings. Here we see clearly the remarkable, seemingly paradoxical fact that living beings are simultaneously quite autonomous (organizationally closed) and at the same time integral to the Earth, since they are dependent on the flow of energy and matter. This coexistence of individual autonomy with embeddedness in the Earth and universe is central to the identity of human and other living beings.

The very Earth is thought by some to be autopoietic. Indeed, it seems this must be so considering that the Earth has come alive on its surface and that the interdependent network of life systems has been sustained for billions of years. In the 1970s microbiologist Lynn Margulis and James Lovelock termed this conception of Earth as "organism" the Gaia hypotheses.[8] (See Margulis and Lovelock 1974; Lovelock 1979; Lovelock and Margulis 1988) In Brian Swimme's words, the Earth is a self-organizing and self-regulating process of astounding complexity and achievement. (Swimme 1984, p. 133). We can observe it, for example, in the temperate rainforests of the Tongass National Forest in southeastern Alaska, an area largely untouched by human activity, where the autopoietic, self-sustaining character of the ecosystem is evident in the luxurious diversity of spruces, hemlocks, eagles, bears and salmon that has sustained itself largely unchanged over centuries.

Consciousness

An important aspect of autopoietic systems is that they are also cognitive systems. The organism's cognition is essential to its survival; it involves awareness of the physical intimacy of the organism and environment. Although cognition is a means of relating living beings to the environment, Humberto Maturana and his colleague Francisco Varela, the Chilean team who have studied and theorized about autopoiesis, see cognition as part of organizational closure, because an organism is selectively coupled with only certain aspects of its environment, not with all the dimensions of its surroundings. Thus a plant may be selectively coupled with the direction of the light, while some deep-sea organisms are not coupled with light at all. Such selective coupling, developed over eons, can trigger needed changes in the autopoietic system, enabling it to maintain its integrity. Maturana and Varela point out that this means an organism constructs *a* world or brings into being *a* world, according to the structural coupling it is capable of, but not *the* world. Much passes it by. (Maturana and Varela 1987, pp. 135, 163, 169)

The Nesting of Parts in Larger Wholes

Arthur Koestler coined the word *holons* for subsystems that are both wholes and parts. A cell is a holon because it is both a self-organizing system and often also a part of a larger whole, the organism in which it lives. Koestler emphasized that each holon has two opposite tendencies: an integrative tendency to function as part of a larger whole and a self-assertive tendency to preserve its individual autonomy. (Capra 1982, p. 43) At each level of complexity we encounter systems that are integrated, self-organizing wholes consisting of smaller parts and, at the same time, acting as parts of larger wholes. There is a kind of nesting of subsystems in larger integrative systems. Each larger whole/part in a living system has distinct emerging properties. There is a reorganization as smaller units (holons) integrate and aggregate into larger units, so they give rise to new rules pertaining to the larger unit. These rules, in turn, constrain and regulate the component subsystems so that they comply with the collective behaviors of the larger system. (Davies 1988, p. 149) Thus living systems cannot be fully understood by analysis of their parts in isolation. A cell can be studied as a functioning unit but not known fully unless it is also studied as part of the larger whole of an organism. People are not fully understood unless their identity as part of the Earth system is also taken into account.

All the matter in our bodies, from the very first, enfolds the universe in some way. Any subtotality up to a point may be studied in its own right, although what is discovered has no final validity because it is necessary to look for laws of larger, relatively autonomous domains in the implicate order. (Bohm 1983, pp. 178, 193) This was recognized in the seventeenth century by the Dutch philosopher Spinoza, who observed that we cannot state the truth of an object in itself because it cannot be isolated from the rest of nature; the whole truth about an object would involve the whole of nature.

Co-evolution is a perspective on evolution that employs the insights about dissipative structures, spontaneous change and the nesting of systems in larger wholes.[9] It describes a complex process involving the interaction of many interdependent systems in a natural, hierarchical (meaning more or less inclusive) order. Within this understanding, evolution is no longer only an interaction of separate parts, as the emphasis on random genetic changes and survival of the fittest suggests. "A structure doesn't appear in isolation either on the macro or the micro level but is a phenomenon born out of an environment in which everything effects everything, like Bohm's holomovement." (Briggs and Peat, p. 196) The production of new forms in the evolutionary processes of the Earth occurs by a combination of self-transcendence characteristic of self-organizing systems, symbiosis and the slower adaptive processes of the trial-and-error aspects of the production of variations that are then acted upon by natural selection.[10] It has been remarkably successful here on Earth, with tens of millions of species having been created since life began. (See chapter 2.)

Discussion

No extrinsic, vitalistic principle is being invoked to explain complexity and the origin of life. The emergence of organized forms and living beings does not involve processes outside of what we call matter but instead arises from the inherent principles of the dynamics of the universe. This includes the inner structure of "active matter," expressed when it is far from equilibrium.

In this recognition of the inherent principles involved in the form-generating capacity of the Earth, we find an avenue of understanding that liberates us from the specter of the "glorious accident." Although there is novelty and surprise, this does not mean things are an accident. There is a direction: toward increased differentiation, subjectivity (autopoiesis), and communion. (Swimme and Berry, p. 71) Matter isn't cobbled together piece by piece, like the colorful wooden model of molecules in chemistry class. No one is a fragment or a chunk of matter, unconnected to the cosmos. The study of self-organizing systems has shown that there is an internal power by which simple and complex systems exhibit order spontaneously.

The person is fully embedded in this deep, creative ordering capacity of things. Order, vast and generative, arises naturally. (Kauffman 1995, p. 25) An answer to the idea of a "glorious evolutionary accident" begins to emerge. The manner in which the creative powers of the universe may find expression in the individual is discussed in later chapters, as the contemplative tradition is integrated with the story.

---

[1] See Gould's article "The Evolution of Life on Earth" in *Scientific American* 271:84–91 (1994).

[2] The reaction involves the oxidation of malonic acid by bromate in a sulfuric acid solution and in the presence of cerium (or iron or manganese) ions. (Jantsch, p. 29)

[3] Equilibrium in this context is the state of maximum disorder in a closed system, from which no further work or temperature gradient can be elicited. For a living system it is the equivalent of death, the endpoint of the second law for that system. Self-organizing systems are in a state of non-equilibrium, or far from equilibrium.

[4] The first formulation of the second law of thermodynamics was made by the French physicist Sadi Carnot in 1824. Carnot based his conclusion that systems tend toward greater states of disorder on his observations of a heat engine. (Talbot 1988, p. 123) The increase in disorder is an increase in entropy, so stated more formally, according the second law of themodynamics, entropy in an isolated system increases until the system has reached thermodynamic equilibrium. (Jantsch, p. 25)

[5] This happens when there is positive feedback, which reinforces and amplifies deviations such that each change adds to the next, leading to destabilization and collapse or, potentially, the development of new forms at the far-from-equilibrium situation.

[6] It is thought that the conditions in the early seas and/or at underwater volcanic vents or even in the hot depths of the Earth favored the formation of complex molecules, and that some became catalysts for a variety of chemical reactions.(A catalyst is a compound that modifies or accelerates a reaction without being altered itself.) Gradually different catalytic reactions interlocked to form complex catalytic webs involving closed loops or cycles. Subsequently these cycles evolved into autopoietic systems that depend on the input of energy from an external source. At some point, membranes formed surrounding different chemical systems and cycles and led eventually to the first autopoietic bacterial cell. (Capra 1996, p. 236)

[7] The production of their own components is accomplished through auto-catalytic cycles. (Jantsch, p. 7) Autocatalysis is the catalysis (a modification of, and especially an increase in the rate of, a chemical reaction induced by material unchanged at the end of the reaction) of a reaction by one of its products.

[8] The Gaia hypothesis states that the atmosphere, oceans, the climate and rocky substratum of the Earth are regulated at a state comfortable for life by the behavior of living organisms. The hypothesis arose from the observation that temperatures of the Earth have remained relatively constant for 3.8 billion years even though the sun's temperature during the Earth's existence has soared by at least 25% above its original temperature. This new knowledge led scientists to ask how the Earth has remained hospitable to life, keeping a steady temperature over that long period. (Swimme 1984, p.134) Another reason the Gaia hypothesis has been put forward is to explain how there has been such fine adjustment and stability between plants and animals and conditions on Earth s a whole if changes on the Earth arise only from the chance events allowed by the scientific assumptions of nineteenth- and early twentieth-century science. In the Gaia hypothesis, Lovelock and Margulis propose specifically that "the temperature, oxidation state, acidity and certain aspects of the rocks and water (the salts) are at any time kept constant and that this homeostasis is maintained by active feedback processes operated automatically and unconsciously by the biota." (As quoted, with commentary, in Barlow 1991, p. 10) This is in contrast to the conventional wisdom, according to which life adapted to planetary conditions as it and they evolved in their separate ways. (See Piel, p. 308.)

Can it possibly be correct that the Earth behaves like a highly integrated organism? Is it in some manner life-like? With much of the Earth comprising inanimate rock and atmosphere and water, it does not seem to make sense to think of the Earth as alive. But it has been pointed out that 99% of a giant redwood tree is composed of dead wood made of lignin and cellulose laid down by the ancestors of a thin layer of living cells. Yet we don't doubt that a redwood tree is alive. The tree is much like the Earth, especially if we realize that many of the atoms of the rocks far down in the magma were once part of the ancestral life from which we all have come. (Lovelock 1991, pp. 10, 12)

There is quite a bit of supporting evidence for the Gaia hypothesis. One of the revelations of the new universe story is that the emergence of life from "non-life" suggests that the physical world is not dead in the manner we have thought. There could have been no fine line between the animate and "inanimate" as life developed in the early seas. This same intimacy between life and the Earth out of which it emerged cannot have disappeared when life took on an apparent independence as it became more complex and the initial conditions changed. And we've seen that the creative co-evolutionary process involves life and non-life in the ongoing changes in the atmosphere. Without living organisms, the atmosphere would contain approximately 98% carbon dioxide, with very little, if any, nitrogen and oxygen, whereas the corresponding figures for our highly improbable atmosphere are approximately 0.03 percent, 79 percent and 21 percent. (Piel, p. 308) The atmospheric compositions of Mars and Venus, reflecting planetary chemistry without the activity of life, are markedly different from that of the Earth. The Earth's atmosphere is thought to be "not merely a biological product, but more probably a biological construction." (Lovelock, as quoted, with commentary, in Barlow 1991, p.12) Lovelock has suggested that the air we breathe can be thought of as like the fur of a cat, bird's feathers and the shell of a snail, not living but an extension of a living system designed to maintain a chosen environment. (Piel, p. 309)

It is the countless forms of life that create and maintain the disequilibrium situation through a cybernetic, self-controlled system. In the aggregate, all the green plants fix approximately 840 trillion kilowatt hours of solar energy per year in the form of biomass. This is more than ten times the amount of energy that all of humankind uses annually, even with its most extravagant technologies. Moreover, that the mean temperature of the Earth has been held fairly stable around 20 degrees C in spite of major perturbations, suggests it is actively maintained. All this implies the Earth has a lifelike character, although not life-like in the sense of being able to reproduce itself.

[9] The insights into co-evolution derive from the work of Ludwig von Bertalanffy, the father of general systems theory in the biological world. He was interested in how biological forms organize to sustain themselves in their environment. Bertalanffy developed the notion of open, nonmechanical systems continuously interacting with their surroundings in order to understand how biological forms organize to sustain themselves in their environment. (Briggs and Peat, p. 192)

[10] This perspective on evolution considers that Neo-Darwinism, which focuses on the survival of organisms in an environment by natural selection, is a limited picture of how biological forms change. (Briggs and Peat, p. 193) While not denying adaptation and the struggle of individuals for survival, it rejects them as a complete explanation for, or an adequate picture of, the holistic unfolding. Thus, scientists working within the perspective of co-evolution, would emphasize the planetary fluctuation in the early oceans and air affecting various autocatalytic chemical reactions. Further fluctuations would result in greater complexity and eventually in life. These living organisms in turn changed the chemistry of the macro (whole Earth) ecosystem so that it also evolved and would again affect the microorganisms. (Briggs and Peat, P. 195)

The co-evolution model incorporates changes in a particular organism. In new forms there are emergent properties and genuinely new characteristics that cannot be described by the sum of single properties or the sum of components and their combinations. (Jantsch, p. 32) When novel events are actualized for the first time and are capable of being replicated, they are candidates for becoming part of the order of the world. Some new forms are carried forward by natural selection to become semi-autonomous parts of the Gaian system.

11

THE DEPTH OF
HUMAN BELONGING

The appropriation of the new cosmology depends upon an understanding of the reality and power of the nonvisible and nonmaterial realm.

— Brian Swimme

THE IMPLICATIONS of the discovery of the creation of complex beings by inherent, ordering, creative principles clamor for our attention. First, let us address common assumptions that can prevent us from recognizing the significance of these discoveries. Perhaps, we may think, DNA fully explains the form of complex beings, or the known physical and chemical laws do. Or does a larger creative, intelligent ordering play an important role in form generation? If so, contemporary insights into form-generation will shed light on age-old ideas about soul.

Is DNA a Formative Power?

It is commonly assumed that DNA can explain the shape and form of the human body and mind—that DNA is a kind of biochemical computer governing the development of an organism. Since there are reports of a gene for almost everything from breast cancer to hair color, it seems that DNA is the sole guide for the growth and development of a person. This idea is further supported by the assumption that evolutionary change results entirely from the mutation of DNA and the reshuffling of DNA in sexual reproduction. However, as biologist Brian Goodwin writes in *How the Leopard Changed His Spots* (1994):

> The sciences of complexity lead to the construction of a dynamic theory of organisms as the primary source of the emergent properties of life that have been revealed in evolution. . . . During morphogenesis [the development of the

complex form of the adult organism from a simple beginning such as an egg or a bud] emergent order is generated by distinctive types of dynamic process in which genes play a significant but limited role. (p. xi)

Goodwin states that while genes may help produce proteins that make the skeleton, they do not determine the shape and form (morphology) of an embryo or an organism. (*New York Times*, Sept. 2, 1997) According to Stuart Kauffman, writing about the science of complexity applied to biology, the genetic information and its capacity to synthesize RNA and the protein molecules for which it codes do not explain form.[1] Instead morphology is a marriage of *underlying laws of form and the agency of selection*. (1993, p. xvii, emphasis added) Thus, it is suggested, form is not determined by genes alone. Science writer John P. Briggs and F. David Peat say it this way: "The existence and form of an organism (that is, the organism as a dissipative co-evolutionary process) develops *using* genetic information." (p. 200) Systems theorist Erich Jantsch writes: "*The structure of DNA and the genes does not contain the life of the organism which develops by* using *this information*." (p. 6, emphasis added) And astrophysicist Freeman Dyson, reflecting the same line of thought, believes that human consciousness has not risen accidentally, with complexity based solely on DNA, as some suggest. In *Disturbing the Universe* (1979), he writes: "I think our consciousness is not just a passive epiphenomenon carried along by the chemical events in our brains, but is an active agent forcing the molecular complexes to make choices between one quantum state and another. In other words, mind is already inherent in the electron." (p. 249)

Embryologist and geneticist C. H. Waddington (1905–1975) thought that developmental processes involved an element of wholeness that represents the expression of the global, epigenetic landscape (landscape affecting development) and are not, therefore, totally determined by DNA. F. David Peat writes: "It appears that Waddington was moving toward a notion of development in which living matter in some way responds to a field of information which exerts a formative power over the processes of a cell." (1987, p. 162).

There is convincing evidence, now available, which comes directly from the new story of the evolutionary universe. It is that *great order appeared very early in the universe, in stars and galaxies for example, before there was any life, much less complex beings with DNA to determine order.* It seems clear that a spiral galaxy, which orders perhaps 100 million stars, cannot have achieved its structure by random processes.

Rupert Sheldrake, English biochemist and speculative thinker, has proposed the controversial idea of morphic resonance as a way of attempting to address gaps in our understanding of the processes of form-generation left by mechanistic perspectives.[2] He also says DNA alone cannot explain the development of complex biological organisms, and that patterns of morphogenesis (the formation and differentiation of tissues and organs) in living organisms are not detected by the reductionist methodology of most scientific investigation. In fact, it is likely that such morpho-genetic principles, if they exist, risk being overlooked in current research. (Davies 1988, p. 199) It is only with new approaches to research, which Sheldrake is attempting, and new ways of looking at complexity in biology that these organizational principles are likely to be discovered.

This search for fundamental formative powers does not negate the central role of DNA, which carries a memory of the achieved complexity of a particular species and thus makes it possible for complex organisms to be reproduced. However, DNA acts within a vast complex of morphogenetic forces that scientists are now studying and which have long been proposed by many philosophers and theologians. (See chapters 12 and 13.)

Do the Known Laws of Physics Explain the Origins of Form?

Perhaps the known laws of physics can explain the complex-ity and self-organization involved in the generation of form, but as Paul Davies points out in *The Cosmic Blueprint*, attempts to do so have met with little success. David Bohm, too, understood that the shaping powers are not fully explained by local forces, and must entail an implicate order (chapter 3). The discovery of these organizing principles, which Davies suggests is imminent, will require ways of thinking about nature that depart radically from traditional science. (Davies 1988, pp. 139, 142) The inadequacy of the known laws of physics to explain form generation becomes particularly clear when we remember that living organisms are unique individuals. Davies quotes Italian geneticist Giuseppe Montalenti: "As soon as individuality appears, unique phenomena originate and the laws of physics become inadequate to explain all the phenomena. Certainly they are still valid for a certain number of biological facts, and they are extremely useful in explaining a certain number of basic phenomena; but they cannot explain everything." (1988, p.147) In dealing with individuality the normal, statistical methods of physics are not adequate.

Unexplored Shaping Powers
of the Implicate Orders and the *Plenum*

Returning again to the work of quantum physicist David Bohm, recall his conception of a fundamental implicate order. Bohm believed that forms, like the fountain in the Italian square, flow out of an order enfolded (implicate) throughout the manifest world. Specifically, he suggested that this *implicate order can account for the origin of forms*, which are then replicated. According to Bohm, formative, or morphic, fields are very subtle aspects of the implicate order that impress themselves on lesser, explicate energies. (Bohm and Weber, 1982, pp. 36, 39, emphasis added) Some of the lesser energies are known. Physicists, for example, study the order governing the electromagnetic, progonic, and electronic fields.[3] However, knowledge of these fields is not to be regarded as having final validity, since larger, more comprehensive domains may be discerned. This insufficiency, now generally acknowledged, contrasts sharply with earlier scientific thought in the West, which, until the mid-twentieth century, was held captive by the conviction that the mechanical laws describing the relations and movement of separated objects that are manifest to the senses and reasoning mind can fully define the nature of things.

Bohm wrote that the true meaning of forms is known by realizing that they are generated and sustained from the *plenum* (1983, p. 192), the immense "sea" of "no-thing-ness" that is the ground of existence of everything. He believes it will never be fully known. "Particles," as well as complex beings constituted from them, are small modifications of the vacuum. "Matter" as we know it with our senses and by our measurements is, in fact, a form of the evolving self-manifestation of *plenum*. (See chapters 3 and 9.) Thus, self-organizing centers of activity, like a tree, a cell, a person, are not fully described as independent separate beings governed by mechanical laws in three-dimensional space, because the unseen organizing of the *plenum* is enfolded within them. In some manner not fully discerned, local laws and random events are caught up in the larger form patterning of the implicate orders and *plenum*.

Another prominent quantum physicist came to conclusions similar to Bohm's. According to F. David Peat, when Werner Heisenberg was trying to make sense of the plethora of elementary particles generated in collision experiments, he suggested that the truly fundamental is not the little wave/particle, as physicists had expected, but abstract symmetries and ordering principles that give form to the wave/particles as they are generated from the vacuum.[4] Peat explains: "The elementary particles themselves would be simply the material realization of these underlying symmetries." (1987, p. 94) The symmetries are not part of ordinary space, time. "These symmetries and ordering principles can be understood as the archetypes of all matter and the ground of material existence." (p. 94) Heisenberg said that separate objects are "shape, nothing but pure shape." This idea of underlying symmetries is related to Bohm's placement of the origin of form in the implicate order and *plenum*. It is related to the classic idea of eternal ideas in the mind of God.[*] Heisenberg is a major figure in the conceptual shift in physics from exclusive emphasis on the part (the atom or particle) to recognition of the whole, as indicated by the title of his scientific autobiography: *Der Teil und das Ganze (The Part and the Whole)*.

It is not only in the discipline of physics that the need to search for unidentified formative powers is now recognized. Thus Paul Davies cites Cambridge zoologist W. H. Thorpe, who saw as early as 1974 that the appearance of new properties at each level of complexity "requires research which is as fundamental as, or perhaps *even more fundamental* than, anything undertaken by the elementary particle physicists." (Davies 1988, p. 145, emphasis added) The suggestion that the research would involve something *even more fundamental* points in the direction of unknown formative powers.

Brian Swimme and Thomas Berry do not see genetic mutation as a random, mechanical, chemical process alone. They describe it as a primal act. It occurs as part of the activity of a universe characterized by ordering movement. It is part of the spontaneous differentiation taking place at life's root. (Swimme and Berry, p. 125) Thus, it is an integral part of the organizing dynamism that arises out of the larger form-generating capacity of the whole. Similarly, Stuart Kauffman suggests that the spontaneous order of biological systems provides the material on which natural selection may act.

We are propelled by these ideas into a stunningly different world, where the energy of the cosmos is continuously inwardly articulated and ordered by the *plenum*.[5] F. David Peat suggests that there are no laws of nature in a juridical sense— imposed from outside; there are only intrinsic, formative, and ordering principles. (1987, p. 87) What if, Peat asks, the laws of nature "are realization, within the world of mind, of something that is creative, generative, and formative, of something that lies beyond mathematics, language and thought?" (p. 88) "Meaningful patterns of the world, which transcend all our attempts to limit

[*] Ewert Cousins: personal communication, 1996.

and encompass them, arise not so much through the mechanisms of external orders but through the unfolding of their own internal significance." (p. 115)

Objective Intelligence and Creative Ordering

F. David Peat proposes the terms "objective intelligence" or "creative ordering" for the generative ordering power in the as yet unexplored realm that brings about the dynamic ordering of matter and mind. (1987, p. 88) These phrases are useful because they avoid the word "mind," which in English is associated almost exclusively with the brain and its activities.

David Bohm, too, was convinced that the ground of all being is permeated with a supreme intelligence that is creative and gives order. He finds the evidence for this in "the tremendous order in the universe, in ourselves and the brain." (As quoted in McInnis, p. 7) Einstein believed we only glimpse the order that lies hidden in nature.

If the world's finest minds can unravel the deeper workings of nature only with difficulty, how could it be supposed that those workings are merely a mindless accident, a product of blind chance? (Davies 1984, pp. 235–236) F. David Peat writes that the laws of nature, written as mathematical formulas and descriptions by mathematicians and physicists, are the realization, within the human mind, of actual laws and patterns that are part of the dynamic universe. They are mathematical manifestations "of something that is creative, generative and formative, of something that lies beyond the mathematics, language and thought. This generative power cannot lie within the mental and material worlds alone, but rather has its place in some, as yet unexplored, ground that lies beyond the distinction of either." (1987, p. 88)

Paul Davies suggests that if nature is so "clever" that it can exploit mechanisms that amaze us with their ingenuity, then we should consider this persuasive evidence for the existence of intelligent design "behind" the physical universe. Furthermore, "the laws which enable the universe to come into being spontaneously seem themselves to be the product of exceedingly ingenious design. If physics is the product of design, the universe must have a purpose and the evidence of modern physics suggest strongly that the purpose includes us." (Davies 1984, p. 243) In the conclusion of *The Cosmic Blueprint*, he puts it this way:

> The very fact that the universe *is* creative, and that the laws have permitted complex structures to emerge and develop to the point of consciousness—in other words, that the universe has organized its own self-awareness—is for me powerful evidence that there is "something going on" behind it all. The impression of design is overwhelming. (1988, p. 203)

Davies also believes science is in principle able to explain the existence of complexity and organization at all levels, including human consciousness, though only by embracing the higher-level laws. Yet he says that even though science may explain all the processes whereby the universe evolves its own destiny, there is still room for a meaning behind existence. (1988, p. 203)

A further indication of creative ordering is found in the unwavering urge to differentiation, subjectivity, and communion in the universe identified by Thomas Berry, following Teilhard de Chardin.[6] Berry observes that the journey of primordial matter through its marvelous sequence of transformations over billions of years is toward an ever more complete "spiritual-physical intercommunion" of the parts with each other, with the whole, and with that numinous presence which has ever been manifested throughout this entire cosmic-earth-human process. ("Spirituality of the Earth," p.16)[7]

The phrase "objective intelligence" signifies the fundamental ordering process present throughout the universe. This realm of objective intelligence is certainly very closely related to Plato's teaching that there are ideal forms in which the forms of the daily world participate and to Plotinus's conception of the *nous,* itself a formative realm. It is startling and heartening to realize how similar their thought is to that of contemporary people like Bohm, as well as others just cited, who also appeal to a hidden, immeasurable form-generating dimension, a dimension not manifest to the senses but constitutive of forms. However significant changes must be made in the Platonic concepts, in the context of an evolutionary universe. Now that we recognize that the world is of great age and that it started from undifferentiated beginnings, any conception of preexistent Platonic ideal forms is precluded. In an evolutionary world we cannot think of the form of a tree waiting billions of years for trees to develop on the Earth. Instead of pre-existent forms, in the evolutionary context it seems necessary to imagine a complexification of the formative realms. It is suggested that we can think of an unfolding of possibility within the generative order. (Bohm and Peat, p. 160)

David Bohm proposes that form develops through a process of projection and injection, reprojection, reinjection, and so on: a "loop of active information." (Peat 1987, p. 194) By the repetition of this process, there is a fairly constant build-up of components. Thus the formative powers are more differentiated in consort with the gradual emergence of complex forms as the universe unfolds.

Along these same lines, Brian Swimme proposes a kind of memory of what is happening in the manifest that feeds back into the formative realm, with the All-Nourishing Abyss "becoming 'more differentiated' in the sense that the activities of the moment, when they dissolve, become 'memories' in the Abyss, and on the basis of the memories the complexities of the next moment are reformed and even improved upon." Such a feedback process would necessarily involve the ongoing, immediate relationship between the formative powers and the manifest, but Swimme indicates there are "nontemporal or eternal aspects too, such as the unchanging urge to differentiation, subjectivity and communion."*

This issue of objective intelligence is fraught with controversy because it can be construed as covert "creationism," and linked with those who oppose the teaching of evolution in schools. The religious conservatives have an important point when they oppose presenting the subject in a manner that suggests it has been

* Personal communication, 1996.

proved to be entirely determined by random, mechanistic events, but they are wrong to oppose the teaching of evolution itself: its occurrence, on Earth and in the Universe, is by now indisputable. Not so its processes, however. In this, there is need for a nuanced approach, with evidence of creative ordering presented as intrinsic both to what we call matter and to the unfolding story, which includes randomness and natural selection.

The Person within the "Emptiness," and Objective Intelligence

Physicists tell us that if we could see the human body in the perspective of particle physics, it would be proportionally as empty as intergalactic space. If all the space were taken out of a human being, she would be a million times smaller than the smallest grain of sand. A person, a tree, a butterfly, in fact all the Earth is more Fecund Emptiness than created particles. (Swimme 1984, pp. 37–38) Since a person is largely Emptiness, and the formative powers, according to Bohm, Heisenberg, Thorpe, and others, are in the realm of Emptiness, it is not difficult to imagine that a person is held in the embrace of those powers and they are part of us—that the formative powers of the implicate order and the *plenum* are integral to or constitutive of the person—that we share in the "objective intelligence."

Along with the recognition that a person is largely Emptiness, it is important to remember, as has been described earlier (chapter 9), that it is not possible to isolate wave/particles from this highly generative Emptiness, out of which they emerge into being. Thus wave/particles and atoms will be ordered within the particular formative activity in the generative Emptiness that is being expressed in the explicate world. Wave/particles remain immanent to the "higher dimensional" reality (the generative Emptiness) and become part of complex organized domains within self-organizing systems. Some complex structures have become autopoietic (self-making, as described in chapter 10). Whatever the degree of complexity, the form-generating capacity is never absent from the explicate world, although it is not visible to the senses. This means that *every form, including the human individual, is held in the embrace of the whole and is subject to its formative powers.*

These are most central insights that connect the person to the heart of the creative universe. We can realize that the formative powers are constitutive of or enfolded within all forms, including the person. And, most important for our purposes, because soul is a formative power, as we shall see in chapter 12, we can connect contemporary ideas about form-generation, developed in relation to the discovery of the evolutionary universe, with traditional insights into the World Soul and the individual soul.

Exploring These Insights

Before turning to the subject of soul, it will be valuable to explore some further issues, which if ignored may impede our embrace of these ideas. One is to ask how the self of self-organizing (i.e., that which organizes) can do the organizing and still be constitutive of that which is organized. This is confusing because it seems to be common sense that things that are to become part of an organized, living being, like sugar in the sugar bowl or the carbon and iron that can sit inert in a jar on the shelf of a chemistry laboratory, are separate entities that would have to be organized by something outside themselves to become part of a living being. Our assumptions in this regard will determine whether we take the formative, soul-like dimension of the person seriously and likewise, assuming we do so, whether it is seen as a dimension intrinsic to the person as part of the Earth or imposed on the physical world from the outside. They will also determine whether we assume soul is given only to people or whether this dimension in found throughout the natural world.

We know, of course, that atoms and molecules regularly enter and leave organisms. The carbon atoms that are at one time part of a plant may be at other times outside the dynamic organizing activity of the plant, as when they are the carbon atoms in atmospheric carbon dioxide. When the conditions are right the carbon atom in the carbon dioxide can again become fully integrated into a living plant. A part/whole (a holon), the carbon atom, can become part of a larger whole (the more complex organized cells and systems of the plant). This is the nesting of part/wholes into larger part/wholes. In some manner the inner ordering of the carbon, iron, and iodine atoms (or the implicate order that is enfolded in them) can be engaged (nested) in the form-generating processes of a living plant or animal. The whole is enfolded within each element so that every aspect of the system is at one and the same time local and global.

David Bohm wrestled with the question of the relation of seemingly inert chemical elements to living beings. He considers a seed that organizes carbon and oxygen, other elements, and energy within itself as it grows. Is it possible, he asks, to make a sharp distinction between what is alive and what is not? Does a molecule of carbon dioxide that crosses a cell boundary into a leaf suddenly "come alive"? Does a molecule of oxygen suddenly "die" when it is released to the atmosphere? "Rather, life itself has to be regarded as belonging in some sense to a totality, including plant and environment." (Bohm 1983, p. 194) Bohm suggests that a tree is built out of the implicate order—"indeed it is the implicate order which makes possible its living qualities. If we perceive the tree in this way, rather than as a bunch of dead particles into which the property of life is somehow infused when the seed is planted, then its aliveness ceases to be such a mystery." (Bohm and Weber 1981, p. 26) The so-called dead molecules are already enfolded in the implicate order, as is the living being they are about to enter. There is a common participation in comprehensive formative dynamics, allowing the molecules to nest into the more complexified local order of the plant.

In the comprehensive order that makes such nesting possible, there is a hierarchical dimension. It is not a hierarchy that imposes order from the outside, but the type recognized by modern psychology and by evolutionary and systems theory, as simply a ranking of events *according to their holistic capacity*. (Wilber 1995, p. 17) Most important, this meaning of hierarchy, unlike that imaged by a patriarchal King or Lord, does not allow us to separate the comprehensive, unifying realm from the unfolding, complex, differentiated world which it orders and integrates. The comprehensive, unifying realm may be distinguished, but the whole may not be pulled apart.

This is an important clarification. The organizing activity is not that which is organized (it's an organizing power), yet this power, this unseen shaping dynamism, is constitutive of that which is organized. The carbon and iodine atoms have within them and around them (after all they are not little bits of particulate finite matter but wave/particles, and they are largely the "nothingness" or "emptiness" that includes the formative powers) the capacity to participate (be nested) in the living being, the larger whole in which they may become a part. In the pages that follow we will look into why it is valuable to distinguish this self-organizing realm, while at the same time we avoid imagining the realm as separate from the organizing, living being.

Formative Powers in Relation to Ongoing Physical Laws

It is difficult to conceive how underlying formative powers could function and not violate the physical laws and physical constants. But it is important to be able to imagine that there is holistic, comprehensive ordering that does not circumvent the physical laws and constants that the astronauts relied upon in their flight to the moon or that we likewise depend upon when we drive the car to the grocery store. If we do not, our identity is diminished, because people try to explain all of human personhood using only the predictable physical and chemical laws. Indeed, we are assaulted by a barrage of ideas from the culture that deny any notion of inner formative ordering or a soul-like dimension of the person. For example, in the video series, "The Glorious Accident" (Kayzer et al.), broadcast on PBS stations, Daniel Dennett, Director of the Center for Cognitive Studies and Arts and Sciences professor at Tufts University, asserts that the self is a rationalization, that "narrative forms our consciousness." A narrative is constructed by the individual to render coherent a set of events. Dennett teaches that there is nobody home other than the sum of processes, memories, and activities, which are constructed into a narrative that serves to provide an identity. It is a position based on the assumption that "an impersonal, unreflective, robotic, mindless little scrap of molecular machinery (macromolecules that have enough complexity to 'do things') is the ultimate basis of all agency and hence meaning and hence consciousness, in the universe." (Dennett, p. 203) Such a conception severely challenges traditional ideas about human identity, including ideas about soul, human worth, and the significance of the experiences we have discussed.

So how *do* we imagine how organizing principles might act in a wholistic fashion and at the same time not contradict the laws of physics as they apply to the constituent components of a complex system? Many writers have offered this analogy: The wholistic principles are like the "software laws" of a computer, which co-exist perfectly well with the "hardware laws" that control the computer's circuitry. Furthermore, the software laws are fundamental in that "they cannot logically be derived from the underlying 'hardware laws' that are the traditional subject of fundamental physics. . . ." (Davies 1988, p. 144)

David Bohm offers another analogy: the radio receiver. "You have a radio wave, sent out from a radio station, that has a form (e.g. music) and this form is carried by a very weak electromagnetic wave that is picked up by the antennae of a particular radio set. Now, when the music comes out of the radio set, almost all of its energy comes from the power plug in the wall socket, but its form comes from the very weak electromagnetic wave picked up by the antennae. In this situation, a very subtle energy (the weak electromagnetic radio wave picked up by the antennae) molds a denser energy (coming from the wall socket)." (Bohm and Weber 1982, p. 39) The organizing principles, Paul Davies says, could harness the existing interparticle forces, rather than supplement them, and in so doing alter their collective behavior in a holistic fashion.[8] (Davies 1988, pp. 143–44)

Don't we, as self-organizing beings who have decided to go for a walk, harness a myriad of "hardware laws" as we stroll through the woods? In a growing seed almost all the matter and the energy come from the environment, so the living seed is continually providing that matter and energy with new information that leads to the production of the living plant. (Bohm and Weber 1981, p. 25) Jungian analyst Edward Whitmont, who is concerned with psychosomatics, homeopathy, alchemy, and psychology, has written: "The dynamism of life does not rest on mere chemistry. It enlists and subordinates and at times even reverses chemistry to serve its own purposes." (p. 28) He offers a telling example. When the ear of a live rabbit is exposed to stomach juices, it will not decompose. But when the animal is dead or when the ear is detached from the body, the digestive effect will occur, and the chemical influences will initiate decomposition. In this example and that of the seed, the self-organizing powers of the living plant or animal are "subordinating" chemistry to serve the organism's own purposes."

F. David Peat is asserting that local order may follow from a global order when he writes that "hidden symmetry will therefore exert a formative influence on how each element behaves and unfolds." (1987, p. 92) Since this formative influence affects both matter and consciousness, it can be the source of intuitive insight and intellectual visions. (See chapter 19.) This is a topic key to our integration, for such insights are part of the contemplative journey, and we will return several times to it. But for now it is enough to note that the recognition of a "creative ordering" in the depth of things, in subtle levels of process "below" even the quantum field, as Bohm suggests (Peat 1987, p. 194), is a reversal of the point of view of much of recent science, in which global order is regarded as purely the outcome of local order. The assumption in my biology classes in college was that chemistry and physics would eventually explain all of biology.

A Practical Application of this 'Way of Seeing'

These reflections about how parts, like atoms and molecules, come to participate in larger wholes can profoundly affect attitudes toward the non-living world. For example, there is a group called the Friends of the Ganges that is working to clean up the River Ganges in India; it grounds its activities in ideas that are closely related to Bohm's insights that life belongs in some sense to a totality. While modern Western people generally think of water as a non-living substance whose molecules are composed of two atoms of hydrogen and one of oxygen, this group seeks to honor the tradition of the holy river to which millions of Hindus make a pilgrimage. Fran Peavy, an American collaborating with the group, describes an alternative way of looking at water, closely related to the tradition of the river as holy, which is to propose that the water is living. Life cannot exist without water, so, she asks, how can water not be alive? "If you put dead water into your body, how can you see through your eyes?" We are not designed to breathe life into water inside us. "If we [thought] of water as part of life, we wouldn't ask it to carry such a burden. It's really the workhorse of our lives. If it's a sacred, holy part of all life, then we really must care for it." (Peavy, pp. 10–12)

A Cosmologically Significant Life

The significance of these reflections on form generation and objective intelligence is that they contradict Dennett's contention that human identity is simply a rationalization formed by a narrative. We do, of course, recognize that many of the complexities of our consciousness, including apparently self-aware consciousness, are emergent properties that arose with the development of the neocortex and do depend on vast numbers of neurons and their interconnections. But to call human beings an accident and to claim that our identity rests only on a constructed narrative assumes that the person is unrelated to more comprehensive orders. The existence of such order as part of human intelligence is suggested not least by the fact that scientists can intuit laws of nature that are later proved to be accurate.

While visiting the American Southwest, Carl Jung had a conversation with Mountain Lake, a member of the Taos Pueblo, who were endeavoring to continue teaching their way of life to their youth. "The Americans want to stamp out our religion.

Why can they not leave us alone? What we do, we do not only for ourselves but for the Americans also. Yes, we do it for the whole world. Everyone benefits by it." In his autobiography, Jung wrote:

> I could observe from his excitement that he was alluding to some extremely important element of his religion. I therefore asked him: "You think, then, that what you do in your religion benefits the whole world?" He replied with great animation, "Of course. If we did not do it, what would become of the world?" and with a significant gesture he pointed to the sun.
>
> I felt that we were approaching extremely delicate ground here, verging on the mysteries of the tribe. "After all," he said, "we are a people who live on the roof of the world; we are the sons of Father Sun, and with our religion we daily help our father to go across the sky. We do this not only for ourselves, but for the whole world. If we were to cease practicing our religion, in ten years the sun would no longer rise. Then it would be night forever.
>
> I then realized on what the "dignity," the tranquil composure of the individual Indian, was founded. It springs from his being a son of the sun; his life is cosmologically meaningful, for he helps the father and preserver of all life in his daily rise and descent. (1965, p. 252)

Although the "inaccuracy" of the Taos Pueblo belief is clear, it supposes a knowledge of direct participation in the cosmos that is remarkable. It brought the Taos Pueblo into a cosmologically meaningful life, one many contemporary people may well envy, as did Jung. The new universe story and insight into the form-generating powers that are immanent in all matter provide a 'way of seeing' that gives us cosmological meaning. The person is placed within a comprehensive, ordering context. Form generation is a creative quality of the universe that cannot be explained in itself. (Swimme and Berry, p. 88) As a form of the universe, the person partakes in the intrinsic, creative quality of the universe. Thus, there is a place for the person at its dynamic heart.

---

[1] "Thus the genome's capacity [the capacity of all the genetic information] to generate a form must depend on very many physicochemical processes constituting a panoply of developmental mechanisms beyond the sheer capacity of the genome to coordinate the synthesis of specific RNA and protein molecules in time and space. Morphology is a marriage of underlying laws of form and the agency of selection." (Kauffman 1993, p. xvii)

[2] The idea of morphic resonance is "that once a new type of form has come into existence, it sets up its own morphogenetic field which then encourages the appearance of the same form elsewhere. Thus, once nature has 'learned' how to grow a particular organism, it can guide, by 'resonance,' the development of other organisms along the same pathway." The fields that Sheldrake has in mind do not act in space and time in the usual causative fashion. (Davies 1988, p. 164)

[3] These fields obey quantum-mechanical laws, implying the properties of discontinuity and non-locality, which themselves may be only abstractions from still more general laws, only some of whose outlines are now vaguely to be seen. (Bohm 1983, p. 178) These more general laws, the holonomy (the overall law), are more fundamental than the relationships between the abstracted and separate forms that are manifest to the senses (and to our instruments). (p. 185)

[4] These symmetries do not exist in individual objects themselves but in the way the elementary particles can be grouped together and mathematically transformed one into another. (Peat 1987, p. 95) The abstract operations by which the particles are related occur in various mathematically defined spaces. (p. 96)

[5] Another perspective on this same idea comes from Eastern thought according to which motion and change are the essential properties of things. The forces causing the motion are not outside the objects, as in the classical Greek view, but are an intrinsic property of matter. So the eastern image of the Divine is not a ruler who directs the world from above, but of a principle that controls everything from within. (Capra 1975, p. 10)

In the history of Christianity, one of the classic, highly controversial debates was over whether nature should be thought of as *natura naturans* (naturing nature) or *natura naturata* (natured nature). I studied this debate in seminary some years ago, not appreciating its significance, but recent attention to the new story of the evolutionary universe and the all important topic of form-generation as constitutive of the manifest world, has helped me to recognize what was at stake. In the theology of the Middle Ages the phrase *natura naturans* (naturing nature) referred to the unseen productive power in nature that gives rise to phenomena. This was in the tradition developed from Aristotle that attributed the power of organizing the autonomous development and behavior of organisms to the vegetative soul. (Sheldrake 1991, p. 88) But, according to Sheldrake, "When the founders of mechanistic science expelled souls from nature, leaving only passive matter in motion, they placed all active powers in God." (p. 80) Nature became merely *natura naturata* (natured nature), the phenomena we observe with our senses without recognizing their inner creativity. The active power intrinsic to nature has been removed. This shift, part of the destructive Cartesian dualism, is only now slowly being addressed. These considerations of the morphogenetic (shape-making) powers help in that process, to the end that we may overcome the dualism in which all the active powers are placed in God, often conceived as a power outside matter, with the result that matter and the Earth are left as a dead objects for our manipulation and commercialization.

[6] Berry writes: "The three basic laws of the universe at all levels of reality are differentiation, subjectivity and communion. These laws identify the reality, the values, and the directions in which the universe is proceeding." (1987, p. 107)

[7] "Spirituality of the Earth" is one of the Riverdale Papers, a collection of unpublished papers written by Thomas Berry during his residence at the Riverdale Center for Religious Research in Riverdale, N.Y. Xeroxed copies of various of these papers, often in loose-leaf binders, are available at some libraries. (See also the bibliography.)

[8] Ideas like this have sometimes been subject to charges of vitalism, meaning that some vital principle is added to the laws of chemistry and physics. But it is possible to be anti-reductionist without being a vitalist. Paul Davies quotes Arthur Peacocke, an English physical biochemist and an Anglican priest, who makes a clear distinction between, on the one hand, espousing vitalism and, on the other, denying the reducibility of nature to the bottom level laws of physics. "It is possible for higher level concepts and theories . . . to be non-reducible to lower level concepts and theories, that is they can be autonomous. At the same time one has to recognize the applicability of the lower level concepts and theories (for example, those of physics and chemistry) to the component units of more complex entities and their validity when referred to that lower level. That is, with reference to biology, it is possible to be anti-reductionist without being a vitalist." (Quoted in Davies 1988, p. 147)

12

SOUL UNFOLDS
IN AN EVOLVING UNIVERSE

What is the work of human works if not to establish, in and by means of each one of us, an absolutely original center in which the universe reflects itself in a unique and inimitable way?

— Pierre Teilhard de Chardin

THERE HAVE been two main traditions regarding the meaning of soul in Western thought. It is important to understand them in order to be enriched by them and also to be able to see where there is continuity or discontinuity between those traditions and recent discoveries about self-organizing processes. Aspects of one based in the Platonic tradition have already been touched on in the discussion about the meaning of contemplation in the mystical philosophy of Plotinus. Recall that for Plotinus, the form-generating dimension of the universe is identified with the divine Intellect. The world soul and the individual soul are emanations from that divine realm, the *Nous*, so that soul is an intermediary between the *Nous* and the world of senses. As an emanation from the *Nous*, it reflects its order and can know that order through intellectual insights.

This is a beautiful tradition because it assumes the possibility of contemplation, the return to the fullness of our being. However, it can so emphasize the person's relationship to the divine realm that it runs the risk of neglecting the body and of thus cleaving the unity of human nature. It has sometimes encouraged a complete detachment from the material world. It has also protected the self-sufficiency of the spiritual world, a position which seems untenable in a universe that has been evolving over 13 billion years.

The second tradition is less concerned with the essence of soul and the possibility of its immortality and more concerned with soul's relationship with the matter it enlivens. According to Aristotle, the soul is the form of the body; it is "that by which we live, feel and especially think." (Quoted in Bouyer 1965, p. 418) In this tradition, the soul could not be thought of without the body to which it gives life (p. 424), and like the body it is mortal. Aristotle spoke of the soul of plants as governing the form of plants as they grow. The Stoics, who belonged to this tradition, held that the soul of the world cannot be differentiated from the world itself, and that the individual soul is but a part of the world soul. The Aristotelian tradition runs the risk of ensnaring the notion of soul within the confines of its earthly existence. (p. 418) It would not recognize contemplation as described by Plotinus.

Both these traditions significantly influenced Christianity. Thomas Aquinas adopted the formula "the soul is the form of the body" from Aristotelian thought and the Judeo-Christian tradition, and thus escapes the danger of a dualism of soul and body. He does name and identify soul, not ignoring this dimension of the person, and thus avoids falling into a naturalism that would have no relation to the immanent divine. (Bouyer 1965, pp. 423–24) Soul is interpreted as the one form-giving life principle of the whole human person, an identification that is congruent with our discussion of self-organizing processes.

The Old Testament holds strongly to the concept of the whole person. It does not have a theory about the nature of soul. The word *néphesh* is used to designate individual people and animals in their total essence. (Gen. 1:20; Ex. 1:5) This is made clear in Genesis 2:7, where the divine breath is blown into the body, and so creates "a living *néphesh*" that is, a person. Thus in Hebrew a person is not a "body" and a "soul," but rather a "body-soul," a unit of vital power. After death, the *néphesh* ceases to exist. The belief in the resurrection in the New Testament necessitated development of thought on the topic of soul, since it seems to imply some form of ongoing personal existence. Here there are views of the soul as a spiritual entity, which continues to exist after death. Saint Paul introduces terms from Greek philosophy into his letters and develops a distinction between the body on the one hand and the intellectual and spiritual character of the soul on the other. Out of its faith and out of disparate metaphysical ideas about the soul, the Christian tradition has sought slowly, over the centuries, to develop a coherent doctrine.

A Contemporary Conception of Soul

In the contemporary discussion about self-organizing processes, the self (of self-organizing) has been identified as an unseen, shaping dynamism that is constitutive of living beings. It is this formative dynamism, personalized in the life of a particular human being (as we shall see in chapter 16), that can be identified as soul. Rupert Sheldrake makes an interesting observation that supports this idea when he observes that although soul has been discarded in contemporary scientific thought, at the same time science has progressively extended the field concept (related to organizing dynamics) to all the natural phenomena that used to be explained in terms of souls. (Sheldrake 1991, p. 86) *Soul in the context of the new universe story refers then to the unseen self-organizing, shaping dynamism of the person.* Jungian analyst Michael Comforti takes the position that Jung's theory of the archetype is the psychological parallel of the scientific theory of self-organizing dynamics in nature. (Comforti 1999, p. xiii) As will be discussed, Jung's archetype of the Self is the near equivalent of soul. Like the self-organizing processes, soul is constitutive of our person. We have previously seen that the formative powers arise in the hidden *plenum*; thus we can recognize that soul as a formative power has its origin in the *plenum*, which we also call fecund Emptiness or Abyss/God. Since soul arises in the more comprehensive formative orders of the Emptiness pervading the person, it plays a mediating role between that creative realm and both the body and daily consciousness. Thus, the creative power of the person arises out of this inseparable, enfolded ground in which the formative soul-powers take shape.

This understanding of soul does not pull the person's loyalties out of the Earth to a transcendent "home," where it has been believed the soul has its origin. Also it is important to recognize this soul-like organizing dynamism is not a specific gift given only to people, but is integral to all beings—animals, plants and other creatures. The soul-like organizing dynamism particular to other beings would be expressed in a manner unique to those beings.

Does Soul Refer Only to the Formative Powers?

By identifying soul as the unseen shaping powers of the person, are we not in grave danger of separating it out as a distinct entity, and thus reestablishing the dualism? Shouldn't we hold to the unity of the person as in the Hebrew conception, and as implied in the new story? Can we separate body from soul? If the organizing powers are folded within the manifest world, shouldn't the word *soul* also designate the whole person? The answer is that we seek to hold to the unity of the person and *at the same* time name and identify the self-organizing, integrating dimension of the person. We resolve the matter in the same way that Carl Jung resolved it with regard to the Self, which is nearly equivalent to the traditional meaning of soul. He conceived of the Self as both the centering, organizing power and also, *at the same time*, the totality of the person it integrates (including the body, emotions, cognitive events, and sensations). This is not a slight of hand trick or an easy compromise to escape a difficult problem. It is a way of distinguishing and naming a dimension of the person (the formative, centering soul processes), yet at the same time recognizing that these processes are constitutive of the whole person and that they are not to be separated from the whole person. The unity of the person is maintained, yet the organizing, integrating soul-powers are identified. *The identification of the formative soul allows us to honor and pay attention to the integrating, centering powers active in us. And it enables us to imagine the connection between consciousness and the creative, generative plenum while at the same time immersing the person in the Earth and the body. The door to contemplation is opened.*

This inclusion of the body as part of the meaning of soul is congruent with what we have previously said about the Old Testament tradition. American essayist Wendell Berry has interpreted the biblical passage in Genesis 2:7— "then the Lord God formed man of dust from the ground, and breathed into his nostrils the breath of life; and man became a living being"— in a manner that presents Hebrew conceptions as not foreign to Jungian conceptions of the Self. He writes that this text has often been misinterpreted so as to support the Western denial of the central place of matter and body in the sacred. In this dualistic interpretation, the formula for man-making is: Man = body + soul. The body is made sacred by embodying soul. However, according to the Biblical verse, God did not make a body and put a soul into it to make it live. The text, Berry points out, specifically says that soul, which refers in Hebrew thought to a whole creature, a living being, is formed of dust and breath, that is, soul = dust + breath. The dust, formed as man and made to live, did not embody a soul; it became soul. (W. Berry 1993, p. 157) At the risk of making too facile an equivalence, one can say that this is quite similar to the ideas just discussed here—that the whole person = that which is organized (dust) + organizing power (breath). The soul/person is a single mystery, which includes the self-organizing, integrating power.

This resolution preserves the insight of the Aristotelian tradition that the soul (the self of self-organizing) is the form of the body and that soul is not known apart from the manifest being: the body and the consciousness of the individual. It also incorporates a Platonic element, because it identifies the formative dynamism arising in the *plenum*—just as the *nous* emanates from the One. Through this origin, the soul is not confined to the limits of the individual physical body, as in Aquinas, who used Aristotle in his synthesis. The Platonic element avoids a dangerous fragmenting fallacy that defines soul as a distinct personal entity confined to the person and thus separated from the comprehensive formative powers in Abyss/God. It also avoids the fragmenting fallacy found in Western science, which has divorced living beings from the unseen self-organizing, formative dimension of the cosmos.

Birth, Death, and Soul

Part of the confusion with regard to understanding soul has come from the way we interpret our experience and observations about what happens to a person at death. We say the soul leaves the body at death because the person is no longer animated (from the Latin word for soul, *anima*). And if the soul leaves at death we easily assume it must have entered from outside the body at some moment. Then we may think of the body as a sort of host or receptacle for soul, or perhaps even a prison from which liberation is found through death or through spiritual advancement. But consideration of the formative dynamism of soul in the context of the evolutionary universe has shown that it is not appropriate to think in terms of adding formative powers to the infant human being, because the formative powers are integral to matter and become expressed in consort with the developing embryo. To think something must be added is a rejection of the fullness of our earthly identity, and represents a failure to comprehend the nature of form-generation in the evolutionary cosmos.

In the encyclical *Humani Generis,* issued in 1950, Pope Pius XII said that Catholics could accept whatever science determined about the evolution of the body, but that "Catholic Faith obliges us to hold that souls are immediately created by God." (par. 64) But in the contemporary context, soul is present as the organizing dynamism rooted in Abyss/God and functions integrally with the development of a new being. The assertion that soul is especially created by God, while not alien to what is being said here since the formative powers do arise in the Abyss/God, must be heard within the context of the evolutionary universe to avoid the suggestion that the formative powers have previously been absent from the Earth and to avoid distinguishing human beings from plants and other animals as the only expression of those powers. There is a dangerous devaluation of the natural order when human beings are singled out by virtue of the special gift, soul. It suggests that the whole unfolding process is deficient until that special gift is given. Thomas Berry writes: "Every being has its own divine, numinous subjectivity, its self, its center, its unique reality." ("Spirituality of the Earth," p. 15) The powerful new origin story makes such a special, divine act as the creation of the human soul, coming after 13 billion years of ongoing creativity, seem quite suspect.

The encyclical's statement apparently also endorses the bifurcation of body and soul. It is important to avoid saying soul is added to the physical body in a manner suggesting a dichotomy between soul and body that can no longer be affirmed. As previously noted, the formative, soul-like powers are constitutive of that which they organize, a proposition that conforms remarkably with Augustine's teaching that the soul is not born prior to the body (the error of Origen, who taught the preexistence of souls) nor begotten as is the body (the error of Tertullian, for whom the soul develops from the "seed" of its parents).[1] (Bouyer 1965, pp. 422–23)

Does the person entirely disappear when she dies, or is there an immortal dimension to the person? We have affirmed that people are integral to an ongoing whole, including the vast *plenum* with its formative realm. A person does not leave the whole when she dies and go somewhere else, although the local formative dynamics cease to operate. The more comprehensive, formative dimensions of our being, which are integral to the Abyss/God, would not die. We die into the sacred realm immanent in all the cosmos.

Structures of the Psyche in the Thought of Carl Jung

Carl Jung's work adds an important contemporary dimension to our conception of soul because his study of archetypes enables us to incorporate the evolved complexity of the psyche that developed in early reptiles and early mammals into our ideas of soul. Jung's concepts, along with those of Paul MacLean, author of *The Triune Brain in Evolution,* connect soul to the millions of years of vertebrate history on the Earth. So our embeddedness in the Earth involves a deep time dimension, during which the formative, archetypal patterns developed. Yet, as we will see below, in our discussion of the Self (comprised of many archetypes), Jung also incorporates a transpersonal dimension in his understanding of the Self, which we can assume refers to grounding of soul in what we call the *plenum* or Abyss/God.

Jung identified common psychological and behavioral patterns in the human being by observing recurring motifs and images in the basic content of religions, mythologies, legends, and fairy tales. He also observed recurring images in dream material which seem to indicate that the same psychological structure and psychic events occur in different people. Through these uniformities of psychic phenomena, Jung identified patterns that are rooted in something beyond the events and relationships in the individual's personal history. For example, he deduced that the profusion of dream symbolism referring to the mother could not be understood adequately in terms of personal history alone. The vast amount of material collected not only by Jung and those influenced by his work but through independent researches undertaken by people trained in different disciplines including ethnology,[2] mythology, and sociobiology is sufficient to establish beyond reasonable doubt the existence of archetypal processes, maternal care included, that must have an origin in the unconscious psyche. (Fordham 1957, p. 8) The mother archetype is seen as closely related to an instinct, and would refer to the structuring element in the human psyche and body that is the foundation for the great commonalities in maternal behavior, including the powerful experiences of bonding and nursing. Jung wrote: "Instincts form a very close analogy to the archetype, so close in fact that there is no reason for not assuming that the archetypes are the unconscious phantasy images of the instincts themselves." (Quoted in Fordham 1949, p. 4) An archetype (*arche*: ancient, and *typos*: pattern) is a given, *a priori*, innate psychic/physical pattern, whose powerful place in the human psyche arises from inherited patterns developed in human and prehuman history.

Jung called archetypes "the deposits of ancestral experience," which is a way of saying that the energy of the organism comes to be channeled according to complex patterns developed over evolutionary time.[3] Archetypes have also been described as like riverbeds along which environmental circumstances might induce libido to flow. (Stevens 1982, p. 143) These universal patterns form the basis of experiences that recur in all human beings, because they organize behavioral and psychic responses to the natural environment, to social groups, and to conditions of the psychophysical organism, like hunger. Archetypes determine the basic pathway of development over the entire life cycle, prescribing "the kind of experience we shall have although what we experience is always individual." (Neumann 1954, p. 349) Our conscious experience of the archetype is the uniquely personal manner in which the transpersonal (archetypal) pattern becomes a lived reality for the individual.[4] (See chapter 16.)

The Psychoid Level

There are two avenues for the study of archetypes, one followed by ethologists and sociobiologists (concerned with behavior) and the other by psychoanalysts (concerned with consciousness and the inner life). As Anthony Stevens, a psychotherapist and psychiatrist in London, explains, they are complementary ways to approach the same universally occurring patterns. (Stevens 1982, p. 22) Thus the mother archetype patterns both physical behavior, like nursing, and psychic events, like the strong mother/child emotional bond. Ethnologists may study fear and flight patterns in people while the analytic psychologist studies dreams of being pursued and trying to run.

After years of work, Jung thought it probable that psyche and matter are two aspects of one and the same thing. (CW vol. 8, par. 418) He sought ways to identify the common ground out of which archetypes are expressed in both behavioral/bodily patterns and psychic images and dreams, postulating that archetypes arise from a level where distinctions between psyche and matter can no longer be made by our minds. He called this the psychoid level. Erich Neumann observes that the "more primitive the psychic level, the more it is identical, or at least indistinguishable, from the bodily events which rule it." (1954, p. 287)

Jung's conception calls to mind the thinking of David Bohm: that matter and consciousness are not the same thing but are mutually enfolded or implicated in one another, and that the mind side and the matter side of things have a common origin in the implicate ground and unfold simultaneously. Bohm says that we do not have any knowledge of mind without matter, or matter disassociated from mind. (Bohm and Weber 1981, p. 25) Jung makes it clear that the psyche is rooted in the organic substrate of the person.

Michael Comforti identifies archetypes as form *in potentia*, a kind of structural coding. Archetypal fields, much like morphogenetic fields (the self-organizing powers discussed in chapter 10), contain the information necessary for sustaining and generating form. (Comforti, pp. 5, 8) They pattern both the psyche and the body. Although Jung's work focused on images in dreams and motifs in myths and legends, "archetypes . . . are *biological entities*. They are present, in related forms, throughout the animal kingdom." (Stevens 1982, p. 17, citing Jungian analyst Irene Champernowne). Modern physiology and psychiatry increasingly recognize that a human is a single psychosomatic whole.

In order to describe the psychoid nature of archetypes, Jung compared them to the light spectrum, where the infrared end of the spectrum represents the dimension of the archetype that is expressed in the body and the ultraviolet end that which is expressed in the psyche. The infrared end of the spectrum, he thought, is largely unknowable to the conscious mind. It is where the more primitive bodily dimension crosses over into the chemical and physical aspects of the body's functions. The ultraviolet end of the spectrum corresponds to the psychic dimension of the archetype, which is mediated by the unconscious to emerge in the conscious mind as images. But he did not limit intelligent behavior to the conscious mind. Jung gave up the idea of the psyche being somehow connected exclusively with the brain and wrote instead of the "meaningful" or "intelligent" behavior of lower organisms, which are without a brain. (CW vol. 8, par. 947) Such behaviors would be part of the ultraviolet end of the spectrum.

The image of the light spectrum makes it clear that Jung's insights into archetypes offer another path to imagining healing the dangerous split between body and mind. It is important to the integration being developed in this book. If we probe matter deeply enough, David Bohm tells us, we will find reflections of the same qualities that are revealed when mind is similarly probed. (Bohm and Weber 1981, p. 26) Analyst Marie-Louise von Franz wrote, "psyche appears as a quality of matter or matter as a concrete aspect of psyche . . . and a decision as to which is mirroring which is scarcely possible." (von Franz 1975, p. 247) William Blake seems to have had the same insight when he described the body as "that portion of the Soul discerned by the five senses." (pl. 4, p. xvi)

Jung assumed there was greater accessibility to the archetypes through dreams than through the body. However, Marion Woodman, a Jungian analyst in Toronto who works with anorexic and bulemic women, is specifically recognizing that the body also expresses archetypes when she requires her clients to pursue some kind of bodywork to facilitate awareness of archetypal patterns in the body. Also, through the use of devices like blood pressure machines, the reactions of the body to stressful situations activating, for example, a flight response, can now be monitored, making the "infrared" dimension accessible to our understanding in a way previously impossible. Now, the study of self-organizing systems in autopoietic, living systems is contributing to our appreciation of patterning in matter.

The Work of Paul MacLean

Paul MacLean's extensive study of the ancient parts of the triune human brain sheds light on the manner in which archetypal patterns developed in Earth history. (See chapter 2.) MacLean has not only identified the ancient parts of the brain anatomically, he has done research in certain reptiles to correlate behavior associated with master routines such as emergence from the den, basking, defacating, foraging and hunting with activity in these areas. (See chapter 2, note 18.) Behavioral patterns that developed in reptiles and early mammals are inherited and carried forward into the modern human, and although people are liberated to some degree from being bound to instinctual patterns of activity by further developments in the brain and in culture, they still play a powerful role. Elaine de Beauport, teacher and educational innovator, recognized many "reptilian" behaviors in her nursery school children. For example, humans have a marked propensity for cooperative behavior with allies and hostile behavior with foes. And we are prone, in a manner reminiscent of reptiles, to congregate in hierarchically organized communities. (Stevens 1982, p.7 and de Beauport, p. 31) The warrior traces his roots to territorial defense and aggression in reptiles and probably in even earlier land animals. De Beauport finds the portion of the brain called the R-complex (R for reptile) speaks to us through our physical body, our behavior, the environment in which we live, and in our dreams. Analytic psychologists are interested in the archetype of the trickster, a pattern one suspects is derived from reptiles, since, as MacLean has noted, deception is one of their basic behaviors. (MacLean, p. 16) Perhaps our propensity to bask in the sun, even to the point of danger of being burned, has the same origin.

New patterns of behavior formed in mammalian evolution, most notably the behaviors associated with nursing, maternal care, and familial life.[5] We can identify human inheritance of such patterns in the fact that human mothers and their infants do not need to learn to bond with each other. They are innately programmed to bond both before birth, and immediately at the birth and respond to each other with great affection and mutual need. And, of course, humans do not have to learn how to fall in love or how to mate and bear children. It is thought that the aversion to strangers in human infants is an evolutionary vestige of the flight response of lower mammals. (Stevens 1982, p. 102)

In other words, the human mind is not an unstructured and unprogrammed *tabula rasa*, owing little to heredity and practically everything to experience, as behaviorists have suggested. Biologist E. O. Wilson proposes, in his theories of "consilience," that altruism, status seeking, parental investment in offspring, territorial expansion and defense, contract formation and the taboo against incest are governed by epigenetic rules, that is, genetically based neural wiring that predisposes the brain to favor certain types of action. (Wilson 1998)

The Objective Psyche

Jung developed the theory of the objective psyche or collective unconscious to describe the common archetypal inheritance of all people. Significantly, it is also called the phylogenetic psyche. In the context of the emergence of humans from early vertebrates, and the work of Paul MacLean, the commonality of the objective psyche of the human being is no longer surprising. Of course the objective psyche will be a common, impersonal (in the sense of not unique to an individual) inheritance in all modern human beings, since we are genetically one species and we possess a definite heredity of psychic and bodily patterns. We are living carriers of psychic history, just as we carry the physical history of the early Earth in our bodies. (See figure 2, p. 40.) There is a veritable interior archeology in each individual. (Boff, p.32). Instead of rejecting this intimate, living connection with our earthly past, we must try to become conscious of the ancient psychic patterns influencing our parental care, sexual relationships, group behaviors, and relationships with other species of the Earth community.

Although Jung referred to the objective psyche as "unconscious," in his conception it has perception, feeling, thinking, volition, and intention, just as if it were a "subconscious." (CW vol. 8, pp. 184–90) He even suggested the possibility that the "unconscious," like daily consciousness, possesses a subject, a sort of ego. (Vol. 8, par. 368) We have mentioned that MacLean thinks the R-complex, like the other formations of the triune brain, operates somewhat independently and has a distinct subjectivity. The ancient reptile itself certainly had a subjectivity, albeit a non-verbal one. Since the reptilian formation, as well as the paleomammalian formation, is carried forward, those modes of consciousness integral to the body do not disappear, and although that subjectivity is no longer dominant in our daily consciousness, it remains nonetheless a powerful presence. The findings of scientists like MacLean and the implications of the new universe story "dramatically corroborate Jung's previously despised assertion that the human psyche, like the human body, has a definable structure which shares a phylogenetic continuity with the rest of the animal kingdom." (Stevens 1982, p. 22)

Part of the urgently needed shift in consciousness to reclaim immersion in the Earth involves recognition of the great influence and power of these ancient, semi-autonomous components of human behavior. In them, though largely hidden from daily consciousness, there exists a direct, profound continuity of human nature with the vertebrate history living in us and the formative patterns of Earth in which the archetypal patterns evolved. They are major factors determining human destiny. We have yet to develop adequate ways of resolving territorial disputes and overcoming human distrust of groups different from our own. Work with these archetypal patterns is part of the task of developing an original relationship with the Earth. Jung's conception of the Self, discussed below, incorporates these ancient dimensions of our being.

The Self in the Psychology of Carl Jung

The Self is the central integrating and ordering principle (or archetype) which unifies the psychic totality, including the ego. It refers, as previously noted, to the self-organizing, creative Center of the person (Neumann 1968, pp. 383–84) and also to the totality of the person. The Self includes everything (Edinger 1973, p. 6). The Self is the organizing principle (the Center), not that which is organized, yet it is inseparable from and constitutive of that which is organized, making a functioning whole.

Thus, the Self can be the organizing Center yet it is also the total person. The Self in its centering function can be distinguished in experience and dreams and discussed rationally, but may not be separated from the whole person. *Jung's conception of the Self orders and unifies the body/psyche and its ancient patterns and thus keeps the individual firmly rooted in the Earth.*

The ego is the center of the *conscious* personality while the Self is the ordering and unifying Center of the total psyche (*conscious and unconscious*). (Edinger 1973, p. 3) The Self is the source of objective identity, to be distinguished from the subjective identity derived from the ego. Although the ego is dominant in daily consciousness, it is only part of the larger Self. The Self is the Center and source of psychic life, and contact with it must be preserved at all cost.

The identification of the Self arose from the observation that the objective psyche operates as if it were directed by a central, guiding entity. People have dreams and intuitive promptings that demonstrate a comprehensive, ordering process, which seeks to maintain the centered, integrated identity of the person. In research using psychedelic (mind-manifesting) drugs, R. E. L. Masters, a pioneer in consciousness research and the mind/body realm, and Jean Houston, a philosopher, psychologist, and cultural historian, observed that the non-personal psyche operates as if it were directed by a central guiding entity or by trans-personal field information. (Masters and Houston, p. 5) Their data strongly suggest a tendency or impetus toward self-actualization and self-healing. An archetypal image may illumine the most important areas of the subject's life needing attention.

In Jung's conception of the Self and the discovery of the self-organizing dynamic, we find an answer to Daniel Dennett's charge that "there's nobody home" in the hustle and bustle of macromolecules. (Dennett, p. 202) The Self is "somebody" that is home. This intelligent, ordering Self is the source of centering identity that arises fundamentally from the differentiating, self-organizing capacity of the universe, with its origins, as we've seen, in the ordering intelligence of the *plenum*. Jung's formulation does not neglect the importance of emergent properties that arose over the course of evolution: There are aspects of human consciousness, like expanded memory, that do arise out of complexity and the activity of the macromolecules. Human ego consciousness in particular comes from the expansion of the neocortex. But the Self that provides the *objective identity* of the person is more deeply rooted, and serves as the organizing principle of the various dimensions of consciousness, which include sensory awareness, memory, emotion, and the archetypal patterns of the psyche and body. The relation of the ego to the larger psyche will be discussed in chapter 15. The constructed narrative of which Dennett speaks is derivative of the ordering authority of the Self, although dependent on the memory and complexity of the neocortex.

Awareness of the Self/Soul

We are not usually directly aware of our Self/soul because we cannot separate ourselves from it in order to be aware of it as an object to the ego; in the same way the eye cannot see itself. Huston Smith writes: "The soul is the final locus of our individuality. Situated as it were behind the senses, it sees through the eyes without being seen, hears with the ears without itself being heard. It lies deeper than mind. If we equate the mind with the stream of consciousness, the soul is the source of this stream; it is also its witness while never itself appearing with the stream as a datum to be observed." (H. Smith 1976, p. 74) But, as it is hoped later chapters will show, there may be occasions when we may experience an alternative "I am" consciousness that *is* awareness of this Self/soul and its origins in the Abyss/God. According to Louis Dupré, "In mystical states we attain a direct, explicit awareness of the soul as such." (1980, p. 460) The Self (or soul), as Jung recognized, also makes itself known in dreams, as a guiding principle, and in the spontaneous appearance of mandala images, considered to be images of the Self. Often empirical symbols of the Self possess a distinct numinosity, that is, an *a priori* emotional value. (CW vol. 6, par. 789) The garden of Eden, with the four rivers flowing from it, is a mandala image depicting original oneness with nature and deity. (Edinger 1973, p. 17) Ezekiel's great vision of the four creatures with wheels beside them, and above them a throne with the likeness of a human person seated on it, is a mandala. Saint Teresa's image of the interior castle discussed in chapter 6 is a mandala image: All the struggle, the trials and joys at different stages of her journey to the contemplative life, take place within the castle, an image of the comprehensive, ordering archetype of the Self/self. Stories of virgin births and Messiahs in various religious traditions are images of the Self, which may be realized through the efforts of the ordinary person. And we will find it in the awakening of human consciousness in the infant, discussed in the next chapter. In the contemplative pathway, people seek to be available to the constant guidance of the Self/soul.

The Person as Image of God

The tradition of the person as image of God is derived from Genesis 1:27: "So God created humankind in his own image, in the image of God he created them; male and female he created them." (New RSV) Jung's thought regarding the Self and the new ideas about self-organizing are remarkably congruent with an important tradition that developed from this text. In the eastern Christian theology, the scriptural text that humankind is in the image of God refers to the indwelling of God's *uncreated* image (the Word) in the person. The word "image" in this usage refers to an *inner pattern*, not a picture or icon that stands apart from that which it images. Dupré writes that the Greek tradition starts with *the identity of the image and that of which it is an image.* There is a distinct presence, which renders the soul an image of God. (Dupré 1984, pp. 13, 17, 27) Origen (c.185–c.254), a Greek contemporary of Plotinus, thought a person is an image of God because the Word— the logos— resides in the person.[6] *The logos is the ordering realm*, related both to the Greek idea of *nous*, which we have considered with reference to Plotinus, and to the Jewish conception of pre-existent wisdom that contains the Law.

Intrinsic to the person, at the heart of human identity, is the fundamental ordering logos. This should begin to sound quite familiar. Louis Dupré writes: "At some point, where the soul touches God's creative act, the soul coincides with the divine Image. God remains present at the core of our existence so our essential depth touches God without any intermediary and invites us to total union." (1984, p. 14)

The Western tradition, in contrast to the Eastern Christian tradition, has commonly been more conservative in its interpretation of the image of God, often carefully delineating the distinction between Creator and creature. Augustine initiated the tradition that the human mind is an image of the triune God insofar as it bears the imprint of the Trinity, which he identified primarily as the relationship and function of the memory, intellect, and will. The human mind is an image of the triune God because it has the power to remember, to understand, and to love. (Dupré 1984, p. 18) Through these powers it can move beyond itself toward union with God. Augustine's later thought, according to Dupré, comes closer to the eastern Christian idea that the image is grounded in identity with God (p. 18), but the idea of superficial resemblance remained dominant in the West for many centuries. In was only with the Cistercians, especially William of St. Thierry (1085–1148), who studied the Greek writers, including Origen and Gregory of Nyssa, that the insight that the deepest essence of the person is identical with God— with the Father, through the Son, in the Holy Spirit—is again understood. Richard of St. Victor and other Victorines, working in the abbey of St. Victor in Paris in the twelfth century, also contributed to this process of claiming the distinct presence of God in the soul, such that a person in her deepest essence is identical with God, in the unity and difference of the full Trinitarian dimensions.[7]

Jan van Ruusbroec inherited this expanded tradition and wrote in a vein very similar to the Eastern tradition, affirming that the soul is from all eternity an archetype (a formative pattern) within God. Man's true essence (*wesen*) is his superessence (*over-wesen*). Before its creation the soul is present in God as a pure image; after its creation this divine image remains its super-essence. Ruusbroec insists that through the mystical transformation *the soul surpasses its createdness and participates actively in God's uncreated life.* (Dupré 1980, p. 462, emphasis added) Following the transformation and healing of the person, a topic addressed in part 5 of this book, the uncreated divine image becomes the essence of the actual living person, making possible a participation in the dynamic ebbing and flowing of the Abyss/God and the ongoing unfolding of the Earth. With this return the person "dwells in God, flows forth from God, depends upon God and returns to God." (Dupré 1980, p. 462)

Jung spoke of the Self as *imago dei*, the "image of God." He believed the dynamism of God lay behind the image or pattern of God he observed moving the individual toward wholeness. Shortly before his death, he wrote to Laurens Van der Post: "I cannot define for you what God is, I can only say that my work had proved empirically that the pattern of God exists in every man, and that this pattern has at its disposal the greatest of all his energies for transformation and transfiguration of his natural being. Not only the meaning of his life but his renewal and his institutions depend on his conscious relationship with this pattern in his collective unconscious." (Van der Post 1975, pp. 216–17) By means of the Self there is an innate capacity to know and express and, according to Christianity, even *be* the Abyss/God in its human form. (See below, chapters 13, 14, 19, 20.)

The Image Tradition in the New Story

We have found in the Eastern Christian tradition, and to a lesser degree in the Western tradition, a powerful, historical recognition of the immanent centering, organizing *logos* constitutive of the person. Fundamentally, this conception of the indwelling *logos* cannot be a different insight from that of the unseen shaping dynamism found by contemporary study to be constitutive of each individual person and of other beings. We find a complementary exploration of a dimension of the human being by both modern science and traditional contemplative spirituality. Since the formative powers are in the realm of the *plenum*, they are integral to the pathway into the contemplative life. Christianity, as discussed in the next chapter, similarly places the ordering realm, the *logos*, within God. This is key to the integration we are seeking, because contemplation—the return that brings participation in one's uncreated image—means we are entering in an integral way into the creative depths of the unfolding whole. And, from the work of Jung, we have added recognition of the phylogenetic psyche to the image tradition, thus incorporating the evolved complexity of the person in the conception of the Self (*imago dei*).

---

[1] Tertullian's error according to the tradition, called Traducianism, would make the soul part of the parent's soul. This was condemned in the canons of Benedict XII against the Armenian error. (Bouyer 1965, p. 422) It should be noted that Tertullian's concern "was opposition to the Platonic ideas about the preexistence of the soul, ideas directly contrary to the text in Genesis, that has been the starting point of this defendant of the faith." (p. 422)

[2] Ethologists study behavior in individual organisms and from this data reach the generalization that certain patterns of behavior are the common instinctual equipment of a given species. We have described some of MacLean's ethological work with reptiles. (See chapter 2, note 18.)

[3] It can be postulated with considerable assurance that some of the instinct-like behavioral patterns now recognized as part of the human psyche were formed during the very long period of early vertebrate evolution on land. J. P. Henry of Los Angeles supports this position, "placing the archetypal systems . . . in the limbic systems and the brain stem." (Quoted in Stevens 1982, p. 263-263) If sufficient information about prehuman ancestors were available, it would be possible to describe the natural history of the archetypes governing behavioral patterns of the human being. This step-by-step development from one pattern of behavior to another, as a species underwent genetic evolution, has been described in some instances. (Stevens 1982, p. 24)

[4] Images of a maternal figure in a dream are not equivalent to the archetype of the mother, but they manifest the individual's life history of the archetype. The actual images depend on the cultural and personal environment, and are not themselves inherited, although comparative studies can reveal the archetypal patterns underlying them. However, Michael Fordham, discussing Jung's thought, says that some images seem to demonstrate little influence from personal history and to maintain a certain autonomy, which in essential respects

corresponds to the instinctual pattern; they are both instinctual and psychic. (Fordham 1949, pp.4–5) The primordial image is the instinct's perception of itself or a self-portrait of the instinct. (Stevens 1982, p. 62, from Jung's Collected Works, vol.. 8, par. 277)

[5] Anna Freud did not recognize any inherited patterns, teaching that the human child learns to display attachment to his mother because she is the primary source of oral satisfaction. (Stevens 1982, p. 4) Others have argued that mother love is a bourgeois luxury dependent on culture, and point to the variety of child rearing patterns, including the eighteenth- century custom of sending well-born infants to a wet nurse. Recognition of archetypal patterns does not deny that the inherited patterns are modified and even temporarily over-ridden by culture. Also, it affirms that the actual physical care of the mother or a substitute is essential to the bonding, as Anna Freud recognized, and that psychic maturation depends on parental care. But in Jung's thought, the child is born with a predisposition to look for its mother and "falls in love with her" at birth. Certainly, as is widely recognized, human behavior is dependent on inherited as well as nurturing and other environmental factors.

To demonstrate that feeding and care and oral satisfaction do not entirely explain infant bonding with the mother or other care-taking person, Anthony Stevens studied infants in an orphanage just outside Athens, Greece. In the orphanage a number of women fed the children but each child still chose one person and established a deep bonded relationship with that woman who became "my nurse" for the child. She was not always the person who fed the child most often. (Stevens 1982)

[6] Both Plotinus and Origen were students of Ammonius Saccas of Alexandria (c. 175–242), one of the early teachers of what would come to be called NeoPlatonism.

[7] The Victorines were the Augustinian canons in the abbey of St. Victor in Paris. Richard of St. Victor and Hugh of St. Victor, his teacher, were their most distinguished representatives. Richard (d. 1173) was a mystical theologian whose work *The Four Degrees of Charity* had wide influence in later centuries. His works *Benjamin Minor* and *Benjamin Major* describe the journey of the soul toward contemplation. Benjamin, the youngest son of Jacob, becomes in these treatises an image of "ecstasy of mind."

13

'ALL AT ONCENESS':
AN INCARNATIONAL WORLDVIEW

Though the originating power gave birth to the universe fifteen billion years ago, this realm of power is not simply located there at that point in time, but is rather a condition of every moment of the universe, past, present and to come.
— Brian Swimme and Thomas Berry

AT A RECENT show at the new planetarium in New York City, a large image of the magnificent Milky Way galaxy floated above the audience. A pointer indicated a bright dot on one spiral arm of our galaxy that is our sun. Its planets are too small to be seen. From this perspective, we residents of the third planet from the sun could see that we were an integral part of the vast display overhead. Although at the time my thoughts did not take precisely this form, the importance of Raimundo Panikkar's statement, previously quoted, became clear to me: "The fundamental unity of reality . . . should not be overshadowed by the diversity of the whole universe. *The variety of beings, including the theological difference between the divine and the created or God and the world should not overshadow the fundamental unity of reality.*"(Panikkar, p. xv, emphasis added) Our traditional separation of God from the physical world fades from the perspective of the new story and the vast cosmos, and instead we are led to recognize, as we saw in chapters 8 and 9, that we are part of a turbulent and magnificent cosmic totality comprising the manifest, physical world and the largely hidden divine within the heart of matter. The person, as a differentiated part of the unfolding whole, participates fully in this sacred wholeness.

One of the great revelations of the new story of the evolving universe is that in it we can clearly see the unfolding unity that becomes diversified and complex while remaining a unity, still composed of the original, primordial particles, now part of complex beings. (See fig. 4, p. 49) Brian Swimme writes that "rather than having a universe filled with things, we are enveloped by a universe that is a single energetic event, a whole, a unified, multiform, and glorious outpouring of being." (Swimme 1984, p. 40; also Swimme and Berry, p.76) This, together with what has been explored in earlier chapters about the manner of form generation, means that people and other beings that develop as the world complexifies are not fragments of things, mere conglomerates of mechanistically conceived matter, but beings whose identity includes the generative, creative depths of the universe. We are thus led to ask, along with Lawrence Kushner: "What if what we call "God" is intimately related to a mode of consciousness and our collective beings that we are not allowed or accustomed to call part of ourselves?" (Kushner, pp. 67–68)

One of the questions over which Meister Eckhart and the Archbishop of Cologne were at odds in Eckhart's heresy trial in the fourteenth century is a question that remains important today: Where is it appropriate to "draw a line" to designate the limits of an individual person? Eckhart is recorded as having preached, "There is something in the soul so closely akin to God that it is already one with Him and need never be united to Him." (As quoted in Dupré 1980, p. 461) This teaching, as well as Eckhart's preaching on the birth of the Son in the soul, challenged the concept of separation of creature from Creator.[1] Other great mystics, including the Dominican John Tauler (c. 1300–1361), a student of Eckhart's, claimed that part of the soul is in eternity (Dupré 1980, pp. 461–62), and as we have seen, the Eastern image tradition assumes that there is a part of the person that is uncreated.

We, as inheritors of the Cartesian/scientific tradition, easily fall back from these implications of the new story into the dualistic mode of thinking that pulls the sacred out of the unfolding whole. Dualism views the relation between God and the world as a relation of pure otherness or difference such that the theological difference between God and the world does "overshadow the fundamental unity of reality." Although there is a promise that the transcendent God will be faithful to human well-being, the world is pulled apart; the sacred is believed to be absent from the person and the natural world. There is a strong bias towards this dualism in Islam, Judaism, and Christianity. The Koran proclaims that Allah is unique and absolutely transcendent. Christianity, which inherited dualistic tendencies from parts of both the Jewish tradition and the Hellenistic world, does counter them with the belief that Jesus, at least, was at once fully human and fully divine, but unfortunately, the full significance of this insight is often obscured because of pervasive attempts to preserve the dualism and to make Jesus of Nazareth a unique, exceptional visitation, an only Son sent to save fallen humanity, not a revelation of the nature of all people and all life.

An attempt to preserve a complete transcendence and separation of God from the person is evident in the work of Karl Barth, a neoorthodox Protestant theologian. He preached and wrote that God is a different order of reality, a different substance, and must be held to be "wholly other" and completely transcendent. He wrote: "There is nothing in man as he actually is which in any way discloses his origin in God." For, Barth said, the "image of God" does not give a person any knowledge of God whatever:: "Man does not know God. His human existence does not point him toward God." (Quoted in Williams, p. 177) God's transcendence was also emphasized earlier by Calvin and Kierkegaard.

While there is a genuine otherness of the Abyss/God in relation to human daily consciousness, and there are very important dimensions of what we will call "true transcendence," these theologies now seem unbalanced. They need to be reconsidered in order to answer the challenge of the worldview of the new physics and the unfolding universe story. It is central to the 'way of seeing' developed in this book to reject a dualism that separates God and the world, yet at the same time to affirm "true transcendence" of Abyss/God, a transcendence that does not contradict immanence. (See chapter 17.)

Unity and Difference

How shall we signify this understanding we are developing from the new story and the new physics, this understanding that avoids dualism yet recognizes a sacred presence within and around all beings? We place it within the tradition of unity and difference, one of three traditional options—the other two are dualism and monism—describing the relationship of God and the world.[2] The unity and difference tradition recognizes real difference (the distinct individuality of Jesus or any other person and of other beings) without denying a genuine unity. It is an independent tradition, not simply a compromise between monism and dualism.[*] The unity and difference position is the one in which Trinitarian thought is placed. (Cousins 1978, pp. 18–20) It is the unity and difference position that is congruent with the identity of the person, revealed by the new story, as a differentiated part of an unfolding, sacred whole. In the context of the new story, the unity, as just discussed, does not refer only to the hidden sacred realm; it includes as well both the non-visible and the manifest, or Abyss/God and the physical world.[3] At the end of this chapter we will consider what is at stake in each of the three positions with regard to how people understand themselves.

It is a major challenge to our dominant ways of thinking in the West to embrace this unity and diversity position because it takes the unity seriously. The unity has been hard to grasp in the context of mechanistic science and the pervasive dualistic theology, and because of the way the ego commonly interprets the world.

A Haiku

The challenge to understand the unity and difference tradition can be considered as a koan, the question posed to Zen students that requires tapping non-rational capacities of the mind to solve. Although we are concentrating on the Western tradition, there

---

[*] Ewert Cousins: personal communication, 1996.

is a haiku that communicates beautifully the elusive unity and diversity we are attempting to fathom:

The old pond, ah!
The frog jumps in:
The water's sound . . .

The haiku is by Bashõ (1644–1694), a Japanese poet. It puts forward an image reflecting an intuitive grasp of reality that awakens to the whole, the unity in the midst of diversity. Thus, the old pond is an image of the Emptiness, the ineffable reality, the source of all things. We are calling it the All-Nourishing Abyss or Abyss/God or *plenum*. When the frog jumps into the pond and we hear the sound of the water splashing, we are led by the haiku to realize that we cannot designate either the frog or the water of the old pond as the source of the sound. Zen master Daisetz Suzuki writes:

> The intuitive grasp of Reality never takes place when a world of Emptiness is assumed outside our everyday world of the senses; for these two worlds, sensual and supersensual, are not separate but one. Therefore, the poet sees into this Unconscious (the Cosmic unconscious, the principle of creativity, the storehouse of possibilities) not through the stillness of the old pond but through the sound stirred up by the jumping frog. Without the sound there is no seeing on the part of Bashõ into the Unconscious, in which lies the source of creative activities and upon which all true artists draw for their inspiration. (pp. 241–42)

Given the pervasive dualism in our culture, we tend to think of "the old pond" as a separate reality, ignoring that the intuitive grasp of Reality (the splashing sound) depends on both the individual (the frog) and the pond, the Emptiness, which Japanese theologian Tokiyuki Nobuhara calls the Trans-individual Reality. The deep mystery of existence comes to us through the frog, the mountains, the wind, Niagara Falls, a person, a flower or a bush!

The 'all at onceness' of the frog and the pond in creating the splash is, it seems, the same insight made by the Christian tradition regarding Jesus of Nazareth, in whom both the "pond" and the living, physical person are recognized as central to his identity—his splash. This is also the 'all at onceness' that William James wrote about and which we discussed in regard to the fullness of the now, in chapter 4. Given this 'all at onceness' in the context of the new story, we can grasp how individuals, including Jesus of Nazareth, can be revelatory of the whole. Recall that Saint Francis loved the finite as such, not just the infinite in the finite. Feminist theologian Carol P. Christ seeks to be faithful to this same unity when she speaks and writes about the goddess (a sacred figure) whose body is the Earth. (Christ 1999) Evelyn Underhill captures the same insight: "There that flux exists in it's wholeness, 'all at once'; in a manner which we can never comprehend, but which in hours of withdrawal we may sometimes taste and feel."(1942, p. 138)

I experienced this 'all at onceness' of heightened individuality as well as communion when my husband was terminally ill. One of the occasions when we are called to enter most fully into our distinct individuality is at our death. We face our death alone because it is our own death and ours alone. The severe sufferings that may accompany it are ours alone to bear. Yet simultaneously death can also be the occasion of the most profound communion and compassion. Our family and friends gathered with my husband, drawn as by a magnet to an event of great magnitude. In an age in which we are "entertained" by the pervasive attractions of the growing entertainment industry, this is true life that we are invited to join.

Trinitarian Thought

It is most heartening to recognize the congruence of the insight from the new universe story concerning diversified unity (unity and difference) and Trinitarian thought, which assumes renewed importance in the new evolutionary context, although it is not applied exclusively to Jesus of Nazareth. The Trinitarian insight in Christianity developed as a way of conceiving of the divine identity of Jesus (a part, an individual) in relation to the one God of the Old Testament. Could an individual be truly divine? Could his divinity be of the same nature as the God of the Hebrew tradition? There also developed a similar need to identify the nature of the Spirit experienced in the early Christian community. The resolution in Trinitarian theology is that the Creator or the one God, called the Father, and that which is brought forth (created), the Son or logos, are one and the same God together with the Holy Spirit.[4] This is an astute formulation, because it was the means by which Christianity would affirm that the divinity recognized in the historical, actual human individual, Jesus of Nazareth, is the same divinity (the same nature) as the Creator or Originating Source (the Father) in the Hebrew tradition. Likewise it asserts that the Spirit, whose fruits—love, joy, peace, long-suffering, kindness, temperance—were identical with the impression Jesus had made, was the Spirit of God. (Pittenger 1974, p. 56) It means, with regard to Jesus' identity, that he did not in some way earn or achieve his divinity; rather it was intrinsic to his very nature. His identity as a human being extends into the fullest 'sacred depth of things.' The Trinitarian formulation is thus a critical insight in the contemporary context, in that it formulates and articulates the grounding of personhood in the hidden sacred depths of the world. It speaks directly to the possibilities of the contemplative life.

Unfortunately the idea of a Trinitarian God has been most difficult to comprehend because of the translation of the original Greek words used to describe it. But it is important to consider the original meaning briefly so that we may try to grasp what was being said. Using the Greek words, Christianity claimed that the Godhead is one *ousia* and three *hypostases*. The unfortunate translation of the Greek *hypostases* to *persona* in Latin has led to great confusion. *Hypostases* are not "centers of consciousness" or centers of awareness, as "persons" seems to suggest, but refers to an abiding or eternal mode of both being and action. Likewise, the translation of *ousia* ("what this or that is itself") as substance has led us to imagine something static and inert, like a physical substance, rather than a dynamic living reality, and moves us away from the vitality and dynamism of God as found in the Jewish tradition. (Pittinger 1974, p. 45) These original meanings, especially with regard to *hypostases*, help us avoid any idea of a self-contained relationship among "persons" somehow next to each other. With the aid of the original meanings, we can relate the Trinitarian insight to the dynamic unfolding of the inner, implicate, formative patterns (the logos) out of the *plenum* (the Father) in the contemporary worldview. We have seen that the formative patterns are constitutive of the person and that these patterns are integral to the *plenum*. And furthermore the ongoing Origin and these formative patterns are not separated, but bonded together in what we call love (Holy Spirit).

Trinitarian Thought in Christianity and Other Traditions

It is most important to our considerations to know that the Trinitarian conception developed in relation to Jesus of Nazareth was not the only occasion when this insight into unity and difference entered human consciousness; it is found in other traditions.* Raimundo Panikkar writes that it "is simply an unwarranted overstatement to affirm that the trinitarian conception of the Ultimate, and with it of the whole of reality, is an exclusive Christian insight and revelation." (p. viii) For example, we find it in the tradition of *bheda-abheda* (difference and non-difference) in Hindu thought. (Cousins 1985a, p. 111) We should not be surprised at this indication of universality, given that the new cosmology and the new universe story show us that people are a differentiated part of a multiform unity.

Ewert Cousins finds that Bonaventure and the Christian Neo-Platonic tradition begins with unity and difference, taking the Incarnation as the paradigm of the entire theological structure. (1978, p.22) Indeed, Bonaventure developed a truly remarkable Christian synthesis. He said there are three books that give witness to the Trinity. They are the book of creation, the book

---

* Ewert Cousins: personal communication, 1996.

of scripture and the book of life. The witness of the book of creation once sufficed to enable people to perceive the light of divine wisdom. But the mirror was made dark and obscure as sin weakened man's sight and the ear of his inner understanding was hardened against hearing the testimony of the book of Nature. For this reason divine providence provided that the testimony of another book, the book of Scripture, was written in accord with divine revelation, "which has never been deficient nor absent from the beginning of the world to the end." (*Disputed Questions*, Art. II; *Breviloquim* 12. 4) Bonaventure taught that the same revelation of divine wisdom is in all three books, it is a threefold book.[5] Here it is clear that in Bonaventure's thought, Trinitarian thought does not refer only to the identity of Jesus. The same inner structure is found in all three books, though expressed differently. Bonaventure's vision is congruent with the insight into unity and difference we are discerning in the new story of the evolutionary universe.

This insight into unity and difference as articulated in a Trinitarian thought is of critical importance to the evolutionary worldview, because it speaks directly to the issue of the identity and essential place of all the many beings in the unfolding whole, an issue that is so central to the new story. If the roots of differentiation did not extend into the Abyss/God or *plenum* (as Trinitarian thought provides), the unfolding of the universe consistent with the nature of the whole could not occur in the various parts. A species of the natural world or a particular person could not act consistently with the whole if they (the differentiated particulars) did not participate in the unitive aspects. Process theologian Norman Pittenger recognizes this when he observes that human beings cannot make a genuine creative contribution to the ongoing direction of the world at its deepest reaches if their works and acts are not at some level identical with God. Thus the Trinitarian insight applies not only to Jesus of Nazareth but also to all the differentiated dimensions of the world, although the divinity of the various parts is expressed and recognized in very different ways and, clearly, the divinity of the person is often not fully expressed.

With the origin of differentiation placed in the Abyss/God, we also avoid making difference primary, as a materialist, atomistic philosophy is bound to do. If difference is recognized, exclusive of unity, we fall into dangerous fragmentation. Herein lies the root of much of our ecological crisis.

The Manifest, Physical World in Unity and Diversity

Is the everyday physical world included in the unity and diversity or does the unity and diversity apply only to the Abyss/God? In chapter 10, we saw how the image of the whirlpool forming in water illustrates unity and difference in a simple way. The whirlpool is a form that persists for a time, yet it is clearly part of the whole, since it is made of the water. But does the ongoing unity of the part with the whole as in this whirlpool/water example also describe the relation of the part and the whole when there is great complexity? David Bohm's thought suggests that it does. We have explored his conception of the holomovement, which describes the unity of the world implied by quantum physics and relativity theory. Furthermore, according to the new story of the evolutionary universe there must be an ongoing unity in the manifest physical world because it is all a complexification of the original primordial soup of elementary particles. There is now great diversity, there is real difference, but at the same time there is a unity. It is a differentiated unity.[6] The formative powers arising in the *plenum* (they are enfolded in or implicate in all the visible world) are constitutive of complex beings and they order the same stuff—the same atoms, the same complex molecules that are themselves differentiations of the primordial soup. There is unity and difference in the manifest, physical world as well as the Abyss/God.[7] So the individual is simultaneously a subject (a part), part of a unity (one with the primordial energy, now differentiated), and deeply in community with other beings.[8]

When the rainforest activist John Seed was taking part in some direct action to preserve the Braintree rainforest in northern Australia from logging, he suddenly realized, "I am part of the rainforest protecting myself. I am that part of the rainforest recently emerged into thinking." (Seed, p. 36) He writes that he found the illusion of separation to be very flimsy, and concludes that there are just a few conceptual filters that prevent us from reuniting with the Earth. We learn from the new story that, by birth, we are of the nature of the whole. It is most important now to include the physical world along with the hidden divine reality in the embrace we enjoy as a part of the unfolding universe.

This inclusion of the physical world in the unity and diversity is crucial because we often speak of our unity with each other in God: It is said that we are brothers and sisters in the Lord. But it is urgent to recognize that we also part of a physical unity, that we are physically brothers and sisters of the other beings of the Earth. We are all born out of the Earth. We are made aware of the intimacy of the human body with the physical world in a multitude of ways: Without fresh water we cannot be healthy and without clean air we cannot avoid asthma and emphysema.

Personal Significance of the Unity and Diversity Tradition

One of the reasons this insight into unity and difference is so important is that by giving it primary place, we avoid the assumption that an individual's experience of the sacred comes only from outside the person. As part of the unity, the sacred is part of the person; Abyss/God is present in the natural world and in our bodies, our very being.

Having personally struggled for many years with the dominant dualistic assumptions of our Western culture arising from both mechanistic science and some theologies, I found the research of R. E. L. Masters and Jean Houston, described in the book *The Varieties of Psychedelic Experience*, a revelation. As noted in chapter 12, in their experiments, a variety of psychological and spiritual experiences became available to a group of ordinary people, who served as subjects, by means of the psychedelic or mind-manifesting drugs LSD-25 and peyote, taken under controlled conditions. (Such research was then legal.) It is thought that the drugs do not determine the content of the experiences, but temporarily remove some type of inhibition to experiences that occur spontaneously without drugs, although with less frequency and typically not without long, maturing preparation of the psyche/body, through meditation, psychotherapy, spiritual direction, prayer, physical disciplines, and the natural maturing that comes from meeting the demands and opportunities of daily life.[9]

In the actual experiments, a trained guide was the companion of each subject who took the drug, and was the observer of the patterns of "descent" and the recorder of the experiences. As a result of experiments with 206 people, Masters and Houston postulated four major levels of the psyche, which they believe are confirmed by classical wisdom on the subject and by subsequent investigations conducted without the use of drugs. (Masters and Houston, p. 258)

The first level involved distortion of temporal and spatial orientation. Then came a second level, named recollective-analytic, which consisted of the repressed emotional material of the personal unconscious, the material that is the focus of Freudian psychoanalytic work and other types of analysis. Subjects relived personal trauma, formative early memories, and unconscious patterns arising from early relationships. The third level, which Masters and Houston called the symbolic level, involved experiences of mythical, ritualistic, and archetypal material like that associated with Jung's work; this material was both universal and particular in that the symbolic element was often shaped and deeply colored by the lived experience of the individual, although sometimes it appeared to be free of personal content. The subject sometimes passed through initiations and ritual observances that were transformative of the personality. Apparently, the symbolic material such as mandalas, and totemic animals and trees, provided the psychic energy for the formation of new attitudes and for the development of more extended and mature states of consciousness. (Masters and Houston, p. 223)

Masters and Houston named the fourth level, reached by only 11 of the 206 subjects, the "integral" level. People who did access this level regarded it as a religious experience. The activity of the guide stopped at the threshold of the integral level, and the subject experienced the final integration unassisted. Regarding the experiences as direct and unmediated encounters with the Ground of Being, God, Mysterium, Noumenon, Essence, Fundamental Reality or the source level of reality, the subjects felt them to be Holy, Awful, Ultimate and Ineffable. They culminated in a sense of total self-understanding, self-transformation, religious enlightenment and possible mystical union. (p. 148) Here is an example:

> I, who seemed to have no identity at all, yet experienced myself as filled with God, and then as (whatever this may mean) passing through God and into a oneness wherein it seemed, God, Being, and a mysterious unnamable One constituted together what I can only designate the ALL. What "I" experienced in this ALL so far transcends my powers of description that to speak, as I must, of an ineffably rapturous Sweetness is an approximation not less feeble than if I were to describe a candle and so hope to capture with my words all of the blazing glory of the sun. (p. 308)

The after-effects were a kind of *post facto* validation of the genuine nature of the experiences: The subjects tended to feel that their encounter with Being had in some way led to the erasure of behavioral patterns blocking their development, and at the same time provided them with a new orientation complete with insight and energy sufficient to effect a dramatic and positive self-transformation. (pp. 149, 276)

The most remarkable thing about these results is that they show that all these various experiences were latent within the average person, waiting, so to speak, to be brought forward. Thus the research confirms the enlarged definition of the person being developed in this book. It indicates that entrance into the various levels isn't a question of some few people being chosen for particular types of experience. Nor is it a question of earning or deserving such experiences, although a preparation for them is often needed: Not everyone in the research was ready for unitive experiences, but perhaps they could have been prepared. Moreover, it is important to note, these various levels of experience are of the same nature as those found in the unfolding of the contemplative pathway and in other traditions. In both situations we see that such experiences are not foreign to the potential of the person; they are not given by a God conceived as external to the personality (although they are acts of grace in the sense of being gifts to the daily consciousness of the person and in bringing healing of the psyche). The experiences were intrinsic to the potential of the subjects, although their realization depended on the fecundity and dynamism of the Abyss/God and the psychological and spiritual preparation of the person.

It is urgent that the discoveries of Masters and Houston and comparable insights, like those of the contemplative tradition, become integrated with the new story of the evolutionary universe. In this new context, we can recognize that the healing and energizing (re-*form*-ation) of the personality occurring in the experiences of the fourth level (and comparably in breakthrough experiences, as described in chapter 6) must be derived from the bonding and dynamic formative processes (powers of the Self/soul) constitutive of the person as a form of the unfolding whole. This is a key insight in changing our 'way of seeing,' which is so important to us individually and to the culture.

Reconceiving the Incarnational Insight in an Evolving Universe

The new story of the evolutionary universe, along with this conception of unity and difference, greatly enlarges and enriches our understanding of incarnation. The early Christians made a remarkable claim: They said that Jesus, a man who came from Nazareth, was divine and even that he was God (assuming a

Trinitarian conception), while remaining fully human.[10] The person of Jesus of Nazareth is described as the incarnation, God become flesh (*caro, carnis*: flesh in Latin). This conception arose within the worldview of much of the Hellenic world, in which it was a radical insight. It was challenged for centuries by those contending that Jesus of Nazareth was not actually divine, but that his sonship was a designation earned by his teachings, the healings, and the quality of his life and sacrificial death. He was thus said to be an adopted son in order to avoid the mythic language of actual sonship, because it was deemed unacceptable that an actual physical person could be given such a holy status. Others by contrast argued that he was a divine being who had assumed the likeness of a human being, but was not actually a full-fledged human being like the rest of us.[11] Thus the implications of the Christian insight have only slowly been assimilated; they are made more accessible within the context of an evolutionary universe.

Now, in the twenty-first century, with the discovery of an unimaginably grand, evolving universe, several considerations regarding the Christian incarnational insight demand our attention. One is that we must abandon our highly anthropocentric stance and recognize that it is no longer appropriate to speak of *the* incarnation. Reference to *the* incarnation as one particular event is dangerously misleading in an evolutionary context, because it would seem to assume that the divine realm was not present within and throughout the world prior to the birth of Jesus and prior to the advent of human beings. It can seem to suggest that the Abyss/God was not an ongoing, generative source throughout the entire 13-billion-year history of the universe. The generative, creative power cannot have been absent from the unfolding story; it had to have always been intrinsic (incarnate) to the manifest world.

Many Christians have not limited the incarnation to one occasion. Louis Dupré writes:

> In Christian piety Jesus plays not merely the role of a teacher of divine Enlightenment (as the Buddha did) or even of a

prophet (as Muhammad or Elijah did), but he himself becomes the object of mystical love. Precisely this incarnational quality has given Christian mysticism in the last seven centuries a marvelously earthy and human quality. Not merely the particular individuality of the person of Jesus becomes an object of reverence, but the entire creation (in all its finite aspects) is virtually included in the incarnated Christ. From this perspective the love of all creatures in Christ implies more than loving them as if they were Christ. What Christians are really invited to love is creaturehood for its own sake. Saints have always understood that the incarnation has united the Christians love of God to the love of the creature. (Dupré and Wiseman, p. 25)

The early church fathers thought that the Word of God (the Son in the Trinity) is not confined to the specific incarnation of Jesus of Nazareth, but is seen operative throughout the cosmos, in all human history and in every person. The Holy Spirit too is operative in the cosmos, in human history and in every person. (Pittenger 1974, p. 17) In the unity and difference tradition, God is incarnate in all beings.

Another consideration in the context of the new story is to affirm that Jesus' life brought a *breakthrough in human consciousness* and human self-understanding, although not a new presence of Abyss/God, to all people and all beings that had existed for untold millennia. We do not know the extent to which there was consciousness of this Presence among the various ancient peoples of the world. As we shall see in chapter 15, however, this breakthrough in the Hebrew tradition was part of an awakening in human consciousness that occurred in several centers of human civilization in the first millennium B.C.E. If we continue to use the word incarnation, it must refer to the divine immanence in all of reality, while pointing to Jesus of Nazareth as the historical occasion when there was an awakening and an important development of human consciousness in relation to that Presence in one culture. In the case of Jesus of Nazareth, it was not just an awakening but an actual living of the human capacity for love, for healing and creativity out of an intimacy with Abyss/God. Within the Christian community there was a new state of affairs, a new time. The chime was different.

It is important to deny that there was only one specific occasion of incarnation in human beings, because, as we have seen in the contemplative tradition, there are individuals who have entered into union with the Abyss/God, although they have admitted this only reluctantly, given the traditional separation of the Creator and the created and the unique role assigned to Jesus.

Affirmation of Difference

One great value of recognizing that the world is a differentiated unity is that difference in the world is given great significance. An atom of gold is not the same as an atom of carbon; nor are daffodils and tulips the same. There are millions of species, each one different from all the others. By the very nature of the self-organizing and autopoietic activity of the universe, there emerge centered, coordinated, organized beings that are rooted in the broader, more comprehensive dimensions of the universe and the full depth of the Abyss/God. A cell, a plant, each individual being is a subject, in the sense of functioning as an organized whole with depth and interiority. In the tradition of Teilhard de Chardin, Thomas Berry identifies subjectivity as one of the primary laws on which the universe functions. (1987, p. 107) The activities and creativity of the many subjects give glorious expression to the potential for magnificence and beauty of the universe.

Although we affirm that difference is indeed a fundamental characteristic of the universe, at the same time, in unity and diversity, we recognize that there are no independent entities. Thus human individuality is not to be confused with independence. We depend on the functioning whole and derive our being from it.

By affirming difference we avoid a pure monism, as found, for example, in the thought of Sankara (788–820 C.E.), the preeminent theologian of medieval India, who proposed the doctrine of *advaita* (not two or nondual).[12] Sankara held that the phenomenal world, with its differences, is illusory, and that there is only one reality, namely Brahman, the divine, ultimate reality. (Cousins 1978, p. 18) When Jalal al-din Rumi, the thirteenth-century Persian poet and mystic, wrote, "There is no reality but God. There is only God," he was expressing a monistic position. (Rumi, p. 16) Classical Christianity rejected monism and upheld the fundamental place of difference when it declared heretical an exaggerated concept of the unity of God, monarchism, which denied any distinction or differentiation within the Godhead (the Trinity). In the *advaitan* position of Sankara, God is homogeneous. But, as we've discussed, the new universe story finds the root of all difference in the Source (Abyss/God). In monistic thought we do not find a place for the origin of form in the 'full depth of things,' so that self-organizing systems that have developed over untold millennia would not be the occasion of true creativity that is integral to the unfolding whole. The part does not have fundamental value, but is merely an appearance or mode of a single reality. Human choice is limited to a passive compliance with what is said to be God's will. There is no true individuation, so people are only carried along by a larger destiny that they do not help create. And there can be a dangerous monistic identification with the perceived will of God that can lead to fanaticism.

Affirmation of Unity, but with Difference Intrinsic to It

Another problematic theology is dualistic. The unfolding, energetic unity revealed by the new story offers great hope for Western culture through its challenge to this dangerous dualism. We find dualistic tendencies in popular spirituality when people speak of the body as a vessel for God, suggesting that the vessel might be empty and that the physical world might be separated from Abyss/God. It is only an alienated, disoriented consciousness that leads us to experience of emptiness. Dualism seems to imply that the physical world is only significant as used by God, and is not itself an integral, essential aspect of a sacred whole.

This dualistic conception of exclusively transcendent ideas of God coupled with a mechanistic view of matter has served to license unlimited manipulation of the natural world by technology and science, often in cooperation with a capitalistic eye for profit. Even people are now commodified, to the level of patenting human genetic information. Wendell Berry describes the great moral failure of such science, quoting the biochemist Erwin Chargaff, who studied nucleic acids for many years at Columbia University: "The wonderful, inconceivable intricate tapestry is being taken apart strand by strand; each thread is being pulled out, torn up, and analyzed; and at the end even the memory of the design is lost and can no longer be recalled." (W. Berry 2000, p. 75)

On a day to day basis, we give primary validity to our daily experience of the diversified world of distinct physical objects and distinct people; this is a necessity for survival and certainly part of our enjoyment of life. But we often fail to recognize any type of unity. When we are told someone visited Niagara Falls and said "That is God," we cannot imagine this is a valid insight. (See chapter 6.) When Keizo Funatsu, the Japanese Antarctic explorer exclaims "I am God" after being buried in the snow overnight, we attribute that to temporary insanity and change what he said when reporting it in a magazine.[13]

It is important to repeat that by rejecting dualism we do not deny important dimensions of transcendence, which we will call "true transcendence," an understanding of transcendence that does not deny the ongoing immanence.[14] Thus our rejection of dualism does not negate the inner, ordering patterns so central to the healing of the person and the relativizing of the ego in the spiritual journey. Some of the dimensions of true transcendence are discussed in chapter 17, on the active universe within us.

---

[1] According to medieval scholar Edmund Colledge, recent scholarship has found that if the commissioners at Avignon had had a better knowledge of the fathers of the Church, both Eastern and Western, they would have found Eckhart's

doctrine of the birth of the Word in the soul in those writings and would not have placed it among the condemned propositions, numbers 10, 11, 12 and 13. (Eckhart 1981, pp. 77–81)

[2] These three types of theology are described by José Pereira in his book *Hindu Theology* (1991).

[3] We choose this designation as more adequate in the evolutionary context than panentheism although it is a panentheistic theology. Panentheism does not adequately address the importance of difference unless it is coupled with a Trinitarian understanding of God. In panentheism, God is immanent to all of reality while at the same time the world is included in God's being somewhat like cells are included in a larger organism. The term was coined by K. F. C. Krause (1781–1832). Theologians Karl Rahner and Herbert Vorgrimler say of this term in *Kleines theologisches Wörterbuch* (Freiburg: Herder Verlag, 1961, p. 275): "This form of pantheism does not intend simply to identify the world and God monistically (God = the 'all'), but intends, instead, to conceive the 'all' of the world 'in' God as his inner modification and appearance, even if God is not exhausted by the 'all.' The doctrine of such a 'being-in' of the world in God is false and heretical when (and *only* when) it denies the creation and the distinction of the world from God (not only of God from the world). . . . Otherwise it is a challenge to ontology to think the relation between absolute and finite being both more exactly and more deeply (i.e. by grasping the reciprocal relation between unity and difference which increase in the same degree)." (As quoted in Cousins 1971, p. 127)

In the context of an evolving universe, however, the assertion of panentheism that the world does not exhaust God's being or creativity is important, because we do not know what is yet to unfold.

[4] The masculine terms are used here temporarily, to describe the tradition.

[5] The first, the book of creation, is efficacious; the second, the book of Scripture is more efficacious; and the third book is a testimony that is efficacious to the highest degree. (Bonaventure, *Disputed Questions*, Art. II)

[6] There is another aspect to the unity to consider. Recall that physicists are not able to find any particulate pieces of matter. The recognition of the demise of the billiard ball view of matter is most important as we wrestle with the issue of the relationship of the differentiated, physical individual to the unfolding whole of the Earth and universe. We need not be knowledgeable about particle physics to see that at this level, the line between the manifest and the generative Source seems hardly to exist. Physicists have discovered that elementary wave/particles take form but remain, at the same time, inseparable from the Generative Emptiness from which they continually emerge and into which they fall back. Wave/particles are sometimes spoken of as a modification of the vacuum. According to David Bohm, "particles" are said to be only an abstrac-

tion of a much greater totality of structure. (Bohm 1983, p. 184) With a somewhat different emphasis, scientists also speak of elementary particles as the material realization of fundamental symmetries or patterns in the ground of material existence. (Peat 1987, p.94) Here is the emergence of difference that remains part of a unity. These descriptions suggest unity and difference because there is difference—wave/particles—yet they remain in some manner inseparable from the Generative Abyss. Since wave/particles remain related to the generative Source, they are thereby also intimately related to each other. Brian Swimme and Thomas Berry write: "The fireball manifested itself as quintillion separate particles and their interactions, but the nature of each of these particles speaks of the universe as indivisible whole." (Swimme and Berry, p. 29) According to quantum physics, "The volume of each atom is the volume of the universe (if you consider that every atom is where its influence is being felt). Every atom is immediately influencing every other atom in the universe, no matter how distant, even if it is billions of billions of light years away. There is still the bonding." (Berry and Clarke, p. 16)

[7] This may be challenged because it seems to violate the principle of contradiction. According to this principle of logic, a thing cannot be and not be at the same time under the same formal aspect. (Cousins 1978, p. 21) So according to this logic, a tree cannot be a distinct tree and also be part of a unity that makes it no longer only a distinct tree. Yet the tree is part of the unfolding whole of the universe. It is one form that the unfolding whole has taken; put another way the great creative Earth has taken the form of a tree. Perhaps there is a way of restating the principle of contradiction in the context of the new story

Commenting on the *advaitan* (Hindu) teaching that God and the world are not either one thing or two different things (similar to simultaneous unity and difference) Raimundo Panikkar wonders if there is a way of passing beyond the law of contradiction, although not negating it in itself. Is there another faculty in a person, he asks, by which she can succeed in grasping simultaneously the truth of the two propositions that God and the world are not either one thing or two different things and their inter-connection, "which is neither complementary nor simply reciprocal but, dare we say it, the truth is of each immanent in the other?" His answer is yes. He finds it in experience, intuition, *anubhava* (Hindu) and at times, grace, faith, gift, and revelation. He writes:

> When one has seen, felt, experienced that God is in all, that all is in God, that nevertheless God is nothing of that which is, . . . then one is close to realization, to the authentic advaita experience which, like all true experience, cannot be communicated or expressed by word, concept or thoughts. (p. 37)

[8] The community may be like an organism. The non-local connections we've described (chapter 9) suggested to Bohm that the relationships in the universe are more reminiscent of those found in organs constituting living beings than parts of a machine. In fact, although he is a physicist, he says flat out that nature

is like an organism, creative and purposeful. (Bohm and Weber 1982, p. 40) Einstein also envisioned the universe as like an organism in which each part is a manifestation of the whole. (Peat 1987, p. 76) Others have drawn similar conclusions. Edward Whitmont suggests we see ourselves as cells in the universe totality. Like a cell in the heart, we are integral to the totality. Whitehead also described the world as "organismic," made up of organically inter-related and organically developing entities, not of static substance or entirely discrete units of matter in motion.

We have discussed briefly how the development of a complex communion on several levels is based on the nesting of organizing systems. (See chapter 10.)

[9] Experiments confirm the notion that provoked alterations in body chemistry and body rhythms are in no small way responsible for the dramatic changes in consciousness attendant upon practices like fasting, flagellation, and sensory deprivation. The severe ascetic practices, such as prolonged fasts, undertaken by Saint Francis and Saint Anthony, are thought to have been significant factors in the dramatic changes in consciousness that they experienced. (Masters and Houston, p. 248)

[10] According to the Chalcedonian formula (451 C.E..), Jesus was "fully God and fully man."

[11] Arius (c. 256–c. 336), an Alexandrian priest, taught that God was transcendent, invulnerable and self-contained, so his essence could not be shared or communicated. Hence Jesus was not of the essence of God and not actually divine. Athanasius, Plotinus's teacher, opposed Arius, wanting to show that the renewal of creation has been the work of the selfsame Word that made it in the beginning. The Council of Nicaea was held in 325 to deal with Arianism, and condemned it. It defined the Logos as "one in being" with God the Father (homoousius, of one substance with the Father).

Docetism was an early Christian belief that Christ's incarnation in human form was a mere appearance. It held that Jesus Christ did not have a real body but only an apparent body, or a celestial (ethereal) body, and hence could no more than appear to suffer and die. Docetism was condemned at Chalcedon in 451 C.E. Also, Monophysitism (Gr.: one nature) was a fifth-century Christological position that there was only one nature, wholly divine, that assumes and dominates the flesh of Jesus Christ. There are monophysite Christian churches today in Syria, Armenia, Egypt and Ethiopia.

[12] There is also a kind of reductive monism in the idea that only matter is real, that is, matter in the reduced atomistic sense of the last century in the West.

[13] It should be noted that Keizo's statement is not fully adequate taken in isolation, and that it was made by a person speaking from an altered state of consciousness. It disregards, temporarily, that Keizo is still the individual human person. Nonetheless, according to the ideas developed here, during the

experience he had while buried in the snow he obtained important insight into a dimension of his identity.

[14] Raimundo Panikkar points out that transcendence precludes a monistic identification, while that of immanence precludes dualistic differentiation. (Panikkar, p.36)

IV

THE DIVIDED SOUL

14

THE AWAKENING
OF SOUL IN THE INFANT

A baby is born through blood and pain and then lies in our arms a mystery, a radiance that belongs to another world.

— Marion Woodman

A FRIEND GREW up in a family that did not belong to a church. His mother was worried when he began attending a Baptist Church during his senior year in high school. She warned against getting "too involved" and urged her son to attend a large state university, where he could discover more of what life had to offer. But what his mother did not realize was that the reason he found that church and its message so attractive was how much the Jesus he was discovering reminded him of her. This is not only a beautiful tribute to a beloved mother, it speaks to the quality of the relationship possible between mother and child.

We need to understand how the immanence of Abyss/God, the *plenum*, discussed in relation to the new cosmology and the unity and diversity tradition, affects the individual. How is this immanent presence of Abyss/God related to the emerging consciousness of the infant and subsequently that of the adult? The quality of the relationship between the mother (or other caregivers) and child is of fundamental importance in determining the capacity of a person to have consciousness of Abyss/God and to receive the guidance of the Self/soul. To begin to understand this, the work of Henry Elkin provides a key first step.

Henry Elkin (1914–1986), an existential psychologist, believed there is an awakening of God-consciousness in the infant that is indeed mediated by the mother—that what he calls the primordial Self is present prior to the emergence of ego consciousness. Recognition of this awakening offers clarification with respect to intrinsic human identity and the foundation of human consciousness, dimensions of the person which much of psychological theory developed in the twentieth century, limited to describing the child's physical, cognitive, and emotional development, has ignored. In addition, by specifying the role of the mother in this awakening, Elkin's work will help us discern a pathway to recovery of access to the primordial Self, if it is lost in the long years of human development.

Henry Elkin's Proposal

Henry Elkin proposed that the awakening of the primordial Self occurs at approximately three months, with the emergence of ego consciousness following at about six months.[1] According to his hypothesis, consciousness does not first appear in conjunction with sensory relations with the daily, physical world, although they accompany the awakening. Instead Elkin postulated a primordial, unitive consciousness that is the initial awareness of the infant and that remains the underlying spiritual, inherently rational ground of human existence even after the ego develops. It is the seat of personhood and psychic individuality. It is "underneath" the relationships of the ego to the external world. Elkin identifies the primordial self with the rational human soul of Western religious thought, with the exception of any reference to the afterlife. He writes of the child younger than six months of age: "Whatever his distinctive qualities, as determined by heredity, environmental influences, and the absorption of the mother's and others' emotional patterns, he is a fully integrated personal being who, unaware of the mother's existence as a separate person, lives in total mystical communion with the primordial Other. . . ." (1972a, p. 399)

Child psychologists generally acknowledge that a sense of personal identity arises no later than the third month of life.[2] (1972a, p. 392 and 1965, p.185) Yet it isn't until six months of age that the infant acquires the first rudimentary body image that makes possible awareness of itself as a distinct physical entity, and with this, the beginning emergence of the conscious ego, which tests and handles reality.[3] Elkin asks, What experience can give rise to the formation of a personal identity or self-image at three months? His answer is that the child's initial self-awareness, the dawning of human consciousness, is an experience that necessarily involves mystical communion with the primordial Other.

Elkin postulates that there are two stages in the awakening of primordial consciousness. These are important because they relate directly to the types of religious consciousness found in the adult. The first type of consciousness is that in which the child has a direct and immediate identification of the Self with God. It is a unitive consciousness. Often the child loses this first, immediate identification of the Self with God because of discomfort, his various needs, and the resulting anxiety if the needs are not met. It is with the repeated experiences of being saved from the loss of primordial consciousness by the merciful intervention of the mother (not identified by the child as a separate person) that the child experiences a renewal of that consciousness. Since the recovery occurs because of the mother's attention, the consciousness is felt to have been given by the Other (carried by the mother). (1958, p.68) This is the second type of consciousness, in which the initial unitive consciousness becomes overlaid by the infant's awareness of the Other (mediated by the mother) as the eternal, numinous Source of Being. (1972a, p.397). Elkin believes religions focus on only one of these two early states: among the major world religions, the Eastern traditions generally focus upon the initial unitive state of primordial consciousness, whereas the Judeo-Christian tradition focuses upon the second phase, when there is awareness of the Other.[4] (1972a, p. 399) However, the unitive consciousness is also found in the Western contemplative tradition, as has been described.

Circumstances of the Awakening of Primordial Consciousness

Elkin tries to imagine the circumstances of the awakening of the primordial consciousness. In the initial months of life, the infant lives in a condition of collective, erotic symbiosis with its surroundings, unaware of either itself or of the mother as separate individuals. Psychic identity is merged with the surroundings. For an infant, subject and object are not yet divided; the self and the surrounding world are one reality: There is just one fact.[5] (Nobuhara, p.146) D.W. Winnicott, an English pediatrician and psychoanalyst, once stated at a conference: "There is no such thing as a baby. . . . If you show me a baby you certainly show me also someone caring for the baby. . . . One sees a 'nursing couple.'"(Winnicott 1958, p. 99) There is a single matrix of mother and child, a single identity, out of which the child must emerge as a distinct, self-aware individual. We can imagine a child living in a shifting field of moving shapes, sights and images, without the distinct people, chairs, table and windows of adult experience. In this situation, while the separate individuality of the mother is not experienced, Elkin thought it is likely that her face, in eye-to-eye contact, is the focal point of a moment of *re-cognition*. Elkin thus suggests that the mother's smiling face is the visual image, the initial sensory image of (mental-spiritual) selfhood.[6] (1972b, p. 260). The occasion for the awakening of the primordial self may occur particularly during nursing. With the repetition of the child's instinctive turning of the head to bring the mouth to the nipple, there is an occasion for the focusing of perceptions and the transformation of the all-encompassing, dimensionless, and shifting field of the child's visual perceptions. This movement must sooner or later bring "a first dim but marvelous apprehension of his own psychic reality—of his primal *Self* in confrontation with an impersonal nonself or *other*." (1958, p. 67) This is the inception of consciousness of the Self. The combination of nursing and seeing the mother's face may be most important. Elkin writes: "The child doubtless experiences this primal Being most fully—certainly most fully gratifyingly—in the blissful plenitude of feeling his lips sucking warm, sweet milk from his mother's nipple into his mouth, while simultaneously delighting in the loving, responsively joyous look in his mother's face." (1965, p.186) *Notice that this awakening of primordial consciousness occurs in an occasion of supreme physical intimacy, when there is a primal connection with the physical world—the breast of the mother, her arms and her smiling face.*

We can imagine that the experience of the infant is like the "I am" mystical experiences which people describe, although because the infant has no consciousness of individual identity, it is a simple "am," known in a wordless manner. Describing an "I am" experience of Alfred, Lord Tennyson, Daniel Merkur, a scholar of comparative religion, writes: "During his experience, consciousness of both external reality and personal identity disappeared. What remained was a sense of 'boundless being.' It was an experience of existing, an experience not of 'I am' but simply 'am.' All else was forgotten." (Merkur, pp. 128–29)

We should also be aware that the awakening and containment *is not only in relation to the human mother but also in relation to "Mother Earth,"* for the child is surrounded by the warm or cold air, various smells, the light, and the feel of the blankets and the mother's clothes. Thus we can see that a failure to find an adequate spiritual/psychological home in the mother may also mean that there is no sense of being at home in the Earth. This in turn may affect largely unconscious assumptions about the individual's relationship to the planet. Since the care of the mother and the surrounding, supporting Earth is essential for the awakening of the primordial Self, we cannot leap over the body and nature in our understanding of the spiritual pathway. This becomes further evident when it is remembered that the roots of the archetypal patterns that emotionally relate infant and mother were established in parent-offspring bonds during the long history of the Earth, especially in the early mammals.

The focusing of identity around the experience during nursing is reflected, Elkin believes, in the mandala which in his view portrays, in transfixed, geometric form, the awareness of primordial Selfhood that originally emerges within the shifting sensory field of infant experience when nursing. This is congru-ent with the discovery that mandalas in dreams restore psychological order during crisis by renewing consciousness of the primordial Self.

The primordial Self is the basis, in the context of maternal care, upon which the child will know he has a body, as the period of merger with the mother is slowly dissolved and a knowledge of a separate existence develops. Elkin maintains that prior to age six months, "The child must at some point become aware of his individual psychic or personal identity," for the child needs some mental representation of himself, or self image, before he can know that his body belongs to himself."[7] A finite system cannot know its finiteness without some other element not imbedded in finitude. Without the initial primordial identity, in Elkin's view, the infant would not have the basis for a self-identity separate from the mother. There is support of this in the thought of William Ernest Hocking (1873–1966), an idealist philosopher at Harvard University, who posited two "selves," the excursive self, which is conscious of the world in which it lives, and the reflective self, which transcends worldly flux and thereby enables the other self to become conscious. Louis Dupré describes Hocking's position as follows:

> The reflective self is not subject to the lapses of the excursive one: steadfastly it maintains itself through the blackouts of consciousness and connects the intermittent stretches of consciousness. The body may be an indispensable instrument in this constant identification process, but it cannot provide its ultimate foundation since the body itself needs to be recognized as identical from one stretch to another. The self, then, surpasses the sum total of psychic phenomena. Indeed, the phenomena themselves remain unintelligible unless we accept a subphenomenal source from which they spring and which gives them their coherence. The founding self depends considerably less upon its bodily environment than the phenomenal self. The former's activity continues uninterruptedly after a withdrawal from the physical world in sleep, in trance, in artistic creation or even in daydreams. Particularly in the latter two states we notice a strange interference of the

unconscious with the conscious self. At such occasions, the self appears to be led beyond the boundaries of its ordinary world and to escape its ruling laws. It becomes expressive rather than reactive, revealing the workings of an inner power instead of those of its bodily world. (1980, p. 450)

The person who denies the assumptions about the nature of human selfhood on which Elkin's hypothesis and observations are based is faced with the problem of explaining how experiences of individual autonomy, creativity, and contemplation could arise out of nothing more than an ego identity formed exclusively in reference to daily sensory and proprioceptive information. The primordial identity that emerges in these early months, in keeping with what Hocking has written, is the basis of a personal subjectivity and freedom that cannot be derived from immersion in and identification with the daily surroundings alone. Similarly, Huston Smith writes that soul underlies "not only the flux of mind but also the changes through which an individual passes; it thereby provides the sense of which these changes can be considered to be his." (H. Smith 1976, p. 74)

In meditation we sit for a long time and learn to watch the various thoughts and emotions that arise in the mind, trying not to resist them, or change them, but simply to watch them without identifying with them or being engulfed by them. In a book about the spiritual life as taught by Meister Eckhart, Cyprian Smith, former novice master of the Benedictine Ampleforth Abbey in Yorkshire, England, instructs us that a meditator can learn by such practice that he must be different from what he is watching. He writes:

> It is like a deep, perhaps even bottomless lake; my various thoughts and emotions are like ripples or waves upon the surface. But below the surface, in the depths, there are no ripples: everything is still. . . . Once the turbulence on the surface has died down and the water becomes quite clear, we can see into the depth and become aware of what lives there. But even this is not the lake itself; it is not me. 'I' am that

which contains it all, the water which is still water, whether it is calm or ruffled, fresh or salt, thronged with fish or totally empty. This is the true, the permanent self, which we may become aware of once we detach from our various projections and activities which are not us but only things we do and functions we perform. (pp. 47–48)

Elkin's Primordial Self and Self-Organizing

We may wonder how Elkin's thought relates to all that has been said previously about Self/soul as organizing power. As the infant develops, a new, highly complex, organized, centered being is coming into existence. The new individual is the occasion when the hidden, self-organizing powers are ordering, giving form to, and centering the identity of the new person. These powers, as we have seen, arise in the *plenum* or Abyss/God. Abyss/God is already inseparably present to the newly forming person such that it may be known in consciousness as the infant develops. Soul, a formative order, also refers to the whole person (chapter 12); it is this whole person that is the occasion, the "place" of knowing the primordial God-consciousness. As the infant develops, the primordial God-consciousness is experienced in that particular individual child. Here is the awakening of the sacred identity of the child emerging out of the unfolding whole. Here, in the infant's awakening God-consciousness, is the very integration we are seeking; it is the consciousness that may be realized again in the contemplative life and, in some individuals, is known throughout childhood.

Loss and Recovery of Primordial Consciousness in the Infant

At first, the child's awakening primordial consciousness is precarious and may be lost when the child is alone too long, uncomfortable or in pain. If the mother is unresponsive, the child loses his primordial awareness and passes through, as Elkin describes it, "a subjective eternity of agonized *primordial doubt* about the existence of both himself and the *other*. . . and passes into a state of numb insensibility, spiritual darkness and despair." (1958, p.68). In this distress, the infant's sensorial perception of the primordial cosmos becomes chaotic (1972a, p.397), and there is a disruption of any "mandala experience" of the primordial Self. But if the mother comes and cares for the child, perhaps nursing him, her attentions save the child from chaos and despair, and are the occasion of the reawakening of primordial awareness. This is a most important event, repeated many times. It is the mother's physical, empathic, personal care that restores the child to primordial consciousness. *Thus the mother has been the embodiment of God for the child, for her care has literally brought a spiritual resurrection. It is through the mother's love that the child is received into his being.*

As the mother cares for her infant, the presence of Abyss/God is known in the psyche of the child. This is the earliest awakening of God consciousness in a particular child. Melanie Klein believed that the good breast is instinctively felt to be the source of nourishment, and therefore of a deep sense of life itself. (Klein 1957, p.3) In the light of Elkin's thought, Klein is correct, because nursing and other occasions of care and love are the occasions of restoring physical well-being and the awakening of the primordial self or soul. Elkin says the child is always aware of this awakening when nursing, whether or not the mother is.

The child realizes with repeated experience of chaos and then recovery of primordial consciousness that the self's very existence depends on the omnipotent and merciful love of the *Other*. It is the mother who embodies the Other for the child, since it is her care that reawakens the primordial self. She is the divine mediatrix, just as the Christian tradition recognizes Mary was for Jesus of Nazareth. Mary is designated *theotokos* (bringer or bearer of God) for this reason. Christ is the image of the divine/human identity that Mary nurtures into being. All mothers who offer loving care of the child are *theotokos*, for they are nurturing this same divine/human identity. Images of the Madonna and child in Western iconography surely derive their power from the observer's own experiences as an infant her mother's arms.

Comparable Insights

Another psychologist has offered ideas about the awakening of a primordial Self that are quite similar to Elkin's. On the basis of clinical observations of infants and children, Jungian analyst Michael Fordham has postulated that the Self is the original totality of the infant prior to the formation of the ego. (Edinger 1973, p.5) In 1951, Fordham put forward some tentative formulations, starting from the assumption that the Self is the original archetype of infancy and, further, that the emergence of the ego is closely related to it. (Fordham 1955, p. 89) We can assume that the Self Fordham describes is quite comparable to Elkin's primordial Self, since the Self as *imago Dei* in Jungian thought can be the occasion of God-consciousness.

Edward Edinger, also a Jungian analyst, likewise describes an original, early state of identity with the Self or archetypal psyche, a time when there is as yet no ego consciousness, although he does not refer to the specific timing of the awakening of the Self in the infant. (Edinger 1973, p.121) During this period of early identity with the Self, the infant's total being and experience is ordered around the *a priori* assumption of deity. Remember the Self is the *imago dei*. There is an original state of unconscious wholeness, which Edinger believes is referred to in the myths of a paradise where people are in union with the gods. (pp. 7–8)

In a 1988 article in *Weavings*, Henri Nouwen, a Catholic priest, author, and teacher of pastoral theology, wrote of his experience caring for Adam, a severely mentally and physically handicapped man in a l'Arche community close to Toronto.[8] Although seeming to be quite useless, Adam became Nouwen's close companion. Nouwen found that Adam could give and receive love. A mutuality not based on shared knowledge or understanding, but rather on shared humanity and shared love, developed. Nouwen observed:

> Often people think that the spiritual life is the last in coming and follows the development of the biological, emotional and intellectual life. But living with Adam and reflecting on my

experience with him makes me realize that God's loving Spirit has touched us long before we can walk, feel, talk. The spiritual life is given to us from the moment of our conception. . . . (p. 29)

This recognition of the "priority of God's loving Spirit" and immanent bondedness is closely related to Elkin's proposal, because they both speak about the priority of a consciousness of Abyss/God that is integral to human identity. It is experienced in the love between mother and child as well as in other special relationships, such as that between Henri Nouwen and Adam.

Congruence with Western Contemplative Tradition

At first glance the idea of an awakening of individual consciousness in an experience of identity with Abyss/God and, with the development of ego consciousness in the second stage, in relation to the Abyss/God as Other rather than in relation to the daily external, physical world, seems very foreign to contemporary secular ideas about the nature of the human being. But we must not reject it too quickly just because it challenges our secular assumptions. There is further support in the Western spiritual tradition for these ideas, although not specifically in reference to the awakening of consciousness in the child. Elkin's proposals have a remarkable congruence with the teaching of John of the Cross that experience of God transcends the faculties; both indicate that *the relation to God is not dependent on the development of a certain adult cognitive and rational capacity, but is more organic and more deeply imbedded in the person.* John wrote of being made to walk in dark and pure faith ("Dark Night" II. 2. 5) because God works in the soul without making use of its own capacities. Thus God consciousness can indeed be of a primordial nature, as Elkin suggests.

Eckhart taught that when the praying person has let go and become disinterested, there may be a breakthrough into an alternative type of consciousness. (See chapter 18.) There is breakthrough into the substance (*ousia*) or essence of the soul, in which there is an alternate knowing that is a unique and direct

awareness of the self. It is a self that precedes all mental differentiation. (Dupré 1980 pp. 459–60) The roots of this consciousness
are in the Godhead because the Ground of the Soul and Godhead
are one. It is this realm of experience, I believe, whose awakening Elkin has identified in the young child.

Eckhart pondered the inadequacy of thought about God as
compared with having God in our being. He wrote in *Counsels
on Discernment*:

> A man ought not to have a God who is just a product of his
> thought, nor should he be satisfied with that, because if the
> thought vanished, God too would vanish. But one ought to
> have a God who is present [alternatively, this may be trans-
> lated "have a God in his being"], a God who is far above the
> notions of men and of all created things. That God does not
> vanish, if a man does not willfully turn away from him. (1981,
> p. 253)

It is remarkable that there are traditions that seem so congruent
with Elkin's ideas of an awakening of primordial consciousness
that is a God-consciousness. Claire M. Owens, the Connecticut
housewife, wonders if mystics are probing a chronologically
earlier, pre-infantile, deep, unconscious level of being, the matrix
of their own identity as well as the source of their humanity.
(Owens, p. 150) Thus she is similarly postulating a primordial,
even pre-infantile level of consciousness.

Notice that in the awakening, as described by Elkin, primordial consciousness simply appears at the appropriate time. Thus
this type of consciousness is entirely natural to the person,
although often not easily accessible to daily adult awareness. But
it belongs to the individual's identity, and is in fact at the heart of
it. Recall Evelyn Underhill's assertion that mysticism is an
"organic pathway toward ever . . . closer identity with the
Absolute." With a certain preparation it is natural to experience
this type of consciousness. Teresa of Avila wrote: " God cannot
resist a prepared soul." Eckhart indicated the immediate availability of this consciousness when he wrote that "your opening and

His entering are but one moment." Gregory of Nyssa said, "participation in the blessed life we hope for is not a retribution for virtue but the 'natural' and 'proper' life of the soul." These statements all assume the presence of a primordial God-consciousness that is available to the person. Elkin's suggestion that it awakens in infancy is reinforced by these other lines of evidence. Together they give us considerable confidence that this consciousness is indeed available to the person.

God-Consciousness and the Ancient Brain

We have seen in the previous chapter that in the phylogenetic psyche there are ancient patterns ordering the body and psyche, which the Jungian community calls archetypes. It may be that, when the archetypal systems of the ancient brains are activated, the more comprehensive and numinous aspects of soul are most accessible for people. This is indicated by the "regressive" phenomena sometimes associated with mystical experience. Indeed, God consciousness is often associated with ritual and repetitive motions that relate to the ancient brain. Symeon the New Theologian (949–1022), an Eastern Orthodox saint, uses the image of God's milk and the divine breast several times in his hymns. In Hymn 28, for example, he addresses God: "You allow Yourself to be seen as a breast that gives light and sweetness." (1975, p. 151) Teresa of Avila uses the image of milk from the divine breasts to describe the way God gives life to the soul: "For from those divine breasts where it seems God is always sustaining the soul there flow streams of milk bringing comfort to all the people of the castle." (*Interior Castle* VII. 2. 6) Meals and eating, a most ancient pattern of behavior, are often occasions of special religious significance. Also, archetypal images, such as icons or mandalas, can be a means of opening to this realm. We will return to this theme as part of our consideration of the preparation for the contemplative life.

Freud attempted to discount mystical experience, explaining it as an oceanic experience derived from regression to the state of undifferentiated merger of the infant with the mother or other caregiver. Henry Elkin's work would support the idea that regression to unconscious early states of being is sometimes involved. But Freud lacked the theology and the knowledge of the nature of matter and form-generation that might have permitted him to recognize the immanence of the Abyss/God in the child's symbiotic merger with the mother. Elkin recognized that there is a unitive, primordial consciousness in this stage of merger, so we need not fear the element of regression in the contemplative pathway. However, this unitive consciousness needs eventually to be known by, or at least reflected in the behavior of, the mature, differentiated adult acting in daily life.

---

[1] Henry Elkin bases his thought on some empirical evidence, including the work of Rene Spitz with smiling faces, which indicates an awakening of consciousness beginning in the third month. Yet Elkin's hypothesis is also based, as he readily states, on philosophical, existential assumptions about the nature of the human being. These are assumptions that are themselves grounded in the Western religious tradition.

[2] The first three months is the period Elkin calls preconsciousness, which is characterized by two features: (1) the infant's mind functions, not by perceptual cognition, but by sensing: vital, psycho-physiological discrimination manifest as attraction-repulsion in terms of pleasure-pain (e.g., if sugar is placed in the infant's mouth, he swallows it; if salt, he spits it out), and (2) the infant is in total collective unity or identity with his surroundings. (Elkin 1972a, p.392)

One piece of evidence that the development of this consciousness begins even before birth is that it is known that human fetuses spend much of their time dreaming (Stevens 1993, p. 23)

[3] One piece of evidence for the development at six months of a rudimentary body image is the fact that the infant begins to cry at the sight of the needle when about to be inoculated a second time by the same doctor in the same office as the first. Now, but not before, the infant being recognizes both himself and the mother, as well as other entities, as distinct physical objects. (Elkin 1972a, p. 391) The development of the body image can be followed, according to Gesell, by the child's use of his hands; the child begins to look at his hands in motion at sixteen weeks, reaches out with them at twenty-four weeks, and grasps and manipulates objects at twenty-eight weeks. (1958, p. 61)

Margaret Mahler has developed an outline of the stages of the individuation-separation process by which the child gradually "hatches out" from the period of symbiosis with the mother. She places the first differentiation phase when there are initial tentative steps to break away physically from the mother, at four or five to ten months of age. (Mahler, Pine, Bergman 1975)

[4] Paul Davies writes as follows about this difference in Eastern and Western emphasis: "Western mystics tend to emphasize the personal quality of the presence, often describing themselves as being with someone, usually God, who is different from themselves but with whom a deep bond is felt. There is, of course, a long tradition of such religious experiences in the Christian Church and among the other Western religions. Eastern mystics emphasize the wholeness of existence and tend to identify themselves more closely with the presence. The Eastern mystical experience is described as follows: 'In the mystical consciousness, Reality is apprehended directly and immediately, meaning without any mediation, any symbolic elaboration, any conceptualization, or any abstractions; subject and object become one in a timeless and spaceless act that is beyond any and all forms of mediation. Mystics universally speak of contacting reality in its "suchness," its "isness," its "thatness," without any intermediaries; beyond words, symbols, names, thoughts, images.'" (Davies 1992, pp. 227–28, quoting Ken Wilber)

[5] Erich Neumann suggests that the initial undifferentiated merger of the infant with the mother recapitulates the early human merger with the environment in the *participation mystique* (see chapter 15). In other words, the young child's experience is a re-experience of very early humanity's psychological experience. (1954, pp. 11–12) Human experience of this archetypal stage in human history and in infancy continues as part of our adult psyche.

[6] A child can recognize outer configurations which correspond to inner archetypal prefiguration. We are prepared for a quite definite world. (Stevens 1982, p. 45)

[7] The fact that an awareness of the body alone does not bring self-awareness is shown by the phenomenon of depersonalization, in which the individual is aware of the body without being aware that it is his. (Elkin 1958, p.61)

[8] L'Arche is an international movement of communities founded by Canadian Jean Vanier. The communities, inspired by the beatitudes, comprise people with developmental disabilities and those who share life with them. Henri Nouwen joined the L'Arche Daybreak community in Toronto.

15

THE EGO CLAIMS CENTER STAGE

Through conscious beings the universe has generated self-awareness. This can be no trivial detail, no minor byproduct of mindless, purposeless forces. We are truly meant to be here.

— Paul Davies

MANY PEOPLE suffer an all-too-common loss of ability to receive the guidance of soul in their artistic and daily activities and to enter into the fullness of their being, as promised by the contemplative pathway, and now by the new story of the evolutionary universe. We can gain some perspective on this alienation by looking briefly at a critical stage in the development of the ego in Western culture and by examining insights from psychology.

Karl Jaspers: An Axial Change in Consciousness

In his book *The Origin and Goal of History*, the German philosopher Karl Jaspers (1883–1969) identifies major developments in human consciousness occurring independently in several centers of civilization between 800 B.C.E. and 200 B.C.E.[1] The social, psychological and spiritual changes were of such a fundamental nature that this was a defining era in world history for much of humankind. Jaspers calls it the first axial revolution. He finds evidence that, prior to this axial change in consciousness, the individual human being participated in the fixed traditional practices of his particular community, to which every member of the society conformed. Such conformity is characteristic of the *participation mystique*, in which there was little sense of independent personal identity apart from the tribe because a strong ego center had not yet developed.[2] (Neumann 1954, p. 105) Jaspers observed that in the axial period, simultaneously in several cultures, revolutionary prophets, teachers, and poets appeared. They include Lao-tzu and Confucius in China; Buddha and Mahavira in India; Zoroaster in Persia; Elijah, Isaiah, and Jeremiah in Israel; Socrates, Plato, and Aristotle in Greece. (Cousins 1992, p. 4) In the cultures they profoundly influenced, a changed, new consciousness emerged in which a sense of distinct individuality, granted by rationalized consciousness, pulled people out of an immersion in the natural order. In the areas influenced by these people, Jaspers contends, the individual psychology of human beings as we know them today came into being. (p. 2) The fundamental categories within which we still think today were created by the self-reflective, analytic, critical consciousness that emerged. Often the psyche subordinated the body to its own purposes. Philosophy appeared and human existence became the object of meditation, as history. There was apparently little cross-fertilization among the developing religious and philosophical movements, which, as Loyal Rue points out, makes the deep formal similarities among them the more impressive. (Rue, p. 30)

During this period five great world religions—Hinduism, Buddhism, Taoism, Confucianism, and Judaism—emerged in their classical forms. Although they differed in philosophy and practice, common to all of them was the growing recognition of the individual within the whole of Being, and the knowledge that an individual can tread the spiritual pathways only as an individual on his own. (Jaspers, p. 4) The individual's spiritual identity is increasingly valued; also, most remarkably, monasticism is found for the first time: In order to sustain a personal search, the individual withdraws from ordinary, daily life. This period opened the search for the pure heart, and the possibility of individual moral consciousness that may stand against the collective. The prophets Elijah, Isaiah and Jeremiah called their people to a new moral awareness. Although the historical person that gave rise to the stories of Moses probably lived in the second millennium B.C.E., his story was told in the time of the axial change in consciousness. After his awakening before the burning bush, an awakening into individual identity in relation to God, he returned to Egypt and led his people out of captivity, thus illustrating the individual strength emerging in the axial period. From the perspective of depth psychology, Jungian analyst Edward Edinger describes the Old Testament as a vast process of individuation taking place in the collective psyche (1984, p. 70), an insight clearly congruent with Jaspers' discoveries. This emphasis on interior subjectivity marks an increase in conscious individuation that continues to this day.

It is important to emphasize that this development of individuality is related to an 'awakening into depth,' that is, the fact that the beginning of the world religions and the beginning of monastic life both occurred in this period would indicate that the change in consciousness was not just a narrow gain in ego strength, as we may tend to think from the perspective of twentieth-century psychology. We can see this 'awakening into depth' exemplified in Ezekiel, a figure from the axial period in the Hebrew tradition. Ezekiel's vision (Ezekiel 1:4-28) is an example of a mandala image of the Self. According to Edinger, in this mandala there is a juxtaposition of strengthened individuality and 'awakening into depth,' because, understood psychologically, it is the numinous appearance of the Self archetype.[3] The Self/soul is a formative power arising in Abyss/God; hence, this mandala image is an 'awakening into depth.' We will consider the relation of the ego to the Self later in this chapter.

The axial shift in human consciousness can be correlated with the development of sophisticated written language—alphabetic in the Near East and South Asia, a highly refined pictographic form in China. David Abram observes that written documents have an independent existence that separates them from the storyteller and the places involved in the story. Their coming into relatively common use beyond the keeping of accounts thus served to break "the spontaneous participation of our eyes and our ears in the surrounding terrain. . . . The scribe, or author, could now begin to dialogue with his own visible inscriptions, viewing and responding to his own words even as he wrote them down. *A new power of reflexivity was thus coming into existence, borne by the relation between the scribe and the scripted text.*" (Abram, p. 107)

With this reflexivity, individuality is thrust forward, with concomitant gains and losses. Although the dates for the origin of such writing systems cannot be given with precision, it is generally agreed that the first alphabet, known as the North Semitic, appeared somewhere on the eastern shore of the Mediterranean between 1700 and 1500 B.C.E. The Greek alphabet developed about 1000 B.C.E., probably from the Phoenician. The fact that these dates precede the axial change in consciousness Jaspers describes may well indicate that written language, having had time to spread, was a factor in the change in consciousness.

Jaspers wrote of this axial period that "no final consummation was attained." (p. 5) The changes in the first millennium B.C.E. and those following have certainly brought great gains and great dangers for the human adventure and the adventure of the Earth. They have involved a vast complex of interwoven cultural and psychological changes, comprising a vast subject of study. These cultural changes—we assume the changes are largely cultural, since a certain type of brain had already been developed[4]— are initiated by individual courage and insight and are made available to other individuals and cultures, allowing for psychological and spiritual horizons not previously attainable.

Development of Ego Consciousness in Hero Myths

There is little recorded history of the changes prior to the first millennium B.C.E., and very little from the axial period, because such a record requires the written language and the axial changes in consciousness only then coming into being. However, according to Erich Neumann, we can glimpse in hero myths the emergence of the ego, like an island appearing out of the great psychic pool of instinct and immersion in the events in the natural order. Just as dreams and fantasies tell us something about the psychic situation of the dreamer, so myths throw light on the stage of human psychic development from which the myths originate, delineating step by step the development of human ego-consciousness. (Neumann 1954, p. 263) Thus, for example, the process by which the culturally newborn, helpless ego becomes a strong, semi-independent system has been imaged in many cultures as the heroic killing of the dragon and the winning of the "treasure hard to obtain." The killing of the dragon represents in the symbolic language of the psyche the manner in which humanity became disentangled from its fusion with nature (fusion in which there is no distinct individual identity) and from collective life by confronting and conquering powers imaged as monsters, beasts and giants. With their defeat, the treasure—energy for the individual, which has been leashed (held captive)—is released (set free) and focused through the ego of the individual. "God, demons, heaven and hell are, as psychic forces, withdrawn from the objective world and incorporated in the human sphere, which thereupon undergoes a very considerable expansion." (pp. 338–39) The ego has gained valuable energy from the psyche for its own self-direction, and gradually moves toward the possibility of a centered, fruitful life.

Although he did not slay dragons, Prometheus stole divine fire for the benefit of humankind and then endured the punishment of being chained to a rock and having his liver fed upon daily by the eagle of Zeus. Edinger identifies the theft of a secret with an increase in consciousness and this myth speaks to the great cost involved in striving for consciousness. (Edinger 1984, p. 107) Now, in the context of the new story and a degraded environment, some people are conscious of the betrayal of humankind's relationship with the Earth. There is a burden that accompanies this increased consciousness, because it brings demands on our behavior, anger from those in denial and a possible cost for faithfulness to the new awareness.

Ego Consciousness: Great Gains and Great Dangers

Jung wrote that in the legend of the Fall we find "expression of dim presentiment that the emancipation of ego consciousness was a Luciferian deed." (As quoted in Edinger 1973, p. 16) There is a sense of disease, and the person is no longer at home in the Garden of Eden. A world of conflict and uncertainty is pictured bringing awareness of deficiency and powerlessness. If a person becomes isolated from the matrix of life, there is a sense of homelessness and alienation. If the ego powers are misused, movement out of the matrix brings suffering and sometimes guilt over the betrayal of the natural world. The same misuse of our personal powers of ego consciousness can bring betrayal of our personal identity, if we cut ourselves off from the larger psyche, the body, and the primordial consciousness of Abyss/God that grounds our identity.

The isolation to which this consciousness has sometimes led can be felt when it is contrasted with this description given by Laurens Van der Post of the "bushmen of the Kalahari":

> Wherever they went, they felt they belonged. Wherever they went they felt known. They felt, as they went, just armed with what life had put out, that they were never alone. The stars knew them. The animals knew them. The plants knew them. They could all exchange personalities. They all participated almost, as it were, mystically in one another's life and one's being. And wherever they went, they had company, not only of human beings, but of animals.*

Much of historical ego development is tied to the development of patriarchal systems of law and order, according to Erich Neumann.[5] He writes: "The patriarchal motto of the ego 'Away from the unconscious, away from the mother,' sanctions all the devices of devaluation, suppression, and repression in order to exclude from its orbit contents potentially dangerous to consciousness." (1954, p. 340) Understood in relation to psychic processes, the dragon represents symbolically the destructive side of the archetypal father and the devouring and terrible side of the archetypal mother, both psychic energies that disempower the ego; their "slaying" frees and strengthens the ego. But the slaying of the dragon has a deeply negative shadow side, in the sense that it represents the energy out of which many men, unconscious of what actually must be "slain," have often destroyed nature and

---

* Sermon at the Cathedral of St. John the Divine, New York City, December 18, 1994.

dominated women.[6] Much of our conquering consists of mutilating parts of the Earth, as in the denuding of forests and, in the West, the poisoning of soils and air with chemicals. We have all supported the heroic efforts of scientists who have conquered polio and smallpox, alleviated hunger in some places by increasing the production of food, and held the cold at bay by discovering the oil and coal reserves that we use to heat our homes. But there has been a lack of discrimination in our achievements, and many people are now beginning to recognize that the historical role of ego-consciousness in its present mode of isolation from its wholistic context must be transformed.

How many of the dangers that human beings are bringing to the planet are the result of weakening and distortions caused by psychological wounding (see chapter 16), and how many are from dangers inherent in the full-functioning of human capacities for self-reflexive thought and independent behavior, is hard to discern. Here we need only emphasize that given the capacities of self-aware ego consciousness, the possibility exists of a further evolution of consciousness; a great "enlargement" of consciousness in the context of the new story and faithfulness to the pathway of the contemplative tradition is now offered to us.

Given the new context, perhaps we may begin finally to move beyond "the narrowly personalistic and rigid personality of the sick-souled modern man." (Neumann 1954, p. xxiii) For we are gaining important perspective on the central, positive role of the ego, as we discern its origins in the larger psyche and in the body, with its roots extending into the structure and origin of the universe. Most important for the 'way of seeing' developed in this book is the power of the ego to become conscious of processes in the body, the objective psyche, and Abyss/God. Each individual is potentially able to embrace in his compass a variety of awarenesses, including mystical/contemplative consciousness. It is a great adventure to gradually awaken through the healing pathway to an enlarged consciousness. If we can embrace the emerging paradigm, with its reorientation of our knowledge of human identity, we can become full citizens of the human community and of the Earth community.

The Ego Is Derivative in Nature

The cardinal discovery of transpersonal psychology, for which it has produced a wealth of supporting evidence, is that the ego is derivative in nature. Erich Neumann wrote: "The collective psyche, the deepest layer of the unconscious, is the living ground current from which is derived everything to do with a particularized ego possessing consciousness: upon this it is based, by this it is nourished and without this it cannot exist." (1954, p. 270; see also p. 297) The ego begins as a child of a royal heavenly family, which corresponds to its original state of identity with the Self or archetypal psyche. (Edinger 1973, p. 121) According to Jung, it is the Self that brings forth ego consciousness. "The Self . . . is an *a priori* existent out of which the ego evolves." (CW vol. 11, par. 391) The ego, Jung wrote, stands to the Self as the moved to the mover.[7] We note that this insight of analytic psychology into the relation of the ego to the Self is congruent with Jaspers' hypothesis that the strengthening of individuality is associated with the breakthroughs into the 'nonvisible, numinous depth of things' that were part of the development of world religions.

Since the ego is derivative of the larger psyche, it can sleep. It can let go in meditative practices. It does not always have to be conscious. The larger objective psyche in the subphenomenal dimension maintains itself during periods of unconsciousness, bridging the gaps and connecting the intermittent stretches of consciousness. (Dupré 1980, p. 450) We saw this was part of Elkin's argument for the awakening of primordial consciousness in the infant and found it in the observations of Ernest Hocking and Huston Smith. (See chapter 14.)

It is empowering and liberating to recognize that the ego is supported and sustained by a complex, balanced system whose wisdom is rooted in millions of years of Earth experience. Ninety-two percent of human actions, it is believed, are unconscious, so we are daily sustained by extensive, complex psyche/body awareness, memory, and intrinsic patterns of behavior. In much of modern culture, our ego consciousness may have lost its grounding, but healing is not far away. It lies within the person. The ego can recover its grounding and embrace its profound and far-reaching dependence on the unconscious. The Self stands behind the ego and can act as a guarantor of its integrity. (Edinger 1973, p. 38) The ego need not be isolated and does not have to make it alone; it can depend on a larger wisdom. There are certainly dangerous distortions in the patterns of personality and mental illness that make many people wary of trusting the psyche, and, indeed, we all must be aware of erroneous patterns in our behavior and our thinking. But we need to learn to honor the potential breadth of human consciousness. The extent to which we can enter into an expanded consciousness, particularly a contemplative consciousness that brings the sacred into daily life, will determine the future of the Earth.

Given its origins, it is of particular importance to note that ego consciousness is an exponent of the creative experiments of the whole. (Neumann 1954, p. 303) As Anthony Stevens has noted, the Self accords itself recognition through that organ of consciousness—the ego—to which it has given rise. (1983, p. 140) This intimate connection between the ego and the Self will be critical when we come to consider the creative side of the contemplative life. The ego stands between the inner world and the outer world, and its task is to adapt to both. In relation to our focus on contemplation, the ego must be the exponent, in daily life, of the inner world, acting "on behalf of" the Self and the Self's immersion in Abyss/God. When the ego system is working properly, it remains affiliated with the whole, combining in itself the executive and the directive functions. (Neumann 1954, p. 297)

The recognition that ego consciousness is derivative of the larger phylogenetic psyche, itself arising as a self-organizing power in Abyss/God, is important, since it indicates the depths of our subjectivity and the depths of our belonging to the Earth. If consciousness were only an epiphenomenon of complexity, as it is in a materialistic worldview, a person would be a conscious automaton governed only by mechanical laws. Consciousness would be like the foam of a raging river that cannot change its course, or the shadow that walks step for step beside us but is quite unable to influence our journey. (Jaynes, p. 11)

Ego Consciousness:
The Self-Reflection of the Universe

From the work of Karl Jaspers concerning the axial change in consciousness, along with that of other thinkers, we have come to see that there have been major changes in consciousness throughout human history. Now, in the context of the new universe story, we see the possibility of further change. *Now, perhaps, we begin to see more clearly what Thomas Berry meant when he wrote, as noted in chapter 2, that the "human is that being in whom the universe activates, reflects upon, and celebrates itself in conscious self-awareness."* [8] *(1987, p. 108, emphasis added) A person is a being emerging from the Earth with real choice and creativity, yet rooted in the deepest ordering and very direction of the universe. It is precisely now, as we are telling the new universe story and seeking to understand its meaning, that this self-reflection of the universe on itself is continuing. We are awakening to the fact that human consciousness has the potential for being an exponent of the creative experiments of the whole.* As Brian Swimme puts it, "The consciousness that learns it is at the origin point of the universe is itself an origin of the universe." (Swimme 1996, p. 112) Our insights and activities can actually be occasions of the original creativity of the universe. We will see in chapters 19 and 20 that this is not at all foreign to the witness of the contemplative tradition.

A Second Axial Change in Consciousness?

A number of modern thinkers are persuaded that a change in consciousness is occurring. Ewert Cousins believes the change is so profound that a second axial consciousness may be emerging.

It would retain the self-reflective, analytic, critical consciousness of the first axial period, while at the same time rediscovering dimensions of the spirituality of primal people and incorporating our roots in the Earth. There would be a recapturing of tribal consciousness, although this time by identifying with humanity as a single tribe. It would not be a mere universal, undifferentiated, abstract consciousness, however, but a more complexified consciousness resulting from the convergence of cultures and religions due to the forces of planetization. Teilhard de Chardin recognized that, following the long period of divergence and differentiation as people spread over the Earth, there would eventually be convergence and planetization, because the Earth is round, which makes unlimited divergence impossible. A complexified consciousness would emerge from what Teilhard calls "center to center unions." Ewert Cousins writes: "By touching each other at the creative core of their being, [individual elements] release new energy which leads to more complex units. Greater complexity leads to greater interiority which, in turn, leads to more creative union. Throughout the process, the individual elements do not lose their identity, but rather deepen and fulfill it through union." (1992, p. 8)

There is an urgent need for an evolution of consciousness. Given that the future is not completely contained in the present and that the creativity of the universe has passed in part into the mode of human self-aware consciousness, a change is possible. We do not live in a fixed situation. Through openness to the origins of the Self, there can be an evolution of consciousness, because qualities that will one day bloom are presently hidden as dimensions of emptiness. (Swimme and Berry, p.76) We need to draw forth the potential of each situation. The ego needs to learn to receive the world in its fullness and wholeness. We now have cosmology within which human consciousness can orient and ground itself subjectively and physically in the whole. The new universe story supports this change in consciousness by transforming centuries of contempt and anger at the body and Earth.

[1] It is stated in a *Dictionary of Philosophy* (New York: Philosophical Library, 1960)that "consciousness is generally considered an indefinable term or rather a term definable only by direct introspective appeal to conscious experiences." (p. 64) This is also expressed by the Scottish philosopher, Sir William Hamilton: "Consciousness cannot be defined: we may be ourselves fully aware of what consciousness is, but we cannot without confusion convey to others a definition of what we ourselves clearly apprehend. The reason is plain: Consciousness lies at the root of all knowledge." (Quoted in Edinger 1984, p. 35) Edward Edinger also points out that the experiential meaning of the term consciousness is almost impossible to convey abstractly. "As with all fundamental aspects of the psyche it transcends the grasp of the intellect. An oblique, symbolic approach is therefore needed." (1984, p.17)

[2] In *The Origins and History of Consciousness*, Erich Neumann outlines the stages in the steady increase in the importance of the ego and personality. He begins with a period in which the individual participated in a world continuum of mana-charged events, such that everything was pregnant with meaning. Everything was potentially "holy." (1954, p. 106) This is the period of *participation mystique*. Through comparative study of mythic material from many cultures, Neumann has identified a group of symbols that include the egg, the circle, and the uroboros (the snake with its tail in its mouth) that demonstrate, he believes, the psychic condition of the period of participation mystique, a period in human history when there was no self-aware ego separating humanity psychically from its living environment.

Many psychologists and ethologists are seeking to discern how self-oriented consciousness emerged from this initial *participation mystique*, in which early human behavior was governed by the functions of the body and by universal instinctual patterns of human response to its human and non-human environment. (Neumann 1954, p. 105) There was little sense of autonomous, individualized personhood distinct from the person's collective position in society and in nature. Within a person's tribe, the individual was organically related to the group as a whole, to life cycles of birth and death, and to nature and the cosmos. There was probably an unconscious identity with the world, so everything inside was outside, all of a person's ideas came to him from outside, as commands from a spirit or magician or "medicine bird," and everything outside was inside. (p. 270) Although the group did not allow the emancipation of a separate ego, this does not deny that there were individual differences with certain limited areas of independence. (pp. 268–69)

Neumann's description of the probable psychic life of early humanity indicates humankind never lived in an idyllic state of nature à la Rousseau, so there were important gains to be made with separation from immersion in the natural world and community. "Life in the psychic cosmos of the primitive is a life full of danger and uncertainty; and the daemonism of the external world, with its sickness and death, famines and floods, droughts and earthquakes, is heightened beyond measure when contaminated with what we call the inner world. The terrors of a world ruled by the irrationality of chance and mitigated by no knowledge of the laws of causality are made even more sinister by the spirits of the dead, by demons and gods, witches and magicians; invisible workings emanate from all these beings, and the reality of these all-pervading influences shows itself in fears, emotional outbursts, orgiastic frenzies and psychic epidemics; seasonal bouts of lust, murderous impulses, visions, dreams, and hallucinations. One has only to know how great, even today, is Western man's primordial fear of the world despite his relatively highly developed consciousness, to understand the world fear of the primitive, and his feeling of endangerment." (1954, pp. 40–41)

[3] The singular importance of this mandala is confirmed by the fact that it is carried forward in Christian mandalas in which the four evangelists take the place of the four creatures of Ezekiel's vision. (Edinger 1984, p. 73)

[4] The neocortex provides much of the neurological substrate of the ego. The ego is sustained in large part by memory and sensory knowledge and bodily information processed by the neocortex. The neocortex contains 75 percent of the 10 to 12 thousand million neurons in the brain.

[5] Repression of the terrible Mother is necessary from the point of view of the patriarchate and of a conscious development with strong patriarchal tendencies. (Neumann 1954, pp. 298, 324) "The development of ego consciousness is paralleled by a tendency to make itself independent of the body. This tendency finds its most obvious expression in masculine asceticism, world negation, mortification of the body, and hatred of women and is ritually practiced in the initiating ceremonies of adolescents. The point of all such endurance tests is to strengthen the ego's stability, the will and the higher masculinity, and to establish a conscious sense of superiority over the body." (p. 310; see also p. 124)

[6] We are increasingly aware that the forces behind the degradation of the Earth are the same as those that subjugate women. The feminist struggle and the environmental struggle are intimately linked. See Heather Eaton's lecture titled "Ecofeminism and the New Cosmology" (Raleigh, N.C., November 1997; available from Lou Niznik, 15726 Ashland Drive, Laurel, MD 20707).

[7] In *The Philosophy of Symbolic Forms*, the German philosopher Ernst Cassirer (1874–1945) demonstrated how the intellectual, cognitive, conscious side of man develops out of "symbolic forms," which from the point of view of analytical psychology are creative expressions of the unconscious.

[8] Paul Davies recognizes that the universe has organized its own self-awareness. (Davies 1988, p. 203)

16

BREAKING THE INTERNAL BONDS TO MOTHER AND EARTH

I never had a mother. I suppose a mother is one to whom you hurry when you are troubled.

— Emily Dickinson

EVIDENCE FOR the existence of a remarkable human identity comes from the implications of the new story of the evolutionary universe, the discoveries of the new physics, and the witness of the experience of contemplatives over many centuries. But why is realization of this identity so elusive; why is it not realized as often as we would wish? The answer to this question is known, at least in part, from the long experience of the contemplative tradition and from contemporary depth psychologies. In this chapter, the aim is to discern the psychological patterns that alienate us from full realization of our personhood: Some key features in the formation of the personality in infancy and childhood will be explored to discover the most common origins of flight from Self/soul and from the All-Nourishing Abyss.

That fact that the reasons for our fleeing are sought should not be taken to suggest that there may not be breakthroughs of Abyss/God regardless of the psychological condition of the person. As we saw in chapter 6, a healing, awakening experience of Abyss/God can occur at any moment. However, the contemplative pathway assumes that a preparation is required to enable Self/soul and Abyss/God to become accessible to the adult consciousness on an ongoing basis, as it is for those like Teresa of Avila who have achieved the unitive life (see chapter 7). If we know some of the reasons why this consciousness has been lost, we will be more prepared to discern the pathway to its recovery.

Personalization of the Archetypes

Recall that we have inherited ancient behavioral and emotional patterns (archetypes) derived from millennia of human and prehuman experience. This seems indisputable. However these patterns do not spontaneously spring into activity; rather, they must be met by a certain reception, a kind of fit with the care of the parents, the human community, and the environment so that the ancient mammalian and human behavioral and attachment patterns of the child can be lived out in relationship. Edward Edinger calls this process the personalization of the archetypes. Erich Neumann wrote: "The transpersonal and timeless structure of the archetype, ingrained in the specifically human psyche of the child and ready for development, must first be released and activated by the personal encounter with a human being." (As quoted in Edinger 1988, p. 264) He spoke of this as a "key and lock phenomenon." An appropriate, empathic, adult response to the natural need and "expectations" of the child in effect ignites, or gives a place for the expression of, the child's instinctual energies and relational capacity.[1] Different stages of development require different responses. Just as language must be learned within a specific period of childhood or the capacity to learn is eventually lost, so there must be response to the needs of each stage of development. The various stages unfold naturally if they are adequately activated and received in the family and community. Nature, the inborn archetypal patterns of bodily and psychological potential, and nurture, the love and empathy and actual physical care of the parents and other personal influences, are inextricably bound together in the development of the child.

Nurture In Human Development: Personalization

Edward Edinger writes that in the process of personalization, "the archetypal image can be successfully experienced and realized only when it is infused with a tangible, personal content through a human relationship." (1988, p. 264) He gives an example of this personal contribution of the nurturing person to an individual's development from his experience as an analyst.

He once offered to reduce his already modest fee for a client who had an opportunity to study music but lacked sufficient funds. This fatherly, caring gift brought forth a dream that indicated the young man was beginning to incorporate a positive father image into his psyche, a dimension that had been lacking because of near psychotic foster parents. The patient had not just projected a father image onto the male analyst, but was also receiving personal experience of a father-like man. Edinger came to recognize that as an analyst he gave embodiment to emerging archetypal forms, which were then incorporated into the personality of the patient, for good or ill. (p. 279) In the same way, the child's experience of a parent is built into the archetypal mother or father image. So in addition to the *a priori* content of the archetype, "the personalities of the parents determine the specific content of the innate archetype as it is experienced by the child." (p. 265)

This personalizing role of parents may seem to be a heavy responsibility, but the English therapist D. W. Winnicott recognized that the essential role of a "good enough" mother is empathic care. If a child is to find an unmuddled, steady presentation of external reality and a faithful mirroring of himself , then, Winnicott emphasizes, the mother must be devoted to the infant and the infant-care task. Winnicott uses the word *devotion* to describe the essential feature without which the mother cannot make her contribution, a sensitive and active adaptation to her infant's needs—needs that at the beginning are absolute. This word *devotion* also reminds us that in order to succeed in her task the mother need not be clever. The steady presentation can be done neither by thought nor mechanically. It can be done through continuous management by a human being who is consistently herself. There is no question of perfection here. What is needed is simply the care and attention of someone who is "going on being" herself. (Winnicott 1965, pp.87–88)

The Maternal Matrix Is Forming

The quality of the personal content that is internalized (or imprinted) in the child's psyche during the process of personalization is of supreme importance. We have seen how primordial consciousness emerges during the early mother-child relationship, following the work of Henry Elkin and others (chapter 14). Recall that if this primordial consciousness is to be sustained, it depends on the mother's ongoing physical care, love, empathy, and mirroring of the child. But what happens when the period of merger ends? There must be an internalized mother that carries on the same receptivity to the primordial self. The reason the meeting of the legitimate needs, described below, is of such fundamental importance is that the mother archetype is being personalized, making possible ongoing access to primordial consciousness after separation from her. It is "she," *now part of the inner person* by the process of personalization, that must continue to mediate this consciousness. The personalization is the means by which the eternal dimensions of the archetypal realm can become incarnate in the daily life of the person. (Edinger 1988, p. 269) This internalized positive mother is sometimes called the "maternal matrix."[2] It is a major component of Self/soul. It is the internalized maternal matrix and other archetypal patterns that sustain, or are the locus of, primordial consciousness. The matrix is *theotokos* (God-bearer). Since Abyss/God is immanent to the body and psyche, it only makes sense that the person must be "at home" in this profound sense of a strong, positive maternal matrix if Abyss/God is to be received.

This archetypal dimension of the maternal matrix is the inner personal manner in which our identity as beings with ancient archetypal patterns become integrated into the ancient Earth and into Abyss/God. If there is a positive personalization, the eternal dimensions of the archetypal realm continue to be available to the developing person. As Alexander Lowen, a psychoanalyst and advocate of bioenergetics, writes in *Depression and the Body* (1973): "We must recognize that true spirituality has a physical or biological basis. . . . Belief is the result of mental activity but faith is rooted in the deep biological processes of the body." (p. 12)

But we are getting too far ahead: We will consider the healing of the maternal matrix and other aspects of healing in chapters 17–19.

Relationship Needs of the Infant

Some of the specifics of the personalization process can be clarified by considering the primary relationship needs of the child and some of the ways in which they are fulfilled, and the ways in which there is failure of fulfillment. The failure or success in fulfilling these needs has important consequences for the condition of the maternal matrix, which in turn affects the contemplative pathway. The primary relational needs of the child are mirroring, respect, attention, touching, caressing, tenderness, steady presentation of the world, acceptance, and understanding.[3] (Miller 1984, pp. 53, 282, 316) Perhaps there are others, not recognized. By fulfillment of these needs, the developmental potential of the child unfolds and the child acquires the roots of his physical and psychological sense of self.

The Story of a Family

There was a family with two young boys, Ken, age five, and David, almost four, living on a farm in New Jersey in the late 1930s. A third child was expected at any moment, when David became ill, perhaps because he contracted a virus when he fell into a ditch one chilly March morning. His illness began as a simple ear infection, but a high fever developed and the family became alarmed. Frances, the mother, stayed up much of the night caring for David, but when labor pains began in the early morning she had to leave for the hospital. The third child, a girl, was born the last day of winter in 1938 in Philadelphia. The next day David was taken to the same hospital, seriously ill with spinal meningitis. Frances was not able to be with her son because there was fear of contagion. Frances felt she heard David call for her, but she could not go to him. Three days after he baby was born, David died. He was buried before his mother and the new baby came home from the hospital. Frances's cousin remembers that Maurice, David's father, was so stricken at the funeral that he looked like a white, stone statue.

One can scarcely fathom the emptiness of the house to which mother and baby returned. So great a grief coupled with the taxing responsibility of caring for a newborn is a nearly impossible combination. In our culture, sometimes parents who lose young children subsequently die themselves; frequently a divorce follows. Frances could not speak about David's death for years. In the weeks and months after David's death, Ken often asked why David could not come back from his "heavenly Father."

I was the infant girl born that March. As a result of David's death, I was not welcomed in a loving, joyful way into the human family. I did not receive the love and attention an infant and young child naturally wants and needs. My parents' attention was captured by their loss and grief. Fortunately, an extended family, with four grandparents and aunts and uncles all living within five miles, helped ameliorate the situation.

Nevertheless, the loss of love and attention left a profound psychological wound, which was unconscious for many years, and which drove me on a long religious and psychological search for healing. I have been compelled to try to understand the relationship between my inner psychological situation and the quest for a satisfying physical, interpersonal, and spiritual belonging. A supportive, patient husband; faithful friends; insights through reading and study; and a Jungian analyst able to relate to the neediness and loss have all been essential in my coming to know how personal, psychological healing is integral to the search of the soul and Abyss/God.

My early experience was by no means a unique experience, although the specifics were unusual. But how many children in war-torn countries are met in a similar way? For a variety of social and psychological reasons parents may not be able to adequately carry out the tasks of parenthood by fulfilling the child's legitimate needs. Affecting the mother may be war, poverty, debilitating disease or death, prejudice, unsupportive or even abusive husbands, disintegrating marriages, misplaced values in the society—all are likely to cause serious impairment in the performance of maternal tasks unless the mother or someone close to the child is unusually strong.[4] Children whose parents survived the holocaust often suffered severe emotional deprivation. How many inner city children are neglected by parents unable and unprepared to cope in a complex, often racist society? These circumstances as well psychological disturbances of the mother herself, described in part in this chapter, may mean that she is not able to be "good enough." Thus my search for a 'way of seeing' and for a spiritual pathway that incorporate psychological trauma addresses a very common need.

The Need for Love

To meet the child's legitimate needs, the mother must provide basic, genuine, caring nourishment that goes beyond being conscientious and providing enough food, security, sleep and healthcare. W. R. D. Fairbairn, an English object relations analyst and theorist, said the critical factor in the formation of the self is the degree to which the child experiences himself as loved for his own sake. In *Psychotherapy and Religion* (1956), Harry Guntrip, also an object relations analyst, wrote: "*The child who was not loved for his own sake and not treated as a person in his own right, never at bottom feels he is one.*" (p.137) The young human person needs a soul mate from his earliest months. For the mother to have this capacity to love she must be at home with her body and her feelings, have self-assurance, accept the natural feelings and demands of the child, and love the child's total being. Techniques of child rearing and manipulation cannot take the place of devoted care and love.

The Need for Mirroring

An essential function of the mother or primary caretaker is to act as a *mirror* to the child. Functioning as a mirror, the mother provides the infant with a reflection of his own experience and gestures. Since the child initially is psychologically merged with the mother and has no separate sense of self, the child absorbs the mother's gaze and attitude and behavior as if they actually depicted and reflected his own personal condition. Sometimes, however, the child does not find himself mirrored in the mother's face, but finds instead the mother's own sufferings and predicaments. My mother's face reflected her suffering. Clearly there will be confusion if the mirroring function of the mother reflects not the child but other information related to the mother's personal situation.

Mirroring is of fundamental importance, serving to awaken the sense of self in a way similar to the awakening that Elkin recognized. The mother gazes at the baby in her arms, and the baby gazes at the mother's face and finds himself therein, provided that the mother is really looking at the unique, small, helpless being. "When I look I am seen, so I exist." (Winnicott 1965, p.61) If the child remains without a mirror through inconsistent, inadequate or missing parental reflection, for the rest of his life he seeks a "mirror" in relation to whom he will be seen and loved as a unique, separate individual. (Winnicott 1971, p.112 and Miller 1981, p.32)

The Need for Empathy

Perhaps the most important capacity of the mother is that she have sufficient *empathy* to perceive and meet appropriately the child's legitimate needs. Given its dependent, helpless situation, the infant requires that there be someone to be aware of the specific care being silently requested. Heinz Kohut, self psychology theorist, regards the empathic perception of the child's needs as of the greatest psychological significance, especially with regard to the child's ability to consolidate the nuclear self. (Kohut 1977, p.95) The mother equipped with a mature psychological organization can realistically assess the child's needs and decide what to do about them. Her emotional and physical response is transmitted to the child via her touch, tone of voice, movement, and expression. (p.86) When the mother is able to resonate with the baby's wants and needs, the latter becomes attuned to his own bodily functions and impulses, which become the basis for the evolving sense of self. (Greenberg and Mitchell, p.193) In other words there has been a fit. As the child's legitimate needs are met, the child is developing automatic, natural contact with his own wishes, which gives him strength and self-esteem. Inner vitality is encouraged; the true self is forming.

The empathic awareness of the mother must extend beyond meeting the child's basic biological needs to empathy for the child's feelings, giving external, objective validity to his inner, subjective reality. If the mother responds with joy and delight in the child's expressiveness, her joy endows the child with a sense of inherent value and worth. But if the mother is joyless, she conveys to the child a sense of worthlessness, attaching a stigma of shame to spontaneous actions and desires. (Elkin 1958, pp.409–10) The child does not know that the mother's joyless-ness or anxiety is the result of the mother's personal situation, since the infant does not see himself as separate and distinct from the mother. The baby can only feel that he is somehow involved in the joylessness and may assume a fundamental guilt as a result. One can readily imagine a child venturing into a new activity such as squealing. If this is met with a joyful responsiveness, the very being of the child is affirmed, whereas if it is hardly noticed, or is discouraged, the child will feel guilty and ashamed of his natural being.

If the mother repeatedly fails to be aware of the infant's situation and does not offer what the child really needs, the infant has to comply and fit into the framework that is given—to learn while still very young to block feelings and responses, thereby pretending normality. Since the infant's legitimate needs are not met and authenticated, the infant does not learn to recognize them and rely on them. Dimensions of the child's own being are not known, because they have not been fully personal-ized. The child forfeits inner vitality because his inner strength has been sapped by having to comply or be defensive. (Horney 1950, p. 20)

The body of the child, as well as the psyche, is affected by the mother's empathic failure. Initially, the child's body is molded to that of the mother, as if his body and that of his mother were merged. It can be a state of bliss and harmony, communicated through the body by caressing, holding, touching, and general physical contact while meeting the child's needs. However, when the mother is upset or angry or tense, these feelings are communicated physically and the child stiffens and pulls away. If the mother's condition is chronic, physical symptoms may result.[5] (Kaplan, p. 28)The child cannot relax into the mother's body, nor later into his own. (Woodman 1982, p. 85) A woman at a conference whose mother had a negative attitude toward her body said that she was raised to be robot-like. She felt she lacked emotion, personal vitality, and contact with the reality of physical life, and had only "machinery" inside. She ran on will.

One common reason for maternal failure of empathy is narcissism.[6] The term *narcissism* is derived from the Greek legend of the youth Narcissus, who fell in love with his own reflection, and is used broadly to refer to the psychological situation in which undue energy and attention are focused on the self. A narcissistic mother lacks autonomy, and still needs to be mirrored herself because her own inner needs were not adequately met at the proper time in her childhood. A poignant phrase used by Alice Miller, a European psychoanalyst, describes a mother who was dependent "on a specific echo from the child that was so essential for her." (Miller 1981, p. 11) In this phrase is the tragic picture of a narcissistic mother, herself desperately needing primary recognition, admiration, mirroring, and confirmation. The most available object for gratification, by means of which she tries to assuage her own narcissistic needs, is her child, who is completely dependent on her. Unconsciously and despite good intentions, her narcissism has a particularly destructive effect on her child because the child, required to respond to the mother's needs, cannot learn to rely on his own developing personhood. To insure she receives the still-needed attention, the mother molds the child to respond and conform to her need, and the child, out of an amazing ability to perceive and respond intuitively to this need, takes on the role that has been unconsciously assigned. (Miller 1981, p. 8) The child does not receive empathic recognition and response in his own right but only as he complies with and gratifies the mother's unconscious needs, which he is forced to do, or else risk overt rejection and the loss of whatever "love" and attention is given. In this deadly psychological situation, the child loses contact with his own impulses, his own initiatives, and his own legitimate feelings and needs, and does not develop a strong sense of self and the capacity to trust himself. The child is "being walked" rather than "walking" of his own volition. (Woodman 1982, p. 34)

In a sermon a minister once remarked with disarming honesty: "We give everything to our children but ourselves." Except in rare moments of insight and painful honesty, parents may not realize that they are only partially available to the child. The consequences of this may be devastating. Lacking adequate response for any of these reasons, the child has no reliable way of learning inner self-regulation through his own feelings. Without individual feeling values, a person observes his own behavior by judging how it looks from the outside, and then switches into false feeling and behaves to please and manipulate others. As a consequence, enjoyment of relationships of genuine interdependence becomes elusive.

For millennia it has been permissible and customary for children to be used to satisfy a wide variety of adult needs. They have provided a cheap source of labor; an ideal outlet for the discharge of stored-up emotion; a receptacle for unwanted feelings; an object for the projection of conflicts, hatred, and fears; compensation for feelings of inferiority; satisfaction of the "need for a specific echo"; and an opportunity for exercising power and obtaining pleasure. (Miller 1984, pp. 196, 312) Often children are the mute receivers of adult projections, the power of which can make life difficult even for an experienced analyst. Unable to defend themselves against the projections, unable to give them back to the adult or interpret them, children are able only to serve as their bearers. This can place a heavy burden on them for the rest of their lives.

Jung observed that the growing child is most strongly influenced by the surrounding affective environment, of which the parents and teachers may be totally unconscious. He wrote: "Concealed dissension between parents, secret suffering, repressed and hidden desires, all engender in the child an affective state that slowly but surely, even though unconsciously, finds its way into the psyche, where it produces the same state. . . . If adults are as sensitive as they are to the influence of their surroundings, then we must expect this to be true to an even greater extent for the child, whose mind is still as soft and malleable as wax." (As quoted in Miller 1984, p. 201) In *Children of the Holocaust*, Helen Epstein describes how the shape of her life was marred because both her parents were survivors of German death camps and were unable to talk about it. She was heavily burdened by her parents' past in spite of the fact that she was born and raised in the United States. (Cited in Miller 1984, p. 183)

Consequences of Parental Failure: Object Relations Theory

Object relations theory, a branch of psychoanalytic theory, has focused on the centrality of relationship in infant and child development. It is a body of sensitive insight into the molding of the human personality in its early relationships. The unfortunate word object is confusing because the object is usually a person, though it can be a body part or an inanimate object.[7]

Object relations theorists make personal (object) relations central to their understanding. They give psychological priority to the need of human beings to relate libidinally and significantly, not aggressively, to other human beings (the objects).[8] (Guntrip 1956, p. 43) Infants enter the world with the built-in assumption of living in relationship. There must be a fit between the infant and the mother, the father, and other caretakers. This is the same idea, within a different theoretical framework, of the need to personalize the archetype.

Melanie Klein pioneered the shift from the Freudian drive model of psychological functioning to the object-relational model.[9] She believed the basic units of mental process are not objectless energy but relational units *ab initio*. She wrote: "There is no instinctual urge, no anxiety situation, no mental process which does not involve objects, external or internal; in other words, object relations are at the center of emotional life." (Quoted in Greenberg and Mitchell, p. 138) Rollo May writes in *Man's Search for Himself* (1953):

> The Human being gets his original experience of being a self out of his relatedness to other persons. . . It is precisely when and because a child is denied the experience of being genuinely personally related to his parents, that he is unable to achieve the "experience of being a self." He then feels empty and unreal in a quite fundamental way underneath all his later experiences in life. (p. 28)

Although object relations theorists do not explicitly recognize the archetypal patterns that must be personalized, they assume an inherited developmental potential and recognize intrinsic patterns of behavior and the need for the object. Their insights regarding parent-child relationships and the consequences of their failure are, of course, applicable when the presence of inherited, ancient patterns of behavior (archetypes) is assumed, although the conception of the results differs in some ways, as described below. They clarify in an important way the manner in which the maternal matrix is affected and why there can be loss of internal receptivity to God-consciousness and the wisdom of Self/soul.

Split-Off Egos and Complexes

Although working with somewhat different conceptions of the structure of the psyche, both the archetypal psychology of Jung and object relations theory recognize the formation of patterns in the developing personality that achieve a certain independence from the central, conscious personality. We are under the influence of these patterns when we say "I don't know what got into me." Object relations people call them split off parts of the ego. Jung called them complexes.

The word *ego* as used by W. R. D. Fairbairn is not just a portion of the personality, as Freud conceived of it, but the primary
psychic self that is originally in a state of wholeness and integration in the infant. Ideally it remains in this condition even as the
differentiated state of the adult develops.[10] Here the word *self* is
used instead of *ego* to describe Fairbairn's conception of the
person so as to avoid the word *ego*, which has been previously
used in discussing Jung's thought. (The word *Self* with a capital
S will continue be used in the Jungian sense to signify the whole
psyche, including transpersonal dimensions.)

Complexes in Jung's thought are described as having an
autonomy "somewhat like a small, secondary mind," such that
they are relatively independent of the central control of consciousness and at any moment liable to bend or cross the
conscious intentions of the individual. (CW vol. 2, par. 1352)
According to archetypal psychology, complexes are usually
formed from negative personalization of part of the original
patterned energy of the child; so, for example, a mother complex
may form from the manner in which the mother archetype is
personalized. Jung's conception of complexes differs in an
important way from the object-relations idea of split-off self
(actually, split-off ego in object-relations vocabulary), in that
complexes coalesce around, or are in some manner related to,
archetypal energies. Thus the Jungian conception goes beyond
object relations theory to connect the woundings of personal
history with ancient energy patterns (archetypes), enabling us to
see, for example, why evil, as a turning of archetypal energy in
destructive directions, is so powerful and seemingly intractable.
We also see why evil can have a numinous quality, since transpersonal energies may be involved in this destructive channeling
of archetypal power. Powerful complexes can overcome the ego.

Something similar, though without the dimension of archetypal energy, is described by object relations theory. If relations
with the mother or other primary caretaker are satisfactory
during the period of merger and the transitional phase, the self
remains integral and whole, with its full libidinal potential

available for relations with actual people (external objects).[11] However, if relations are unsatisfactory, the self is divided by the formation of an internalized replication of the actual parent-child relationship. Instead of being related to a person in the world, the child's relationship-seeking is turned toward an inner figure, called an inner object.[12] A relationship-seeking (object-seeking) aspect of the child, having identified with the rejecting aspect of the mother (bad object), becomes active inwardly, with the result that the child rejects aspects of his own self in the same manner he was rejected. As a consequence of the splitting, the self grows in active relationship not only with external objects but also with the internal objects, which form the personal unconscious. A complex set of internalized object relations is established, so that fantasies and anxieties concerning the state of one's internal object world become the underlying basis for one's behavior, moods and sense of self. (Greenberg and Mitchell, p. 125) The splitting-off of the internalized inner system leaves a weakened central self and an impoverished capacity for relationship with external objects. The degree to which a person achieves normal development is governed by the intensity of the affects of the internal relationships. Splitting is considered to be present in essentially everyone in varying degrees of severity.[13] Recognizable characteristics of the two systems of splitting, described below, can be seen in even very stable people at all phases of life on the way to maturity.

Two Types of Split-off Selves

There are two basic patterns of splitting which clarify the broad types of unconscious patterns that underlie much of adult behavior, profoundly affecting our physical, psychological, and spiritual lives. The spiritual problems caused by these inner patterns have been recognized throughout the centuries in writings about the spiritual pathway, although under different names and conceptualized differently, of course.

As described by Fairbairn, the two types of split-off portions of the self are called respectively the anti-libidinal ego (or self), which will be signified here by the easier name of "dragon" or "evil emperor," and the libidinal ego, which will be called the "wolf."[14] The anti-libidinal ego acts against the basic life energy (libido) of the child. The libidinal ego seeks relationship with an enticing but unfulfilling inner object. Typically the initial patterns of "dragon" and "wolf" have their origin in bodily experience, primarily in relation to the mother or others intimately involved with the child prior to the phase of separation. (Elkin 1965, pp. 187–88)

The Inner Dragon: Response to Parental Commission

One type of split-off self, the "dragon" or "evil emperor" (the anti-libidinal ego), is formed in reaction to the rejecting parent, who consistently spurns the child's advances, crossly threatens, attacks, and frightens him. When the rejecting parent is internalized, becoming an inner object, a part of the child is split off from the central self and continues in relationship with that inner object, repeating internally the pattern initially established in relation to the threatening, rejecting parent. It is an internal censor, the internal judging "parent" that sabotages the personality; hence, it is anti-libidinal.[15] Fairbairn called this split-off part of the self the internal saboteur, because it is turned against the child's own needs out of a now internalized fear of parental disapproval and rejection. The terms dragon or the evil emperor are used for it here because it sabotages all the child's active, spontaneous, and creative self-expression.[16] (Guntrip 1956, p. 81) Depression arises as hate and anger become internalized and directed toward part of the self, the part identified with the parent. Fairbairn called this psychological configuration the depressive position.

Harry Guntrip calls the quality of the child's love in this split-off portion of the self "love made angry" (p. 97), and the anger of the evil emperor can be very great. The child wants to smack the parent who smacks him and reject the parent who rejects him, until fear makes him lock up his anger inside and even turn it against himself, so that he becomes inhibited and develops the basis for obsessional, hysteric, and psychosomatic illness. (p.79) The anger and hate may be so intense that the child fears unconsciously he will destroy the very person he needs and loves. If the adult the child becomes is threatened by a challenge to identity or by an insult, the rejection may unleash repressed fury and rage. It can be a rage against life from which one has been excluded. The inner anger may cause the person to "show them," to punish authority, punish the weaker, or to perceive the falseness of parental figures in many guises of authority. Furthermore, he may have learned not only not to be *attuned* to his own basic human needs, such as the need to relax and care for body and soul, but to be hostile toward them, sometimes driving and manipulating the body, starving it or overeating, to obtain comfort. There can also be a rage against God, who has not protected the vulnerable individual.

The internalization of parental attitudes initially has survival value, because the child cannot leave the parents and so must preserve the nearly unbreakable ties with them at all cost. The identification and repression reduce the inclination to express both dangerous desires and aggression toward them. Furthermore the child cannot consciously feel and tolerate repeated misuse and neglect, since this is too painful, isolating, and threatening to the developing sense of self. Splitting relieves him from experiencing unbearable awareness of helplessness, fear, isolation, and betrayal. Thus the internalization of the destructive relationship has short term gains, because it allows the child to make the people in the environment "good" by taking upon himself the burden of their "badness" and thus to make his environment more tolerable. (Fairbairn 1954, p.164) But the defensive attempt to establish outer security is purchased at the price of inner security, since it leaves the self at the mercy of inner persecutors.

The formation of this type of split-off self means that there has not been adequate separation from the mother (father, caretaker). The child, and later the adult, is still unconsciously reacting to the rejecting parent, now internalized as an inner object. In Jungian thought, the ego has not separated from the archetypal mother. It is important to realize that, however disruptive, the anger is still relational in nature and contains enormous energy that may be used productively by the conscious personality if it can be reintegrated to the central self.

The Inner Wolf: Response to Parental Omission

The other type of split-off self is the inner wolf (the libidinal ego). The split-off self in this type of repressed relationship system continues actively—hungrily, like a wolf—to seek relationship with other people (object seeking). The person wants recognition and a place in life, legitimately needed but not granted by the mother. The object to which the split-off portion of the self is attached internally is exciting and enticing, but not satisfying. Harry Guntrip calls this unfulfilling aspect of the mother the "desirable deserter," since she was tantalizing but finally failed to satisfy the child's needs. The mother was libidinally exciting, arousing the child's desire (libido) to be valued and understood, and to be the recipient of genuine interest. Although the child's desire to be loved, comforted, and caressed, and to enjoy bodily intimacies with her mother, were awakened, they were not satisfied, and the child was left hungry for full relatedness and in a constant state of unsatisfied desire.[17] The person is always hungry for love and attention and can be greedily devouring of those with whom he seeks to be related. This split-off self is often described as the unconscious, hungry, needy, inner child.

So, the child's love in this split-off portion of the self becomes "love made hungry," which is felt by the person to be a dangerous impulse that can lead to the draining, exhaustion, and destruction of the love-object. (Guntrip, p. 98) Deep in the unconscious, sexual need is felt as a desire to suck, to eat, to swallow and incorporate the object. The person seeks to prove worth and gain admiration and acceptance. Because of the fear that the needy love itself may become so strong as to be destructive, he may withdraw and become aloof, hostile to his own needs. But in spite of the fear, the "wolf" is a valuable portion of the self, worthy of attention, because it still seeks relationship. There remains an inner hope that satisfactory, fulfilling, relationship may be found.

In an adult, the presence of this wolf-like hunger means the individual remains unconsciously bound and attached to the now internalized, unfulfilling mother—an attachment expressed in many forms in relation to the actual mother and to other people or physical objects. There are often repetitions of the original unfulfilling situation, although healing relationships fortunately can be found. (See chapter 18.) The wolf is the part of the self that may ardently seek God, but it does not know how to receive the desired fulfillment; the person is instead in flight from the central self that can receive the fullness of our being. The wolf is unable to fully relate to Abyss/God and to join the community of life.

The relationship with people other than the mother may affect the early splitting for better or worse, thus either ameliorating or aggravating the inner situation. Commonly a composite, complex structure is derived from relations with both parents. In the course of time other people—siblings, acquaintances, teachers, workmates, bosses, friends and enemies—contribute to the mental elaborations of the internal relationship system, described below, which is the central self that is not split-off in relation to the internalized ideal object. Notice that both the inner figures (inner objects) derived from identification with mother or father or other close figures, are ungratifying. Both types of split-off selves have their own inherent energy (libido) that continues to be object seeking, but are now separated from awareness of the conscious central personality (the central self or ego in object relations terms).

An inner environment that is not supportive of a strong conscious central self has been internalized into the developing personality. Tragically, with self splitting there is a loss of the primary unity of psychic life, with the result that individuals are internally at odds with themselves. The energy available to the still conscious central self has been diminished and weakened by the splitting.

Archetypal Psychology

Complexes, as mentioned, are formed as personal experience coalesces with archetypal patterns. In the thought of Jung, rather than the splitting of the self, the personalization of the mother archetype results in the formation of mother complexes of various types. There are, of course, other complexes, such as the father complex. The complex, with an inner life of its own, influences the life of the conscious person according to its autonomous energy patterns. In archetypal psychology, a mother archetype involves transpersonal energies, so the complexes will likewise involve them. Thus an addiction (an expression of the wolf-like need) involves a craving for God, a longing for the sacred. Jungian analyst Marion Woodman explains that in eating a symbolically important food, the addicted person searches for a loving mother and contact with God. But because the addiction is based on the neediness of the split-off self tied to the internalized, negative mother (object) who did not mediate divine reality for the person, there results no nourishment of the soul and personhood. Abyss/God cannot be found because the wolf-like neediness continues to be related to an object that fails to fulfill—there is no established pattern of god-consciousness and inner fullness of being. Woodman describes a "muffaholic" for whom bingeing on muffins is a misdirected attempt (misdirected in object relations terms because of the turning of inner libido toward negative inner objects) to find in eating muffins what the church calls the transubstantial Christ. (Woodman 1982, p. 56) For there to be a receptivity to God, the addiction must be sacrificed and the demonic ritual of bingeing replaced by the sacred ritual in which our Self/soul receives God's body as the fruit of the Earth.

Long Term Consequences

These patterns of splitting buried in the psyche are not a passing phase of childhood, but can persist throughout life, perpetuating past ties along with their accompanying hungers and angers. People maintain an inner pattern of old internal attachments and allegiances to early significant others, no matter how ungratifying they may have been and how detrimental they are to the personality. There is more than ample evidence for the persistence of these patterns, as most people could testify. W. R. D. Fairbairn once examined a large number of delinquent children from homes rife with drunkenness, quarreling, and physical violence. Only very rarely could the children be induced to admit, far less volunteer, that their parents were abusive and violent. Instead the child takes the side of those who frustrate and hurt him, and so identifies internally with them that he himself feels bad, turns the aggression against himself, and in the end is unable to separate himself from the unsatisfactory inner figures.[18] (Guntrip, p. 86) Thus, psychologically, a person's major problems are caused by unshakable primary emotional loyalties, which perpetuate the world of infancy and early childhood. Edinger suggests that a person clings to the original experience of the parent, even if negative, because it is the aspect of the image that has been personalized and therefore has an element of security, even though it is negative.[19] (Edinger 1988, p. 266)

As a result of such repressed relationship patterns, people live outwardly in the present and inwardly in the past at one and the same time. We are commonly largely unaware that the character of the conscious and socially adapted personality is not only an adjustment to the demands of the outer world, but also a means of control over, and a defense against, internal dangers threatening from the inner world of the unconscious. The inner life out of which basic emotions arise is hidden away during waking hours behind an iron curtain of repression, while the outer world engages the conscious attention.

The consequences with regard to attempts to follow the contemplative pathway are significant. Both the neediness and/or anger unconsciously mold and dominate the personality. There cannot be a relaxed "at-homeness" or letting go. We do indeed run away from our Self/soul and Abyss/God, and from the totality of our being, often largely unaware that we are doing so. Consciously aware only of our attempts to seek, the patterns by which we seek in a false manner or reject and flee are largely unconscious. The personality has agendas of which we are largely unaware. People may suffer from both the anger and the hunger and oscillate between them. We create a society of fear, lack of trust and aggression because of the power of these hidden systems. As Jung said, what we don't bring to consciousness, we live out unconsciously. (Cited in Woodman 1993, p. 125)

The Central Self (Ego) and the Idealized Self

There is a further tactic of the psyche that compensates for the splitting of the self. The central self, the part of the self that remains conscious after the splitting-off of parts of the self, is in relationship with the ideal object, the gratifying aspects of the mother and father. Since the enticing and rejecting aspects of the parents are split-off and repressed, the actual parent with whom the central self relates is quite idealized: The child comes to see one or the other, if not both, of his outer real parents as better than they are, and unconsciously experiences his inner, repressed, mental versions of them as worse than they are. Often people think they had an ideal family with a happy childhood, yet they are disturbed in dreams by terrifying figures which are in fact the repressed bad side of their parents.

The central self is the part of the person still available for relations with real people in the external world and partakes in personal growth. This is the functioning central core of the personality to which split-off portions of the self can be reintegrated when they lose their autonomous power, healed by love, mirroring and empathy in the context of new relationships.

Accompanying the idealization of parents is a self-idealization. In the face of the threatening energies of the repressed dragon and wolf, the child needs knowledge of his own value, of his own power and significance. This is provided by the idealized self, with which the child identifies, and to the actualizing of which he turns all available energy. (Horney 1950, p. 24) The personality has been structured to get along as well possible without the inner, receptive maternal matrix that would have resulted from internalization of a positive relationship with a caring adult. Armed with an array of defense mechanisms to avoid recognition of its true personal condition and its internal divisions, the self-idealization can often be quite successful at its assigned task of providing a form of identity. Considerable achievement may ensue.

The idealized self serves to cover up, and distract attention from, painful and frightening feelings of emptiness, anger, loneliness, inferiority, needy restlessness, and an inability to receive emotional nourishment. The need to actualize the idealized self is compulsive, since it feels like the solution so desperately required. But this "solution" is particularly tragic with respect to the contemplative life, since the idealized self has its own god-like agenda, often filled with false pride. It must be the subject and it must be in control. The pharisaic person who achieves a kind of external moral perfection exemplifies the idealized self, but such moral perfection is covering (and covering for) an angry, needy, divided person who is not related to his actual situation, to others, to his Self/soul, or to the encompassing Abyss/God in a personally fulfilling manner. Commonly the pharisaic person is plagued by hidden secret desires and angers as the split-off selves, presenting their own neediness and anger, do not comply with the ideals of the conscious person. Whatever his accomplishments, the price paid by the person is the loss or diminishment of wholeness.

With the idealization of the conscious self that compensates for splitting, a fundamentally dualistic pattern, recognized since the early ages of humanity as an antagonism of body vs. mind, is established. (Guntrip, p.85) The neediness of the inner "wolf" is often of a physical and sexual nature, making the body seem to be foreign and in need of control. And, at the same time, energy and attention are focused on the idealized self, often around moral and spiritual, or perhaps military, ideals. The ideals may be valuable in themselves, but dangerous when pursued in a manner alienated from body and soul. Furthermore without the neglected body and soul, the ideals will not be realized.

Concluding Reflections

Clearly it is important to understand how a strong maternal matrix can be restored so the person knows he belongs and that the world holds him. With awareness of the deep embeddedness of the human in the Earth, embraced through the maternal matrix, the so-called feminine dimensions of life are recognized for their great value and no longer denigrated. The person is able to relax, to be at home in himself and to receive his physical, psychological and spiritual reality.

---

[1] Although the developmental patterns in human beings are highly complex and variable in their expression, we can illustrate the release of instinctual, patterned behavior with an example in an animal. A newborn gull stands next to the mother's beak ready to be fed. It has been determined that it is the red spot on the mother gull's beak that evokes this positioning of the baby gull. The red spot, and it must be red, is a specific stimulus, the "sign stimulus." In the development of animal behavior there are commonly more than one "sign stimulus" with long and complex reactions that occur in chains. When one stimulus has been exhausted, another takes over and so on. Studies of the sign stimuli in gulls and in other animals have determined that the selection of the sign stimuli out of the perceptual field releases the instinctual response from inhibition. (Fordham 1957, pp. 12–13) This conforms with the assumption that the pattern is innate, not learned.

In human beings the patterns are emotionally and physically complex and difficult to study, but nonetheless there is ample evidence that a comparable signal or recognition of some kind between the mother and the infant is required for development. René Spitz, a psychiatrist who did research in infant development, has shown that two eyes moving up and down in the manner of a nodding head elicited the staring and smiling responses of two-month-old babies. The response is strengthened if a hair-line is drawn on the dummy to emphasize the nodding and if a crude mouth is added with its corners turned up to represent a smile. (Stevens 1983, p. 57) Recall that Henry Elkin has suggested that eye-to-eye contact and the smiling face are part of the reception of the mother of the child when primordial consciousness is awakening.

[2] In object relations terms, the "maternal matrix" would be referred to as an empathic inner object. (See Miller 1984, p. 302.)

[3] These needs are sometimes called narcissistic needs, but that has an inappropriate pejorative connotation that does not recognize the needs of the infant as natural, legitimate needs, appropriate to the infant's situation of dependence and helplessness. Many authors reserve the term narcissistic to describe self-directed love that develops secondarily in the personality if the primary relationship needs are not met.

[4] We will assume it is the mother who is the primary care giver, although it will sometimes be the father or some other person. We will refer to the mother as the care giver because of the significance of the bonding between the woman and child during pregnancy and at birth, and because it is the mother who may nurse the child.

[5] According to Alice Miller, there are babies who are so highly sensitive that they sense their mother's distress and rejection in their first contact with her breast in the first days of life, and express their anxiety in various physical symptoms. (1984, p. 276)

[6] American psychoanalyst Heinz Kohut describes three elements in the mother's personality that prevent the development of the creative personality in the child: (a) *self-absorption* which may lead to a projection of the mother's own moods and tension on to the child with consequent faulty empathy on the part of the mother; (b) *overresponse* to certain moods and tensions in the child that correspond to her own narcissistic tension states and preoccupation; and (c) *unresponsiveness* to the moods expressed by the child. (1971, p.65)

[7] For Fairbairn "natural objects" or "primary objects," that is, objects which the libido seeks prior to any deprivation or interference, are simply other people. (Greenberg and Mitchell, p. 158)

Although Freud recognized that drives have an object, in his thought the object was not inherently or originally connected with the drive, although there could be no expression of drive demand without at least an implicit object.

[8] "Libido" is the psychoanalytic term for the basic life-urge, the desire and drive to live, to love, to achieve good relations with the object world. Freud regarded it more narrowly as the sexual drive, though he broadened the definition of sexual. For Fairbairn, libido is the primary object seeking life drive. He regards the sexual drive as only a part of libido. (Guntrip, p. 42)

Analyst Louise Kaplan describes the need to relate to the object as follows: "In the beginning the baby is bound to his mother's presence by virtue of his physical excitements and appetites. By three months he is already bound to her by his psychological desire for human dialogue. The fear of loss of dialogue with his mother will become more central in the baby's life than his fear of humger and inner tension." (Kaplan 1978, p. 95) Fairbairn belived that from the moment of birth the mother-infant relationship is potentially fully personal on both sides, in however primitive and undeveloped a way this is felt by the baby. (Guntrip 1964, p. 184)

[9] Melanie Klein's contribution to the shift from the Freudian drive model to an object-relational model was to explore infantile fantasies and to recognize the fact that the ego has relationships with mentally internalized objects, both good and bad. She developed an analysis of endopsychic structure in terms of object relations, although she never abandoned the Freudian structure of the personality the way Fairbairn did. However, her perspective represents a fundamental shift from Freudian thought with regard to the motivation of the individual. Pleasure seeking is directionless and impersonal for Freud, not object seeking. (Fairbairn 1954, p. 176)

[10] Fairbairn rejected Freud's hypothesis of an innate division in the psyche in which the ego and superego must control the unruly libido of the separate, impersonal id, where instinctual energy resides. Fairbairn had a quite enlarged conception of the ego compared to Freud, because he conceived of the ego as having its own inherent libido. The unitary, originally whole ego differentiates into organized structured patterns under the impact of the experience of object relationships after birth. The dimension of the personality that Freud called the id is considered by object relations theorists to be a secondary development that is a consequence of a division in the ego ("splitting"). It is not innate, but it is created from a split-off portion of the ego unacceptable to consciousness and separated from the awareness of the conscious personality.

[11] Recall that in the first six months of infancy, psychologically speaking there is no such thing as an individual baby because the infant is intensely involved with its mother in a state of integration or symbiosis. Fairbairn thought the child is in such total merger with the mother as to "preclude his entertaining any thought of differentiation from the maternal body, which constitutes his whole environment and the whole world of his experience." (Fairbairn 1954, p. 275) The separation is very gradual. The inability of the child to separate and distinguish feelings and events in the environment from self continues long after the period of merger, as shown by the feelings of guilt that children typically feel over the divorce of their parents or perhaps the death of a parent or sibling. The work of Margaret Mahler and Louise Kaplan suggests that it is only during the third year that a psychological being possessing selfhood and separate identity is born, in a process they refer to as the second birth or psychological birth. (Kaplan, pp. 15, 30)

[12] Inner objects are formed, Melanie Klein postulated, in response to the painful feelings of frustration in infancy and childhood and the intense aggression associated with these feelings. (Discussed in Sutherland 1963, p. 113) These objects are described as introjects, the internalization of the experience of relationship.

[13] A basic assumption of object relations theory is that splitting of the self is found not only in overtly schizoid states but also in the psychoneuroses, and indeed in psychopathological conditions generally. (Fairbairn 1954, p. 162)

[14] Technically the two split-off portions of the self are called the anti-libidinal ego and the libidinal ego. Fairbairn has described two main categories of inner bad objects and two main ways the divided ego (or self) behaves towards these two types of objects. The libidinal ego is related to the enticing bad object and the anti-libidinal ego to the rejecting bad object.

The respective characteristics of the split-off portions of the self are derived from the quality of the repressed, still-object-related aspects of the self. One bad object is the outright denying and rejecting mother (or father), in relation to which the split-off self is angry and *dragon*-like. The other bad object is the promising, enticing mother (or father) who does not satisfy, in relation to which the split-off self is hungry and *wolf*-like.

[15] The inner object can have an antibody-like quality. In a 1987 article titled "Introducing Not Self," Leopold Stein, a Jungian analyst in London, helps us conceive just how serious the consequences may be if there is not an adequate reception of the child. He distinguishes what is incorporated in the sense of self and not incorporated in it using the terms self and not-self taken from the field of immunology. It is by means of the immune system that the body recognizes what is self and not self, and maintains its organismic wholeness as distinct from foreign bodies. The body recognizes (from Latin *re*: again, and *cognoscere*: to know) its own individual characteristics and rejects what is not self to preserve an intact self.)

An instructive example comes from the development of antibodies in a pregnant woman that then harm the fetus (antibodies defend the organism against invading foreign substances). Stein writes: "In mammals the unborn offspring participates in the mother's blood circulation in the womb and thus obtains the necessary nutriment. The unborn baby is, it must not be forgotten, separated from his mother by the placenta. It seems that sometimes cells from the embryo's blood pass this barrier, enter the mother's bloodstream and induce antibody formation. Antibodies then re-enter the baby's blood and cause serious harm to the red blood corpuscles (hemolytic disease). It can be seen that mother and baby are by no means always biologically compatible." (p. 100)

In this example the reaction by the mother's body to what is foreign to her body subsequently causes the child to react against part of his own self, via the absorbed antibodies. Using this and other immunological analogies Stein suggests that because of the reactions of the mother, the developing psychosomatic self of the child can apprehend its own constituents in the wrong sense, and defend itself against part of itself as if its were not-self. (p. 101) Stein's work makes it easier to imagine the confusing issue of inherited potential and the rejection of that very potential. We may wonder if this antibody analogy is too extreme an image. But there are numerous cases in which a psychosomatic disorder gradually develops as a belated expression of basic incompatibility between mother and child.

[16] It is the same psychological configuration as the superego described by Freud.

[17] Fairbairn called this split-off portion of the ego the libidinal ego, a phrase referring to its desirous seeking and longing for the enticing promise of relatedness, and called this type of splitting the schizoid position. The libidinal ego is comparable to Freud's id.

The reason for calling the split-off libidinal ego the wolf is that this animal symbolically represents hunger and measureless greed in many myths and fairy stories. We speak of "wolfing" food to mean eating with a kind of passionate greed. Marie-Louise von Franz comments that because of unhappy childhoods, thousands of children become lonely wolves, suffering from isolation and greed and the inability to make human contact. (von Franz 1980, p. 217)

[18] See the work of W. R. D. Fairbairn for an explanation of the repression of bad objects as a primary defense.

[19] Edinger writes: "For such a person [with a largely destructive parental experience] to encounter the positive aspect of the archetype is threatening because this side has never been personalized, it carries a transpersonal magnitude which threatens to dissolve the boundaries of the ego." (1988, p. 266)

V

THE CONTEMPLATIVE
JOURNEY AND ITS FRUITION

17

THE ACTIVE UNIVERSE WITHIN: SOURCES OF HEALING AND HOPE

You are quite right, the main interest of my work is not concerned with the treatment of neuroses but rather with the approach to the numinous. But the fact that the approach to the numinous is the real therapy and inasmuch as you attain to the numinous experiences you are released from the curse of pathology. Even the very disease takes on a numinous character.

— Carl Jung

A CRITICAL PHASE in this exploration of a 'way of seeing' is an inquiry into the pathway to becoming conscious, active participants, in a supremely personal manner, in the unfolding universe story. It has been known for centuries that the journey to full realization of our identity is a most difficult journey. We should have confidence, however, as Marion Woodman reminds us:

> We plant our fat amaryllis bulb, we water it, put it in the sunlight, watch the first green shoot, the rapidly growing stock, the buds, and then marvel at the great bell flowers tolling their hallelujahs to the snow outside. Why should we have more faith in an amaryllis bulb than in ourselves? Is it because we know that the amaryllis is living by some inner law— law that we have lost touch with ourselves? (1985, p. 15)

Many women are in a privileged position when it comes to appreciation of the organic processes of growth because of their experience with pregnancy and childbirth. There is a type of knowing offered to women in the course of these remarkable events, for the experience of pregnancy is that of participating in an inexorable and miraculous process that is occurring within the body. The woman has no control over the growth of the baby, although her support of the process with good nutrition, rest, and health care is important. She simply must wait out the months until the birth of the child, which itself happens spontaneously and in its own proper time. While we must have a more conscious, active involvement in the rebirth and transformation of our personhood, the experience of pregnancy and childbirth is deeply instructive with respect to the orientation the ego must take when confronted with the larger processes of the spiritual journey.

The pilgrim—the would-be contemplative—is faced with the mysterious task of allowing to develop within herself a transformed life that cannot be willed to develop. We seek to embrace our full being, and this includes embracing the consequences of tragedy and the failures in love that are buried in the body and psyche. Although the journey is often difficult, it is of supreme importance, for we know its realization will not only be of profound personal significance, but will affect our relationships with others and the total Earth community.

Active and Passive Dimensions of the Journey

We will explore two dimensions of the organic, healing process that can lead to the contemplative life. These are the active aspect, in which our conscious choices and cooperation are involved, and passive events, which occur spontaneously without conscious choice.

Teresa of Avila clearly emphasizes both the active and passive dimensions of the contemplative journey. In *The Interior Castle*, the seven places in which one may dwell in the castle, or seven states of being, are, as we saw in chapter 7, stages in the contemplative life and in contemplative prayer, as a person moves toward the central dwelling place, the unitive life imaged as marriage to God. Teresa describes the active role of the person when she tells her sisters that they have a part to play in building the castle. "There is no edifice as beautiful as is a soul pure and full of virtues. The greater the virtues, the more resplendent the jewels." (*Way of Perfection* 28. 9) She also uses the image of a silkworm weaving a cocoon from which a butterfly will emerge. She writes: "Let us be quick to do the work and weave this little cocoon by taking away our self-love and self-will," and then gives a variety of recommendations appropriate to a monastic spirituality. Yet seeming to contradict her advice about the active role of the person, Teresa also writes that we cannot enter God's dwelling place: His majesty must place us there. (IC VII. 2. 9 and VII. 1. 3) The grace of the various forms of contemplation are a pure gift; they are passively given states of prayer. In Book VI of *The Interior Castle* she describes a gold reliquary containing a precious stone of highest value and curative powers. She writes that "the manner of opening this reliquary is known solely by the one to whom the jewels belong . . . and [He] will open it . . . when he desires to show us the contents, and he will take the jewel back when he wants to, as he does." (IC VI. 9. 2)

The word passive is traditionally used in the contemplative tradition, but we should be warned that it may easily be misleading. The events that are designated as passive from the perspective of daily consciousness actually refer to ordering, healing dimensions of Self/soul, itself nested in the indwelling, creative, active, All-Nourishing Abyss (Abyss/God). These dimensions of our being are not passive, but very much alive and active. For example, nightly we are offered in dreams several remarkably creative dramas depicting in symbolic language something about the state of our inner life. The wisdom of the body plays an active role in the contemplative journey. We have recounted several breakthrough experiences in which the Generative Emptiness has made itself known in people in an active manner. So this "passive" dimension of the contemplative journey is precisely the dimension of it in which we can recognize, at a very personal level, our immersion in a creative, dynamic Earth and Universe as they are taking expression in the individual.

Since the so-called passive dimensions of the journey are considered in this chapter and the active ones in the next, it is important to remain cognizant of the fact that this separation into active and passive is somewhat artificial. While the passive and active aspects can be distinguished, recall that the ego, the instrument of conscious choice in the active aspects of preparation, rests on the foundation of the larger psyche, so its choices are not independent of the condition of that larger psyche and the "passive" events that may be occurring. Yet at times it is our conscious awareness and choices that are a decisive dimension of the journey, since they bring changes offered by the larger psyche or soul into daily life. Thus, the two aspects of the journey are deeply intertwined and both essential to the journey.

The Passive Dimensions of Preparation and Healing

Awakenings, breakthrough experiences, and subsequent dramatic events or peaceful nudges, come as a great surprise to the person. The person is passive before them. They may occur in many forms, including a quiet breakthrough of spirit, subtle feelings of presence; a physical healing; near death experiences; a major dream, sometimes involving a mandala; flashes of insight and understanding; and visionary and auditory events. They may occur in many contexts, including an awakening to the demands of justice as the value of persons is known; a sacramental celebration; in meditation and prayer; through nature, art, or literature; with exposure to the Word of God in the Bible or other sacred literature; in war; in love-making; through an encounter with a great historical spiritual figure or an inspiring, living person. One may have a breakthrough experience in a time of severe crisis or great despair. Sometimes awareness of an emptiness or profound longing motivates a person to seek therapeutic help or to begin meditation with a teacher. This can eventually lead to breakthrough experiences in either subtle or dramatic ways. We will explore various consequences of these experiences for the personality after first considering their fundamental nature in the light of the 'way of seeing' we have developed.

The Nature of Passive Breakthrough Experiences

To understand the passive dimensions of the awakening and preparation for contemplation, it is necessary to recall briefly what has been said about the nature of the person. The organizing activity of the universe brings forth centers of creativity, with each being given its unique existence. (Swimme and Berry, p. 74) We have identified the unseen, self-organizing, shaping capacity constitutive of the person as Self/soul, and we have located the genesis of form-generation in the implicate order of the generative *plenum* or Abyss/God, thus recognizing that the human being and other beings of the natural world are permanently and inseparably rooted in the ongoing creative power of the universe, at the Center, the omnipresent Center. We humans *are* predominantly this realm of ultimate creativity, a creative Nothingness (which we have seen in chapter 8 is actually a fecund, generative reality, the ultimate source of the manifest world).

In the light of this description of the person, we can identify the nature of an awakening. It is the reawakening of the primordial God-consciousness of Self/soul. It is the consciousness of Abyss/God known in the form (soul) of the particular individual. The awakening itself is the gratuitous showing forth (epiphany) or explication (unfolding) in human awareness of the *plenum* or Abyss/God. It is the awakening of the depth of the Self. As Erich Neumann put it, the numinous substratum bursts through the given cosmos. (Neumann 1968, p. 412) It is a passively given awakening of our deepest roots, such that we know that our identity extends into the origins of the universe, into the very font of holiness. (Swimme 1985, tape 1) Such a breakthrough results in a great augmentation of the consciousness of the person.

There is a wide range in the intensity of awakening experiences. Awakenings can be such that the All-Nourishing Abyss so dominates daily consciousness that it is briefly the sole content of experience, or they may not interrupt ongoing, daily self-awareness. They may or may not be accompanied by a wide variety of visual, auditory, cognitive, and physical events in various combinations. This discussion will be limited to non-dual experiences, defined below, and "I am" experiences, since they help us grasp what is happening in passive awakenings. Accompanying visions and auditions add important personal content to the experience, but do not change the essential nature of the breakthrough.

Non-Dual and "I Am" Experiences

Non-dual experiences refer to occasions when the person does not experience any separation between what is known and himself as the knower. It is a unitive knowing, such that the knower experiences himself to be one with what is known. In this type of experience, the mind escapes the duality of ordinary consciousness. (Dupré 1980, p. 459) It is not possible to describe such experiences in the words of daily discourse, because they involve an alternative type of knowing or loving. Abyss/God cannot be an object to the ego. Lawrence Kushner laments that "we are condemned to (re)discover time after time that you cannot behold that of which you are made without ceasing to be who you are." (p. 105) We are what we seek to study. The Hellenistic Jewish philosopher Philo Judaeus of Alexandria observed: "As in the case of light, which can only be seen by means of light, so too, God is not to be conceived except through Him: The questers after truth are they who envisage God by means of God, light by means of light." (Quoted in Kushner, p. 105) Evidence from interreligious dialogue demonstrates the great commonality of these experiences, since, given their non-cognitive nature, cultural factors hardly play a role in them.

Although words cannot adequately explicate the nature of unitive experience, Teresa of Avila wrote after return to herself from such a moment that the soul "can in no way doubt that it was in God and God was in it." (IC V. 1. 9) However difficult their communication, these events are of central importance, because they demonstrate, at least to the satisfaction of the subject, that we can have an immediate experience of God, the absolute or ultimate reality. (Cousins 1990b) Similarly, Brian Swimme once said, "You can go directly into an infinite, bottomless intimacy in the universe." (1997, p. 10)

There is a type of experience during which the consciousness of daily personal identity and external reality temporarily disappears. (Merkur, p. 129) In chapter 6 we quoted Tennyson's report that "individuality itself seemed to dissolve and fade away into boundless being." However, the "loss of personality seemed no extinction, but the only true life." Daniel Merkur describes this as an experience not of "I am," but simply of "am." All else is forgotten.

In Mark's gospel, it is recorded that Jesus heard these words at his baptism: "Thou art my beloved Son, with Thee I am well pleased." (Mark 1:11) Although we cannot know the inner experience of Jesus, and the phrase is thought to be a composite from scripture (Psalms 2:7 and Isaiah 42:1), we can assume that there was a divine breakthrough. To be considered a Son suggests Jesus knew a remarkable divine intimacy, even union with God; in other words, Sonship would seem to be an image of "am" consciousness. Such a knowing would be the basis of the remarkable dedication, and the healing and creative powers he demonstrated throughout his life. The claim of the early church that Jesus was fully human and fully divine supports the assumption of an early unitive experience to which he was supremely faithful and which was probably repeated often.

On some occasions there is an "am" consciousness even when the ego continues to function. Here is a description of an "I am" experience of a young woman that does not involve the disappearance of daily identity, although it carried a transforming value for the person. It is taken from the work of Rollo May:

> I remember walking that day under the elevated tracks in a slum area, feeling the thought "I am an illegitimate child." I recall the sweat pouring forth in my anguish in trying to accept that fact. Then I understood what it must feel like to accept, "I am a Negro in the midst of privileged whites," or "I am blind in the midst of people who see." Later on that night I woke up and it came to me this way, "I accept the fact that I am an illegitimate child" but "I am not a child any more." So it is, "I am illegitimate." That is not so either: "I was born illegitimate(ly)." Then what is left? What is left is this, "I am." This act of contact and acceptance with "I am," once gotten

hold of, gave me (what I think was for me the first time) the experience, "Since I am, I have the right to be."

What is this experience like? It is a primary feeling—it feels like receiving the deed to my house. It is the experience of my own aliveness not caring whether it turns out to be an ion or just a wave. It is like when a very young child I once reached the core of a peach and cracked the pit, not knowing what I would find and then feeling the wonder of finding the inner seed good to eat in its bitter sweetness. . . . It is like a sailboat in the harbor being given an anchor so that being made out of earthly things, it can by means of its anchor get in touch again with the earth, the ground from which its wood grew; it can lift its anchor to sail but always at times it can cast its anchor to weather the storm or rest a little. . . .

It is like going into my very own Garden of Eden where I am beyond good and evil and all other human concepts. . . . It is like the globe before the mountains and oceans and continents have been drawn on it. It is like a child in grammar finding the *subject* of the verb in a sentence—in this case the subject being one's own life span. It is ceasing to feel like a theory towards one's self. (Quoted in Edinger 1973, p. 58)

The experience of "I am" or "am" is not a bestowal of an identity on a person who is otherwise empty. It is the awakening of the very origins and ground of the individual into the consciousness of the person. A self greater than the young woman's culturally given identities was discovered. This new identity gave freedom from the imprisoning images.

In "I am" or "am" experiences, there is penetration into the divine ground, known through Self/soul, as it comes forth into consciousness in the particular individual. The person has a direct, "*knowledge of ultimate selfhood*—an immediate awareness of presence to oneself and to the transcendent source of the self." Such an experience "neither needs nor provides any rational justification for itself." (Dupré 1980, p. 460, emphasis added) There is a discovery of our fundamental identity, as Abyss/God is given voice in the particular, unique individual. It is the basis of true individuation.

Understanding "I Am" Experiences: Historical Perspective

The historical perspective offered by the work of Karl Jaspers describing the axial change in consciousness (chapter 15), with its cultural shift towards emphasis on individual spiritual identity, helps us understand why these passively given "am" experiences are so central to the healing of the person.

The awakening described in the literature of the people of Israel was part of the axial change. Lawrence Kushner writes about the Hebrew tradition in *The River of Light*, saying that, initially, the "I am the One of Being" is heard as other than the person, but that it has also been heard as internal to the person.[1] He calls the voice that Elijah heard the internal innermost private side of the ineffable voice of being. (p. 62) The Lord was not in the wind, the earthquake, or the fire, but Elijah heard a "still small voice." (I Kings 19:12) This awakening into depth is the basis of greater individual differentiation, as Jaspers pointed out. The "I am" experiences are, I believe, the "I am the One of Being" heard internally. The awakening represented by Moses and also by Elijah is the awareness of the One of Being in the person— remember, it is not a subject/object consciousness, but an "am" consciousness of the person—which is a God consciousness known as Self/soul. With "am" awareness there could be a development of individuality in the manner Jaspers described. This is also true for the contemporary person, and is why such passively given awakening experiences are so important.

Kushner describes the event at Sinai as the recognition of the roots of consciousness. Not until Sinai, he writes, did we become conscious of the medium by which we are conscious. (p. 52) Similarly, mysticism historically has been understood as the birthplace of consciousness, because the primordial "am" is the basis of the differentiation of the individual from the surroundings. Sinai and other events were awakenings that allowed people to transcend their identification with their social status quo as slaves, and the individual to transcend identification with the physical status quo and with the wounds of the past. They do indeed bring an increase in strength, individuality, and personal freedom, as Jaspers recognized, and they can do so in profoundly healing ways for the contemporary person.

Understanding "I Am" Experiences: Revisiting the Work of Henry Elkin

Another way to understand the nature of an "I am" or "am" experience is to recall the insights of Henry Elkin and others about the awakening of a primordial consciousness in the infant (chapter 14). We have already suggested in our earlier discussion of Elkin's work that the experience of the infant is a simple "am" known in a wordless manner. When a relationship with the Self has been compromised, eventually there must be a re-emergence of Self/soul and its primordial God-consciousness in order to restore wholeness to the psyche. Elkin describes mystical experience as follows:

> On the one hand, it is a most sublime experience of profound conversion, or spiritual rebirth. In any case, the fact that total mystical experience involves the disruption or the regeneration of the self, or soul, indicates that it is, essentially, a re-experience of the original process of spiritual birth and creation: *the emergence of the self and of the primordial cosmos out of the chaos of sensation-feeling in the earliest, collective-erotic phase of infancy.* (1958, p.67)

Erich Neumann makes similar assumptions when he describes what he calls "source mysticism," which extends back into an unknown sphere prior to the emergence of the ego, into the earliest beginning of personality. (1968, p. 415)

A Personal Experience

I was twenty-nine years old, alone in my apartment in New York City going about my household chores on an ordinary day.

I had just walked into the bedroom when suddenly I felt compelled to kneel, a posture foreign to me and to my religious tradition. I knelt and was surrounded by an unseen, vibrant presence so real that I felt as if touched on my left shoulder. It overpowered my normal, daily consciousness. I do not know how long the experience lasted, but I emerged from it saying to myself, "I know the answer to humanity's problems." This knowledge was not a rational conclusion, it arose from the type of "knowing" inherent in the experience itself. I could only think, "I must have met God," whatever that might mean. It also came to me that I would write a book about what I now knew, but at the time this was impossible because I had few words and no images to put on paper.

Emerging from the experience, I understood for the first time what the words "the courage to be" mean. The experience was a form of "I am" consciousness. I had not been able *to be* in the sense of acting and living in the world in a way that involved a fully grounded identity because of the psychological consequences of the tragedy of the death of my brother and its effect on my mother and father. Thus this experience was a re-emergence of the Self/soul and primordial consciousness, the beginning of the difficult journey to restore wholeness, to embrace that identity.

For more than a month following the experience, I was a different person. A profound healing had wiped away my ingrained habit of hiding and my lack of self-confidence. I felt free and quite joyful. Regrettably, the change did not last, yet in the years that lay ahead, as I struggled with difficult psychological and spiritual issues I could hope to become that changed person again in the future.

Awakenings of this nature are a *re-ligio*, a re-connection (or re-linking) to our origins. However, the experience of the adult is significantly different from the experience of the infant. The kind of reality experienced by infants may certainly be "primal Reality," but the significance of their knowledge is lost in the amorphous content of their psyches and is therefore unavailable to consciousness. (Owens, p. 146) In the differentiated adult consciousness, the significance of the experience may be grasped; it can change self-understanding and transform consciousness and behavior. The ego is greatly enriched by being related to the larger psyche and discovering that it can depend on its support and guidance.

It seems very likely that animals also have this "am" experience, but not the self-aware consciousness to act in accord with it, except as they naturally do as part of their instinctual life; and apparently some people have a kind of communion with this consciousness of animals. Given human reflective consciousness, the human task is to make wise choices out of this awareness of the sacred origins of daily consciousness.

The Perspective of the New Story

If we are not carefully reflective, the source of awakening experience is imagined to be from a source exterior to the person, totally "above" or "higher than" the person. Images of God as a male authority like a King or Lord, and patterns of contemporary ego consciousness, predispose us to this. The context of the new story of the evolutionary universe is highly valuable in helping the person avoid a dualistic understanding of "am" experiences and other forms of spiritual awakening. We have identified the unity and difference tradition that enables us to avoid the dualism, yet retain what we are calling "true transcendence." Some of the aspects of true transcendence are described later in this chapter. If the source of these experiences is not understood to be intrinsic to the person and to all of the unfolding whole, the individual is left isolated when experience is withdrawn; indeed there is a deep self-negation involved in the projection of such experience into an exclusively transcendent source and the resulting narrowing of human identity.[2] If the individual is denied knowledge of ongoing participation in the numinous, creative reality of which she is an integral part, she will inevitably feel empty and without value, believing that the human body/psyche is limited to the mechanistically viewed natural order and that God is spatially separate and distant except for occasional visitations. *When the referent of experiences of great worth and value is pulled out of the Whole, the manifest world becomes a hollow shell denuded of intrinsic worth.*

If God is described as "on high," we may think we must "fetch God from outside." When this does not work, and it often does not because of the initial manner of seeking, we are left angry at Abyss/God or at ourselves and perhaps at life. We are left powerless and stuck, not knowing that the nourishing *plenum,* the Abyss/God, is immanent to our being.

The new story and the recognition of the indwelling *plenum* help us avoid assuming that experiences of grace and mystical experiences are a gift given by a Father imagined to be outside the person. Although it is very important not to deny the gratuitous aspects of "am" experiences and other awakenings vis à vis the conscious personality, they must not be thought of in a way that denies the ongoing immanent presence of Abyss/God. There is great danger if a person's most valued experiences of the numinous and most profound hopes are seen as "belonging" to the separate transcendent God. Since experiences of grace and of contemplation usually occur only occasionally, we may deduce they must be someone's to give and to take away. We conclude that all one must do is await a gift from a transcendent source, and so may fail to realize that there is an organic pathway to healing that is an essential preparation for the full flowering of the sacred in the person.

There is also the important question of where we place our emotional allegiance, which is captured as a consequence of mystical/contemplative experience. When this allegiance is placed in God understood in an exclusively transcendent, dualistic manner, the result is tragic displacement of our most profound loyalties out of the natural world and the human community. We do not understand that our mystical experiences bring us into the very heart of life, and so are isolated from the adventure of the Earth. According to Whitehead, such conceptions of God as "eminent" reality separated from the universe, as a totally transcendent deity imposing his will upon heaven and Earth, are responsible for the tragic persecutions and inhumanity which have been so prominent in some phases of Christian, Jewish, and Islamic history. (Discussed in Wilmot, p. 44) People act in His name, out of a righteousness and ego ideal, separated from organic wholeness, and reject and sometimes kill whatever does not conform.

Experiences in Nature

The active universe is also encountered by the person in experiences that occur in relation to nature. Recall that Jacob Boehme gazed into the very heart of things even as he continued to be aware of the herbs and grass (chapter 5). Given the intimacy of Abyss/God with the entire manifest world, we can expect that such perceptions will occur in a vast number of encounters with nature: Niagara Falls, mountains, the sea and the night sky, fountains, birds and wild animals have awakened these knowings. Such experiences can lead to a passionate desire to spend as much time as possible in the natural world. John Muir hiked and camped in the Sierras for months at a time, year after year, in search of them. They are avidly sought because they bring a personal awakening: The recognition of Abyss/God in nature occurs within the inner experience of the person and can have a healing effect.

Images and Their Transformative Power

Images that touch us deeply in dreams, and in paintings, sculptures and religious icons, may claim a kind of authority, objectivity, and healing power. For Jung, the meaning of images in dreams extends far beyond the cognitive sphere, because they are creative entities coming out of the body as well as the psyche, and potentially exert a transformative power upon us. According to David Bohm, images manifest the implicate order. They may be part of the healing process that demands a re-imaging of self and world.

Marion Woodman says that some images may be metaphors. She cites that word's Greek origin, from the verb "to transform."

If instinct-like archetypal patterns are frustrated in their aims, they activate images that redirect their energy into new channels. Energy enters at one level and is transformed into another level. She sees metaphors as refining the raw energy patterns of the unconscious (the archetypal, instinct-like patterns) into forms that can be assimilated into consciousness.[3] (1993, p. 54) Through the capacity of images to transform instinctual energy there is healing, because energy caught in complexes becomes available to consciousness.

The power of images is seen in the effects of the ordinary process of dreaming, especially big dreams that are archetypal in nature. A woman in a dream group described a dream in which she held a black bird with a red head and golden feathers on its back. "As I held it," she reported, "I noticed its hands and its feet had become human hands and it changed into a light brown skinned baby girl." This signified a redirection of psychic energy into a more human form, away from a less grounded channeling. Usually it is not one dream that can transform us but a long sequence of images in several dreams. Masters and Houston observed in their research that several experiences of the third archetypal level (the level dealing with archetypal material) over the course of a number of sessions were often sequential in nature. A sequence of encounters with inner patterns was required to resolve an issue and bring an erasure of old behavioral patterns.

When we respond to an archetypal image the psyche makes a step toward wholeness.[4] Jungian analyst James Hollis writes: "The archetypal imagination seeks, through affectively charged images, to connect us to the flow of energy that is the heart and hum of the cosmos." (p. 10) This linkage is well known to visionaries, artists and prophets. Hollis says it is the archetypal imagination that generates the image, which may be a bridge to the mystery. Through the ordering of soul and increment in wholeness, we are opened to Abyss/God.

Marion Woodman recommends trying to find the image that will take us into healing. If there is an immediate relationship to the image, and we allow ourselves to see freshly by means of the image, the conscious orientation may be altered. Although it is produced spontaneously by the psyche (and is thus given passively from the perspective of the ego), and has brought a change in the flow of energy, there must still be a conscious cooperation with the change or we fall back into old patterns. This is a topic that will be discussed further, since it concerns our active participation in the transformative process.

Images are central to artistic creations and are often called inspirations. Louis Dupré writes concerning the inspirations of the poet and other artists: "At such occasions, the self appears to be led beyond the boundaries of its ordinary world and to escape its ruling laws. It becomes expressive rather than reactive, revealing the working of an inner power instead of those of its bodily world." (1980, p. 450) We become gods when we create. Matisse said, "I believe in God when I'm working." (In Woodman 1993, p. 127) The artist gives form to the inspiration in the painting, the sculpture, the music. Among Eastern-rite Christians, icons of saints are intended to give form to the presence of God in the image that is painted. Icons may thus offer a way of knowing for those responsive to that tradition.

Recollection of Primordial Consciousness in Images

One type of transformative image that is an important source of passively given healing comes from the early experience of merger with the mother. In the work of Jung and others, including particularly Henry Elkin, one finds the insight that there are healing resources in the initial containment and primordial consciousness experienced by the infant (chapter 14). Recall that we have tried to imagine smpathetically the experience of an infant. Elkin proposed the infant's consciousness awakens with an initial primordial God consciousness, although subsequently that consciousness may be felt to come from the Other, because the recovery of primordial consciousness was due to the care from the mother. The infant initially lived in a world continuum of mana-charged events; everything was potentially "holy." In the adult, the embedded "memory" of this early experience of unity with the mother and the surrounding world is still alive, buried but sometimes accessible. It exists in the person in a bodily way. (Neumann 1954, p. 284) Lawrence Kushner writes that ultimately "all we seek to learn is what we as children knew in the Garden but forget in order that we might live as real people." (p. 45) Given the sacred nature of this early experience, an experience of the pattern/memory of it can be transformative to human consciousness. Although the occasion of recall is regressive in nature, if the ego is sufficiently strong, it can be a decidedly positive, healing experience. It can be negative, however, in the life of the neurotic. (Neumann 1954, p. 278)

In Jungian thought, the symbols of the egg, the uroboros (the snake with its tail in its mouth) and the circle are thought to reflect the period of merger with the parent and the surrounding world.[5] Erich Neumann found the uroboros to be the archetypal image most evocative of the pre-ego stage of infancy. It refers to a time when the infant human being was linked, "at the deepest level, with the unconscious and with nature, between which there subsisted a fluid continuum that courses through man like a current of life." (1954, p. 106) As an archetypal symbol in the psyche, the uroboros is the ongoing psychic basis of ideas about the original unity and of an original state of perfection, wholeness, and beatific containment. Also, the image of the primordial Earth Goddess, the all-sustaining Great Mother, can call forth the early containment in the sacred and in the Earth. Given the ancient roots and the power and importance of our early unitive experience, all these symbols may have transformative power in the psyche. They may appear in dreams and indicate an important healing transformation in the personality

Such images refer to a place of great creative potential because the original merger contained what would unfold into the conscious person and is continuing to unfold. The potential lies in the assumptions that there is more to the person that is yet to unfold. The images, which include the grail and the vessel in the Catholic mass, make available in imaginative thinking a "pre-worldly" source of wisdom that finds its origins prior to the ego and the coming of daily consciousness.[6] This "memory" includes instinctual patterns that involve a knowledge of reality infinitely superior to our conscious knowledge, even today. (Neumann 1954, p. 285) The task is to undertake the journey to reappropriate or rediscover this "memory," so that we may experience again the elemental bond with the world of nature and the primordial knowing. To do so involves a heroic, difficult journey that is part of the contemplative pathway.

Sustained by Divine Milk

In her writings on the prayer of quiet, Teresa of Avila beautifully describes the actual experience of this life-giving contact with God, using language that clearly suggests it occurs in a psychological state that is regressive in nature, yet at the same time remarkably generative. First she is careful to teach us that we must recognize that the soul needs initially to "return often to the stage of an infant and a suckling." In other words, there needs to be a regression to the pre-ego stage of development.[7] She elaborates in a remarkable way: "In this life the soul doesn't grow like a body, even though we say it grows—and in fact it does. After a child grows up and develops a strong body and becomes an adult, his body doesn't dwindle and grow small again. But in the case of the soul, the Lord desires this to happen." (*Book of Her Life* 15. 12) Similarly, she had advised earlier that there is not "on this journey a soul so much a giant that it has no need to return often to the stage of an infant and suckling. And this should never be forgotten. . . . There is no stage of prayer so sublime that it isn't necessary to return often to the beginning." (13. 15)

Teresa insists that we must not turn away: "In this prayer [the prayer of quiet] the soul is not yet grown but is like a suckling child. If it turns away from its mother's breasts, what can be expected from it but death?" (*Interior Castle* IV. 3. 10) It seems clear that these references all demonstrate that the prayer of quiet was firmly associated in St. Teresa's mind with what would now be called a generative regression in which God is imaged as a mother nursing her child even "without the babe's effort to suckle." (*Way of Perfection* 31. 9)

The regression does not only involve a regression to the pre-ego stage of development in the personal history of the individual person. Simultaneously, it involves touching into the archetypal systems of the ancient parts of the brain, particularly, in this case, the mother archetype. It may be that the immanent divine presence is most accessible to people when the archetypal systems of the ancient brains are activated. We have just seen this in the association of the prayer of quiet with nursing. Nursing and care of the infant are paleomammalian patterns. In shared meals we may find a special communion. God-consciousness is often associated with ritual and repetitive motion that relates to the ancient brain. Henry Elkin says that mystical participation is spontaneously aroused by physical closeness, collective patterns of rhythm and movement, tones of voice, simple melodies of song and speech—sensations that reactivate the original, pre-conscious collective-erotic unity of mother and child. (1958, p. 62) Certain positions, asanas, dances and sometime sexual activity may bring an alteration of being such that Abyss/God is known in the archetypal pattern.

Major Consequences of These Awakenings

These awakenings and primordial images have the most profound consequences for the person. One is that a very great desire is awakened within the individual to enter again, or enter even on a permanent basis, into the world to which she has been introduced. The hope that one could know again such meaning and love, such fulfillment and satisfaction, compels a search for its rediscovery. In these awakening experiences there is clearly an attractiveness that transcends an individual's daily goals, hopes and desires.

Many people describe how they were allured into growth, relatedness, love, and the fullness of life by an awakening. The better love they have known heals and kindles hope, so that a person may abandon appetites and loves of little value, and be drawn into the blossoming and integration of the personality. Like the urgency and movement of a child learning to walk, the person is propelled into movement, entering into the organic process of the contemplative pathway. This allurement is a great gift, because, as Erich Neumann wrote: "Only modern Western man in the rigidity of his ego, in his imprisonment in consciousness, can fail to recognize man's existential dependence on the force which mystically changes him, the force by which he lives and which lives within him as his creative self." (1968, p. 380)

The allure, it is thought by some, exists primordially in God. God, Norman Pittenger says, works in the individual by enticement, by tenderness and persuasion, calling forth a response. (1969, p. 25) Process theologian Daniel Day Williams wrote that it is the essence of God to "move the world" toward new possibilities. Plotinus felt that the contemplative return is initiated by the allure of the One. And Whitehead referred to "the one who calls us forward." This emotional and spiritual non-coercive attractiveness is a central way in which the Abyss/God intimately affects the person such that the course of a life may be changed.

Edward Edinger would describe awakening experiences as initiating the recovery of the ego-Self axis, that is reconnecting the ego to the larger psyche. The allure and desire, in the early stages of the journey, are themselves coming from the beginnings of a living connection between the ego and the Self, although this is not yet consciously realized or fully known. The struggling conscious ego is beginning to become realistically related to the Self and its wisdom and transpersonal energy. The allure is the intrinsic attractiveness of experiences of wholeness.

The Organic Healing Process is Activated

Another profound consequence of awakening is the setting free, or you might say "jump starting," of the self-organizing processes of Self/soul that have become stalled or distorted in some way. The organic process that can lead to contemplation, as described in chapter 5, depends on the organizing power constitutive of the person—power that is within the p*lenum* or Abyss/God. The central guiding, organizing entity has been identified as the archetype of the Self. Healing then, as Jungian analyst Edward Whitmont writes, is "a reconciliation with the appropriate superordinate pattern— with Self, World, Tao, God or whatever we choose to call it."[8] This is very good news to a wounded person: The fact that the self-organizing principle is at work within each individual means there is an intrinsic possibility for healing, for a creative revolution and reorientation of the psyche and body within the great intelligence and harmony and ongoing creative dynamism of the Earth and Universe. We are invited to recognize and trust the guidance and wisdom of the Self, as opposed to clinging to the isolated ego and often feeling undermined and threatened by the "dragon" and the "wolf" and other unconscious forces. However, as described in the next chapter, there often needs to be a great deal of healing before this trust is possible. Although the gratuitous, natural process of the active, self-organizing universe exists within us, we must have the courage to cooperate actively with the healing, because old, imbedded psychic patterns are tenacious indeed.

True Transcendence and Healing

We have seen that there is actual healing of the body and psyche in these experiences; for this to take place, it is evident that there must be some kind of transcendence of Abyss/God because the body and psyche are reordered or re-formed in healings. What is the nature of this transcendence? How are we to understand this in the context of the new story? We have discussed how it is possible to accept the true transcendence of Abyss/God while not conceiving of it as outside the time-developmental universe. In chapter 13, we said that the immanence of Abyss/God throughout the world does not preclude what I am calling "true transcendence," a transcendence that does not contradict immanence. The divine immanence does not refer to a God who is enclosed in our being, nor can true divine transcendence be reduced to the aspect of exteriority or even the "otherness" of God. (Panikkar, p. 30) Rather, our conception encompasses the transcendence of that which is inner to our being—an "ordering realm" transcendant not in the "spacial" sense of "outside" or "above," but in the sense of more comprehensive.

The complete denial of transcendence is false to the manner in which the world is ordered, as the healings indicate. We must vigorously avoid collapsing everything into this- worldliness, in the narrowly mechanistic manner of understanding the Earth and universe common in the West. We cannot dull our sense of being allured toward a Center of greater value and worth, of being invited to joy and deeper engagement in life by the "One Who Calls Us Forward." We have identified a hierarchical feature in the cosmos, meaning a ranking of orders of events according *to their holistic capacity or more integrative capacity*. (Wilber 1995, pp. 17–18) This comprehensive, ordering realm is a source of healing—a re-*form*-ative realm.

An example of this conception of hierarchy is found in Jung's thought about the Self. Recall from chapter 12 that the Self, like the traditional idea of soul, is the central integrating and ordering principle that unifies the psychic totality, including the ego. As a unifying Center it has a hierarchical aspect, in that it centers and orders the entire body and psyche. The Self is the organizing principle, not that which is organized, yet it is inseparable from and constitutive of that which is organized. Teresa of Avila's image of the interior castle made of clear crystal (chapter 7), an image of God, incorporates this aspect of true transcendence. The transformation of the personality occurs within the castle.

True transcendence refers, among other things, to this comprehensive ordering and grounding.[9] How may we have hope of emerging from our entrenched patterns and from hopelessness if we cannot be transformed by more comprehensive, creative, healing depth? Louis Dupré notes that even a creative theory of man, like that of Marx, for example, runs into difficulties with a concept of freedom that lacks transcendence. Dupré writes: "To lose one's God, then, is to lose one's deepest self, to become 'unfree,' to be reduced to a 'substance,' a part of the world." (1980, p. 452) I believe that we can be fully immersed in the unfolding of the Earth, but at the same time, because of true transcendence, we can surpass ourselves.Soul is more than an individual soul because the ' ground of the soul' far surpasses the boundaries of individual personhood. (Dupré 1980, p. 461) On this basis, the person is given freedom, creativity and self-transcendence. A person is not to be totally identified with her personal and cultural history. Eckhart, among many others, bases the action of the contemplative on God, who operates in the 'ground of the soul.' (See chapter 20.)

Healing and re-*form*-ation in body and psyche are reported by a wide range of people. David Bohm asserts that the subtler manifestations of matter, or matter-energy, have the power to transform the less subtle ones. With regard to the healing effects of insight, he writes: "The insight being supreme intelligence, it is able to rearrange the very structural matter of the brain which underlies thought so as to remove that message which is causing confusion, leaving the necessary information and leaving the brain open to perceive reality in a different way." (Bohm and Weber 1978, p. 35) Likewise, co-authors Robert Augros, a philosopher, and George Stanciu, a physicist, cite neuroscientist Roger Sperry in asserting that the higher properties of mind and consciousness are in command and can result in physical and psychological healing of a person. "They envelop, carry and overwhelm the physico-chemical details," Sperry says. (Augros and Stanciu, p.33) Based on a similar assumption, Jung asked, "'How can we be lifted from our pathologies if we are not imaginatively open to the depths of those energies which both conflate us and tumble us in harness to the sea?' The approach to the numinous, Jung insisted, is the true therapy." (Hollis, p. 123) Masters and Houston report that one of their subjects felt that his encounter "with Being has in some way led to the erasure of behavioral patterns blocking his development, and at the same time provided him with a new orientation complete with insight and energy sufficient to effect dramatic and positive self-transformation." (p. 267) However, for these changes to be sustained, there must be consciousness of the nature of the change, because it must be actively supported and reinforced through changes in the way of living.

Masters and Houston suggest that the healing results from a psychical organization, restructured in such a way that ineffectual and self-damaging behavior patterns are effaced and overlaid in a kind of imprinting or re-imprinting process. The subject may be strengthened, energized; made more serene, creative, and spontaneous. They report that "the subject knows with perfect conviction that he will in the future respond in terms of the new insights and new orientation instead of making the old, painful, and non-productive responses he has made in the past." (Masters and Houston, pp. 148–49)

Jungian analyst Michael Fordham writes that it is common to find that the discovery of the meaning or pattern behind a psychological disorder will often remove symptoms in a variety of physical states. Insight may bring healing to physical expressions of anxiety: some forms of dermatitis, ulcerative colitis, infantile eczema, and a good many allergies and infectious diseases of the respiratory tract, especially in children. (Fordham, 1974)

In sum, it is the allure of wholeness within the immanent divine presence, the activation of the Self and its self-organizing, healing powers, and actual physical and psychological healing that summon forth the human person. As Teresa responded to that call and moved toward that central reality, her life reached a remarkable fullness and effectiveness. Her great book, *The Interior Castle* and her autobiography, *The Book of her Life*, are a testimony to the emergence of full personhood in response to the allure of Abyss/God and the organic, ordering process. Each of the seven dwelling places in the interior castle is a metaphor for a step in the self- organizing, re-*form*-ative process. As a result of the call, the isolated ego gives way to the mystery of the Center and the integrating powers of the psyche, and the personality is fundamentally changed.

[1] Notice that these two manners of knowing God are the same as those that Elkin postulates for the child: in identity with the Self or projected as the Other, known through the mother. This change from hearing the voice externally to hearing it internally is often replicated in the individual journey, and will be discussed in chapter 19.

[2] German philosopher Ludwig Feuerbach (1804–1872), declared that the very ideas of God and Absolute are mere projections of the human spirit, that it is man's nature to idealize, and that this aspect of his nature has been objectified and split off from its true basis in the human spirit and declared to be God. Having posited all his goodness in God, man is left with only negative aspects and so prostrates himself before his self-made deity and accuses himself of having no good in him. (Discussed in Wilmot, p. 4)

[3] Michael Fordham writes with regard to images that "because they are psychic, yet at the same time effective representatives of instinct, they are the means through which libido can be transformed, and they consequently form the basis of spiritual, intellectual and social life." (1949, p. 4)

Erich Neumann writes about the role of symbols as follows: "The world of symbols forms the bridge between a consciousness struggling to emancipate and systematize itself, and the collective unconscious with its transpersonal contents. So long as this world exists and continues to operate through the various rituals, cults, myths, religion, and art, it prevents the two realms from falling apart, because, owing to the effect of the symbol, one side of the psychic system continually influences the other and sets up a dialectical relationship between them." (1954, p. 365)

[4] In alchemy and other like-minded traditions, the image, as distinct from the thing, is called the subtle body. (Woodman 1993, p. 41)

[5] Erich Neumann includes pictures of the uroboros from Mesopotamia, Babylon, Nigeria, Mexico, and a drawing made by a five-year-old English girl, in his book *The Origins and History of Consciousness*.

[6] Marie-Louise von Franz wrote that the vessel in the grail legend and in the mass is a feminine symbol, *a maternal womb* in which the figure of the God-man is transformed and reborn in a new form. (1975, p. 271, emphsis added)

[7] Claire M. Owens, like Jung, sees regression beyond the personal memory to the deeper collective unconscious as a normal part of a natural rhythmic movement forward to the conscious mind and backward to the unconscious. (p. 141) Jung held that mysticism is derived from the collective unconscious and entails union with the impersonal source of life, attained through regression. (Owens, p. 141)

[8] Whitmont describes the self as a transpersonal field.

[9] The various dimensions of true transcendence are most important but beyond the scope of this book to discuss adequately. However, the discussions of the previous chapters, it seems to me, persuasively point to a generative realm present throughout the world and inseparable from the unfolding whole. It is the same fecund Source at the beginning and at the present time, which is generating the cosmos. It is a creative reality. Particles boil into existence out of sheer emptiness, which is the basal generative power of the universe. It is immanent to the extent of being intrinsic to the very atoms, and it is the ground or condition of all there is. So one aspect of "true transcendence" of Abyss/God is the stupendous fecundity and power required to generate the cosmos. It is the ongoing source of the manifest world, and we are totally dependent on it and integral to it. This is a dimension of true transcendence.

True transcendence also refers to the recognition that the Abyss/God is bottomless and without definable limit. David Bohm's estimate of the tremendous power in a cubic centimeter of "space," and his suggestion that matter is a comparatively small excitation on the enormous "sea of energy nothingness" have been discussed. According to him, the implicate order has infinite depths, so that only a small part of it is expressed in explicate fashion. (Bohm and Weber 1978, p. 26) Whitehead said that God is not exhausted by expression in the finite world. Note that in both of these meanings of transcendence, no distance or separation from the manifest world is implied. This is key to true transcendence.

18

"GOD CANNOT RESIST A PREPARED SOUL"

Where and when God finds you ready, he must act and pour himself out into you, just as the sun must pour itself into the air if it is clear and pure and cannot help doing so.

— Meister Eckhart

ONE OF JESUS' parables warns dramatically of the importance of being prepared. According to Matthew he taught:

> Then the kingdom of heaven shall be compared to ten maidens who took their lamps and went to meet the bridegroom. Five of them were foolish, and five were wise. For when the foolish took their lamps, they took no oil with them; but the wise took flasks of oil with their lamps. As the bridegroom was delayed, they all slumbered and slept. But at midnight there was a cry, 'Behold, the bridegroom! Come out to meet him.' Then all those maidens rose and trimmed their lamps. And the foolish said to the wise, 'Give us some of your oil, for our lamps are going out.' But the wise replied, 'Perhaps there will not be enough for us and for you; go rather to the dealers and buy for yourselves.' And while they went to buy, the bridegroom came, and those who were ready went in with him to the marriage feast; and the door was shut. Afterward the other maidens came also, saying, 'Lord, lord, open to us.' But he replied, 'Truly, I say to you, I do not know you.' Watch therefore, for you know neither the day nor the hour. (Matthew 25: 1–13)

Teresa of Avila wrote: "If the soul does not fail God, He will never fail, in my opinion, to make His presence known to it." (IC VII. 1. 8) In contemporary psychological language, Erich Neumann wrote: "The epiphany of the numen is dependent on the personality's stage of development." (1968, p. 394) This same idea can be found in mythic material. In archetypal lore there is the idea that if one prepares a psychic place, the Being, the creative force, the soul source, will hear of it, sense its way to it, and inhabit it. These ideas are most compelling in the context of the new story, for they entail the possibility of engaging in the full creative depths of the unfolding adventure of the Earth and its communities. Because the teachings of the contemplative tradition offer great promise of a transformed identity, and the new story offers great promise of the possibility of creating a viable future given that the universe is an ever-transforming reality, we must now consider how this active preparation is accomplished.

A note of warning to prevent misunderstanding before we begin: Recognizing the importance of preparation does not mean denying that contemplative experiences sometimes occur spontaneously; more commonly, however, they follow prolonged psychological, moral, and meditative preparation and general faithfulness to the demands of life. Also, the reflections that follow on the active side of the journey should not be interpreted as advocating a works righteousness, which is actually based in an effort to maintain the idealized self. (See chapter 16.) Nor is this preparation a Pelagian effort to earn salvation by will power and free choice alone.[1] Instead, it involves active cooperation with the organic process that includes the passively given events described in chapter 17.

The Hero's Journey: Preparing for Contemplation

The preparation for contemplation has qualities of a hero's journey because it requires great courage, dedication, honesty, suffering and tenacity. The hero we are describing is not one who has slain the outer enemy, who has sought glory through military victory, or "conquered" and subdued nature, but one who has confronted the inner enemy and integrated into the conscious personality the energy held captive from the splitting of the self. According to Erich Neumann, this hero has a revolutionary quality, in that he "dares the evolutionary leap to the next stage and does not, like the average person who clings to the conservatism of the existing system, remain the inveterate enemy of the new." (1954, p. 312) We can embrace the hero's journey as a way of talking about much of the contemplative journey because the supreme goal of the hero, expressed in mythological language, is to experience the fulfillment of "I and the Father are One." (p. 360) The capacity of the person to undertake the hero's journey is an expression of the self-organizing processes intrinsic to the person, the inner ordering dynamism that makes healing and further individuation possible. We urgently need people to join with those who are already undertaking the journey, because they can speak and live and teach as Earth beings from a centered identity grounded in the All-Nourishing Abyss.

The Necessity of a Descent

Hero myths tell us the dragon that guards the treasure must be confronted and dismembered if the captive treasure is to be liberated. The killing of the dragon depicts, in the symbolic language of the psyche, the manner in which early humanity, by killing "monsters, beasts and giants," became disentangled from its fusion with nature and with collective life.[2] In an individual life, the same type of fusion—with destructive parental and social patterns—can rob the ego of freedom, centered focus and energy. We have seen this fusion in the split-off selves, the angry dragon and the hungry wolf. When we recognize that the splitting involves archetypal power, as complexes are formed, it becomes clear that recognizing and confronting the inner beasts and dragons is a heroic task.

This chapter looks at the manner in which there can be a healing of the split (or healing of the complexes), so that the maternal matrix (chapter 16) can function positively to mediate the immanent sacred mystery. An open, trusting inner environment that is created by the re-integration of the self is the occasion for the re-emergence of primordial Abyss/God consciousness. Since, concomitant with this healing, the ego is no longer at the mercy of unconscious complexes, it is strengthened and able to assume its proper role as the center of conscious life. This is essential, since only a strong ego can surrender to the larger comprehensive, loving, creative orders.

Desire

Why do we undertake the difficult descent? Because there has been an activation of the healing, self-organizing processes, and an awakening of a powerful desire. It is the desire to enter again into the world into which we have been introduced, and to be relieved of suffering, that propels us on the journey. The desire must be very strong, because it must overcome great unconscious resistance. I felt on several occasions that I would have preferred to remain unconscious rather than feel again and endure the suffering and loneliness of my childhood and early adulthood.

Hardly a classic author fails to mention over and over again the importance of desire. Bonaventure wrote that we must be people of desire to follow the soul's journey. Augustine said that everything is drawn by God's love; we love what attracts us. Recall the experience of Johannes Anker-Larsen while he waited to go to the train (chapter 6): He expresses the strength of his desire to know again the "infinite tenderness" when he declares that he would not exchange "all the food in the world in one dish, all the wine in the world in one glass, all its tobacco in one cigar . . . and all the honors of all the kings" conferred on him if it meant renouncing the possibility of experiencing again a meeting with the Eternal Now. John of the Cross taught that to have the courage to enter the darkness of the night of sense requires "a more intense enkindling of another, better love (love of one's heavenly Bridegroom)." ("Ascent of Mount Carmel" I. 14. 2). Jesus taught, "Ask, and it will be given you; seek, and you will find; knock, and it will be opened to you." (Matthew 7:7)

In *Practical Mysticism*, originally published in 1914, Evelyn Underhill comments on the importance of pressing forward with "the sharp dart of your longing love":

Nothing but your apathy, your feeble and limited desire, limits this realization [of a more perfect and unmediated union with the Substance of all that is]. Here there is a strict relation between demand and supply—your achievement shall be in proportion to the greatness of your desire. The fact, and the impressing energy, of the Reality without does not vary. Only the extent to which you are able to receive it depends upon your courage and generosity, the measure in which you give yourself to its embrace. (1942, p. 134)

Suffering

The journey into self-kowledge and healing requires an entrance into painful suffering. I suffered greatly as I became conscious of the consequences for me of my parents' very great sorrow over the loss of their four-year-old son. As a baby, I was inevitably not fully loved, not adequately responded to, or welcomed into the family. It took a long time for me to recognize this deeply buried suffering. Reliving it was required, not because suffering in itself is in some way good, but because it is necessary to experience the suffering again so that one may become conscious of the inner splitting that has resulted, and more importantly, so that the knowledge can be received with compassion. It has helped in the acceptance of the wounding and its consequences to know they resulted from the most difficult human circumstances. By embracing the pain, and realizing that my problems were not due to personal fault or some original sin, I could instead recognize that my suffering was the suffering of the human community. We partake of both cosmic celebration and profound human travail.

In her book *The Wounded Woman*, Jungian analyst Linda Leonard describes well this process of acceptance of buried suffering. She writes: "Since I had denied any value to my father after he 'drowned' in the irrational Dionysian realm [of alcohol], I needed to learn to value that rejected area by letting go of the need to control. But this required experiencing the negative side, being plunged into the uncontrollable chaos of feeling and impulses, into the dark depth where the unknown treasure was hidden. Ultimately, to redeem the father required that I enter the underworld, that I value the rejected areas in myself. . . . I had to learn to live with my father again so I could reconnect to his positive side." (Leonard, pp. 157–58)

The pathway to healing is often elusive. It is impossible to outline in advance because each individual pathway is tied to the life circumstances of the person from earliest infancy. In the poem that begins, "The Malay – took the Pearl" (*Complete Poems*, no. 452), Emily Dickinson is aware that the pathway to recovering the pearl may be through a dark, hidden aspect of the personality that cannot be consciously grasped:

> The Malay – took the Pearl –
> Not – I – the Earl –
> I – feared the Sea – too much
> Unsanctified – to touch –
>
> Praying that I might be
> Worthy – the Destiny –
> The Swarthy fellow swam –
> And bore my Jewel – Home –
>
> Home to the Hut! What lot
> Had I – the Jewel – got –
> Borne on a Dusky Breast –
> I had not deemed a Vest
> Of Amber – fit –
>
> The Negro never knew
> I – wooed it – too –
> To gain, or be undone –
> Alike to Him – One –

According to Theodora Ward, an editor of Emily Dickinson's letters, Dickinson's conscious superior self was defrauded of the pearl because of her fear of the unknown and a sense of unworthiness that was part of the religious conflict from which she had suffered since her adolescent years. (Ward, p. 63)

At a conference organized by Michael Comforti in 1998, a man asked if there is meaning in suffering or if it only has the meaning we give it. The question was phrased in such a manner that a good answer was not likely to be found. The first part of the question "Is there meaning in suffering?" seems to involve the assumption that there might be a structure to things, perhaps a reward system, such that suffering per se is always, automatically meaningful. Actually suffering may or may not have meaning, depending on how the individual and the community engage with it. The second part of the question, whether suffering only has "the meaning we give to it," appears to suggest that the only alternative is that the person willfully imposes meaning on suffering, or consciously attributes meaning to it, with the implication that the suffering does not sometimes involve some actual experience of meaning in the midst of engagement with a particular situation. It is looking for knowledge through ideas rather than by *being*. Instead, the question should be about *entering* into suffering, at least the psychological kind being discussed, with an openness to the discovery of its origins and of the pathway by which the psyche may relate to it in a different manner. Suffering in this way can have tremendous meaning, since it is part of the healing of the maternal matrix. The place that Abyss/God cannot resist is being prepared.

A person often bears unconscious, buried suffering not only from personal history but from generations of human suffering carried forward in families and societies. We have a choice about how we respond to it. We have the "power to accept the suffering, to refuse to pass it on to another, to forgive, to end the needless torment, and, most of all, to transmute evil into energy for the vitality of the whole." (Swimme 1984, p. 81) When we no longer deny our own suffering or that of others, we may have compassion (*pati* in Latin is to bear, to suffer) for ourselves and for others. This meaning of our suffering does not imply a blanket acceptance of unnecessary suffering from injustice and unwarranted aggression, but it does entail an embrace of our life as it is given. It means desisting from the deep anger and rebellion at our earthly condition that has characterized so much of human history. It can be an important factor in the transformation of our relationship to the Earth.

The Suffering of the Body

Marion Woodman believes that the eating disorders of her anorexic and bulemic clients are an acute expression of a pervasive cultural alienation from the body. She has discovered that an essential element in healing for these women is finding a firm base of bodily feeling. Past experiences, she teaches, are always inscribed in the body. Personal psychological history is built into the very musculature of the person, as the body receives the pain that the mind cannot endure. (1985, p. 130) Restoring the maternal matrix must include attention to the body by noting its posture, its manner of relating to other bodies, its weight, images in dreams that relate to the body, symptoms of ill health and signs of tension, like back and neck pain.

A rejection of body/matter occurs in the self-splitting that results from the early maternal relationship because that relationship is so fundamentally physical, as well as psychological and spiritual, in nature. When the repressed relationship systems are formed, in order to protect the person from the enticing or rejecting aspects of mother, a physical self-alienation results because the ongoing inner rejection of legitimate need necessarily involves the body. Particularly when the mother was not sufficiently at home in her own body, she cannot confer a basic bodily security on the child. Furthermore, if a person is maintaining an idealized self, she is not present to an inner grounded, physical reality and lacks a primary at-homeness in bodily existence. Since it is the mother who mediates primordial awareness of Abyss/God for the infant, and since subsequently it is the internalized mother (the maternal matrix) that is the medium of mediation between Abyss/God and the person, the absence on the physical level of a positive, empathic internalized mother means the child and subsequently the adult does not have the capacity for internal mediation. She is alienated from and rejects unconsciously the very physical reality that is an essential part of the 'all at onceness.'

The common fact that people ignore the body and use it as a dumping ground for undealt with feelings is a sign of physical alienation. Clear examples are compulsive overeating and alcoholism. Harry Guntrip, the object relations theorist whose work we considered in chapter 16, observes that while human beings generally shrink from pain, mental pain is ultimately more unbearable than bodily pain. (p.28) As a result, the body is made to carry the person's mental pain and is identified as the cause of his problems. Dr. Bernie Siegel, the advocate for cancer patients, says it is easier for us to tell our neighbors we have to have surgery than to tell them we are seeing a psychiatrist. We must be aware that the body often expresses the inner personal situation and therefore plays a vital role in the spiritual pathway.

It is essential to seek to recognize unconscious patterns of body movement or body tension that reveal the nature of our imprisonments. Marion Woodman describes body movement as a waking dream: "What is important to realize is that releasing the body into spontaneous movement and play constellates the unconscious in precisely the same way as does a dream." (1982, p. 178) The body does not lie, but presents the unconscious in its most immediate and continuous form. The body as an expression of the unconscious has the advantage over dreams in that its inner patterns cannot be forgotten the way dreams often are, and because it is possible to work directly with the waking dream of the body by becoming involved as participating agents in its movement. The body will reveal the nature of our psychological prison if we give it occasions to speak in movement and learn to listen to it and embrace its reality as an integral part of our identity. It may speak in the form of faulty actions, involuntary gestures, and/or physical symptoms. "In its spontaneous movements the body is like an infant crying out to be heard, understood, responded to, much as a dream is sending out signals from the unconscious." (p.79) Therapist Don Johnson describes a man with chronic headaches who discovered that when he spoke to his boss his neck began to hurt and the pain radiated into his head. This reaction occurred each time he saw his boss and was a repetition of the way he had always reacted to his father. (Johnson, p. 5) He shrank from his boss as he had shrunk from his father when a little boy; his body was the voice of the unconscious child in him and a reliable source of self-knowledge. Through this type of discovery, the person can recognize how his spontaneous feelings have been locked in the musculature, making natural responses and feelings unavailable.

Through a persistent physical symptom, a woman whom we will call Rebecca was led to important self-knowledge that profoundly transformed her religious life. Rebecca spent several weeks traveling with a younger person as a companion and friend. During their time together the younger woman became angry and abusive, but Rebecca forced herself not to respond, feeling unable to face a confrontation. The exigencies of travel and the angry feelings left her exhausted and suffering from persistent diarrhea. She knew the physical problem was related to the anger, because it followed a pattern that was familiar from similar conflicts in previous years. In her search for healing she was brought to reconsider her earliest memory, from about age three. An angry woman was leaning over her shouting and scolding as she clamored for attention in a playpen. The woman was not her mother, but a nurse employed to help the family during a time when the child's mother had a miscarriage. Pondering this early memory and later occasions in childhood when she was subject to verbal abuse, Rebecca became aware that she was paralyzed when confronted by anger and that she herself became hurt and angry in return. Her response to anger had been to walk away, to force herself to be silent, leaving the feelings unattended and unacknowledged. As she became conscious of this pattern, acknowledging and accepting her own anger (the dragon) and her fear of the anger of others, she began to be able to respond to anger with words of strength. The symptoms disappeared. Her prayer became quieter and deeper as she brooded less on angry relationships.

Relationships

Once, in a women's spirituality group, a young woman, a mother of small children, talked about her prayers for healing of the consequences of trauma in her childhood. Another woman in the group suggested that instead of praying for healing, she pray for and look for a healer. This insight wisely recognized that the course of our journey is most profoundly influenced by our relationships. Process theologian Daniel Day Williams reminds us that we are not looking for some detached love. He writes:

> To love eternal being as a different kind of being is to miss the real point about God's love, that it is manifest not only in his eternity, but in his temporality. It is the essence of God to move the world toward new possibilities, and his being is "complete" only as an infinite series of creative acts, each of which enriches, modifies and shapes the whole society of being. (pp. 183–184)

We may find a teacher whose wisdom guides us. Or we may find a good therapist. Unconscious split-off portions of the self enveloped in complexes surface in a therapeutic relationship and thereby are made available to healing within a relationship in which they may receive the mirroring and empathy for which they have waited. Dante's attraction to Beatrice allured him into a lifelong search, ultimately given full expression in *The Divine Comedy*. Jesus of Nazareth has been an alluring figure for millions of people, who have recognized a truthful and deeply revelatory life and have been changed by a deep inner connection with his humanity and his divinity. Finding a healing relationship is sometimes a risky, dangerous process, characterized by misplaced promises, but even when there are human failings, they may become a source of knowledge of the split-self and hence part of the pathway to healing.[3]

Theologian Norman Pittenger beautifully expresses the cosmic nature of the unifying love: "The love wherewith that Man [the Man of Nazareth] loves, in his tenderness and in his courage, his humility and his boldness, is the very love which moves the sun and the other stars." (1968, pp. 213–14) This is the basis of communion with other beings and the potential our loves carry for healing and differentiation. Just before he died,

Freud was asked, "How does psychoanalysis really cure the patient?" Freud hesitated for a long time. He then answered: "At one moment in analysis the analyst loves the patient and the patient is able to know it and the patient is cured." So one can think of all therapies, which in many ways consist of the clearing away of the defensive, psychic superstructure so that the patient can know he is loved—be known and still be loved. (NYSEPH Newsletter, vol. 8, no. 1)

It is particularly in the struggles and joys of a long marriage and long committed relationships that we have an occasion for self-knowledge and differentiation. We are drawn into powerful erotic intensities. To sustain the love, we need great honesty and humility, because in such relationships our "wolf" and our "dragon" inevitably surface. Also, sexual love can be an occasion that is still available in modern life to experience our primal, energetic, desirous being. It may be an occasion of both union and of personal healing. Two people united in this way may be totally present to each other and to that deeper mystery out of which both the universe and we ourselves have emerged.

James Carse recognizes the importance of relationships when, reflecting on Nicholas de Cusa's classic *The Vision of God*, he writes in *Breakfast at the Victory*: "Since we can only be as we are seen, whoever looks at us plays a part in creating us and the world we live in. . . . We cannot see the face of God. Instead we see a multitude of faces around us, earthly faces, in each of which is a hidden seer." (pp. 117–18) We have discovered this same idea in Henry Elkin's work. The mother is God-bearer (*theotokos*) for the child, as she looks with loving attention at her infant. Carse goes on:

> To the degree that every glance at us participates in the creation of our world, every glance participates in God's vision of us. . . . It follows that our own seeing participates in the vision of God quite as much as any other. The vision of God, therefore, is not our vision *of* God but God's own vision by which all things are created. To the degree that we see anything at all, we see with the eye of God. (p. 118)

Meditation and Prayer

Meditation and prayer are clearly central to both the active and passive aspects of preparation. There is a vast literature on these topics, including the writings of Teresa of Avila describing active recollection, the prayer of quiet, and the prayers of union. (See chapter 7.) David Bohm's thoughts on meditation are particularly helpful in the context of the new story. Bohm suggested that the realization that we are enfolded (implicate) in a spiritual order requires another kind of research than that undertaken by scientists, including quantum physicists like himself. He proposed that a meditative method is demanded, that indeed meditation would constitute the experimental method for "tuning in" to implicate resonances of a higher order than those detectable by physicists. (Toolan, p. 566) Bohm also maintained that "every individual is in total contact with the implicate order, with all that is around us." (Bohm and Weber 1978, p. 40) By meditative and contemplative practices, the "common sense" view of every day life is profoundly informed, and gradually even transformed; as we see freshly, we may begin to enter the way of seeing offered us by the new story and the contemplative tradition.

The desire to make us over into love permeates the universe, so we may find the allure in many places and people. "All that is required," Brian Swimme tells us, "is that you fall in love. Fall in love as deeply as you can." It is not a question of theoretical or abstract ideas about love, "but immersion in the actuality of love and love's activity." (1984, p. 64) Elaine de Beauport encourages us to observe carefully what allures us, and to trust in the erotic element of allure. (de Beauport, p. 223) By succumbing to the allure of mountains where we may walk, the garden where we may dig in the Earth, the music we may sing, or special people we may love, we are being drawn into being.

Rebuilding the Maternal Matrix

In the context of healing relationships, and with the quieting of the ego and its defenses during meditation and prayer, startling self-knowledge sometimes springs into consciousness. We must summon the courage to enter our areas of deep suffering and become conscious of our dragons and wolves. From our earlier discussion of the splitting of the personality, we can imagine that dismantling these "monsters" releases energy for rebuilding the castle. The very captive, split-off parts of the personality are themselves then part of the treasure, because their reunion with the central self rebuilds the maternal matrix with its capacity to mediate consciousness of Abyss/God. Erich Neumann writes: "Liberating the captive and gaining precisely that captive as a treasure releases a flood of productivity in the soul, causing the individual to feel himself akin to the gods in this creative act." (1954, p. 208)

One way the liberation of the captive is described is as a process of "breaking up, digesting and then rebuilding the objects of the world and the unconscious, in exactly the same way as our bodily digestive system decomposes matter physiochemically and uses it for the creation of new structures." (Neumann 1954, p. 318) This process of re-*form*-ation depends on the self-organizing powers of the Self/soul, which bring the energies of the psyche into a more integrated whole. Often this is assisted by image formation. With new images, the energy mediated by that image acting as a metaphor (a transformer) is turned in a different direction, and conscious assimilation is made possible. (See chapter 17.) The process of dismembering the wolf and the dragon and freeing the "captive treasure" must be repeated several times for each complex, and as different complexes are unearthed. Each digestion and reassimilation allows the person to obtain more energy (libido) for the ego and to move toward a positive embrace of the body-psyche.

Descent and Healing in the Life of Teresa of Avila

Recall that Teresa of Avila taught that active recollection is the gateway to contemplation. It is like a meditative practice that focuses attention inwardly. She lamented that for years she was unable to practice it. (*Book of Her Life* 11. 9) In her writing she described with remarkable honesty the personal problems that prevented her from practicing recollection. She identified three of them as attachment to friends, false humility and excessive concern over honor. We can look at just one of these, her attachment to friends, to illustrate the manner in which the descent and healing of the split-self can enable recollection.[4] Teresa confesses that she was led seriously astray as a consequence of her attachment to friends. (*Life* 37. 4, 11. 9, 7. 17) We can identify this as the "love made hungry," the inner wolf that arose, we can assume, from some combination of unsatisfied but legitimate need for attention, mirroring, and recognition in infancy and early childhood. For Teresa, this inner wolf meant that she was torn between her prayer on the one hand and on the other the pleasures of the company of friends and admirers and of conversations in the parlor of her convent. She describes it this way:

> I should say that it is one of the most painful lives, I think, that one can imagine; for neither did I enjoy God nor did I find happiness in the world. When I was experiencing the enjoyments of the world, I felt sorrow when I recalled what I owed to God. When I was with God, my attachment to the world disturbed me. This is a war so troublesome that I don't know how I was able to suffer it even a month, much less for so many years. (*Life* 8. 2)

Evidently, Teresa's attachment to friends was so strong that while seeking to recollect, she was preoccupied by thoughts and emotional conflict concerning them. The split-off part of the self had its own agenda. We do not know precisely how the inner wolf lost its power, but she persisted in her prayer. Images and rituals from the church— she was especially fond of St. Joseph and of communion—were apparently healing for her. And her relationships with spiritual directors and her sisters must have played a role. We do know that with the healing of her attachments, there was a reassimilation of the split-off portion of the self. When this happens, the diffuse contents of consciousness are knit into a single system. (Neumann 1954, p. 315) For Teresa, this and other healing brought a gradual restoration of the maternal matrix and with it the beginnings of the contemplative life.

This type of healing is of great importance with respect to our integration into the Earth, because it can mean a change in our attitude toward our identity as Earth beings. For both men and women, this means a positive relation to the maternal matrix and, by extension, to the nurturing aspects of the Earth, which is central to finding a fruitful human-Earth relationship. We leave behind any ideas that the world is fundamentally alien or any attempt to separate ourselves from life in some manner (except in the sense of avoiding a commercialized "worldliness," meaningless secular entertainment, excessive consumption, and imprisoning addictions), and instead seek to penetrate deeply into the body, the larger Self and its mysterious depths.

Strengthening of the Ego

We receive confusing messages about the role of the ego in this transformative process. Is it strengthened or is it defeated? Many have written about the "naughting" (negating) and marginalizing of the ego. (Carse, p. 82) Others describe the initial encounter with the Self as a defeat for the ego. In object relations theory, there is an initial defeat of the defensive, idealized, often proud ego ideal that formed to compensate for the splitting. But far more important than any emphasis on defeating the ego is the healing of the split, so that the defensive projects of the personality and its false inflations are no longer necessary. As a result of the process of digestion and reassimilation and re-organization, the person is no longer at the mercy of the split-off figures and no longer needs to be a slave to the ego ideal and its domination. The central self is strengthened. In Jungian terms the ego is strengthened as it becomes strong enough to break away from the negatively personalized archetypes. The ego-self axis is being restored, so the ego is strengthened by receiving guidance from the Self.

Although the ego-ideal must be defeated, the ego, as Marion Woodman explains, must become strong enough to surrender to thrusts from the unconscious—strong enough to "let-go" and "let-be" (see below). The lower levels of contemplation may begin as the ego recognizes that it is not the center of the entire personality and seeks the larger guidance. It has recognized its subordinate position and is prepared to serve the totality and its ends rather than make personal demands. (Edinger 1973, p. 96) The healing has prepared daily ego-consciousness to be an instrument for the operation of our creative urge, our intelligence, our compassion and truth. (Bohm and Weber 1978, p. 49) In this sense there is a loss of ego-centeredness, although at the same time the ego is stronger, able to reflect and trust the flow of various internal states, and to witness the many dimensions of the personality.

Letting Go and Letting Be

As preparation, Meister Eckhart taught "letting be" (*gelassenheit*) and detachment (*abgeschiedenheit*). Unfortunately, the word *detachment* seems to suggest a kind of aloofness or lack of interest in the world, just the opposite of what would be required for an integration of the contemplative life and our immersion in the unfolding Earth. The German word *abgeschiedenheit* is better translated as *disinterest*. It refers to something like the stance required of laboratory investigators in pure science, which enables them to distinguish between what they might desire of the truth and what the truth appears to be. (Blakney, p. x) Disinterest would be the opposite of addiction. Thus, contrary to our assumptions, the traditional idea of detachment actually describes a kind of "worldliness" and a capacity to be among things without being a prisoner to fixed ideas and personal wolf-like needs or dragon-like demands.

Eckhart taught that this "letting be" and disinterest applies to our thinking. It first concerns letting go of fixed, perhaps rigid ideas and assumptions. For example, we may have inadequate images of God. Eckhart wants us to drop incomplete notions of

God—even of God as good, as a Spirit, as "Father, Son and Holy Spirit"—because we are continually in danger of belonging to our images and automatic associations, and not to the unknowable mystery. The intellect must be empty and in a state of receptivity, available for illumination and insight. Through our disinterest we are free to enter the soul's ground and to rest there. This is the openness to fresh seeing recognized in the first chapter of this book as necessary for embracing the implications of the new universe story and our integral embeddedness in the Earth.

John of the Cross taught that the *night* of thought is the light of perception. ("Dark Night" II. 9. 3) He recognized that our fixed ideas and inadequate images are one source of disordered consciousness that separates us from the Source.

In *Practical Mysticism* Evelyn Underhill uses a compelling image to remind us of the danger of the most positive beliefs and ideas if they isolate us from the world and the deepest experience of its demands and its gifts:

> It is useless to offer your spirit a garden—even a garden inhabited by saints and angels—and pretend that it has been made free of the universe. You will not have peace until you do away with all banks and hedges, and exchange the garden for the wilderness that is unwalled; that wild strange place of silence where "lovers lose themselves." (p. 136)

Eckhart's teaching regarding "letting be" and disinterest also addresses the preparation of the will. The word *gelassenheit*, translated as "letting be" or "releasement," means to restore freedom, to untie. He who has learned how to "let be" restores all things to their primitive freedom; he leaves all things to themselves. We no longer regard objects and events according to their usefulness, but accept them in their autonomy. (Schürmann 1978a, p.16) With "disinterest" and "letting be" Eckhart is recommending that we no longer willfully insist on fixed plans and results, to which we may have been captive. Psychologically, this would mean that the wolf and the dragon no longer control us. Eckhart even taught us to be free of a possessive relationship with a God who we have insisted must conform to our expectations and needs. Eckhart is pushing beyond a certain image of God and into freedom even from doing God's will as we may perceive it. (1981, p. 203) The "letting be" extends to being free for the working of God in Himself. According to Eckhart, important things happen when the will loses all its objects and is receptive; it will remove rather than erect dams around the person's inner being; it opens itself to things and lets them enter in their illness into its very core. (Schürmann 1978a, p.17)

Contrary to the initial impression that "letting be" and detachment instruct us in a certain aloofness, Eckhart actually intends a dwelling in "this present now." We are able to be with the present situation as opposed to living in the past or in the future because we have given up our ardent claiming and grasping (the wolf), and we have loosened our grip on things. We have broken through the rigid barriers of isolated individuality and entered a form of communion with the world. Note that this is not an elevation of the soul into some cosmic contemplation, but a certain way of living among things. There is no rejection of the body. Eckhart is invoking a special awareness of the meaning of everyday life, aimed at penetrating the ordinary to reveal the extraordinary. He is not looking for unusual, ecstatic experience, although these may be part of the pathway. There can be a kind of spaciousness, serenity, and receptivity before the larger energies of life as we embrace a new, freer, life-giving self-understanding.

Eckhart describes the person who is free of false and alien images and expectations as virgin. The virgin has "let himself be, has let God be, and lives in wandering joy." Jesus is a model of the detached and released person, "free and void and virginal in himself." (Quoted in Schürmann 1978a, p. 17) In the sermon "Jesus Entered," Eckhart preached about the radical nature of being virgin:

> If I were so rational that there were present in my reason all the images that all men had ever received, and those that are present in God himself, and if I could be without possessive-

ness in their regard, so that I had not seized possessively upon any one of them, not in what I did or what I left undone, not looking to past or to future, but I stood in this present moment free and empty according to God's dearest will, performing it without ceasing, then truly I should be a virgin. (1981, p.177)

Eckhart recognized a gradual process of preparation for ever deeper levels of releasement. He spoke of the remaking or rebuilding of a person by a process of assimilation to the image of God. When there is actualization of the divine ground of the person, as in breakthroughs, there is healing and then, in turn, the possibility of ever deeper intensities of releasement. According to Reiner Schürmann (1941–1993), who was for many years Professor of Philosophy at the New School for Social Research in New York City, the fruit born of breakthrough is man himself; he is delivered to himself, brought back from dispersion. And, we would add, brought back into integral participation in the new story of the evolutionary universe.

---

[1] Pelagius was a fifth-century British or Irish monk and later a fashionable teacher in Rome, whose teachings were opposed by Augustine and finally condemned by a council in Carthage in 418. Although his teachings are known only through the writings of his opponents, Pelagius apparently denied original sin inherited from Adam, taught that people can live without sin and rejected salvation by infused grace. His teachings are thought to be defective in their insufficient recognition of people's weakness and insufficient acknowledgement of their dependence on God. The issue in the Pelagian controversy concerned clarification of people's fallen condition and consequent need for divine help in relation to belief in free will and responsibility.

[2] Neumann discerns a number of stages in the ego's separation from immersion in the matrix of its origins in human history, and finds similar stages in the personal ego development of every individual. (1954, p. 131) Thus in his view, in broad terms these myths are models for what has become a pathway for every individual. Although this is disputed, it seems to me that, in the context of the evolutionary universe, it is probably broadly true.

[3] By identifying the importance of allure in relationships, are we not in danger of advocating chasing false gurus and other people with a certain charisma? There is always danger, but this does not deny the necessity of finding healing relationships in the spiritual pathway. We must find out if a guide has support

and training in his or her religious community or therapeutic tradition. The allure requires great discernment, because our needy "wolf" arises in many guises. And we must recognize that not all attractions are on the same level of significance. Yet behind the hungry wolf is the larger attraction of a wholeness within the great Mystery.

[4] For a fuller discussion of the type of wounding involved in the three problems she identifies and the relationship of their healing to the practice of recollection, see my article "The Pathway to Recollection: St. Teresa of Avila's Descent into the Personal Unconscious" in *Spiritual Life*, Summer 1994.

19

KNOWINGS THAT CHANGE CONSCIOUSNESS: ENTRANCE INTO THE UNITIVE LIFE

The experience of the book [his *Answer to Job*] was for me a drama that was not mine to control. I felt myself utterly the *causa ministerialis* of my book. It came upon me suddenly and unexpectedly during a feverish illness. I feel its content as the unfolding of the divine consciousness in which I participate, like it or not.
— Carl Jung

TERESA OF AVILA was in her fifties when, as she put it so charmingly in *The Interior Castle*, she was brought into the wine cellar. (IC V. 1. 12) This is an image of the unitive life, the realization of the return to the fullness of her being, imaged as living in the center of the castle made of one large crystal. As time had passed and the healing of the body and psyche had occurred, the nature and quality of her relationship to God had gradually changed. Her initial experiences of contemplation brought a gentle centering of the personality, and then the prayer of quiet made the recollection more profound. (See chapter 7.) The next experiences of contemplation were for her at the unitive level. According to Teresa, a sure sign of union is that when a person returns to herself after a unitive experience, "it [the soul] can in no way doubt that it was in God and God was in it." (IC V. 1. 9) The very purpose of the contemplative journey—that is, to surpass daily consciousness and to rest in the dark sources of the conscious self—has been accomplished. (Dupré 1980, p. 451) While initially unitive experiences are sporadic, eventually, we are told, the unitive consciousness becomes permanent, running concurrently with, and in some way fused and integrated with, daily consciousness. For this to happen, further transformation of consciousness, beyond the psychological, emotional healing, is often necessary. Thus, before we consider the unitive life later in this chapter (and its active expressions in the next), insights and illuminative visions that bring this further transformation must be explored.

First, let us address a possible lingering question. We may worry that Teresa's experience of the unitive life is quite rare and nearly unattainable. But history tells us that the various forms of contemplation, whether the so-called lower forms like the prayer of quiet, or the higher, unitive forms, have been realized over and over again. They were once considered the normal evolution of the Christian life. The 'way of seeing' ('*theoria*') explored in this book may encourage us to recognize contemplation as an inherent human possibility. It is part of our deep belonging to a sacred Earth, and is, I believe, central to the changes in consciousness required if we are to address the ecological, cultural, and political issues before us. *And even if the unitive life is not attained, knowledge and understanding of it and seeing that the contemplative life is integral to the new story of the evolutionary universe will encourage us to seek to live in accord with the worldview they both make manifest.*

Insights and Illuminative Visions

These illuminative "visions" that are part of the journey, it should be noted immediately, are not visual in nature, like hallucinations, but a kind of insight. Louis Dupré writes about privileged instances of intellectual intuition, in which the mind literally perceives as directly as the senses ordinarily do. (1980, p. 451) He says the impact of this type of experience is one of insight, even all-surpassing insight; there is direct mental intuition. (pp. 459–60) Such "visions" may also be called experiences of objective intelligence, following F. David Peat (chapter 11).

Ewert Cousins makes an interesting observation about one of the participles of the verb "to see" in Greek, which supports the idea that an illumination is a kind of direct perception akin to seeing. He refers to *eikon*, or idea. The word is used to refer to "ideas" in the divine mind (ideas from the intrinsic ordering, ideas that are deeper than language), and since it is a form of the verb "to see," it suggests that these ideas are conceived through a type of perception. An *eikon* gives intellectual clarity; it is like an image that allows us to see and is, of course, the root of the word *icon*.[*]

A central component of the 'way of seeing' proposed in this book is the recognition that there are ways of knowing in which there is direct perception derived from our integral belonging to the larger whole. It is a knowing distinct from our sensory knowledge and from the subject-object mode of rational knowledge. For the individual, these direct perceptions are a vital way of participating in the unfolding Earth. Unfortunately, such modes of knowing have largely been discredited in recent centuries, because they cannot be tested by experimental methods using controls. Trained by the assumptions and preferences of Western culture to focus almost exclusively on the explicate order, we screen out and suppress vast dimensions of our own implicate nature. The great psychological and spiritual cost of this has been noted by a number of writers. However, we now realize that such alternative forms of knowing are possible because we understand that the creative ordering and formative processes and symmetries integral to the world manifest themselves not only in physical structures, but also in the internal structures of the mind.[1] (Peat 1987, pp. 94, 96) Carl Jung recognized this when he compared the influence of archetypes to the light spectrum, with the infrared end representing the expression of the archetype in the body and the ultraviolet end corresponding to its expression in the psyche (chapter 12).

The great physicist Wolfgang Pauli regarded Jung's ideas about the psychoid nature of the archetype as a major contribution to our understanding of the "laws" of nature. Recall that Jung thought archetypes arise from a fundamental level of being, the psychoid level (chapter 12), where distinctions between psyche and matter can no longer be made by our minds. He thought it probable that psyche and matter are two different

[*] Personal communication, 1997.

aspect of one and the same thing. In his writings, Pauli offered an explanation, based on Jung's insight, of how it is possible for there to be scientific intuitions that are subsequently proven to be accurate by experimentation. Anthony Stevens explains:

> The psychoid archetype represented a sort of "missing link" between the world which is the legitimate study of science, and the mind of the scientist who studies it. . . . [According to Pauli], the relationship between the physical reality we perceive and our cognitive formulations concerning that reality is "predicated upon the fact that the soul of the perceiver and that which is recognized by perception are subject to an order thought to be objective." The archetypes which order our perception and ideas are themselves the product of an objective order which transcends the human mind and the external world. (1982, p. 74)

Louis Dupré's important statement should not be forgotten: "Following the years of gradual change, the real is no longer an object that reason places before the mind, but rather a totality of which the mind constitutes an integral dynamic part." (1989b, p. 21) We've accepted this in the context of having recognized that the formative powers and unknowable mystery of the Abyss/ God are constitutive of the person, as well as also extending beyond the person. That the person is able to know subjectively something of the totality of which she is an integral dynamic part is cause for joy and excitement. One of the most important consequences of the recent recognition that the person is so deeply embedded in the evolutionary universe and that consciousness arises in the non-manifest is that it lends such strong support to the claims of the contemplative tradition that a person can engage in a kind of participatory, alternative knowing—a knowing that can move us to a profound awareness of our belonging to the unfolding whole and perhaps, in the process, to identify our personal calling as such participants in the ongoing story.

Illumination of Selfhood
and Illuminations in the Natural World

Two types of illuminations have already been discussed. One is insight into the one's own identity. From all evidence, Louis Dupré says, we confront in certain illuminative experiences a unified state of consciousness that allows the soul to contact its own core. (1980, p. 459) There is a knowledge of ultimate selfhood in which what is known is not a different thing from the knower. Such intuition brings the person into awareness of his or her unity with Abyss/God. The "I am" or "am" experiences, as described in the chapter 17, involve direct illuminative perception—not a bestowal of identity on a person who is otherwise empty but an awakening that is a direct knowing of the very origins and ground of personhood.

When Keizo Funatsu, the Japanese explorer of the Antarctic, said, "I am God," he had an intellectual perception awakening him to an identity much larger than the physical person with a certain personal history. Another example of such an illumination would be that of Catherine of Genoa, who wrote: "My Me is God, nor do I recognize any other Me except my God Himself." (Quoted in A. Huxley, p.11) Catherine came to an ongoing knowledge of this divine identity—a fact that no longer shocks us in the context of the new story and all that has been discovered about form generation and the plenum or fecund Emptiness that is integral to all matter. These discoveries from the experiential side, as reported by Catherine and so many others, along with those from science, could not be more important to our self-understanding.

The second type of illumination already discussed is perceptions of this participatory type that reveal the presence of Abyss/God throughout the natural world. Here are three examples, given previously in chapter 6:

> Richard M. Bucke reported a mystical experience that included an intellectual vision or illumination he thought was

impossible to believe: that "the universe is not composed of dead matter but on the contrary is a living Presence."

A contemporary American, "N.M.," had the following intellectual intuition: " I had no doubt that I had seen God, that is, had seen all there is to see; yet it turned out to be the world that I looked at every day." (In Stace 1960, p. 73)

A friend of mine realized "That is God" when he saw Niagara Falls.[2]

David Bohm describes these perceptions as insights. They are not thoughts. They are "perceptions through the mind." (1983, p. 51) In them, as Brian Swimme teaches, ultimate reality is emerging in consciousness. It is interesting in this regard that Evelyn Underhill, closely paralleling Bohm, writes that the method by which you will attain to "your place in the Eternal World . . . is strictly analogous to that by which you obtained a more vivid awareness of the natural world in which you grow and move. Here too it shall be direct intuitive contact, sensation rather than thought, which shall bring you certitude—it's like 'tasting food, not talking about it' as Bonaventure says." (1942, pp. 142–43) Her use of the phrase "intuitive contact" shows the immediacy of the experience.

The Human Capacity for Insight

Along the same line of thought—that the mind constitutes an integral, dynamic part of the real—Brian Swimme writes: "*The dynamics that fashioned the fireball and the galaxies also fashion your ideas and visions. . . . In your specific personal dreams and desire, the whole process is present in your personal self.*" (1984, p. 135, emphasis added) In some manner the mind creates images not only from patterns of intelligence that are inner to the person but also from patterns or fields that it shares with the larger world.[3] Scientific discovery of this ordering can be through images, since the person is fully embedded in the deep ordering of the universe. David Bohm said that "the source of what we perceive both of the so-called external world and of ourselves, our so-called inner processes, lies in this nonmanifest . . . and the nonmanifest itself lies in something immensely beyond that." (Bohm and Weber 1978, p. 33) We have considered how the implicate orders of the whole are present in the part. They are manifest in both psyche and in matter. If our being is an explication of the implicate patterns of the underlying whole movement, it makes sense that we can know this inner patterning in an intrapsychic manner. We do not experience form only through information from the senses; we see form through the intelligibility of things.* This intelligibility involves patterning present throughout the parts.

After indicating the manner in which memory and thought are basically mechanical processes, Bohm describes how they can respond to intelligence in an unconditioned act of perception, which he calls "intelligent perception."[4] It occurs when the "the brain and nervous system respond directly to an order in the universal and unknown flux that cannot be reduced to anything that could be defined in terms of knowable structures." (Bohm 1983, p. 53) Specifically he writes that "the ground of intelligence must be in the undetermined and unknown flux, that is also the ground of all definable forms of matter." (p. 52) When there are flashes of intelligent perception there has been an opening to the ground of intelligence.[5] There is an opening to original and creative insight, without any fixed limits or barriers, such that our overall worldview ceases to be rigid, fragmentation ends, and our life comes into harmony. Original and creative insight *is* the action of the immeasurable.(p. 25)

In science as in art, it is necessary to allow for the emergence, in creative perception, of new generative orders. Paul Davies observes: "We, who are children of the universe—animated stardust—can nevertheless reflect on the nature of that same universe, even to the extent of glimpsing the rules on which it runs. How we have become linked into this cosmic dimension is a mystery. Yet the linkage cannot be denied." (1992, p. 232) Indeed, it is this linkage that has made possible the very discovery

---

* Ewert Cousins: personal communication, 1997.

of the new universe story that is itself transforming our consciousness.

Insights and intellectual visions sometimes occur in the context of scientific work. When Einstein wrote down the field equations for relativity theory, he was, as Brian Swimme puts it, "a form of these very dynamics, he jotted down as the field equations." Swimme describes Einstein's discovery of the field equations as follows: "This chunk of the Milky Way jotted down the dynamics of the Milky Way. This region of space-time rich with the interactions of the universe jotted down the interactions of the universe. This fleshy portion of the world transformed its insides into graphite to reveal the harmonies at work throughout the fleshy world." (1996, p.108) The equations did not derive from images, but were a direct perception that *permeated* Einstein—his mind, his muscles, his viscera. Through Einstein's consciousness, the universe itself broke into a reflection on its own grandeur. It is most important to be aware, as we have noted, that the confirmation of his ideas (his "seeing") came *after* his insight. The movement of the whole was expressing itself in explicate form in Einstein's prepared and creative mind. Einstein himself marveled that the world is intelligible.

Johannes Kepler (1571–1630) believed that his delight in scientific discovery was due to the mental exercise of matching ideas or images already implanted in his mind by God with external events perceived through his senses. He spoke of his innate ideas and images as "archetypal." (Stevens 1983, p. 45) Fred Hoyle's sudden intuition about the mathematics of a cosmological theory of electromagnetism (chapter 6) shows the remarkable capacity for insight and creativity available to the person.

The intelligibility of things in general and that occurring on specific occasions when there is a kind of alternative knowing and insight (traditionally called illuminations) are central to this integration of contemplation into the new universe story. The person knows experientially that she is embedded in a larger, ordered whole. The contemplative tradition has recognized occasions of insight that have great meaning to individuals and to their communities. In the integration being developed in this book, such insights are precisely available to all people as embedded earthlings. They are the source of wisdom and of healing for the individual and for people in relation to the Earth both of which are so desperately needed.

This issue of the intelligibility of things is very difficult for Western people of the twenty-first century to comprehend, because science has often taught that knowledge of the very small, such as the movement of atoms and their components, will fully explain more complex events. However, as discussed earlier, following Bohm and others, there are indications from within science itself that the *immeasurable* contains the essential formative causes of all that happens in the manifest world, although not negating the known physical laws. The studies of form generation have shown that local order may follow from global order. Hence the local order of the human mind may be affected, often in a healing manner, by more comprehensive orders. One can get a sense of what is involved in saying this by recalling our ponderings in chapter 11 about the manner in which a non-living carbon atom in carbon dioxide (a local order) can become integrated into a living being because the carbon is already part of larger comprehensive orders that make it possible for it to nest in the living being. Similarly, the spin of coupled particles is somehow determined instantaneously by their participation in a larger field and, perhaps, in some unknown dimension to which they both belong. Given this comprehensive ordering embracing local forms, it is possible to see that an insight or an image involved in a scientific discovery or a contemplative illumination is the movement of the comprehensive order acting through the local self-organizing processes of Self/soul, expressing itself as the insight of the particular seeker. This comprehensive ordering is one of the qualities of true transcendence, as previously noted.

The issue of the intelligibility of things is difficult for another reason: that we cannot observe the form generating, archetypal patterns through our senses. Only their effects can be discerned.

We do not see matter, we see form through the intelligibility of things.* It is not just sensory information that allows us to know things. The self or identity of a tree or an elephant or a human being is a reality immediately recognized by intelligence, even if invisible to the senses. (Swimme and Berry, p. 75)

Still another reason we have difficulty with these alternative ways of knowing is the inadequacy of the words with which the direct perceptions become linked. We have to avoid a naïve conception of equating the language and assumptions by which someone may try to explain her illumination and the actual content and nature of the experience. Problems in understanding this level of knowing are further complicated by the variety of languages—Chinese, Aramaic, Greek or German—each with words with subtle nuances of meaning that are used to describe the experiences, as well as by differences in worldviews and even in the ways languages structure the mind. These problems of individual and cultural interpretation are now being addressed through extensive interreligious dialogue. A communion of understanding, like the noosphere of Teilhard de Chardin, may be gradually developed in the context of the clarifying revelations of the new story of the evolutionary universe and the wholistic perspective it demands.[6]

Theology and Self-Understanding Change with the Journey

"Direct illuminations" of various kinds are often a key component of the ongoing change in consciousness that is part of the organic process of the contemplative pathway. Many people have recognized that the initial encounters with Abyss/God or with numinous archetypal levels of the psyche are often experienced and interpreted differently by a person new to the spiritual life than comparable events will be interpreted after twenty or thirty years of arduous transformations of personality. For example, it is commonly assumed following an awakening experience that there has been an encounter with an order of

---

* Ewert Cousins: personal communication, 1998.

being totally distinct from the self; it seems certain that it is "not me." There is often a marked sense of otherness and transcendence. Consequently, after an awakening experience, a person will initially not believe the claim that the unitive life is possible. I, myself, once did not believe it.

But after a long education, both painful and joyous, the ego is able to recognize that what seemed so foreign is intrinsic to all things, yet still entails true transcendence. There is a gradual shift away from reliance on the subject/object manner of knowing and an openness to letting the world and the depth of the Self reveal itself to us. According to Louis Dupré, "The mystic begins by asserting the 'otherness' of God with respect to the creature, but the final vision must be one of identity." (Dupré and Wiseman, pp. 24–25) Similarly, Daniel Merkur says experiences that commence as an interpersonal encounter change so that God ceases to be felt as distinct, and one's normal or realistic sense of oneself is replaced by an ideal Self who is seemingly God.[7] (p.143) As already noted more than once, the heart of the matter is stated very well by Louis Dupré when he writes that "following the years of gradual change, the real is no longer an object that reason places before the mind, but *rather a totality of which the mind constitutes an integral dynamic part.*"(1989b, p. 21, emphasis added) The "I" that set out is different from the very same "I" that has returned. (Kushner, p. 142)

Carl Jung's description of the process of individuation incorporates this same recognition of a profound change in the person. In his conception, God and man are initially opposites, meaning that God is first experienced by the ego as the "not-I" and the "other." Through the individuation process involving *coniuntio* (unconscious content is brought into the conscious psyche), the Self, a consciousness of wholeness, is realized. There is a union of opposites called a *coniuntio oppositorum*. It is of the nature of a *unio mystica*, a mystical union. (Edinger 1984, p. 16) There results a profound shift in the sense of identity as the locus of identity shifts to the Self. This change in consciousness clearly takes on particular importance in the context of the new story.

I once thought God was to be found entirely outside my person. After that initial breakthrough experience, when I was twenty-nine, I spent many years seeking and praying for another visitation to be given me. Because the initial experience was so gratuitous, I assumed that, wiith patient waiting, further experience would be gratuitously given. I had no understanding that the awakening experience I had had was a reordering experience, which had launched me on the pathway of much needed healing and change. Slowly over the years, through therapeutic work, study, various insights and illuminations, and, finally, learning the implications of the new story of the evolutionary universe, my 'way of seeing' has been transformed, in the manner suggested in this book.

The Unitive Life

Eventually, we are told, the unitive consciousness becomes permanent, running concurrently with, and in some way fused and integrated with, the normal or common consciousness. Teresa was able to attend to the many affairs of her reformed Carmelite order while also being able to turn to an inner unity with God. In last-stage mysticism, there is an achievement of uninterrupted transparency; the stage of discontinuous encounter with the self is transcended. (Neumann 1968, p. 414)

The Flemish mystic Jan Ruusbroec describes the unitive level as a regaining of one's uncreated image, the archetype or pattern within God. He writes that the soul "beyond all its faculties, beyond all its powers, attains its naked essence. It is not a self-enclosed state but an opening to the superessence of God." (As quoted in Dupré 1984, pp. 33–34) This recovery of the uncreated image is critical because the divine reality is dynamic. With the regaining of the image, the person becomes a participant in the fecundity and fertility of God's uncreated life. Elucidating Ruusbroec's thought, Dupré writes: "At the highest level of union where God alone works, the contemplative person must, in union with the distinct Persons of the Trinity, move out again into activity." (pp. 35–36) Eckhart preached about the "birth of the Son in the soul," described in the next chapter on the active, fruitful life.

In the Jewish tradition, the unitive life is sometimes described as the actualization of Messianism, which the Hasidim formulated as "the redemption of the divine sparks in all times and all places." The work of the Messianic age, which is to make the Godhead and the world that is bound up with it "whole and complete" again, is done by the individual. Baal Shem Tov (1698–1760), the founder of Chassidus, an important Jewish religious movement, taught that "the coming of the Messiah does not depend upon anything supernatural, but rather upon human growth and self-transformation. . . . The world will only be transformed . . . when people realize that the Messiah is not someone wholly other than themselves." (Quoted in Kushner, p. 72)

This actualization of Messianism is what Erich Neumann calls last stage mysticism. It is described as "adhesion." Free from the narrow confines of ego identity, the soul has now become attached to the divine Nothingness. Thus the person is no longer in the condition when the ego sees only itself and the contents of its ego-world. (1968, p. 408) Neumann writes: "The mature mystic of the final phase . . . lives in a permanent trans-parence. His self has attained lasting transparence, and so has the world without and within him. With this in mind we shall be in a position to understand the ultimate and central content of last-stage mysticism, its vision of unity." (p. 411) For the mystic of this phase, life in the world is possible; he needs no heaven, no hereafter, no messianic kingdom, for all this is present in the world, though veiled and hidden. (p. 411)

Everyone can seek to participate in the 'way of seeing' we are discovering. Human life is no longer simply a private, personal affair or an affair of the human community alone, although it engages the human community and defines our individual life within the unfolding whole in the most personal and profound way possible. *As a form of the unfolding Earth, each human life is simultaneously that of an individual with personal concern and also a life that is part of the unfolding, sacred Earth.* This is the unity and diversity explored earlier, and understanding it portends an important shift in our emotional loyalties. We are freed from the isolated self as we join not only the human community, but the natural order as well.

The Contemplative Enters the Eternal Now

According to Alan Watts, an interpreter of Eastern philosophies to the West, "The central core of mystical experience seems to be the conviction, or insight, that the immediate *now*, whatever its nature, is the goal and fulfillment of all living." (p. 437) One of the implications of the new story is that there is "only the present now, the present is the only thing that has no end." (See chapter 4.) The confluence of insight into the potential fullness of the 'present now' from both the contemplative tradition and the story of the evolutionary universe greatly enriches the 'way of seeing' we are describing. *The phrase "Eternal Now" used in the contemplative tradition does not simply mean that the numinous Abyss is accessible to individual consciousness only in the present chronological moment; more fundamentally it means that the present is always characterized by an immediacy between the Abyss/God and its manifestation.* We have seen that there is no going away from the ongoing Origin. We recognize in the context of the new story that we may enter the "timeless realm" at no other time than 'this present now' and in no other context than the current state of affairs. Describing a breakthrough experience, R. M. Bucke wrote, "I became conscious in myself of eternal life. It was not a conviction that I would have eternal life, but consciousness that I possessed eternal life then." (In Coxhead, pp. 7–8) Bucke's awakening was an experience of the immanent Presence, which is a condition of every moment of the universe. To live in the Eternal Now and to partake of Eternal life does not imply a withdrawal from day to day life (although this may be an important part of the journey on occasion). The contemplative enters into awareness of the fullness of the 'present now' in the midst of daily life. Thus we find an integration of the radical news from the new universe story with the power and fruitfulness of the unitive life.

We can appropriate the subject/subject relationship with the natural order as found in the traditions of indigenous peoples. Although not considered an accurate historical document, Chief Seattle's reply to the Great Chief in Washington who wished to buy the land of the Northwest Indians resonates with recognition of the sacredness of the natural world: "Every part of the earth is sacred to my people. Every shining pine needle, every sandy shore, every mist in the dark woods, every clearing and humming insect is holy in the memory and experience of my people. . . " (Seed et al., p. 68) Mircea Eliade writes from his study of indigenous peoples: "All that exists fully has mana," a mysterious but creative power. (Eliade, p.24) It is certainly not only indigenous people who have recognized the subjective depth of plants and animals. Francis of Assisi could talk to a bird as one interiority to another, as an "I" to a "Thou." Thomas Berry writes: "The sense of communion at the heart of reality is the central force bringing the ecological age into existence. Thus the birth of a new overwhelming spiritual experience at this moment of Earth history." (1988, p.121)

---

[1] F. David Peat writes that the mind may contain, in some enfolded form, the whole nature of the ground. In this way the patterns of synchronicity, which manifest themselves in both matter and mind, represent the unfolding of a deeper order that lies beyond the distinction of either. (1987, p 82)

[2] Sometimes the contemplative/mystical insight is not in relation to a particular bush or falls like Niagara or a person but is more comprehensive in scope and applies to "everything." The person may not use the word God but may speak of a unity or oneness. Eckhart wrote as follows: "All that a man has here externally in multiplicity is intrinsically One. Here all blades of grass, wood and stone, all things are One. This is the deepest depth." (As quoted in Otto, p. 61.) Here is a report of another experience describing a oneness from William James's collection: "I felt myself one with the grass, the trees, birds, insects, everything in Nature. I exulted in the mere fact of existence, of being a part of it all — the drizzling rain, the shadows of the clouds, the tree trunks, and so on." (James, p. 310, n. 12)

When the world is known in this manner, the mystic literally experiences it as One, despite an ongoing awareness of difference. That which is known in mystical experience to be a unity is still recognized simultaneously as distinct entities.

[3] As explained by Michael Talbot, the most recent theoretical formulations of David Bohm and Karl Pribram provide a profound new way of looking at the world: "Our brains mathematically construct objective reality by interpreting frequencies that are ultimately projections from another dimension, a deeper order of existence that is beyond space and time: The brain is a hologram enfolded in a holographic universe." (1991, p. 54)

[4] The mechanical aspects of our memories and thoughts are demonstrated by the fact that often they are irrelevant and unsuitable to a situation. (See Bohm 1983, p. 53.) Thought (which for Bohm includes the intellectual, emotional, sensuous, muscular and physical responses of memory) is part of a person's response to each actual situation. Thought and memory are basically material processes that are inseparable from electrical and chemical activity in the brain and nervous system and concomitant tensions and movements of muscles, and are thus basically mechanical.

[5] This ground of intelligence is the metaphysical undergirding of our "reflections and intuitions." (Nobuhara, p. 144) Bohm explains that when an insight occurs, "the source cannot be within ideas already contained in the field of measure (i.e. those things that are not immeasurable) but rather has to be in the immeasurable, which contains *the essential formative cause* of all that happens in the field of measure." (Quoted in Coxhead, p. 117, emphasis added; see also Stevens 1982, p. 58.)

[6] The first part of the word *noosphere* comes from the word *nous*, the Greek word for mind that is not the rational mind, but the mind of intuitive vision that sees things s a whole. The noosphere is a sphere of thinking, of knowing, of acting, and of collaborating that came into existence with the human being and will spread over the Earth, as has the biosphere.

[7] Although we are drawing largely on the Western tradition, philosopher David Loy writes regarding the yoga that the subject works to transform a particular type of experience from a dualistic to a nondualistic mode. (p. 287)

20

THE ACTIVE AND FRUITFUL LIFE

For us an adequate knowledge of the psyche is probably a matter of life and death. If the emergent God that wants to be born in man is not humanized and transformed by a sufficient number of conscious individuals, its dark aspect can destroy us.

— Edward Edinger

IT TAKES A minimal knowledge of less than a century of history to be aware that humanity is hurtling, largely blindly, into a dangerous, even desperate future. To allay our almost subliminal, gnawing fear, we choose leaders who collude in hiding the dangers by predicting a better and better future. Still, we are aware of a number of alarming situations. For example, more than 80,000 different industrial chemicals are used worldwide, only a small portion of which have been tested for their effects on the human being, much less the rest of the natural world. Some of them can cause destruction of genetic information, some are carcinogenic, and some mimic naturally occurring hormones, disrupting endocrine function. The loss of biodiversity as species become extinct, the destruction of ancient forests and plains, the loss of topsoil and the disruption of genetic information cannot be remedied, because the universe is a continuing sequence of irreversible transformations. If our understanding and the focus of our concern and attention do not change, the road we are taking will lead to more poverty and disease, increased human displacement from stable cultures, less beauty, fewer vocational choices and mounting violence exacerbated by competition for shrinking fresh water, food supplies, and natural resources.

The 'way of seeing' developed in this book enables us to envision the possibility of an integrated, organic pathway into a future with hopeful possibilities for the individual and the Earth community. The source of this hope lies, in part, in actions that may arise from transformed personhood in the context of the new story. The creative, active side of the contemplative life, long recognized by the tradition, becomes now an urgent matter for human survival and the creation of a viable future.

After the person rests in "the dark sources of consciousness," there is intrinsic to this unitive realization participation in the fecundity and productive power of Abyss/God. Plotinus believed that contemplation of the Source is the only way we enter the fullness of living and productive power available to us, and taught that creation is impossible apart from contemplation. (*Enneads* III. 8. 30) As Lawrence Kushner says, "You fall back into your source and forward into your destiny." (p. 132) In unity with the creativity and fecundity of the depth of things (Abyss/God), the person is able to be an exponent of the creativity and unity of the whole as it is expressed in a particular situation. It is precisely to this capacity that the contemplative tradition speaks. To discuss the fruitful, active life, we turn again to Meister Eckhart, because he writes so compellingly about the active life that becomes possible with the developing contemplative capacity.

The Active Life of the Contemplative: Meister Eckhart

Eckhart preached that an intrinsic dimension of the contemplative life is a fruitfulness and fertility arising in the person "from the most noble ground."[1] (1981, p. 179) This fruitfulness and fertility is the completion of "letting be" and disinterest. The Godhead is fertile or fecund; as a consequence, the person who has broken through into the ground of the soul, which is one with the Godhead, also becomes fertile and fruitful. Eckhart describes the creativity and love that come with breakthrough and contemplation as a "going out," a "speaking forth," a "boiling or even a boiling over" and a "melting." The oneness flows out of itself.

In a brief anecdote recorded in the Gospel of Luke, Jesus praises Mary, who has been sitting at his feet listening to him talk, but admonishes Martha, who is anxious and troubled while busily serving the guests. (Luke 10:38–42) In contrast to the parable, Eckhart did not preach that Mary's behavior was superior to the active life of Martha, but that Martha's life of action was the perfection toward which Mary should strive—a life of action that flows out of the return to the Ground of the self. To Eckhart, Martha is a more mature person, and further advanced in the spiritual life, for she knows about contemplative rapture but does not cling to it; what matters to her is to act in the way made possible by the opportunity and demands of each occasion.

Eckhart held that inner silence is entirely compatible with outer activity. He, himself, led a very active life as an administrator in the Dominican order and as a preacher throughout the Rhine valley. Breakthrough into contemplation, in Eckhart's thought, is not just an isolated experience or a type of prayer and meditation. It involves an openness and responsiveness to what is required of us at any given time. In "On Detachment," he said the active life was like the planks of a door, which move while the hinges, on which the door pivots, are at rest. (1981, p. 291)

On another occasion, Eckhart describes the fruitfulness he honored in Martha as that of the virgin who has become the wife. The virgin has let go and broken through and is free of alien images (the disinterest), but it is the wife who participates in the fecundity of the Godhead. In the sermon "Jesus Went Up" he preached:

> Now mark what I say and pay careful attention! For if a man were to be a virgin forever, no fruit would come from him. If he is to become fruitful, he must of necessity be a wife. "Wife" is the noblest word one can apply to the soul, much nobler than "virgin." That a man conceives God in himself is good, and in his conceiving he is a maiden. But that God should become fruitful in him is better; for the only gratitude for a gift is to be fruitful with the gift, and then the spirit is a wife, in its gratitude giving birth in return, when he for God gives birth to Jesus into the heart of the Father. . . .
>
> The virgin who is a wife brings this fruit, and this birth about, and everyday she produces fruit, . . . becoming fruitful

from the noblest ground of all—or, to put it better, from that same ground where the Father is bearing his eternal Word, from that ground is she fruitfully bearing with him. (1981, p. 178)

Here, Eckhart makes it clear that the active life of the contemplative has origins deep in the heart of things, and is not to be confused with the busyness and unexamined social conformity of much of life, with which we are all too familiar. Eckhart described this as being lost in "multiplicity" and "alien images." Only through contemplation, which involves immersion of the person in the larger order of things, will one's activities reflect the order and beauty of the intelligible world.

Birth of the Son in the Soul

Eckhart not only describes the creative and fruitful dimension of contemplation as becoming a Martha or a wife, but more radically, calls this aspect of contemplation the birth of the Son in the soul. The capacity to give birth to the Son in the soul is based on the nobility of the soul, which refers, in Eckhart's preaching, to the capacity of the ground of the soul to unite itself to the ground of God.[2] (Schürmann 1978b, p. 299) Eckhart asserts that the disinterested and released soul, the one who with true poverty of Spirit has reclaimed its unity with the Godhead, "co-bears" the Son.[3] There is a simultaneous and identical bearing of the Word in the released human being and in the bosom of the Father. In order to emphasize that he is speaking of the Son in his divinity, Eckhart adds that this fruit is very great, "neither more nor less than God."[4] (As quoted in Schürmann 1978a, p.23) Here in the birth of the Son in the soul out of its nobility is the crucial grounding of personhood in the sacred depth of things. The birth of the Son means a transformed personhood and transformed presence in the world. With regard to the use of the phrase "the birth of the Son," recall the discussion in chapter 13, where we sought to understand how the Trinitarian conception grounds personhood in the sacred depths, thus valuing individual subjectivity, while not removing the person from the ongoing unity.

Much of our study in earlier chapters about the nature of matter and the processes of form generation has been undertaken precisely in order to show that there is evidence and support in the new story for this grounding of personhood in the dynamic depth of things. Since, as Swimme says, "Creation comes from emptiness, so creation comes from us in so far as we identify with the Emptiness" (1984, p. 37), we see that the creativity can emerge in individual self-aware consciousness. This is what Eckhart is preaching when he makes the powerful claim that the person takes part in the emanation of reality (in its human expression) from the simple unity of the Godhead, or in more orthodox Christian terms, from the Father.

The Person and God Are Jointly Given Birth

The birth out of the noble ground is described by Reiner Schürmann in the selection that follows. He is commenting on Eckhart's phrase: "He gives me birth, me, his Son and the same Son" (Eckhart 1981, p. 187):

> Being reborn in the Father as Son of God, as the unique Son, is becoming fertile "out of the most noble ground." . . . Out of the "same" ground from which the Father engenders his eternal Son, the detached man engenders the same Son at the same time. The "same" ground, the "same" Son, the "same" time: this implies clearly that the identity of God and man is altogether related to the birth of the Son. *The Father begets, and man begets jointly with him.* . . . At each instant the detached man engenders the eternal Son of the Father. (1978a, p. 23, emphasis added)

Could our embeddedness in the heart of things be more complete? When Eckhart teaches that "man begets jointly with him," he is integrating human creativity and fruitfulness with the central fecundity and creativity at the heart of the creative powers of the universe. We have deep roots with many fine tendrils in the cosmos. At the heart of the integration developed here is this recognition that the rebirth of the individual into the unitive life (the son being born in God) and the birth of God in the active life of the person (the son born in the soul) are not to be separated. There is a simultaneous and identical bearing forth of the Word, in the "disinterested" and released human being and in the bosom of the Father. (Schürmann 1978a, p.26) *The creative heart of the world dwells within and among us and within and among the natural world. The individual is no longer an isolated entity grasping for a place in the world, but is given a remarkable intrinsic place, a place that is sacred.*

When Eckhart preached about the birth of the Son in the soul, he was not speaking about an ongoing event in a realm spatially transcendent to the individual, but about an event that is enfolded within and inseparable from the individual's actual body and psyche.[5] He preached: "For the Father begets his Son in the soul exactly as he does in eternity and not otherwise. He must do so whether he will or not. The Father ceaselessly begets his Son. And what is more, he begets me as his Son—the self-same Son!"[6] (1941, p. 181) So we are talking about a rebirth in a person in which divinity finds expression in a particular occasion in daily life. Or, stated another way, the event in Bethlehem is being fulfilled now, in this present time.

Eckhart's concept of the birth of the Son in the soul is not unique within Christianity, since it is in the radical image tradition (from Genesis 1:27) of the Greek fathers of Christianity. (See chapter 12.) In addition, he develops the ancient formula of the church fathers Irenaeus and Athanasius: God becomes Man so that Man might become God. Eckhart preached:

If anyone were to ask me, Why do we pray, why do we fast, why do we do all our works, why are we baptized, why (most important of all) did God become man?—I would answer, in order that God may be born in the soul, and the soul be born in God. For that reason all the Scriptures were written. God created the world and all angelic natures: so that God may be born in the soul and the soul be born in God. (1979, p. 215)

Jan Ruusbroec also wrote of the birth of the son in the soul.[7] He is considered the person in the Western tradition who most fully understood the spiritual meaning of the mystery of the Trinity. (Dupré 1984, p. 26)

This same recognition that the person and God are jointly given birth is present in the fundamental incarnational insight of Christianity. That the human being, Jesus of Nazareth, should be described in mythic language as the son of God and therefore be a divine person, implies that his personhood is in some manner integral to the nature of God and the full meaning of the word God. This conception eventually came to be expressed in Trinitarian formulas, as we have seen (chapter 13). God's being in the world involves this human person. In the context of the new story, the life of Jesus of Nazareth must be understood as not only a revelation about the particular unique person that he was, but a revelation of the nature of things, which includes this joint birthing in the prepared person in the 'fullness of the present now.'

There is further remarkable testimony to this simultaneous birth of God and the person from "love mystics." The German mystic and religious poet Angelus Silesius (1624–1677), for example, wrote that we shelter God:

> There are but you and I, and when we two are not
> The heavens will collapse. God will not more be God.

> God shelters me as much as I do shelter Him
> His Being I sustain, sustained I am therein.
> (Quoted in Dupré 1985, p. 23)

In the light of these radical insights, we can see why the integration of the new story and the contemplative tradition is of crucial importance. In the unitive life the person enters into the 'all at onceness' we have found both in the new universe story and in the contemplative tradition. This 'all at onceness,' this fullness unfolds from the state of affairs of the 'present now.' Each person, as she is prepared (chapters 17 and 18) or "worthy," as Eckhart describes it, is a power participating in the cosmos-creating endeavor in each present moment.

Becoming Conscious

Brian Swimme expresses the radical integration we are describing when he says: "The consciousness that learns it is at the origin point of the universe is itself an origin of the universe." (1996, p. 112) The contemplative has developed this consciousness. Lawrence Kushner writes in *The River of Light* of the role of consciousness: "It is as if the primary act of creation is simply becoming conscious and that through becoming conscious we—like God—create ourselves. The first and most important creation that human beings (and through them the One of Being) and the One of Being (and through the One of Being, human beings) can give birth to is consciousness. Awareness. Eyes open, remade for wonder. Eyes that see. Ears that hear. Hands that feel." (p. 108)

The creation of consciousness was central to Carl Jung's personal myth. Edward Edinger points out that Jung recognized that the divine service which man can render to God is to make it possible for light to emerge from the darkness, for the Creator may become conscious of His creation and man conscious of himself. (Edinger 1984, p. 16) Further, Edinger writes, when "enough individuals are carriers of the 'consciousness of wholeness,' the world itself will become whole." (p. 32) He thought that what both "Christ and Buddha have in common is the idea of being a carrier of consciousness." (p. 22) Erich Neumann wrote of the renewal of the world by the change in consciousness brought by encounter with the numinous: "The world and history are the places in which the numinous manifests itself, that numinous which transforms its elect by revelations and mystical encounters and through them renews the world." (1968, pp. 402–3)

A snowy egret and an ancient oak each give expression to the numinous. But it is in human consciousness that changes affecting the planet are occurring very rapidly and precipitously.

Now there is no longer just slow biological evolution, but evolution in human culture. In the videoseries *The Earth's Imagination* (1998) Brian Swimme reports that it has been calculated that the rate of creativity is a thousand times greater than with genetic change. *With human influence on the planet so pervasive, a change in human consciousness becomes urgent. The Abyss/God needs to be given a fuller personal face, a full human expression of itself in each person.* The individual is rooted in the creative depth of things, with responsibility and work that are as filled with meaning—as fundamentally important—as the rituals of the Taos Pueblo in tending, as they saw it, to the rising sun. The creativity that may be ignited in us is that which fashioned the galaxies. A human life can be an activation of the deep, creative dimension of the universe. We are called to extend and deepen this activation. This is a sacred role, a sacred capacity.

A Personal Place in the Great Story for Everyone

We have found a very personal place for the individual in a vast cosmos. The word *personal* is used to mean that we are affected in the Center of our being by the immanent presence of the All-Nourishing Abyss, whose dynamism awakens and "moves" us, affecting us in profoundly intimate ways. It shapes and informs our dreams and our self-understanding in a life-transforming manner. *Daily life gains reality and meaning and creativity by participating in the sacred realm.* Our very existence brings us into the nexus of the wholistic qualities of the universe. It is a depth of belonging which is actually more intimate and personal than that offered by the image of the transcendent Father caring for a child. As Brian Swimme says, we tell the story of our origins in order to establish ourselves in vital relationship with reality's core.

The 'Present Now'

We all live in the 'present now' with its particular chime. As we enter physically and spiritually into the heart of things in the contemplative mode of consciousness, we bring a particular "take" on a situation and bring forth what would otherwise be absent. A prepared person will often be conscious of dimensions of the world that she would not otherwise have been open to, and thus be enabled to act in ways previously unavailable to her. The contemplative mode of consciousness may lead to a simple act of kindness or of compassion. This act may seem to be only the replication of a cultural pattern, but in spite of its familiar appearance, it can be a fresh, creative, loving action, bringing what never existed before into being. Something is done on a particular occasion by a unique person in a present moment which has never existed before and is not to be repeated. Daniel Day Williams reminded us that to love God is to set the highest value on temporality as well as on eternality.[8] (Williams, p. 184) In innumerable ways a person may contribute to a situation that would be diminished or impoverished without a particular creative insight or a gesture of caring or practical work.

The consciousness may lead to confrontation with entrenched injustice. Martin Luther King and the courageous acts of many people changed the patterns of racial segregation in the southern United States. Rosa Parks said that when she refused to stand in the bus so a white woman could have her seat, she was not tired, she was not old, and she was not doing it for a political goal; instead the decision was a deeply personal one, made for the sake of her own identity and integrity. (Palmer, p. 168) The individual can indeed act with nobility, and on occasion the action is a decisive factor in future developments. We may find the nobility of which Meister Eckhart wrote, and the dignity which Jung recognized in the Taos Pueblo, in innumerable acts of courage, faithfulness, and endurance in ordinary daily life.

Although we are stunned by the creativity of educated minds like Einstein's, of gifted musicians like Mozart, of great writers and artists and leaders of movements for social change, we also can engage in the creativity of the unfolding whole through simple, fresh ideas and often humbling insights that lead to changes in our personal lives and in the lives of our family and community. Though often invisible to the outside world, these creative insights and acts of love can make all the difference in the quality and felt value of life and in our relationship to the Earth. If we fail to acknowledge and embrace the 'all at onceness' in the 'present now' and the direct, very personal vocation of each person in the birth of the unfolding of the future of the Earth community (like the Taos Pueblo who believed they helped the sun to rise), many of us are likely to continue to seek expression of their energy and creativity in illicit, often dangerous, rebellious, and sometimes unsatisfying ways because we are denied a place of fundamental meaning and authenticity.

Is it possible that this 'way of seeing' could make a person feel falsely puffed up, perhaps encouraging her to believe she is uniquely in possession of some ultimate truth or to assume too facilely that she is destined to carry out some divinely appointed mission? It might seem so. But dangerous claims such as these arise from a disturbed psyche, and are made regardless of any particular worldview or theology; in particular, such "inflation" occurs when the ego is unconsciously identified with the transpersonal Center, that is, when it is not strong enough to be the *conscious* Center of the personality.[9] Such pathologies are largely precluded when the maternal matrix is restored (chapter 18). Then the ego can consciously relate to the Self and its transpersonal Center without being identified with it. (Edinger 1973, pp. 7, 13, 96).

A more serious challenge is that claims to the unitive life would seem to suggest a person might be God. Some people have suffered greatly when reluctantly making this claim, so easily misunderstood. Certainly a person is not God if by that word we refer to a separate, distinct supernatural being. But in the context of the unfolding story, we *are* a form of the whole that includes the creative, largely unknowable depths we are calling the *plenum*, the generative Nothingness or Abyss/God. A dimension of our being *is* the generative Nothingness. When we hold together unity and difference, as we have been seeking to do, we must accept this seeming paradox that a dimension of the person is Abyss/God and the individual may give expression to Abyss/God while being at the same time a distinct, particular individual. Gordon Cosby, of the Church of the Savior in Washington, preached: "Our real work in the world is to be that little piece of God's being so that God's nature is released into the world whenever we show up."* The union is in the more comprehensive reality, in Abyss/God, yet finds expression in the individual being.

A Humbling Position

The message of the simultaneous birth of Abyss/God and the person actually points us in the opposite direction from that of inflation; it is humbling to realize that we are part of a larger whole, much of it without a voice. We awaken to know we must live out of our integral belonging to the Earth, which is filled with joy and with suffering, beauty and ugliness. As we become freer of our hungry, addictive attachments and our dragon-like angers, there emerges a closer relationship to the body and to the Earth. And this in turn requires a kind of humility, as we identify with the Earth community and are called to speak for its integrity. It takes humility to sustain nobly the suffering that is part of human life; we are humbled when we are led to difficult changes in the direction of our lives. The contemplative experience in the context of the new universe story may sometimes call us to renounce the security of our carefully laid plans in deference to larger callings emerging in relation to the Earth and the creative Abyss/God.

There is a pervasive quality of self-offering and self-giving throughout the universe. It was the sacrifice of a supernova that synthesized some of the elements in our bodies. The sun consumes four million tons of hydrogen every second as it pours forth the energy that sustains us. The early organisms of the Earth ate the energetic molecules in the oceans. Animals feed on plants and/or on other animals. Some cultures have rituals of gratitude for the sacrifice of plants and animals for human

* Sermon, June 17, 2001.

sustenance. John Grim, who is a professor of religion, writes: "In the primal time of myths, one seminal feature of this bond with the natural world is an understanding that animals and plants had sacrificed their bodies so human beings might live. They sang songs which provide life direction and reflection on the shared sacrifice and interdependence of all life." (pp. 47–48) There is a sacrificial dimension at every level. True altruism—the giving away of something without return—goes on everywhere in nature. (Thomas 1981, p. 52) With a compelling vision and experience of meaning, we willingly join the self-offering.

There are severe limits to human hubris built into the Earth's systems. Just as our numbers grow and our technological skills extend our dominance over the Earth, we are at the same time recognizing that we are totally dependent on its ongoing vitality and fruitfulness. It is only in concert with a viable biosphere that the human adventure can be sustained. The threat of global warming, and the resulting abrupt (in geological terms) changes in climate, which seem already to be upon us, constantly reminds us of this. There are severe limits to any grandiose conceptions of being God in the sense of thinking we control things: It has been said that only when the last tree is gone and all the fresh water is polluted will we realize that money is useless. The creative, divine potential of the person can be expressed only within the continuing healthy functioning of the Earth.

Furthermore, it has long been understood that all claims of divine representation must be carefully tested by the process of community discernment, including, of course, weighing any proposed activities in relation to their influence on the ongoing viability of the Earth and to issues of justice and peace in the human community. It may be important to wait for a period of time before undertaking some action, to be sure it's not just a passing enthusiasm. All of a person's actions and words are always those of the particular individual, so a constant process of discernment in relation to the well-being of the human community and of the various ecosystems on which it depends is necessary.

The Integration

Full participation in the ancient, unfolding universe, a whole permeated with creative, interpenetrating numinous depth, grants us great nobility and intrinsic worth. The contemplative awakening is no longer just a reawakening to private, subjective knowledge of Abyss/God and the action that comes from that; in the light of the integration just developed, the person is simultaneously brought into intrinsic participation in the unfolding whole. It is true that only "those who have this experience of the identity of the human with the entire order of things can be considered as possessing a completely human mode of being." (Swimme and Berry pp. 197–98) Full expression of the unitive life would therefore include living in a sustainable manner, so the Earth may continue to be fruitful. We would no longer tolerate seduction into needless consumerism and waste production. Several communities that integrate a contemplative spirituality and a sustainable manner of living are developing. At Genesis farm in Blairstown, New Jersey, the new story is taught, careful food preparation is taught, and organic food is grown by community-supported agriculture. A new monastic community, based on the revelations of the new story, is being founded in New England, under the leadership of a Catholic sister, Gail Worcelo. A family in Ohio is starting a community called *greenfire,* in which there will be both communal contemplative life and, as part of that contemplative life, an intention to live on the land with Earth-healing and regenerating life-ways.

A woman once found great joy in cooking, but lost a sense of its importance when she learned it is seen by some as slave labor in a capitalistic society. However, she could recover that joy and sense of value in the context of the new story, when she recognized that as she cooked for her friends and family using wholesome food, "slow food," she was giving fresh expression to a beautiful, self-nourishing universe. Many people leave their car in the garage whenever possible, plant native species, shop for local produce . . . This activism comes out of the kind of consciousness that is emerging from the new story and the contemplative tradition.

The integration may also be given expression in costly ways. In the mid-seventeenth century, Quaker John Woolman traveled extensively by foot and by horse as an itinerant minister to Quaker meetings throughout the eastern colonies. It was the depth of communion with the suffering of his fellow human beings that led him to an early witness against slavery, which in turn shaped the future witness of the Society of Friends against slavery. When he walked long distances on foot instead of traveling by horse or carriage, it was by choice, in order that he might feel first hand the condition of slaves. In his travels he would customarily receive the hospitality of Quakers, some of whom owned slaves, but this caused "a difficulty . . . in [his] mind with respect to saving [his] own money by kindness received, which appeared to [him] to be the gain of Oppression." (Cady, p. 95) He sometimes left money for the slaves or gave it to them directly, and on one occasion he quietly left before the meal was served in the elegant home of a family he was visiting because it was attended by slaves. The family later freed their slaves, saying they could not continue to keep slaves "if they are going to cost the friendship of such a man as John Woolman." Earlier, in his life as a merchant, Woolman had refused to write wills if they provided for the passing on of slaves as part of the inheritance. In later years he began to wear undyed clothing, because the production of dyes was dependent on slave labor in the West Indies. This caused him great suffering, because the pale white color of his clothes made him conspicuous. He refused to ride long distances in carriages in England, because of the cruel exhaustion of the horses. Rufus Jones, a twentieth-century Quaker leader, said of John Woolman: "Here was a mysticism—and it was the type to which I dedicated my life—which sought no ecstasies, no miracles of levitation, no startling phenomena, no private rapture, but whose overmastering passion was to turn all he possessed, including his own life, into the channel of universal love." (Vining, p. 262) Jones felt that a mysticism that did not find expression in creative serving remained incomplete.

A Second Axial Change: Ecozoic Consciousness

Crisis moments are a time of stupendous creativity that can draw forth great change. (Swimme 1990, p. 89) Energies directed toward the preservation of the species and the Earth are emerging from a level below our rational preoccupations, so that the changes in consciousness now glimpsed in many places are not just a frantic grasping at straws by worried residents of an Earth under great stress.

Ewert Cousins suggests that we are now involved in another axial change in consciousness occurring simultaneously all around the Earth. (See chapter 15.) It is bringing about an unprecedented complexification of consciousness through the convergence of culture and religion.[10] (Cousins 1992, pp. 7, 10) When Thomas Berry identifies the twentieth century as the end of the Cenozoic Period (the last 67 million years, when the mammals flourished) and the beginning of the Ecozoic Period, he refers to a complex of issues that includes the change in consciousness brought by the new story of the evolutionary universe. In the Ecozoic Era, humans will be present to the Earth in a mutually enhancing manner. Berry is playing a key role in awakening us to the very great significance of the discovery that we belong to an evolutionary universe, which he sees as the context for a contemporary shift in consciousness in many disciplines. Loyal Rue calls the story a "wisdom tradition" tolerating a diversity of interpretations, yet a means for global solidarity and cooperation. (Rue, p. 136)

With more than 6 billion people living on the Earth and many ecosystems severely weakened or destroyed, it will be extremely difficult to shift to sustainable cultures. Faced with major threats, do we dare to recognize that there are signs of hope? Are not small communities and individual lives, however heroic, very fragile and nearly insignificant before the enormous, unprecedented devastation of the great wars of the last century? What of the vast numbers of migrants living in poverty on the periphery of large cities and the children dying daily of hunger? Dare we believe that we are at a major evolutionary threshold? Could it really be the case, as Teilhard de Chardin observed, that "Today something is happening to the structure of human consciousness. A fresh kind of life is starting"?

But it is a fact that now, in the context of the new universe story, we *are* becoming aware of the power for transformation grounded in the inexhaustible fecundity at the root of reality in every region of the universe in this present moment. Based on all that has been presented in the previous chapters, I believe that we are indeed now offered a 'way of seeing' that allows us to take heart and recognize the potential that lies within us and within the Earth. The evidence is there. To think that the contemplative life with its inner realizations and its outer creative expression is insignificant is to fail to realize that mind and mental events have a status matching that of the material world. Many remarkable individuals have witnessed by their lives to the possibility of a fundamental change in human consciousness and to the possibility of joining in a larger, creative, trustworthy order to effect great change. Besides, as Brian Swimme says, the universe is addicted to surprise: How can we be without hope? Joanna Macy, an American Buddhist and activist, considers it an "enormous privilege to be alive now, in this Turning, when all the wisdom and courage we ever harvested can be put to use and matter supremely." (Quoted in Ryan, p. 77)

In our direct participation in the point of creativity that produces things out of "nothingness," we find the freedom within which we are able to choose to participate in the building of a sustainable future. We are placed right in the heart of things physically and spiritually in the 'present now.' By becoming conscious of our full identity we find it highly possible to choose ways of transforming our relationships with the Earth and all its peoples, with our close human and other than human companions, and with the institutions that govern and teach about these relationships.

Nelson Mandela included this poem, "Let Your Light Shine," in the speech he gave when he was inaugurated president of South Africa in 1994. It speaks to the invitation we are offered to the contemplative life within the great evolutionary story. It was read at the funeral of the college-age son of a friend.

Our deepest fear is not that we are inadequate
Our deepest fear is that we are powerful beyond measure.
It is our light, not our darkness that most frightens us.
We ask ourselves, who am I to be brilliant, to be gorgeous, to be talented?
Actually, who are you not to be?

You are a child of God;
your playing small does not serve the world.
And there is nothing enlightened about shrinking
So that other people will not feel insecure around you.
We were born to make manifest the Glory of God that is inside us.
It's not just in some of us, it's in everyone
And when we let our own light shine,
We unconsciously give other people permission to do the same.
As we are liberated from our own fear,
Our presence automatically liberates others.

---

[1] The word *ground*, as Meister Eckhart uses it, refers to some interior region of man, of an unsurpassable intimacy. (Schürmann 1978a, p. 23)

[2] In his work *The Book of "Benedictus": Of The Nobleman*, Eckhart wrote that one should remember, based on our Lord's teaching in the gospel, "how noble man has been created in his nature, and how divine that is which he can attain by grace, and also how man should attain to it." (1981, p. 240)

[3] Eckhart called the condition of the person who is prepared for contemplation "poverty." In true poverty of spirit, a person is free of things and all works and so has become a place only for God. In this condition of poverty of spirit, "God performs his own work and the man is in this way suffering God to work, and God is his own place to work in, and so God is his own worker in himself. Thus in this poverty man pursues that everlasting being which he was and which he is now and which he will evermore remain." (1981, p. 202) He also wrote: "God

asks only that you get out of his way, in so far as you are creature, and let him be God in you." (1941, p. 127) These ideas about poverty of spirit could be read as a denial of the importance of the body and psyche, but they simply assume there has been a letting-go and a letting-be such that there is an availability to these primal, creative emanations of Abyss/God in the healed and ordered personality. Through the formative powers of the soul, constitutive of the person, this birth is realized in the whole person.

The conception of the "birth of the Son" is based on the emanation tradition of God as self-diffusive goodness. The divine essence, the Godhead as ontological source emanates the diffusion of the three persons of the Trinity. The creative aspect is described in Christian terms as the birth of the son from the Father. At times Eckhart follows the authority of Augustine, where unity is ascribed to the Father as the origin and source of the divinity of the other Persons.

"We have . . . two contrasting formulations of the relationship between the breakthrough to the Godhead and the birth of the Son. In the one, the breakthrough to the Godhead is *more radical* than the birth of the Son and indeed the ground and basis of it. In the other, the birth of the Son *crowns* and *perfects* the unity with the Godhead as fruitfulness perfects virginity." (Caputo, p. 224)

[4] Eckhart's statement of the simultaneous and identical bearing forth of the Word in the detached human being and in the bosom of the Father raised many questions that rancored the inquisitors in Cologne. Eckhart's writing have numerous passages stressing the identity of sonship between the good or just man and Christ. (McGinn 1981b, p. 52) For the inquisitors, the apparent claim of the identity of the individual and Christ challenged the uniqueness of Christ. Eckhart's statements about the birth of the Son in the soul could be accepted as orthodox for the inquisitors if the birth of the Son refers to an eternal, immanent process of birth from the Father within the Trinity, prior to the distinction into substance (i.e. creation), but when the birth of the Son seemed to mean that the actual whole physical person (the existential subject in the world) is a Son of God, it was challenged.

[5] We can understand this birth of the Son to mean that, in the divine reality, immanent to the person, there is a "boiling up" or emanation within the divine essence, and that this immanent event is part of the being of the person in the ground of the soul.

[6] Reiner Schürmann states it most clearly: "Out of the same ground from which the Father engenders his eternal Son, the detached man engenders the same son at the same time." (Schürmann 1978a, p. 23) Here again Eckhart is in the tradition of the Greek Fathers of Christianity, who spoke of the divinizing power of grace. The birth of Christ in the believer is a way of expressing the mystical union of the soul and the Logos. (McGinn 1981b, p. 50) However,

according to Schürmann, the extension of the meaning of divinization to the preaching of the simultaneous and identical bearing forth of the Word in the detached human being and in the bosom of the Father cannot be corroborated by patristic sources. (Schürmann 1978a, p. 26)

[7] Ruusbroec also wrote of the birth of the son in the soul, staying carefully within the framework of the ongoing dynamic process in which each Person of the Trinity remains eternally involved. (Dupré 1984, p. 41) The contemplative accompanies God's own move from hiddenness to manifestation within the identity of God's own life. The reader is referred to Louis Dupré's book *The Common Life: The Origins of Trinitarian Mysticism and Its Development by Jan Ruusbroec* (1984).

[8] In classical theology God was in no sense really temporal. Augustine asserted the superiority of loving God to loving the world because God is eternal and the world is temporal. But time— in the sense we have come to understand it in the context of the evolutionary universe, that the present is the only thing that has no end—includes the divine dimension. Abyss/God shares in the world's temporality and its becoming. However, there remains an "atemporal" aspect, not in the sense of beyond time as we understand it in the new story, but in the sense of more than mere successiveness and change in a time-developmental universe. There is a 'timeless' factor in every timebound experience. Whitehead addressed this question in his ideas of the primordial and consequent nature of God.

David Bohm also addressed this question; he asserts that the implicate order is manifested or displayed in the explicate order, so the implicate order is thus intimately involved in the visible, temporal world. But at the same time, in a discussion of the origin of new forms, Bohm said that the implicate order has a deep purpose and intentionality that does not necessarily show up in its surface and explicate forms. This deep purpose is creative and relates to the form of new wholes; its creativity is illustrated by the fact that complex forms appear that are not explained by the mere requirement of survival. (Bohm and Weber 1982, p.39) We could consider this an "atemporal" aspect of Abyss/God. It is an aspect of true transcendence.

[9] Psychosis is extreme ego-Self identity.

[10] Cousins observes that ironically, while the meeting of religions is having a positive effect, the secularization of culture is threatening the very survival of the world's religions. The technology that has made possible the meeting of spiritual paths is engulfing the human spirit in an atmosphere of materialism. Cousins finds that this secularization is a global phenomenon. (1985, p. 3, and personal communication)

BIBLIOGRAPHY

Abram, David. 1996. *The Spell of the Sensuous.* New York: Pantheon Books.

Ancelet-Hustache, Jeanne. 1957. *Meister Eckhardt and the Rhineland Mystics.* New York: Harper Torchbooks.

Armstrong, A. Hilary. 1940. *The Architecture of the Intelligible Universe in the Philosophy of Plotinus.* Cambridge.: The University Press.

———. 1979. "Salvation, Plotinian and Christian." *Plotinian and Christian Studies.* London: Various Reprints, pp. 126–39.

———. 1996. Preface. *Plotinus.* Vol. 1, pp. vii-xxxii. London: William Heinemann Ltd..

Augros, Robert M. and Stanciu, George N. 1954. *A New Story of Science.* Chicago: Gateway Editions.

Augustine of Hippo. *Confessions.* Translated by Rex Warner. New York: New America Library, 1983.

———.*City of God.* Translated by Gerald Walsh, S.J.; Demetrius Zema, S.J.; Grace Monahan, O.S.U.; Daniel Honan. Garden City, N.Y.: Doubleday, 1958.

Balas, David L. 1966. "Metousia Theou: Man's Paraticipation in God's Perfections According to St. Gregory of Nyssa." *Studia Anselmia* 55:94 (Romae, I.B.C. Libreria Herder).

Balint, Michael. 1968. *The Basic Fault.* London: Tavistock Publications.

Barlow, Connie C., ed. (1991) *From Gaia to Selfish Genes: Selected Writings in the Life Sciences.* Cambridge, Mass.: M.I.T. Press.

———. 1994. *Evolution Extended: Biological Debates on the Meaning of Life.* Cambridge, Mass.: M.I.T. Press.

Barrow, John and Frank Tipler. 1986. *The Anthropic Cosmological Principle.* Oxford: Clarendon Press.

Bernard of Clairvaux. *Sermons on The Song of Songs.* In *Selected Works.* The Classics of Western Spirituality. New York: Paulist Press, 1987.

Berry, Thomas. 1987. "Twelve Principles: For Undestanding the Universe and the Role of the Human in the Universe Process." In *Thomas Berry and the New Cosmology*, edited by Anne Lonergan and Caroline Richards. Mystic, Conn.: Twenty-Third Publications.

———. 1988a. *The Dream of the Earth.* San Francisco: Sierra Club Books.

———. 1988b. "The Cosmology of Religions." *Teilhard Perspectives*, vol. 21, nos. 1 & 2, pp. 1-6.

———. 1999. *The Great Work.* New York: Bell Tower.

———. "The Spirituality of the Earth." Riverdale Papers. Riverdale Center for Religious Research, 5801 Palisade Ave. Riverdale, NY 10471.

Berry, Thomas, C.P. with Clarke, Thomas S.J. 1991. *Befriending the Earth, A Theology of Reconciliation Between Humans and the Earth*. Mystic, Conn.: Twenty-Third Publications.

Berry, Wendell. 1989. *The Hidden Wound*. New York: Farrar, Straus and Giroux.

———. 1993. "Christianity and the Survival of Creation." *Cross Currents* 43: 2, pp. 149–63.

———. 2000. *Life Is a Miracle*. Washington, D.C.: Counterpoint.

Bertalanffy, Ludwig von. 1968. *General Systems Theory*. New York: G. Braziller.

Blakney, Ramond B. 1941. Preface. *Meister Eckhart: A Modern Translation*. New York: Harper & Brothers.

Blake, William. 1975. *The Marriage of Heaven and Hell*. London: Oxford University Press.

Boff, Leonardo. 1995. *Ecology & Liberation*. Maryknoll, N.Y.: Orbis Books.

Bohm, David. 1983. *Wholeness and the Implicate Order*. London and New York: Ark Paperbacks.

Bohm, David and Peat, F. David. 1987. *Science, Order and Creativity*. New York: Bantam Books.

Bohm, David and Weber, Renée. 1978. "The Enfolding-Unfolding Universe: A Conversation with David Bohm." *ReVision* 1:24–51.

———. 1981. "The Physicist and the Mystic: Is a Dialogue Between Them Possible?" *ReVision* 4:22–35.

———. 1982. "Nature as Creativity." *ReVision* 5:35–40.

Bonaventure. *Soul's Journey Into God*. The Classics of Western Spirituality. New York: Paulist Press, 1978.

———. *The Life of St. Francis*. The Classics of Western Spirituality. New York: Paulist Press. 1978.

———. *The Breviloquim*. Translated from the Latin by José de Vinck. Vol. II in *The Works of Bonaventure*. Paterson, N.J.: St. Anthony Guild Press, 1963.

———. *The Disputed Questions on the Mystery of the Trinity*. Introduction and translation by Zachary Hayes, O.F.M. Vol. III in *The Works of Bonaventure*. St. Bonaventure University, St. Bonaventure, N.Y.: The Fransciscan Institute, 1979.

Bouyer, Louis. 1965. *Dictionary of Spirituality*. Translated by Rev. Charles Underhill Quinn. New York: Desclee Co., Inc.

———. 1982. *The Spirituality of the New Testament and the Fathers*. New York: The Seabury Press.

Brady, Ignatius, O.F.M. 1976. "St. Bonaventure's Doctrine of Illumination: Reactions Medieval and Modern." In *Bonaventure and Aquinas, Enduring Philosophers*. OklahomaCity: Oklahoma University Press.

Briggs, John P. and Peat, F. David. 1984. *Looking Glass Universe: The Emerging Science of Wholeness*. New York: Simon & Schuster, Inc.

Buber, Martin. 1965. *Between Man and Man*. New York: MacMillan Publishing Co.

Cady, Edwin H. 1965. *John Woolman*. New York: Washington Square Press.

Capra, Fritjof. 1982. *The Turning Point*. New York: Bantam Books.

———. 1996. *The Web of Life*. New York: Anchor Books (Doubleday).

Capra, Fritjof and Steindl-Rast, David. 1991. *Belonging to the Universe*. San Francisco: HarperCollins.

Caputo, John. 1978. "Fundamental Themes in Meister Eckhart's Mysticism." *The Thomist* 42:197–225.

Carse, James. 1994. *Breakfast at the Victory: The Mysticism of Ordinary Experience*. San Francisco: HarperCollins.

Chaisson, Eric J. 2001 *Cosmic Evolution: The Rise of Complexity in Nature*. Cambridge, Mass.: Harvard University Press.

Christ, Carol. 1999. *Find Inner Goddess*. New Dimensions audiotape no. 2688. New Dimensions Foundation, Box 569, Ukiah, CA 95482.

Cloud of Unknowing, The (14th century). Introductory commentary and translation by Ira Progoff. New York: Dell Publishing Co., 1957

Cobb, John B., Jr. 1969. "The World and God." In *Process Theology: Basic Writings,* edited by Ewert Cousins. New York: Newman Press.

Cobb, John B., Jr. and Griffin, David Ray. 1976. *Process Theology*. Philadelphia: The Westminster Press.

Cobb, John B., Jr. and Griffin, David Ray, eds. 1978. *Mind in Nature: Essays on the Interface of Science and Philosophy*. Washington, D.C.: University Press of America.

Coelho, Mary C. 1987. "St. Theresa of Avila's Transformation of the Symbol of the Interior Castle." *Teresianum-Ephemerides Carmeliticaes* 38:109–25.

———. 1994. "The Pathway to Recollection." *Spiritual Life*, vol. 40, no. 2, pp. 100–110.

Comforti, Michael. 1966. "On Archetypal Fields." *The Round Table Review*, vol. 4, no. 2, pp. 3–8.

———. 1999. *Field, Form and Fate*. Woodstock, Conn.: Spring Publications Inc.

Cousins, Ewert, ed. 1971. *Process Theology: Basic Writings*. New York: Newman Press.

———. 1978. *Bonaventure and the Coincidence of Opposites*. Chicago: Franciscan Herald Press.

———. 1985a. "Eckhart's Christian Advaita." In *Global Spirituality: Toward the Meeting of Mystical Paths*. Madras, India: Radhakrishnan Institute for Advanced Study of Philosophy, University of Madras.

———. 1985b. "Nature Mysticism in Francis of Assisi and Bonaventure." In *Global Spirituality: Toward the Meeting of Mystical Paths*. Madras, India: Radhakrishnan Institute for Advanced Study of Philosophy, University of Madras.

———. 1990a. "The Self and Not-Self in Christian Mysticism: Augustine and Eckhart." In *God, the Self and Nothingness.*, edited by Robert E. Carter. New York: Paragon House.

———. 1990b. "Future Study of Mysticism in the Light of the Problem of Pure Consciousness." Panel, audiotape. AAR/SBL meeting, November 17-20, New Orleans, La. Emory University, Atlanta, Ga.: American Academy of Religion.

———. 1992. *Christ of the 21st Century*. Rockport, Mass.: Element, Inc.

Coxhead, Nona. 1985. *The Relevance of Bliss*. London: Wildwood House.

Curtis, Helena and Barnes, N. Sue, eds. 1989. *Biology*. 5th ed. New York: Worth Publishers, Inc.

Davies, Paul. 1983. *God and the New Physics*. New York: Simon and Schuster, Inc.

———. 1984. *Superforce*. New York: Simon and Schuster, Inc.

———. 1988. *The Cosmic Blueprint*. New York: Simon & Schuster, Inc.

———. 1992. *The Mind of God*. New York: Simon & Schuster, Inc.

de Beauport, Elaine. 1994. *Las Tres Caras de la Mente*. Caracas, Venezuela: Editorial Galac, S.A.

Dennett, Daniel C. 1995. *Darwin's Dangerous Idea*. New York: Simon & Schuster, Inc.

d'Espagnat, Bernard. 1979. "The Quantum Theory and Reality." *Scientific American* 241:158-80.

Dicken, E.W. Trueman. 1963 *Crucible of Love*. New York: Sheed and Ward.

Dickinson, Emily. *The Complete Poems of Emily Dickinson*. Thomas H. Johnson, ed. Boston and Toronto: Little, Brown and Company.

Dionysius the Areopagite. *The Divine Names and Mystical Theology*. 5th ed. Translated by C. E. Rolt. London: SPCK, 1971.

Dossey, Larry. 1989. *Recovering the Soul*. New York: Bantam Books.

Dupré, Louis. 1976. *Transcendent Selfhood*. New York: Seabury Press.

———. 1980. "The Mystical Experience of the Self and Its Philosophical Significance." In *Understanding Mysticism*, edited by Richard Woods O.P. Garden City, NY: Doubleday & Co.

———. 1981. *The Deeper Life*. New York: Crossroad Publishing Company.

———. 1984. *The Common Life*. New York: Crossroad Publishing Company.

———. 1985. Preface. *John Russbroec, The Spiritual Espousal and Other Works*. Mahwah, N.J.: Paulist Press.

———. 1989a. Introduction. *Christian Spirituality III: Post Reformation and Modern*. New York: Crossroad Publishing Company.

———. 1989b. "Unio Mystica: The State and the Experience." In *Introduction to Mystical Union and Monotheistic Faith*, edited by Moshe Idel and Bernard McGinn. New York: MacMillan Publishing Co.

Dupré, Louis and Wiseman, James, O.S.D., eds. 1988. *Light from Light*. Mahwah, N.J.: Paulist Press.

Dyson, Freeman. 1979. *Disturbing the Universe*. New York: Harper and Row Publishers.

Eckhart, Meister. 1941. *Meister Eckhart: A Modern Translation*. Translated by Raymond B. Blackney. New York: Harper & Brothers.

———. 1979. *Sermons and Treatises*, vol. I. Translated and edited by M. O'C. Walshe. Worcester, G. B.: Element Books.

———. 1981. *Meister Eckhart: The Essential Sermons, Commentaries, Treatises and Defense*. New York: Paulist Press.

Edinger, Edward F. 1973. *Ego and Archetype*. Baltimore, Md.: Pelican Books.

———. 1984. *The Creation of Consciousness*. Toronto: Inner City Books.

———. 1988. "The Relation Between Person and Archetypal Factors in Psychological Development." *Pychological Perspectives* vol. 19, no. 2.

Eiseley, Loren. 1957. *The Immense Journey.* New York: Time, Inc.

Eldredge, Niles. 1991. *The Miner's Canary.* New York: Prentice Hall Press.

Eliade, Mircea. 1958. *Patterns of Comparative Religion.* New York: Sheed & Ward.

Elkin, Henry. 1958. "On the Origin of the Self." *Psychoanalysis and Psychoanalytic Review,* vol 45, no. 4, pp.57–76.

———. 1961. "The Emergence of Human Being in Infancy." *Review of Existential Psychology and Psychiatry* 1:17–26.

———. 1965. "The Unconscious and the Integration of Personality." *Review of Existential Psychology and Psychiatry* 5:176–89.

———. 1972a. "On Selfhood and the Development of Ego Structures in Infancy." *The Psychoanalytic Review* 59:389–416.

———. 1972b. "Towards a Developmental Phenomenology: Transcendental-Ego and Body-Ego." *Analecta Husserliana* II: 258–66.

———. 1977. "On Existentialism, Phenomenology and Psychoanalysis." *The Psychoanalytic Review* 64:551–58.

"Espagne, Age D'Or." Tome IV, col. 1127–78. *Dictionnaire de Spiritualité.* Paris: Beauchesne, 1971.

Fairbairn, W. Ronald D. 1952. "Object Relationships and Dynamic Structure" In *Psychoanalytic Studies of Personality.* London: Routledge and Kegan Paul.

———. 1954. *An Object Relations Theory of the Personality.* New York: Basic Books.

Fordham, Michael. 1949. "A Discussion of Archetypes and Internal Objects." *British Journal of Medical Psychology* 22:3–7.

———. 1955. "On the Origins of the Ego in Childhood." In *Studiem zur Analytische Psychologie C.G. Jung,* vol. 1. Zurich: Rascher and Cie, AG.

———. 1957. *New Developments in Analytical Psychology.* London: Routledge and Kegan Paul.

———. 1974. "Jungian View of the Mind-Body Relationship." *Spring* (annual publication of the Analytical Psychology Club of New York).

Fox, Matthew. 1983. *Original Blessing.* Santa Fe, N. Mex.: Bear & Co.

———. 1985. Commentary. *Illuminations of Hildegard of Bingen.* SanteFe, N. Mex.: Bear and Co.

———. 1988. *The Coming of the Cosmic Christ.* San Francisco: Harper and Row.

Freemantle, Anne, ed. 1965. *The Protestant Mystics.* New York: New American Library.

———. 1991. *Creation Spirituality: Liberating Gifts for the Peoples of the Earth.* San Francisco: Harper

Galleni, Lodovico. 1992. "Relationships Between Scientific Analysis and the World View of Pierre Teilhard de Chardin." *Zygon* 27:153–66.

Gilson, Etienne. 1938. *The Philosophy of Bonaventure.* New York: Sheed and Ward.

——. 1955. *History of Christian Philosophy in the Middle Ages*. London: Sheed and Ward.

Goodenough, Ursula. 1998. *The Sacred Depths of Nature*. New York: Oxford University Press.

Goodwin, Brian. 1994. *How the Leopard Changed Its Spots*. New York: Charles Scribner's Sons.

Gould, Stephen J. 1981. *The Mismeasure of Man*. New York: W.W. Norton.

Greenberg, Jay R. and Mitchell, Stephen A. 1983. *Object Relations in Psychoanalytic Theory*. Cambridge, Mass.: Harvard University Press.

Griffin, David Ray. 1986. "Bohm and Whitehead on Wholeness, Freedom, Causality, and Time." In *Physics and the Ultimate Significance of Time: Bohm, Prigogine and Process Theology*, edited by David Ray Griffin. Albany, N.Y.: State University of New York Press.

Griffin, David Ray and Smith, Huston. 1989. *Primordial Truth and Postmodern Theology*. Albany, N.Y.: State University of New York Press.

Grim, John A. 1993. "Native North American Worldviews and Ecology." In *Worldviews and Ecology*, edited by Mary Evelyn Tucker and John A. Grim. Lewisburg, Pa.: Bucknell University Press.

Guntrip, Harry. 1956. *Psychotherapy and Religion*. New York: Harper and Brothers.

Hadot, Pierre. 1986. "Neoplatonist Spirituality I: Plotinus and Porphyry." In *Classical Mediterranean Spirituality: Egyptian, Greek and Roman*, edited by A.H. Armstrong. New York: Crossroad Publishing Co.

Happold, F.C. 1973. *Mysticism*. London: Penguin Books.

Harding, M. Esther. 1973. *Psychic Energy*. Princeton, N.J.: Bollingen Paperback Series, Princeton University Press.

Helleman-Elgersma, Wypkje. 1980. *Soul-Sisters: A Commentary on Enneads IV 3 (27), 1-8 of Plotinus*. Amsterdam: Rodopi N.V.

Hollis, James. 2000. *The Archetypal Imagination*. College Station, Tex.: Texas A&M University Press.

Hoorneart, Rodolpe. 1931. *Saint Teresa in Her Writings*. Translated by Rev. Joseph Leonard. London: Sheed and Ward.

Horney, Karen. 1937. *The Neurotic Personality of Our Time*. London: Kegan Paul, Trench, Trubner and Co. Ltd.

——. 1950. *Neurosis and Human Growth: The Struggle Toward Self-Realization*. New York: W. W. Norton and Co.

Huxley, Aldous. 1945. *The Perennial Philosophy*. New York: Harper and Brothers.

Huxley, Thomas H. 1896. "On the Hypothesis That Animals Are Automata, and Its History" (1874). In *T. H. Huxley's Works: Collected Essays*, vol.I: Methods and Results. New York: Appleton.

Idel, Moshe and McGinn, Bernard. 1989. *Mystical Union and Monotheistic Faith*. New York: MacMillan Publishing Co.

hapter
14 & 15

HY

1. *The Varieties of Religious Experience.* New York: Collier

The Self-Organizing Universe. New York: Pergamon Press.
Christian and Islamic Spirituality. Mahwah, N.J.: Paulist

The Origin and Goal of History. Translated by Michael Bullock. New Haven, Conn.: Yale University Press.

Jaynes, Julian. 1976. *The Origin of Consciousness in the Breakdown of the Bicameral Mind.* Boston: Houghton Mifflin Co.

John of the Cross. "The Ascent of Mt. Carmel." In *The Collected Works of John of the Cross.* Translated by Kieran Kavanaugh, O.C.D. and Otilio Rodríguez, O.C.D. Washington, D.C.: Institute of Carmelite Studies Publications, 1979.

———. "The Dark Night," in *The Collected Works of John of the Cross.* Translated by Kieran Kavanaugh, O.C.D. and Otilio Rodríguez, O.C.D. Washington, D.C.: Institute of Carmelite Studies Publications, 1979.

———. "The Living Flame of Love," in *The Collected Works of John of the Cross.* Translated by Kieran Kavanagh, O.C.D. and Otilio Rodríguez, O.C.D. Washington D.C.: Institute of Carmelite Studies Publications, 1979.

Johnson, Don. 1983. *Body.* Boston: Beacon Press.

Jones, Mary. 1986. "Rufus Matthew Jones." *Mystics Quarterly XII,* March.

Jung, Carl G. 1960. *Collected Works.* Vols. 2, 6, 8, 10, 11. Princeton, N.J.: Princeton University Press.

———. 1965. *Memories, Dream and Reflections.* New York: Vintage Books.

Kaplan, Louise J. 1978. *Oneness and Separateness from Infant to Individual.* New York: Simon and Schuster.

Kauffman, Stuart A. 1993. *The Origins of Order: Self-Organization and Selection in Evolution.* New York: Oxford University Press.

———. 1995. *At Home in the Universe: The Search for the Laws of Organization and Complexity.* New York: Oxford University. Press.

Kaufman, Gordon. 1993. *In the Face of Mystery: A Constructive Theology.* Cambridge, Mass.: Harvard University Press.

Kaufman, William J. III. 1985. *Universe.* New York: W. H. Freeman and Co.

Kavanaugh, Kieran, O.C.D. 1976. Introduction. *The Collected Works of St. Teresa of Avila,* Vol. 1, translated by Kieran Kavanaugh, O.C.D. and Otilio Rodríguez, O.C.D. Washington, D.C.: Institute of Carmelite Studies Publications.

———. 1980. Introduction. *The Collected Works of St. Teresa of Avila,* Vol. 2, translated by Kieran Kavanaugh, O.C.D. and Otilio Rodríguez, O.C.D. Washington, D.C.: Institute of Carmelite Studies Publications.

———. 1984. "St. Teresa and the Spirituality of 16th Century Spain." In *The Roots of the Modern Christian Tradition.,* edited by E. Rozanne Elder. Kalamazoo, Mich.: Cistercian Publications.

———. 1987. Introduction. *John of the Cross: Selected Writings.* Mahwah, N.J.: Paulist Press.

Kayzer, Wim; Kamer, Nellie; Sacks, Oliver; Sheldrake, Rupert; Dennett, Daniel Clement; Toulmin, Stephen; Dyson, Freeman; Gould, Stephen. 1994. *A Glorious Accident: Understanding Our Place in the Cosmic Puzzle.* 8-part video series. Princeton, N.J.: Films for the Humanities.

Keating, Thomas. 1986. *Open Heart, Open Mind.* New York: Amity House.

Kelley, Carl Franklin. 1977. *Meister Eckhardt on Divine Knowledge.* New Haven, Conn.: Yale University Press.

Klein, Melanie. 1957. *Envy and Gratitude.* London: Tavistock Publication Ltd.

Knoll, A. H. 1991. "End of the Proterozoic Eon." *Scientific American* 265: 64–73.

Knowles, David O.S.B. 1966. "The Influence of Pseudo-Dionysius on Western Mysticism." In *Christian Spirituality,* edited by Peter Brooks. London: S.C.M. Press, Ltd.

Kohut, Heinz. 1971. *The Analysis of the Self.* New York: International Universities Press, Inc.

———. 1977. *The Restoration of the Self.* New York: International Universities Press, Inc.

Kushner, Lawrence. 1981. *The River of Light: Spirituality, Judaism and the Evolution of Consciousness.* San Francisco: Harper and Row.

Lamprecht, Sterling P. 1955. *Our Philosophical Traditions.* New York: Appleton-Century-Crofts, Inc.

Lean, Geoffrey and Hinrichsen, Don. 1992. *Atlas of the Environment.* London: Helcon Publishing Ltd.

Leonard, Linda. 1983. *The Wounded Woman: Healing the Father- Daughter Relationship.* Boston, Mass.: Shambhala.

Lonergan, Anne and Richards, Caroline, eds. 1987. *Thomas Berry and the New Cosmology.* Mystic, Conn.: Twenty-Third Publications.

López-Baralt, Luce. 1982. "Santa Teresa de Jesús y el Islam." *Teresianum* XXXIII, I/II: 629–93.

Lovelock, James E. 1979. *Gaia: A New Look At Life On Earth.* Oxford: Oxford University Press.

Lovelock, James E. and Margulis, Lynn. 1988. *The Ages of Gaia: A biography of Our Living Earth.* New York: W. W. Norton, Inc.

Lowen, Alexander. 1973. *Depression and the Body.* Baltimore, Md.: Penguin Books, Inc.

Loy, David. 1988. *Nonduality: A Study of Comparative Philosophy.* New Haven: Yale University Press.

Macy, Joanna. 1991. *Mutual Causality in Buddhism and General Systems Theory.* Albany, N.Y.: State University of New York Press.

Mahler, Margaret S. 1979. "Separation and Individuation." In *The Selected Papers of Margaret S. Mahler,* Vol. 2. New York: Jason Aronson.

Mahler, Margaret S.; Pine, Fred; and Bergman, Anni. 1975. *The Psychological Birth of the Human Infant: Symbiosis and Individuation.* New York: Basic Books, Inc.

Margulis, Lynn and Lovelock, James E. 1974. "Biological Modulations of the Earth's Atmosphere."*Icarus* 21:471–489.

Margulis, Lynn and Sagan, Dorion. 1997. *Microcosmos*. (Originally published 1986) Berkeley: University of California Press.

Marshall, Ian and Zohar, Danah. 1997. *Who's Afraid of Schrödinger's Cat?* New York: Quill (William Morrow).

Martin, Marcelle. 1996. "The Inward Teacher Among Us Today." *Friends Journal*, April 1996, pp.13–15.

Maslow, Abraham. 1962. *Toward a Psychology of Being*. Princeton, N.J.: D. Van Nostrand.

Masters, Robert E. L. and Houston, Jean. 1966. *The Varieties of Psychedelic Experience*. New York: Holt, Reinhart & Winston.

Maturana, Humberto R. and Varela, Francisco. 1980. *Autopoiesis and Cognition: The Realization of the Living*. Dordrecht, Holland: D. Reidel Publishing Co.

———. 1987. *The Tree of Knowledge: The Biological Roots of Understanding*. Boston: Shambhala.

May, Rollo. 1953. *Man's Search for Himself*. New York: W. W. Norton and Co.

McDargh, John. 1983. *Psychoanalytic Object Relations Theory and the Study of Religion*. New York: University Press of America.

McGinn, Bernard. 1981a. "The God Beyond God. Theology and Mysticism in the Thought of Meister Eckhardt." *Journal of Religion* 61:1–19.

———. 1981b. Introduction (Theological Summary): *Meister Eckhart: The Essential Sermons, Commentaries, Treatises, and Defense*. New York: Paulist Press.

McInnis, Noel F. 1995. "Bridging Science and Spirituality." *Noetic Sciences ReSource* V:1(Winter/Spring).

MacLean, Paul D. 1990. *The Triune Brain in Evolution*. New York: Plenum Press.

McMenamin, Mark A. 1998. *The Garden of Ediacara*. New York: Columbia University Press.

McNabb, Vincent, ed. 1907. *The Decrees of the Vatican Council*. London: Burnes and Oates.

Merkur, Daniel. 1989. "Unitive Experiences and the State of Trance." In *Mystical Union and Monotheistic Faith*, edited by Moshe Idel and Bernard McGinn. New York: Macmillan Publishing Co.

Miller, Alice. 1981. *The Drama of the Gifted Child*. Translated by Ruth Ward. New York: Basic Books.

———. 1984. *Thou shalt Not Be Aware*. Translated by Hildegarde and Hunter Hannum. New York: Farrar, Straus, Giroux.

Milne, Lorus and Russell, Margery and Franklin. 1975. *The Secret Life of Animals*. New York: E.P. Dutton & Co.

Montefiore, Hugh, ed. 1975. *Man and Nature*. London: St. James' Place.

Moyers, Bill. 1993. *Healing and the Mind*, edited by Betty Sue Flowers. New York: Doubleday.

Muir, John. 1983. *Orion.* Spring.(complete)

———. 1986. "Religion Is in the Rocks." *Sierra Club Magazine*, July- August.

Murchie, Guy. 1978. *The Seven Mysteries of Life.* Boston, Mass.: Houghton Mifflin Co.

Nasr, Seyyed Hussein. 1981. *Knowledge and the Sacred.* New York: Crossroad Publishing Co Inc..

Needleman, Jacob. 1970. *The New Religions.* Garden City, N.Y.: Doubleday.

Neumann, Erich. 1954. *The Origins and History of Consciousness.* Translated by R. F. C. Hall. New York: Pantheon Books, Inc.

———. 1968. "The Mystic Man, the Mystic Vision; Papers from the Eranos Yearbooks." Translated by Ralph Manheim. *Bollingen Series XXX,* 6:375–415. Princeton, N.J.: Princeton University Press.

———. 1989. *The Place of Creation.* Translated by Eugene Rolfe. Princeton, N.J.: Princeton University Press.

Nobuhara, Tokiyuki. 1995. "How Can Pure Experience Give Rise to Religious Self-Awareness and Then to the Topological Argument for the Existence of God Cogently?: Nishida, Whitehead, and Pannenberg." *Process Thought* 6:125–150.

Nouwen, Henri. 1988. "The Peace That Is Not of this World." *Weavings*, vol. III, no. 2, pp. 23–34.

NYSEPH (New York Milton Erikson Society for Psychotherapy and Hypnosis) Newsletter 8:1.

Ogden, Shubert M. 1966. "The Reality of God." In *Process Theology*, edited by Ewert Cousins. New York: Newman Press, 1971.

Otto, Rudolph. 1932. *Mysticism East and West.* New York: MacMillan Publishing Co.

Owens, Claire M. 1972. "The Mystical Experience: Facts and Values," In *The Highest State of Consciousness*, edited by John W. White. (Garden City, N.Y.: Doubleday and Co.

Pagels, Heinz R. 1982. *The Cosmic Code.* New York: Bantam Books.

Palmer, Parker. 1998. *The Courage to Teach.* San Francisco: Jossey-Bass Publishers.

Panikkar, Raimundo. 1973. *The Trinity and the Religious Experience of Man.* New York: Orbis Books.

Peat, F. David. 1987. *Synchronicity: The Bridge Between Matter and Mind.* New York: Bantam Books.

———. 1990. "Unfolding the Subtle: Matter & Consciousnes." Audiotape. Philadelphia: Center for Frontier Sciences, Temple University.

Peavy, Fran. 1998. "Living Water and a Politics of the Heart." *Earthlight* (111 Fairmount Ave., Oakland, Ca 94611) Spring, pp.10–12.

Pereira, José. 1991. *Hindu Theology.* Delhi: Motilal Banarsidass Publishers PVT. LTD.

Pert, Candace B.; Ruff, M. R.; Weber, R. J.; and Herkenham, M. 1985. "Neuropeptides and Their Receptors: A Psychosomatic Network." *J. Immunol.* 135:820S–824S.

Piel, Gerard and Segerberg, Osborn Jr., eds. 1990. *The World of René Dubos.* New York: Henry Holt and Co.

Pittenger, W. Norman. 1967. *God in Process.* London: S.C.M. Press.

———. 1968. "Bernard E. Meland, Process Thought and the Significance of Christ." In *Process Theology: Basic Writings*, edited by Ewert Cousins. New York: Newman Press, 1971

———. 1969. *Alfred North Whitehead.* Richmond, Va.: John Knox Press.

———. 1974. *The Holy Spirit.* Philadelphia: United Church Press.

Plotinus. *The Enneads.* Translated by Stephen MacKenna. New York: Pantheon Books, 1969.

Prince, Raymond, and Savage, Charles. 1972. "Mystical States and the Concept of Regression." In *The Highest State of Consciousness*, edited by John W. White. Garden City, N.Y.: Doubleday.

Rue, Loyal. 2000. *Everybody's Story.* Albany, N.Y.: State University of New York Press.

Rumi. 1994. *Say I Am You.* Athens, Ga.: Maypop.

Rutledge, Dom Denys. 1964. *Cosmic Theology, The Ecclesiastical Hierarchy of Pseudo-Denys: An Introduction.* London: Routledge and Kegan Paul.

Ruusbroec, Jan van. *The Spiritual Espousals and Other Works.* Edited by James A. Wiseman, O.S.D.Mahwah, N.J.: Paulist Press, 1985.

Ryan, M. J., ed. 1998. *The Fabric of the Future.* Berkeley, Calif.: Conari Press.

Schrödinger, Erwin. 1951. *Science and Humanism.* Cambridge: Cambridge University Press.

Schürmann, Reiner. 1978a. *Meister Eckhardt, Mystic Philosopher.* Bloomington, Ind.: Indiana University Press.

———. 1978b. "The Loss of the Origin in Soto Zen and in Meister Eckhart." *The Thomist* 42:281–312.

Seed, John; Macy, Joanna; Fleming, Pat; and Naess, Arne Naess. 1988. *Thinking Like a Mountain.* Philadelphia: New Society Publishers.

Sheldrake, Rupert. 1992. *The Rebirth of Nature: The Greening of Science and God.* New York: Bantam Books.

———. 1995. *The Presence of the Past. Morphic Resonance and the Habits of Nature.* Rochester, Vt.: Park Street Press.

Smith, Cyprian. 1987. *The Way of Paradox.* Mahwah, N.J.: Paulist Press.

Smith, Huston. 1976. *Forgotten Truth, The Primordial Tradition.* New York: Harper & Row, Publishers.

———. 1982. *Beyond the Post-Modern Mind.* New York: Crossroad Publishing Co Inc.

———. 1990. "Future Study of Mysticism in the Light of the Problem of Pure Consciousness." Panel, audiotape. AAR/SBL meeting, Nov. 17–20, New

Orleans, La. Emory University, Atlanta, Ga: American Academy of Religion.

Sölle, Dorothee. 1996. "Visiting Professor Dorothee Sölle Revisits Union." Union Theological Seminary (New York) *Union News* Winter/Spring.

Stace, W. T. 1960. *Mysticism and Philosophy*. London: MacMillan.

Steere, Douglas. 1975. "Contemplation and Leisure." *Pendle Hill Pamphlet 199*, Wallingford, Pa.: Pendle Hill Publications.

Steger, Will and Bowermaster, Jon. 1990. *Saving the Earth*. New York: Alfred A. Knopf.

———. 1992. *Crossing Antarctica*. New York: Alfred A. Knopf.

Stein, Leopold. 1967. "Introducing Not Self." *The Journal of Analytic Psychology* vol. 12, no. 2, pp. 97–113.

Stevens, Anthony. 1982. *Archetypes, A Natural History of the Self*. New York: Quill (William Morrow)

———. 1993. *The Two-Million-Year-Old Self*. College Station, Tex.: Texas A&M University Press.

Stoudt, John Joseph. 1968. *Jacob Boehme: His Life and Thought*. New York: Seabury Press.

Strollo, Charles P. 1981. "The Primacy of Love in *The Cloud of Unknowing*." *Review for Religious* 40:736–58.

Sutherland, J. D. 1963. "Object Relations Theory and the Conceptual Model of Psychoanalysis." *British Journal of Medical Psychology* 36:109–21.

Suzuki, Daisetz T. 1959. "Zen and Japanese Culture." *Bollingen Series LXIV*. New York: Pantheon Books.

Swimme, Brian. 1984. *The Universe Is a Green Dragon*. Santa Fe, N.Mex.: Bear and Company, Inc.

———. 1985. *Canticle to the Cosmos*. 12-part video series. Center for the Story of the Universe, 311 Rydall Ave., Mill Valley, CA 94941.

———. 1989. "Cosmos as Primary Revelation." *Teilhard Perspectives* vol. 22, no. 2.

———. 1990. "Science: A Partner in Creating the Vision." In *Thomas Berry and the New Cosmology*, edited by Anne Lonergan and Caroline Richards. Mystic, Conn.: Twenty-Third Publications.

———. 1996. *The Hidden Heart of the Cosmos*. Maryknoll, N.Y.: Orbis Books.

———. 1997. Interview. *Earthlight* (111 Fairmount Ave., Oakland, CA 94611). Summer.

———. 1998. *The Earth's Imagination*. 8-part video series. Center for the Story of the Universe, 311 Rydall Ave., Mill Valley, CA 94941.

———. 2001. "Comprehensive Compassion." Interview by Susan Bridle. *What Is Enlightenment?* (PO Box 2360, Lenox, MA 01240), Spring/Summer.

Swimme, Brian and Berry, Thomas. 1992. *The Universe Story*. San Francisco: HarperCollins.

Symeon the New Theologian. 1975. *Hymns of Divine Love*. Translated by George A. Maloney S.J. Denville, N.J.: Dimension Books.

Talbot, Michael. 1988. *Beyond the Quantum.* New York: Bantam Books.
———. 1991. *The Holographic Universe.* New York: HarperCollins.
Teilhard de Chardin, Pierre. 1959. *The Phenomenon of Man.* New York: Harper and Row.
———. 1960. *The Divine Milieu.* New York: Harper and Row.
Teresa of Avila. *The Book of Her Life.* In *The Collected Works of St. Teresa of Avila,* vol.1. Translated by Kieran Kavanaugh O.C.D and Otilio Rodríguez O.C.D. Washington, D.C.: Institute of Carmelite Studies Publications, 1976.
———. *The Interior Castle.* In *The Collected Works of St. Teresa of Avila,* vol.2. Translated by Kieran Kavanaugh O.C.D. and Otilio Rodríguez, O.C.D. Washington, D.C.: Institute of Carmelite Studies Publications, 1980.
———. "Meditation on the Song of Songs." In *The Collected Works of St. Teresa of Avila,* vol. 2. Translated by Kieran Kavanaugh O.C.D. and Otilio Rodríguez O.C.D. Washington, D.C.: Institute of Carmelite Studies Publications, 1980.
———. "Spiritual Testimonies," in *The Collected Works of St. Teresa of Avila,* vol. 1. Translated by Kieran Kavanaugh, O.C.D. and Otilio Rodríguez, O.C.D. Washington, D.C.: Institute of Carmelite Studies Publications, 1976.
———. *The Way of Perfection.* In *The Collected Works of St. Teresa of Avila,* vol. 2. Translated by Kieran Kavanaugh, O.C.D. and Otilio Rodríguez, O.C.D. Washington, D.C.: Institute of Carmelite Studies, 1980.
Thomas, Lewis. 1981. "Debating the Unknowable." *Atlantic Monthly,* July 1981.
———. 1984. *The Lives of a Cell.* New York: Bantam Books.
Thomas of Celano. *The Second Life of St. Francis.* In *St. Francis of Assisi: Writing and Early Biographies.* Chicago: Franciscan Herald Press, 1975.
Tillich, Paul. 1959. "Two Types of Philosophy of Religion." In *Theology of Culture.* New York: Oxford University Press.
———. 1965. *The Future of Religions.* New York: Harper and Row.
Toolan, David. 1980. "Psychology's Theological Quantum Jump." *Commonweal,* Oct. 10, pp. 562–67.
Toulmin, Stephen. 1982. *The Return to Cosmology, Postmodern Science and the Theology of Nature.* Berkeley and Los Angeles: University of California Press.
Tucker, Mary E. and Grim, John A. 1993. *Worldviews and Ecology.* Lewisburgh, Pa.: Bucknell University Press.
Underhill, Evelyn. 1942. *Practical Mysticism.* (Originally published 1914.) Canal Winchester, Ohio: Ariel Press.
———. 1955. *Mysticism.* (Originally published 1910.)New York: Meridian Books.
———. 1992. *The Mystic Way.* (Originally published 1913.) Atlanta, Ga.: Ariel Press.
Union News. 1996, Spring/Winter. Union Theological Seminary (3041 Broadway, New York, NY 10027).
Van der Post, Laurens. 1975. *Jung and the Story of Our Time.* New York: Pantheon Books.

——. 1996. *Hasten Slowly: The Journey of Sir Lauren van der Post*. Film produced and directed by Mickey Lemle, Lemle Pictures, Inc.

Varela, Francisco J. 1991. *The Embodied Mind: Cognitive Science and Human Experience*. Cambridge, Mass.: MIT Press.

Vedfelt, Ole. 1999. *The Dimensions of Dreams*. Translated by Kenneth Tindall. New York: Fromm International.

Vining, Elizabeth Gray. 1958. *Friend of Life: A Biography of Rufus M Jones*. Philadelphia: J. B. Lippincott Company.

von Franz, Marie-Louise. 1975. *C.G. Jung: His Myth in Our Time*. Translated by William H. Kennedy. Boston: Little, Brown and Company.

——. 1980. *Shadow and Evil in Fairy Tales*. University of Dallas, Irving ,Tex.: Spring Publications, Inc.

von Hügel, Friedrich. 1909. *The Mystical Element of Religion*. London: J.M. Dent; New York: E.P. Dutton & Co.

Wapnick, Kenneth. 1980. "Mysticism and Schizophrenia." In *Understanding Mysticism*, edited by Richard Woods O.P.Garden City, N.Y.: Doubleday and Co.

Ward, Theodora. 1961. *The Capsule of the Mind*. Cambridge, Mass.: The Belknap Press of Harvard University.

Watts, Alan W. 1972. "This Is It." In *Highest State of Consciousness*, edited by John White. Garden City, N.Y.: Anchor Books (Doubleday)

White, John, ed. 1972. *The Highest State of Consciousness*. Garden City, N.Y.: Anchor Books (Doubleday)

Whitehead, Alfred North. 1926. *Science and the Modern World*. Cambridge: Cambridge University Press.

——. 1929. *Process and Reality: An Essay in Cosmology*. New York: MacMillan Publishing Co.

——. 1933. *Adventure In Ideas*. New York: The MacMillan Co.

Whitmont, Edward C. 1993. *The Alchemy of Healing*. Berkeley, Calif..: North Atlantic Books.

Wilber, Ken. 1977. *The Spectrum of Consciousness*. Wheaton, Ill.: The Theosophical Publishing House.

——. 1979. *No Boundary: Eastern and Western Approaches to Personal Growth*. Los Angeles: Center Publications.

——. 1983. *Up from Eden: A Transpersonal View of Human Evolution*. Boulder, Colo.: Shambhala.

——. 1995. *Sex, Ecology and Spirituality*. Boston, Mass.: Shambhala.

Williams, Daniel D. 1968. "God and Man." In *Process Theology*, edited by Ewert Cousins. New York: Newmann Press, 1971.

Wilmot, Laurence F. 1979. *Whitehead and God*. Waterloo, Ontario, Can.: Wilfrid Laurier University Press.

Wilson, E.O. 1984. *Biophilia*. Cambridge, Mass.: Harvard University Press.

——. 1998. *Consilience*. New York: Alfred A. Knopf.

Winnicott, D.W. 1958. *Collected Papers: Through Paediatrics to Psychoanalysis.* London: Tavistock Publications.

———. 1965. *The Maturational Processes and the Facilitating Environment.* New York: International Universities Press, Inc.

———. 1971. *Playing and Reality.* New York: Basic Books Inc.

Wolf, Fred Alan. 1989. *Taking the Quantum Leap.* New York: Harper & Row.

Woodman, Marion. 1982. *Addiction to Perfection.* Toronto: Inner City Books.

———. 1985. *The Pregnant Virgin.* Toronto: Inner City Books.

———. 1993. *Conscious Femninity.* Toronto: Inner City Books.

Woods, Richard. 1980. *Understanding Mysticism.* Garden City, N.Y.: Image Books.

———. 1986. *Eckhart's Way.* Wilmington, Del.: Glazier.

Yungblut, John R. 1974. *Rediscovering the Christ.* New York: Seabury Press.

———. 1995. *Walking Gently on the Earth.* Pamphlet. Southern Yearly Meeting of the Religious Society of Friends, 1114 NW 40th Dr., Gainesville, FL 32605.

Zohar, Danah. 1990. *The Quantum Self.* New York: William Morrow and Company.

Zukav, Gary. 1980. *The Dancing Wu Li Masters.* New York: Bantam Books.

INDEX

ABOUT THE AUTHOR

MARY COELHO brings to this work an academic and practical background in both biology and theology. She has an MA in biology, has taught biology and worked in a research laboratory. She has studied at both Union Theological Seminary (MDiv) and Fordham University (PhD in historical theology) and worked as Co-director of the Programs in Spiritual Direction at the Center for Christian Spirituality at General Theological Seminary. She is the author of several articles and coauthor with Rev. James Neufelder of *Writings in Spiritual Direction by the Great Christina Masters*. She has been a member of the Steering Committee of the Friends Committee on Unity with Nature and is on the board of The American Teilhard Association. She has led a number of workshops on the integration of the epic of evolution and the Western contemplative/mystical tradition. By avocation, Mrs. Coelho is a watercolorist, exhibiting and selling her cityscapes and landscapes in the northeast.